DUBLIN THROUGH SPACE AND TIME

'*Dublin through Space and Time* ... written from geographical and historical perspectives, is straightforward and logical. There is no easy nostalgia, no pedantic swipes. It is the product of the visionary multi-disciplinary, contextual approach that has consolidated Irish historical geography's status as an exciting and practical force in Irish scholarship. Above all, it showcases the value of maps as the geographer's eye. Sources are acknowledged and throughout the text is the sense of footsteps, the layers of lives lived and of history made.

Every aspect of life is covered, from the amount of stabling once needed in a city with a commercial life dependent on the horse, to the brewers, to the long-gone merchants and clothes shops whose very names formed part of Irish social history.

... This is yet another of those superb books quietly published by an Irish publisher and it testifies to the quality of current Irish scholarship in these fields – and the clarity of its thought.

... *Dublin through Space and Time* is fair-minded, honest; eloquent and exciting. It is also a valuable book that records the triumphs, the tragedies and the history, that has created the Dublin of today – often victim, always witness and, most definitely, survivor.'

Eileen Battersby, *Irish Times*

The making of Dublin City

GENERAL EDITORS
Joseph Brady and Anngret Simms, Department of Geography,
University College Dublin

1 Joseph Brady and Anngret Simms (eds), *Dublin through space and time,*
   c.900–1900

2 Ruth McManus, *Dublin: building the suburbs, 1910–1940*

3 Joseph Brady, *Living in the city, 1940–2000: a social and economic geography*

Dublin

THROUGH SPACE AND TIME
(*c.*900–1900)

Joseph Brady & Anngret Simms

EDITORS

FOUR COURTS PRESS

Set in 11 pt on 14 pt Garamond by
Carrigboy Typesetting Services, County Cork for
FOUR COURTS PRESS LTD
Fumbally Court, Fumbally Lane, Dublin 8, Ireland
e-mail: info@four-courts-press.ie
http://www.four-courts-press.ie
and in North America for
FOUR COURTS PRESS
c/o ISBS, 5824 N.E. Hassalo Street, Portland, OR 97213.

First printing 2001
Second printing with corrections 2002

ISBN 1–85182–610–6 hbk
ISBN 1–85182–641–6 pbk

Printed in England
by MPG Books, Bodmin, Cornwall

Contents

Grafton Street and environs — George's Street and environs
Westmoreland Street and D'Olier Street
Sackville Street (O'Connell Street) and environs
Concluding comments

Acknowledgments

This book grew out of our years of teaching in University College Dublin and the many stimulating discussions that we had with colleagues and students. We have seen interest in urban studies grow so that it now represents a major component of the geography syllabus and we are part of an ever-growing international network of urban scholars. To this has recently been added a new Urban Institute in University College Dublin. Our sincere thanks are due to all who have shared their knowledge and experience with us.

There are a number of people to whom we owe a particular debt. Howard Clarke and Patrick Wallace gave generously of their time to read drafts of the section on early Dublin and helped us clarify our thinking. Willie Warren facilitated access to bore-hole readings, kept in the Geological Survey of Ireland, which helped to reconstruct the physical landscape of medieval Dublin. John Andrews' comments and advice on the appendix on Dublin maps were crucial and deeply appreciated. Barbara Mennell gave us much-needed advice at the early stages of this project and helped smooth the path. The comments provided by the anonymous referees were very useful and challenging.

Our contributors, Edel Sheridan and Jacinta Prunty, friends and colleagues both, deserve our thanks for putting up with the multiplicity of demands that were placed upon them. Many of the graphics are the work of Stephen Hannon, the cartographer in UCD, and we are lucky to have his skill at our disposal.

Most of the illustrations come from the private collection of one of the editors, Joseph Brady. However, we are very grateful to Mary Clark, City Archivist, for permission to reproduce some of the Wide Streets Commission's drawings as well as a number of other graphics from the City Archive. Dublinia kindly gave permission to include a photograph of the model of the medieval town, while we are indebted to the Royal Irish Academy for Figure 6.

Our sincere thanks are also due to the National University of Ireland and to University College Dublin for very generous publication grants which permitted the inclusion of so many illustrations. We are grateful to the Ordnance Survey of Ireland for permission to reproduce some map extracts (Permit 7251).

Finally, our thanks to Anne and David without whose patience and encouragement this project would never have been completed.

Introduction

The story of the development of the city of Dublin stretches back over a thousand years and during this time there have been many influences on the landscape of the city. The town began as a Viking sea-port in the ninth century, when Dublin was a more important trading place than Berlin and Stockholm. Following the invasion by the Anglo-Normans in the twelfth century the town developed into a borough with a charter, as occurred in other European countries during this time period. Dublin's great monastic houses played an active role as developers in the suburbs outside the medieval walls. The sixteenth century saw the beginnings of the transformation of the landscape of the city as these monastic precincts were dismantled and the land passed into both civic and private ownership. It reached its greatest flowering, perhaps, by the end of the eighteenth century when the city had grown to be one of the most elegant capital cities in Europe, but it was a divided city as the élite differed in religious and ethnic terms from the majority of the population. The nineteenth century was less kind to the city, and the popular, though limited, image is one of poverty and neglect. However the twentieth century saw Dublin re-emerge as the capital of the newly independent Ireland and it expanded on an unprecedented scale into the metropolis of today. Once again, it is part of a great trading empire that will soon encompass the whole of Europe.

All of these events are recorded, to a greater or lesser degree, in the streetscape of the city, and this book is an attempt to explain and interpret this landscape. It is the first volume in a new series on urban landscapes under the general editorship of Joseph Brady and Anngret Simms. Both editors are geographers and we are therefore most concerned with explaining the landscape of the city and its spatial character. Cities are not only economic and social entities; they exist in time and space and need to be understood from this perspective. Spatial planning has become one of the catch-phrases of our current economic development but a spatial approach has always been the stock-in-trade of geographers. It is hoped that the reader will be able to understand the city in an holistic way and see how its various components interact; what many would see as a living organism. We hope that the book, based on a great deal of original research, will appeal to the general reader as well as provide a much-needed text for third level students. It is lavishly illustrated because the geographical approach is strongly visual and the graphical material is central to what we are trying to say. The first volume is designed to set the scene for the subsequent volumes and provides an overview of the city from its earliest origins to the first decades of the twentieth century. Given the timespan involved we thought it best to ask a number of authors to contribute to this volume but subsequent volumes will be the work of individual researchers. Our aim is to provide fresh and interesting insights into the city in a format that is accessible to all.

Both editors teach in the Department of Geography in University College Dublin and all of the other contributors to this and subsequent volumes have undertaken graduate research in this department. Anngret Simms was drawn into research on medieval Dublin in the wake of the campaign to protect the archaeological excavations at Wood Quay in the 1970s. In the first chapter, she introduces the reader to the early development of the city in a multidisciplinary approach that links the work of medieval historians and archaeologists with her own geographical research. She attempts to reconstruct the layout of medieval Dublin using the cartographic evidence for property boundaries from Rocque's detailed eighteenth-century map, the earliest surviving large-scale plan of the city.

The second and third chapters are written by Edel Sheridan. She takes up the story of Dublin from about 1660 when a new spirit of confidence imbued the city. There was a determined effort to fashion a city worthy of its status as the capital of a kingdom which could boast to be the second city of a developing empire. The Corporation of Dublin played a key role in the late seventeenth and early eighteenth centuries by improving the city's economy and encouraging building. They promoted early quay construction and undertook work in Smithfield, but pride of place must go to their development of St Stephen's Green. There were problems that they found intractable, not the least of which was traffic congestion in the narrow streets and lanes. Ultimately a solution was found in the creation of a commission in 1757 with wide statutory powers that over-arched the Corporation and controlled the city's growth for almost a century. The Commissioners for making Wide and Convenient Ways, Streets and Passages, or Wide Streets Commissioners as they became known, aimed to do more than just widen the streets of the city. They had a vision of European urbanism that they wanted to see reflected in Dublin and so they set out to create streets of unified architecture in keeping with the best planning theories of the day. They played a key role in developing the city's distinctive character in what we now call the Georgian style. Fortunately they also created wide streets and it is through their legacy that the city centre manages to function at all today. It was not just public agencies that were central to the development of the city. Private land owners, both property speculators and titled families, were also of key importance. People such as Jervis, Gardiner and Fitzwilliam are immortalized in the names of the streets and districts they created. These three groups, Corporation, Wide Streets Commission and private developers, interacted to build a new city beyond the boundaries of the medieval town. Edel Sheridan details how this was done using primary source material and weaves a fascinating story of the development process that has many resonances today. For the first time the extent of the property held by great estate-owners in Dublin is shown on a map. However grand Dublin might have been, it was also a deeply socially segregated city. In the second of her chapters, Edel Sheridan looks at the social geography of the city. A picture emerges of how urban form contributed to social control. The contrast was between the western sector of the city with its proto-industrial activities and the eastern side, particularly the south-eastern sector where the social elite built their residences, closely associated with symbols of power.

The fourth chapter by Jacinta Prunty concentrates on a less happy city. Dublin lost much of its grandeur in the period following the Act of Union in 1801. It was no longer a capital city with its own parliament, and many of its wealthiest citizens removed to London. Of even greater importance, the better-off section of society was increasingly attracted to the new suburbs that were developing beyond the boundaries of the city. Though they were very close to the city centre, just beyond the canal, these suburbs or townships were legally distinct from the city of Dublin and thus the tax base of the city contracted. Added to this was an influx of poor into the city from the depressed countryside. Dublin was an important staging point for emigration but many migrants remained in the city. Unfortunately, Dublin did not have a demand for this level of unskilled labour and so it was not long before the city developed an image of poverty and neglect. Jacinta Prunty describes how the worst problems were created by overcrowding and bad sanitary facilities, which led to epidemics of infectious diseases, especially cholera. The General Valuation of Ireland, the 'Griffith Valuation' (1854), shows how widespread was the distribution of low-value residences in the city. The poor lived in tenements, the former grand residences now converted to multi-family occupancy, cottages, cabins and cellars. It is only after 1848 when the Public Health Act and the Nuisance Removal and Diseases Prevention Act were passed that we begin to see a slow progress towards improvement. Dublin Corporation worked with commercial agencies such as the Dublin Artizans' Dwellings

Company or with philanthropic bodies such as the Iveagh Trust but it was not until towards the end of the nineteenth century that it began to be directly involved in meeting the crisis of poverty. By then the scale of the problem was so great that it was almost the end of the twentieth century before the last slum clearances were completed.

But it was not all gloom. The better-off lived in the suburbs but the city was where they did business, shopped and enjoyed themselves. In the final two chapters, Joseph Brady looks at the commercial and economic life of the city. The city is presented as it was portrayed in the guide books and advertising of the day. The nineteenth century had seen many improvements to the infrastructure of the city – water, roads, bridges – and there had been some important civic projects, though not on the scale of the previous century. The ensemble of the National Museum, the National Library, the National Gallery and the National History Museum, which clustered around Leinster House was probably the single most important addition to the landscape of the city. The changing political climate found physical expression in the city's streets. A nationalist Corporation commemorated the heroes of Ireland such as Daniel O'Connell while attempts were made to remove the memorial to Nelson on the grounds that it was a hazard to traffic.

The final chapter adopts a specifically geographical approach to the city. Here Joseph Brady is concerned with the distribution patterns of the city's economy and with the character of its main streets. Using commercial guides, advertising publications and other documentary sources, he attempts to recreate the city centre as it would have been seen and used in the early years of the twentieth century. What emerges is a picture of a very complex city with many different patterns interwoven. Industry was centrally located and intimately associated with retail activity. Many shops have had manufactories close by their retail outlets, if not on the actual premises. The quality of life of the better-off is clearly delineated in the variety of specialized services available to them. The business and commercial world was more dispersed across the city centre in those days but the core streets then, as now, were Grafton Street on the southside and Henry Street on the northside.

Despite the passage of a thousand years, Dublin was still quite a compact city at the turn of the twentieth century. All was soon to change. Speculative builders increasingly turned to suburban locations to meet the demand for middle class housing while the city authorities, with greater reluctance, found that only in suburban locations could public housing on the required scale be provided. The city expanded as it had never before. In the second volume of this series Ruth McManus will tell the story of this expansion from the early decades of the twentieth century to about 1940. She will detail the creation of the great local authority estates such as Marino and introduce the reader to the people who drove this process. She will also look at the speculative builder, focusing on a number of key individuals. She will show that there were close links between private builders and local authorities and that the differences between public and private housing were not as clear as might be imagined.

Volume 3 continues this discussion and concentrates on the period from about 1940 to the present day. Joseph Brady will look at the growth and development of the city during this time period. As the city got bigger so it developed a clear spatial structure, a mosaic of different social worlds. The book will look at the structure of these social areas in some detail as well as many other aspects of the character of the city.

Together these three volumes will provide a comprehensive analysis of the growth of the city. Subsequent volumes will expand on particular aspects of the city's structure.

In tracing Dublin's development through the ages, as we have done in this volume and others will do in subsequent volumes, we have written the historical geography of processes that combined to create the public and private spheres of our capital city. The spaces of modernity that we take for granted in our city today are the result of innovations that dispersed throughout Europe, whether it be electricity supply, sewage disposal or communications. Just as important as these functional aspects is the city as a mediator of cultural memory. Different cultural traditions have left their own mark on the form of the town. Often institutions, which symbolized a specific social and political aspiration, as for example Trinity College Dublin, which was founded by Queen Elizabeth for the children of her civil servants, have become an integral part of Irish life.

Knowledge of the past of our city creates collective memory, which in turn helps to create community. How does society remember its own history? The answer is manifold. We encounter our history in poetry, music, paintings, the findings of archaeologists and the writings of scholars. We can also learn to recognize elements of the past in the built environment around us. Our cultural identity depends on our memory and as a group of citizens we can only experience our identity by active memory. Of course, cultural memory can have an integrating as well as an alienating effect, it all depends on the spirit in which the images of the past are recalled. But there is no doubt that they have to be mastered, if we want to be at ease with the symbolic messages in our capital city today.

This book presents research that has been carried out by geographers in University College Dublin on the major growth phases of our capital city. As geographers we are mainly interested in the topographical transformation of the city from the small Viking trading town on the confluence between the Liffey and the Poddle to the elegant eighteenth-century city with gracious public buildings and Georgian squares to the capital of an independent State in the early twentieth century. We believe that a contextual approach is most important for such a study, as writing about urban landscapes without any reference to contemporary thought would deprive the reader of a fuller understanding of their meaning. But we consider it beyond our scope to go into any great detail about the political, social and economic history of the town, as these issues are dealt with by experts in their own field.

We hope that this volume will encourage many potential students of Dublin's historical and contemporary geography to undertake their own work. Our advice for these future researchers is that even the best-known collections of manuscripts and maps still contain much untapped information. It always depends on the questions that you ask. For example, there are many issues still to be resolved in relation to environmental problems of Dublin's past history.

This book wishes to enable Dubliners and visitors to the town to recognize those elements in its urban landscape which immortalize the endeavours of a very long line of former generations, reaching back into Viking times, who have contributed to the making of this vibrant capital city.

JOSEPH BRADY, ANNGRET SIMMS
Department of Geography
University College Dublin

Origins and early growth

ANNGRET SIMMS

Introduction

Dublin is one of the oldest European capitals outside of the areas that were once part of the Roman Empire. During the tenth and eleventh centuries it developed into an important coastal trading station within the Viking trading-network that connected the Irish Sea via the North Sea with the Baltic and extended as far as the Black Sea. The town and its hinterland were ruled by Scandinavian dynasties. As Viking and Gaelic culture fused in the eleventh and twelfth centuries, historians speak of Hiberno-Norse Dublin – 'Norse' being used interchangeably with 'Viking' to describe the inhabitants of Viking-age Dublin. In the late-twelfth century after the capture of Dublin by the Anglo-Normans, the town was granted a royal charter by the English King Henry II and thereby acquired the status of a borough, like medieval towns in England and continental Europe at the time.

Under the Vikings, Dublin had been a semi-independent kingdom, but under the Anglo-Normans it was reduced in status. It became a regional capital, the focus for the feudal lordship of Ireland. Under these new circumstances the fate of the Dubliners was closely linked to that of the Anglo-Norman colony as a whole. While the colony shrank in the fifteenth century to include only the capital and its hinterland, known as the Pale, medieval Dublin did survive more or less in splendid isolation. In the seventeenth century it provided the platform for the re-conquest of Ireland by the English.

Medieval Dublin constitutes a very small area in the centre of the large capital city of today (Figure 1). It is not easy to find relict features of Dublin's rich medieval past in the present day city, for only a few major medieval buildings have survived. These include the two cathedrals, Christ Church and St Patrick's, which retain medieval masonry in what are largely nineteenth-century reconstructions. The Church of Ireland parish churches of St Michan's, north of the Liffey, and St Audeon's south of the Liffey signal their medieval origins by late-medieval towers, which were largely rebuilt in the seventeenth century. Dublin Castle, although reconstructed in the classical idiom of the eighteenth century while retaining two of its corner towers, still reflects a medieval layout. With so little of the medieval fabric left, the medieval street-pattern, which has survived to a greater extent, takes on a particular importance.

By the first half of the twentieth century, the medieval town had become increasingly derelict and public memory of the historical importance of that part of the city had faded away. It has only re-emerged in the recent past through the results of archaeological excavations in the medieval core of the city carried out by the National Museum of Ireland over a period of twenty years from 1962 to 1981. The work undertaken by Patrick Wallace at the Fishamble Street and Wood Quay site was a watershed in many respects. Not only did the site reveal so much, the findings of these substantive excavations are now being published jointly by the National Museum and the Royal Irish Academy, but they placed urban archaeology on the public agenda.

In their haste to complete the Civic Offices, Dublin Corporation would have ended the excavations prematurely but for the intervention of the Friends of Medieval Dublin, an interdisciplinary research group, founded in 1976 for the promotion of research into medieval Dublin and the preservation of medieval fabric in the town. It was F.X. Martin, then Professor of Medieval History at University College Dublin and the first chairman of the group, who took the vital court case that succeeded in having the excavation site north of Christ Church cathedral declared a national monument. Despite this, with the aid of formal legal proceedings the Corporation persisted in trying to end the excavations. The subsequent occupation of the site and the protest demonstration by 17,000 people showed the growing acceptance of the need to understand and preserve our heritage. Unfortunately not even a resolution passed by the Council of Europe calling on the Irish Government to preserve the Viking settlement at Wood Quay as a European monument had any impact (see Bradley, 1984 for an account). The best that was achieved was that the Irish Government conceded that the excavations could continue for another five months. A unique opportunity was lost to preserve *in situ* the beginnings of the city but some good came out of this disaster. These stormy events prompted new research, which is reflected in the growing number of publications that are now available on different aspects of medieval Dublin. Over the last decade a large number of rescue excavations have been carried out in the city and some, for example at Patrick, Francis, Nicholas and

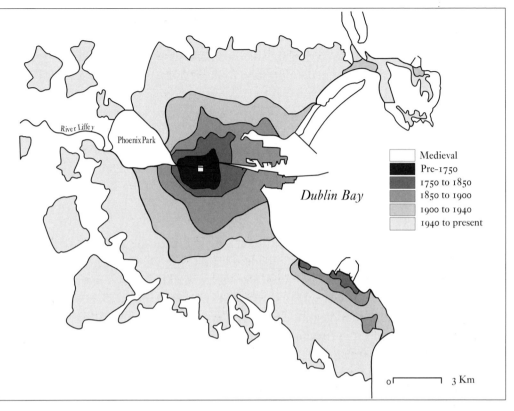

Medieval
Pre-1750
1750 to 1850
1850 to 1900
1900 to 1940
1940 to present

River Liffey

Phoenix Park

Dublin Bay

0 — 3 Km

1 The walled medieval town (small white area) in relation to the modern city.
Zones have been generalized.

Winetavern Streets as well as those in Temple Bar, have been published in excavation reports. Most recently Linzi Simpson (2000) has provided a chronologically organized report of archaeological investigations in medieval Dublin over the last four years. A city archaeologist has been appointed by Dublin Corporation and a heritage centre for medieval Dublin, called Dublinia after the medieval Latin name of the city, has been established. Its major attractions are a scale-model of late-medieval Dublin and the display of artifacts from the Anglo-Norman layers at Wood Quay as well as historical information in maps and text.

This chapter explores the changing topography of medieval Dublin, that is to say the layout of the medieval town in response to its major growth phases. It also attempts to establish how much of the medieval town has survived in the modern city and the degree to which the layout of the oldest core of the city still reflects a medieval origin. We shall try to recreate the topography of medieval Dublin with the help of the earliest surviving maps of Dublin, John Speed's map of 1610 and John Rocque's map of 1756, respectively the first accurately surveyed plan of Dublin and the first to show property boundaries. Speed's map is discussed in detail by John Andrews (1983) who has also analyzed Rocque's maps of Dublin city and county in an introduction to a reprint of these plans (1977). The city maps have been recently reprinted in book form with a very useful gazetteer to the city's streets (Ferguson, 1998). These maps will be used in conjunction with evidence produced by archaeologists and medieval historians. (See the appendix for a short guide to maps of Dublin.)

Viking-age Dublin: the historical background

The origins of Dublin as a town are closely linked to the activities of the Vikings. These came to Ireland as raiders, mainly from the Norwegian fjords, in the ninth century and sailed up Irish rivers to plunder wealthy monasteries and capture prisoners whom they sold as slaves to Iceland and on the continent. It was only in the middle of the tenth century that the former raiders began to be transformed into merchants and craftsmen and their strongholds became coastal trading settlements. In spite of the overlordship by Gaelic families, particularly during the eleventh century, these settlements survived as distinct places until the Anglo-Normans conquered their towns in the late-twelfth century.

Some historians refer to the time when the Vikings plundered rich monasteries and withdrew again in their ships as the 'hit and run' period. It lasted from 795 to 836. In 841, according to the Annals of Ulster, the Vikings set up a permanent camp at the mouth of the Liffey. It was described in the Irish sources as *longphort oc Duibhlinn*. This was the beginning of the *longphort* phase, which lasted from 841 to 902. We will return to the thorny question of where the *longphort* was located.

At the end of the ninth century Irish resistance to the *longphort* increased and in 902 the Irish managed to defeat the ruling Dublin Norse and to expel them. The elite of the Viking families and their followers sailed across the Irish Sea to the Isle of Man, England and to southern Scotland. But fifteen years later they came back from exile and re-established their settlement at Dublin. This event effectively marks the second major phase of Viking settlement in Dublin and constitutes the *dún* phase (917–1014).

Patrick Wallace has expressed the belief that when the Vikings returned in the early-tenth century they brought with them a well-developed urban concept resembling the Anglo-Saxon towns which they would have seen during their enforced stay in England. In this view the Vikings were catalysts through whom the germ of urbanization was transferred from England to Ireland (Wallace, 1990, p. 77; 1992b, p. 36). The move from raiding into trading, with intermittent emphasis on one or the other, would probably have been common all over the Viking world of the time. For example, the Varangians (largely Swedish Vikings) settled in the west of modern-day Russia and the Ukraine in the ninth century. Between then and the eleventh century they gradually shifted from plunder to trade, thus sowing the seeds of the Russian State (Stone, 1990). The subtlety of the situation in Dublin is indicated, as Charles Doherty (1980, p. 81) has pointed out, by the fact that in Irish the word for market is *margad*, which is a borrowing from the old Norse *markaðr*. Obviously intermittent warfare coexisted with economic development.

From the late-tenth century onwards the Irish high kings successfully exerted pressure on Dublin and their forces captured the town on different occasions. In 989, according to the Annals of the Four Masters, when Dublin was temporarily under Irish overlordship – the pretext for celebrating Dublin's millennium in 1988 – the high king Mael Sechnaill levied a tax of one ounce of gold on each house plot in the town. This would certainly support Patrick Wallace's idea that Dublin had an orderly layout at that time. These events initiated the 'Hiberno-Norse' phase that was to last until the arrival of the Anglo-Normans in 1170.

In summary, following Howard Clarke's (1990a) work on early-medieval Dublin which is based on documentary evidence, we can distinguish a number of phases in the development of Viking-age Dublin which were preceded by a 'hit and run' phase and interrupted by a short period in exile.

795–836	'hit and run' phase
841–902	*longphort* phase
902–917	defeat and exile overseas
917–1014	*dún* phase
980–1170	Hiberno-Norse phase

(Clarke, 1996, pp 341–53)

This short outline confirms that towns were not an innovation that the Vikings brought fully-fledged from Scandinavia to Ireland. On the contrary, a place like Dublin, located at a pivotal site in the expanding Viking-age trading-network, was the product of the Viking age itself. Early medieval

Dublin was a vibrant place. Its inhabitants would have spoken Norse, English and Irish. It must have been a contested cultural space, particularly when it was dominated by Irish overlords for much of the second half of the eleventh century.

The physical environment of medieval Dublin

The area on which the medieval city of Dublin was built is almost entirely composed of boulder clay, deposited by the last ice-sheets that spread across the region some 10,000 years ago. This boulder clay is derived from the under-lying limestone. Bore-hole readings in the vicinity of St Patrick's cathedral, taken when the Poddle was culverted at the end of the nineteenth century, show that *c.*4 metres of boulder clay rested on the limestone bedrock (MGS, 1903, p. 88). However, over time the Liffey has eroded the boulder clay from its riverbed in Dublin so that there is now only a thin layer of alluvial loam or silt which overlays a thick layer of flood gravels which in turn rests on the limestone bedrock.

The existence of a steep river terrace, rising up to 12.5 metres above the present river, was of key importance in choosing where to build the first town. At normal tides this terrace would have been above the floodplain of the river and it was on this terrace, following the 11 to 12 metre contour line that long stretches of the Viking-age town wall were built. Circumstantial evidence for the site of the first bridge and the location of St Saviour's church as well as the towers at the western and eastern end of the medieval wall along the quays has led John de Courcy (1996, p. 28; 2000) to believe that there were pockets of firmer ground protruding into the river that were used as building sites as well as numerous bays. However, the records of boreholes that were sunk at the turn of the nineteenth century in the immediate vicinity of the river in preparation for building work show deep deposits of river gravel but no boulder clay. On the north side of the river near the Four Courts, close to the oldest bridge, there was over 3 metres of river gravel before limestone was reached. At the opposite side of the river at Usher's Quay there was about 5 metres of river gravel below the road surface under one metre of alluvial soils and at Fishamble Street limestone had not been reached after passing through 5 metres of gravel (MGS, 1903, p. 89). More recent borings carried out at Merchant's Quay in 1988 by the Geological Survey of Ireland recorded 3.4 to 4 metres of grey silt followed by 4 to 5 metres of river gravel, reaching limestone bedrock at about 9 metres under ground level. There seems to be no doubt that river gravel is the dominant layer within the floodplain. On Rocque's map we find a reference to a small landing place west of Arran Quay called 'Gravel Walk Slip'.

Dublin is located at the mouth of the Liffey at its entry to Dublin Bay. The river is tidal, with a tidal range of about 3 metres. Before the quays were built the shoreline of the river changed with the fullness of the tide. Today's great riverside buildings, the Custom House and the Four Courts, could only be erected after land reclamations and the completion of the new quays in the early-eighteenth century. The main difference between the river as we see it today and as it presented itself to the Viking settlers was the vast extent of shallow water covering large areas that were to become built-up land in later centuries (Figure 2).

In the ninth century when the Vikings first came into the Liffey estuary, tidal waters reached as far as Chapelizod and the Poddle was tidal as far as its confluence with the Coombe stream. As the Liffey rises in the Wicklow Mountains and has a large catchment area, strong rains would swell it and cause severe flooding before it entered the sea. This threat was eliminated only in the twentieth century by building dams further upstream at Poulaphouca, Golden Falls and Leixlip (de Courcy, 1996, p. 24). The Poddle has shown that it is still capable of causing severe flooding in the Harold's Cross area of the city.

We do not know for certain how the coastline would have looked to the Vikings. Taking the boundary between the distribution of river deposits (alluvium) and boulder clay gives a reasonable approximation of the line between river and dry land. This coastline is shown in Figure 2. Archaeological excavations at Wood Quay confirm that in the Hiberno-Norse period in c.1100, the Liffey came right up to the town wall and left behind marine deposits, coinciding, in this instance, with this boundary.

North of the Liffey, both of the church sites that predate the Anglo-Norman period, St Michan's and St Mary's abbey, are located just off the projected early-medieval coastline. South of the Liffey the location of the recently sculptured 'Viking Long Stone' (at today's junction of Pearse Street and D'Olier Street) is an indicator of the earlier shore-line. This granite pillar is reminiscent of the original Long Stone which the Vikings had erected, probably in the tenth century, at the mouth of the river Steine to mark their first landfall in 841 and also as a guide for sailors (Figure 2). The original Long Stone was removed in the early-eighteenth century but its well-documented existence makes it necessary to abandon the geological boundary as the indicator of the former shoreline at this point. Instead we must assume that, over time, the coastline extended into the bay as the result of natural processes and human actions. This adjustment allows the pre-Anglo-Norman religious house of All Saints priory, which after the dissolution of the monasteries in the sixteenth century became the site of Trinity College, to stand on dry ground. Another good indicator for the shoreline in the Viking period would have been the *Thing Mount*, the site of assembly of all free men, which was usually to be found near the shore. The Thingmount in Dublin was erected near the confluence of the river Liffey with the river Steine at the present site of St Andrew's church, now the offices of Dublin Tourism at the junction of Suffolk Street/St Andrews Street. In order for Viking-Age settlers to get to the Thingmount, there must have been a ford and later a bridge across the Poddle. The monument was levelled in 1685 and the soil was used to raise the level of present-day Nassau Street, which was liable to flooding. This explains the height difference between this street and the grounds of Trinity College (Clarke, 1998).

Because the ridge on which medieval Dublin was built runs parallel to the river we must assume that on the southern side the river bank was relatively straight as far as the confluence of the Liffey with the Poddle. Here there was a deep inlet and to the east, the river widened considerably (see Speed's map). Further downstream, the Steine, a small stream, flowed into the Liffey estuary at what is now Aston Quay. On Speed's map this river goes underground in a locality that was to become Trinity College.

Between the mouth of the Steine, an Old Norse word, and the spit of Ringsend the river Dodder joined the Liffey in a wide delta. Beyond this point the estuary opened up and only two features would have been landmarks at high tide – Clontarf Island on the northern side, now incorporated in land reclamations, and the spit of Ringsend on the southern side. When in 1986 Hurricane Charlie caused widespread flooding in Dublin, the road over the spit at Ringsend was the only one to provide access from Sandymount to the city as all the land reclaimed in post-medieval times was again temporarily under water.

On the north side of the Liffey there seems to have been firmer ground in the vicinity of the first bridge across the river. But downstream from this site the riverbank was not well defined because the small river Bradogue flowed into the Liffey through extensive mud-banks and produced a large water inlet known as the 'Pill by the Water', which is shown on Speed's map (Figure 9).

One of the fascinating characteristics of medieval towns is how natural terrain was used to the maximum advantage. It is, therefore, most revealing to

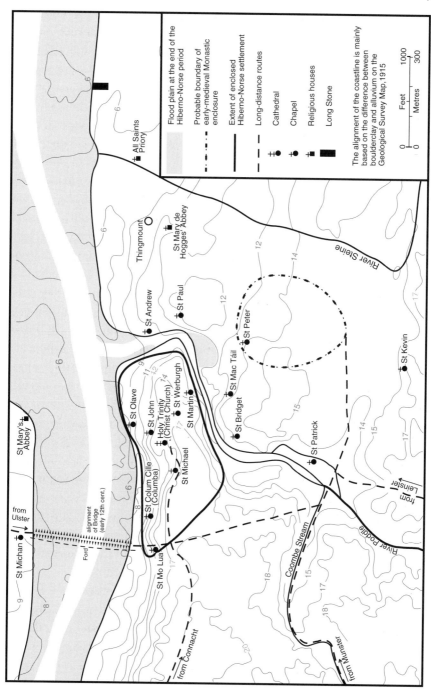

2 Viking and Hiberno-Norse Dublin (917–1170). (Based on Clarke and Simms, 1984, p. 36. The alignment of the hurdle ford is based on Simms, 1979, p. 30.)

look at a contour map of medieval Dublin (Figure 3). The ground level in the medieval city is now almost 3 metres higher than it would have been in medieval times and some mental adjustments must be made in deriving the medieval from the modern contour lines. All the same, it is obvious that the dominating feature on the contour map is the long narrow ridge, *c.*17 metres high, running parallel to the Liffey on its southern bank as far as the confluence with the Poddle. The main landmark on this ridge today is Christ Church cathedral, as it has been throughout the centuries. The increase in height from medieval times is well illustrated when we look at the way in which the entrance to the two medieval cathedrals, Christ Church and St Patrick's, lie below the present street level. The explanation lies simply in the build-up of rubbish over time. The wooden houses of medieval Dublin would have lasted little longer than one or two generations before they had to be replaced, the ground being then levelled and a new house erected. Refuse from cooking and probably also from domestic animals would have remained on the individual house plots and contributed to the build-up of the surface level.

As already mentioned, in the medieval period the Poddle was a tidal river almost as far as St Patrick's cathedral (Figure 2). The little stream flowed around the southern and eastern edge of the ridge and, as we must expect that its bed was marshy, it would have made access to the ridge difficult even at low tides. The ridge therefore provided an excellent defensive site with steep slopes ending in marshy land to the north, east and south and only leaving the western flank without a natural boundary. The site has such locational advantages for defence that it is not surprising that it is here that the Vikings built their stronghold.

South of the ridge the 12.5 metre (35 ft) contour line indicates a depression that in early-medieval times was likely to have been flooded. The same contour also represents the shoreline alongside the old stone city wall on Wood Quay which we have already identified. Therefore we can assume that in the early-medieval period this hollow was flooded at high tide and this must have been the site where the Vikings beached their boats. Its location near the sea at the confluence of a smaller with a bigger river would have been ideal for this purpose, because the banks of the side stream provided the necessary firm ground for the ships to be pulled up, while the estuary afforded protection against currents and waves (Ellmers, 1978, p. 178). It has been suggested that this was the 'black pool' (*dubh linn*), which is mentioned in contemporary documents in relation to an early Irish monastery that must have been located at this pool (Clarke, 1977), (Figure 2). The Vikings adopted a Norse version

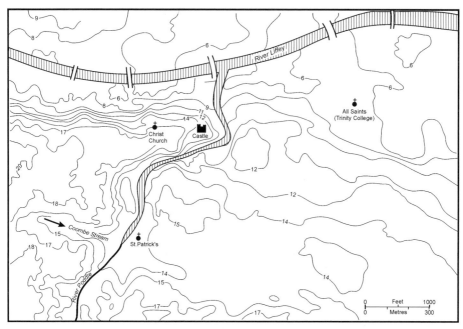

3 Contour lines in the area of medieval Dublin (based on 1:10,560 Geological Survey map, 1915) converted from feet to metres. The Liffey is shown within its modern banks. Only the most westerly bridge on this map (today's Father Mathew Bridge) existed in the medieval period.

CATHEDRAL of CHRIST CHURCH.

4 Christ Church as it appeared in the eighteenth century prior to its restoration.
(Pool and Cash, 1780, following p. 76.)

of the Irish name, *Dyflinn*, for their enclosed permanent settlement on the ridge south of the Liffey overlooking the Black Pool and this eventually became Dublin in English.

Before a bridge was built in the early-twelfth century, a hurdle ford linked the road from Brega, north of the river, to the Kingdom of Leinster south of the Liffey. The hurdles consisted of stems of trees laid on piles of stone placed at intervals in the stream (Haliday, 1882, p. 214). A settlement would have developed on the southern banks of the river in association with the hurdle ford and took its name from the ford – *Áth Cliath*, the ford of hurdles. Tidal fluctuations and the danger of flashes associated with strong rain made this ford dangerous and crossing was restricted to the times of low tide. In the absence of archaeological evidence it is difficult to determine the precise form and location of this ford. We must assume that the ford had a considerable width that would have reduced the danger of it being swept away. As to its location all we can do is to seek it in the context of the ancient roads and the configuration of the river banks. The old road from Munster coming down the Coombe stream and the old road from Leinster crossing the Poddle at St Patrick's joined and formed the road leading northwards towards the river, probably on the alignment of present-day Francis Street. Speed's map (Figure 9) supports the conclusion that the continuation of this street was cut off by the building of the town's defences, but might originally have continued to present-day Bridge Street. On his sketch-map showing the Liffey shoreline at Dublin in 850 John de Courcy (1996, p. 28) draws attention to a 'hard spot' in the river where the Four Courts are located today. He suggests that this 'hard spot' provided a convenient bridging point. It might be assumed that the people who built the original hurdle ford, which predated the Viking age, used this natural advantage, just as their successors did in the early-twelfth century when they built the first bridge across the Liffey at this point. It would have been beneficial to build the permanent bridge close enough to the ford to benefit from its barrier effect. The fact that St Michan's, a pre-Anglo-Norman foundation, is located on the road continuing from the projected early river crossing supports the argument that the ford would have run close to the alignment of the later bridge. The suggestion is that there was continuity of site from the hurdle ford to the later bridge across the Liffey (Simms, 1979, p. 30).

The existence of the two early settlement sites at Dublin explains why the Irish annalists refer to two placenames for Dublin – the *Duibhlinne* settlement by the black pool and *Áth Cliath*, the settlement by the hurdle ford, one ecclesiastical in origin and the other secular. A passage from the biography of

St Mo-laga equates the two places. It says, in translation (Clarke, 1990a, p. 59) '… and to the coastal town, which is called *dún duibhlinne* or *áth cleat*.'

The last major feature that contributed to the physical environment of early-medieval Dublin was the Poddle. This small river meandered across a shallow valley and split up into a main stream and a side stream. The island between the streams became the site of the pre-Norman church of St Patrick's, referred to as 'St Patrick's on the island' in a document of 20 April 1179, which confirmed the metropolitan jurisdiction of Archbishop Lorcan Ua Tuathail (McNeil, 1950, p. 3). On James Malton's eighteenth-century print of St Patrick's cathedral a street sign on a house near the cathedral says 'Cross Poddle'. The nearby confluence of the Poddle with the Coombe stream was probably the nearest point to the town at which the Poddle was fordable. It was, as we have mentioned earlier, an important intersection for long distance routes coming from the south and west and leading north across the Liffey.

The harbour suited the Vikings in this early period because their sailing vessels had a shallow draught (1 m or so) and so could navigate the significant sandbars in the bay. With the Anglo-Normans came larger trading craft that found navigation in and out of the city both difficult and dangerous. Throughout the Middle Ages ships coming in and out of Dublin encountered the danger of sandbanks, low water channels and no shelter against high winds. When Stanihurst wrote about Dublin in the 1570s, he mentioned that the only fault with the city was the shortcomings of its harbour (Lennon, 1988a). In the eighteenth century, when the Ballast Office, a State agency, took on the task of improving the harbour, it dredged the sandbars and constructed the Great South Wall and the Poolbeg Light House, thereby providing a better protected harbour. Later the Great North (Bull) Wall was built from Clontarf to improve tidal scour and thus maintain the channel. The Great South Wall is probably one of the most dramatic marine walls built in the eighteenth century and it still constitutes one of the best-hidden marvels of present-day Dublin.

The layout of Viking-age Dublin: the longphort at Áth Cliath

The reconstruction map of early-medieval Dublin shows a number of churches in the area south of the Black Pool that were founded before the arrival of the Anglo-Normans. These are considered contemporary with the Hiberno-Norse settlement on the ridge (Bradley, 1992). They include St Patrick's, which became the cathedral church and gave its name to Patrick Street, and St Bridget's, which gave its name to Bride Street. The latter church is shown on Rocque's map but has since been demolished. There was also the church of St Michael le Pole in Ship Street, which is not shown by Rocque, although its round tower, recently identified by Margaret Gowen as a late-twelfth-century bell tower, was demolished only in the late-eighteenth century. Rescue excavations on this site have also uncovered finds connected to graves that were dated to the middle of the eighth century (Simpson, 2000, p. 18). St Kevin's church, which gave its name to Kevin Street, was rebuilt in the eighteenth century but is now in ruins in a small public park. There was also the early-medieval church of St Peter's which has vanished but if you look at the modern-day map of the city Whitefriar Street and Stephen's Street Upper and Lower have a circular alignment reminiscent of early-medieval monastic enclosures (Clarke, 1977). Unfortunately, this suggestion is not supported by the archaeological investigations undertaken by Margaret Gowen in that area. The eastern part of this suggested monastic enclosure would have been greatly changed in the seventeenth century with the laying out of one of the early city estates, the Aungier estate, with its regularly planned street-pattern focused on York Street (Burke, 1972).

This leads us finally to the question of the location of the *longphort*, the fortified ship harbour mentioned in the Annals in 841. The word *longphort* is a Latin loan word originally meaning 'landing place'. The *Annals* do not provide a description of a *longphort* but it probably consisted of an earthen bank with wooden palisades on top thrown up on the landward side of a harbour area or, as recently suggested by Howard Clarke (1998), on an island in the mouth of the river, in order to protect the ships. It was from these *longphort* that the Vikings conducted their plundering forays to monastic sites. The term may very well have come to describe the encampment for the Viking seafarers when they stayed in Ireland over the winter. The problem is that until recently archaeologists could not find any evidence for mid-ninth-century Viking occupation in Dublin. Over a hundred years ago a Viking-age burial place dated to the mid-ninth century was found in Kilmainham, Islandbridge, about one and a half kilometres upstream from Dublin. Because this site is also the location of an old ford across the river, it has been suggested that the cemetery with Viking goods was associated with some kind of early Viking settlement at this site (O'Brien, 1998).

Howard Clarke has argued that the documentary evidence suggests that the Dublin *longphort* of 841 should be located in the vicinity of the Black Pool, because in documents of the mid-ninth century the Dublin Norsemen are linked with Duibhlinne. Raghnall Ó Floinn (1998) believes that the *longphort*

5 A reconstruction of Dublin in the medieval period from the Dublinia exhibition.
Reprinted with kind permission of Dublinia. The picture looks towards the north with
St Patrick's cathedral in the lower centre. The Castle can be seen in the upper right.

might indeed have been located within the monastic precincts of Linn
Duachaill, located at the Black Pool. At the beginning of the tenth century the
Annals record that the Vikings were expelled from the *longphort* at Áth Cliath.
This change in the description of the Dublin *longphort* led Clarke (1998) to
believe that the location of the *longphort* might have changed to Usher's
Island, a site just upstream of the old hurdle ford, which in the tenth century
still constituted a proper island and which would have been a good defensive
site. This suggestion is attractive except that the river was liable to devastating
floods before the building of dams further upstream in recent centuries.
Limited archaeological excavations on Usher's Island have not confirmed any
Viking settlement (Simpson, 2000, p. 21). The first archaeological hint for
mid-ninth-century settlement structures came in 1993 from the excavations at
Parliament Street, which produced some tentative evidence for activity along
the west bank of the Poddle (Simpson, 1994, p. 4). From the locational point
of view it would indeed make sense if the *longphort* was located at the site of the
present castle, with the boats beached and protected in the vicinity of the Black
Pool. This location combines elevated ground with speedy access to the sea.

The excavations at Temple Bar West, directed by Linzi Simpson, have further
confirmed ninth-century Viking habitation on the eastern side of the ridge. A

number of structures belonging to small buildings (2.25 metres by 3 metres) with floors sunk into the ground were also found and it is believed that these are the earliest Viking habitations in Dublin. They were dug into the boulder clay and bedrock (Simpson, 1999, p. 13). Radiocarbon analysis of one of these structures suggests a ninth-century date. There were no hearths in these structures and according to Simpson they seemed to have a common cooking place outside the houses. They were not laid out in a regular pattern, nor did they show any signs of property boundaries. The excavator suggests that these structures relate to the *longphort* phase of Viking-Age Dublin inhabited by a small community living along the banks of the Poddle. By the late-ninth century these sunken structures were backfilled and were superseded by post-and-wattle houses surrounded by property fences, as we know them from the Wood Quay excavations.

What is puzzling is the apparent lack of a defensive bank at this early site, as by analogy with the Scandinavian evidence one would expect the *longphort* to have been defended. It is therefore necessary to return to the suggestion that the *longphort* was indeed located on the site of the present day castle. This proposition is based on the likelihood of continuity from the ninth-century *longphort* to the tenth-century stronghold of the Viking and later Hiberno-Norse town to the thirteenth-century castle of the Anglo-Norman borough. The contour lines (Figure 3) indicating higher lying ground surrounded by water make this sequence very likely on purely topographical grounds.

The earliest archaeological record for Viking-age Dublin comes from Linzi Simpson's excavations in Temple Bar inside the eastern enclosure of the Viking stronghold. She found sunken floored structures, used as houses, together with boundary fences and pathways, which she dated to the late-ninth century. In the Wood Quay excavations, carried out by Patrick Wallace, the earliest excavated levels, consisting of the foundation of houses and plot boundaries, date from the early-tenth century. It was during this period that the oldest Viking-Age settlement by the banks of the Poddle developed into an industrial area with some form of metal working. It may be that there was a deliberate upsurge of residential activities in the area of Fishamble Street at that time (see below). The other interesting point is that according to the archaeological evidence there seems to have been continuity of settlement right through the early-tenth century as Leslie Simpson (2000, p. 24) hints at. This means that the years of exile in England (902–917) for the Dublin Vikings might only have affected the warrior families and that merchants and craftsmen continued to live in Dublin, this time under Irish overlordship. There is as yet no historical evidence to back up this suggestion.

The Viking stronghold-settlement: Dún Dublinn

When the leading Viking families returned to the Liffey estuary in the early-tenth century, it was recorded in 917 that they returned to *Áth Cliath* but by the middle of the century the name *Dún Dublinn* had come into use. According to Howard Clarke (1998, p. 358) the first mention of the word *dún* (stronghold) in relation to Dublin appears in the records in 944. This might imply that a stronghold had been built by this stage, possibly in the vicinity of the present castle. The juxtaposition of a landing place for ships and a stronghold, constructed of wood, on higher ground is typical of early trading places as comparison with Lübeck on the western Baltic suggests. We must assume that in the second half of the tenth century Dublin grew from the harbour area uphill to the vicinity of the stronghold on the ridge (Simms, 1979; 1990). This suggestion has been born out by the archaeological evidence at Fishamble Street (Wallace, 1985).

Towards the end of the tenth century, that is to say towards the end of the *dún* phase, the Irish high kings successfully exerted pressure on Dublin and on different occasions captured the town. According to the Annals of the Four Masters, in 989, when Dublin was temporarily under Irish overlordship, the high king Mael Sechnaill levied a tax of one ounce of gold on each house plot in the town referred to in the Annals as *garths*. Examples of such *garths* may have been uncovered in the form of rectangular house plots and enclosures at Fishamble Street, where Patrick Wallace (1992a, 1, p. 36; 2, p. 42) has found evidence for the regular layout of the tenth- and eleventh-century town. The excavations revealed the division of the site into a number of contiguous plots, obviously the forerunners of later burgage plots, separated from each other by post-and-wattle fences (Figure 6). At one point the property fences went through three different centuries of debris, indicating the continuity of property boundaries from the later tenth to the twelfth century. This archaeological evidence suggests that houses were built along this street in the eleventh century and probably earlier with long narrow yards stretching towards the Liffey. At the end of these yards the archaeologists found the remnants of wooden structures and concentrated accumulations of dung. This reminds us that the Viking settlers and Hiberno-Norse would have kept their own domestic animals.

This settlement, which writers of the time referred to as *dún duibhlinne* was protected by two parallel earthen banks, about two metres wide each, dating to *c.*950 and *c.*1000 respectively. The best-preserved section of these banks had stockade-like wooden palisades on top, whilst on the inside the bank was

PLOT BOUNDARIES (HYPOTHETICAL) — —· — — —

EXTENT OF EXCAVATIONS   — · — · — · —·

PROBABLE ANCIENT LINE
OF FISHAMBLE STREET   — · — · — · — · —

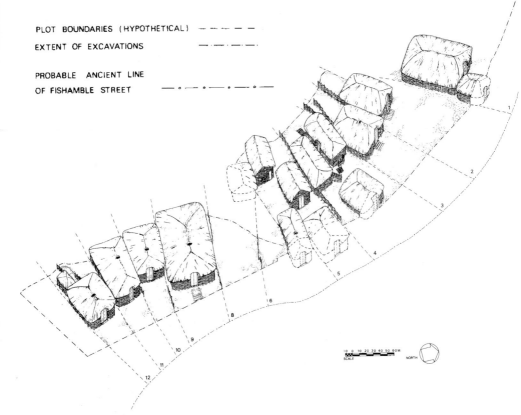

6 Reconstruction of Viking-age streetscape in Fishamble Street dated to the late tenth/ early-eleventh century (Wallace, 1992a, p. 42). Reprinted with kind permission of Royal Irish Academy.

faced with post-and-wattle work. The exposed sections resembled ramparts for defensive purposes, but they are also reminiscent of dikes built elsewhere for protection against flooding. The excavations can provide only a partial answer to the question of how extensive was the area of the Viking settlement as they only exposed small sections of these ramparts.

7 (*opposite*) Growth-phases of medieval Dublin within the town-walls, superimposed on John Rocque's map, surveyed in 1756 (Simms, 1979).   **A** First plan unit – probably identical with the *dún* phase (tenth century), enclosed by an earthen bank.   **B** Second plan unit – probably an extension of the Viking-age town in the Hiberno-Norse phase (eleventh and most of twelfth century). The Hiberno-Norse town (units A and B) was surrounded by a stone-wall from the early-twelfth century onwards.   **C** Third plan unit – land reclamation carried out by the Anglo-Normans (early-thirteenth century). Extension of the town-wall to the river in the mid-thirteenth century.

Rocque's map is in four sheets and it has been necessary to join two to produce this extract. The parallel dots between zones A and C indicate the location of sections of the two parallel-running tenth-century enclosing banks excavated by Patrick Wallace (see Figure 8).

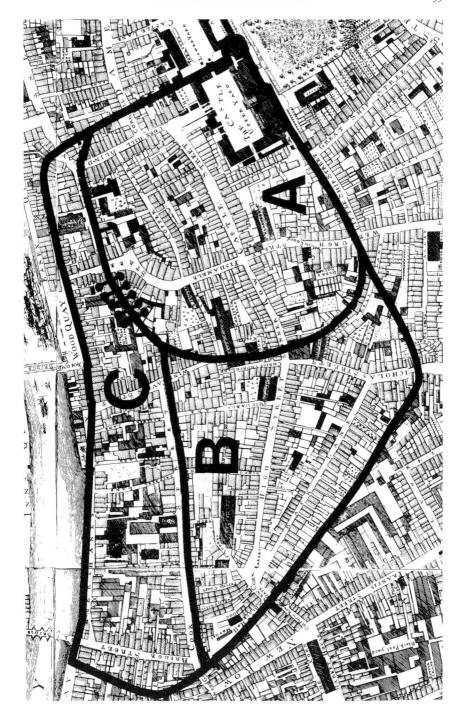

It is at this point that the cartographical method of town-plan analysis may help to provide the answer. By identifying the street-pattern and the alignment of property boundaries on Rocque's map, surveyed in 1756, it will be possible to suggest three major growth-phases or plan-units for the walled town. Unfortunately, it appears that Rocque had no interest in antiquarian matters, as he failed to show remnants of the medieval stone wall which were still standing in 1756. Fortunately, the break in plot pattern that the wall had produced particularly on the south-western side of the walled town is so striking that it is possible to superimpose the medieval wall and its predecessors on the map. The street and plot pattern suggest that the walled area of the town consisted of three different plan units, reflecting three different growth phases – an eastern unit, a western unit and a third unit between these and the Liffey (Figure 7).

The eastern unit (A) is the earliest one and the one that we identified as the probable site of the early *longphort*, and which became the focus of their stronghold after the Vikings returned to Dublin in 917. The dominant feature is the east-west axis of Castle Street and Skinner's Row (now Christchurch Place) which is crossed by the north–south axis of Fishamble Street and Werburgh Street. We know from archaeological evidence that these streets were densely settled by the late-tenth century. Castle Street and Skinner's Row run along the edge of the ridge without any change in street level. Fishamble Street and Werburgh Street led down steep slopes in opposite directions. The marked bend in Fishamble Street may have arisen to avoid an even sharper break of slope.

Looking at the representation of the castle on Rocque's map (Figure 8) it should be remembered that the much smaller structure of the Viking stronghold was replaced by the thirteenth-century stone-built Anglo-Norman castle, which in turn was replaced by the eighteenth-century rebuilding (see Maguire, 1974). Excavations carried out by the Board of Works in the 1960s underneath the castle have produced evidence of the eleventh-century town wall, which ran at a right angle to the upper castle yard across Cork Hill down to Blind Quay. Excavations in the castle carried out in the 1980s by Anne Lynch and Con Manning (1986) uncovered clear traces of the eastern ramparts of the Viking-age town. The earliest of these was a bank with dry stone facing built on the shore of the Poddle estuary.

Thus far, the evidence from our town-plan analysis suggests that the area between Christ Church and Dublin Castle, marked as A, constitutes the first plan-unit of the medieval town. Archaeological evidence confirms that,

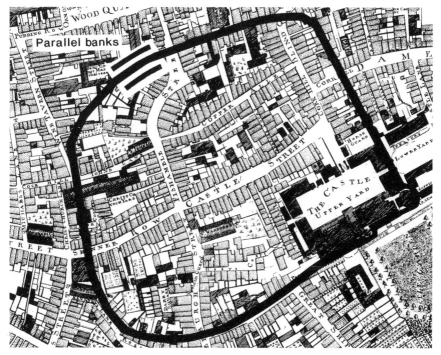

8 Detail of unit A, the first plan unit of medieval Dublin.

enclosed by an earthen bank, this area is identical with the initial Viking
stronghold settlement of the tenth century, and as such it constitutes the pre-
urban nucleus. This then raises the question of how to identify the alignment
of Dublin's first enclosing banks on Rocque's map? At Wood Quay, Patrick
Wallace excavated sections of two parallel running banks, dated to *c*.950 and
c.1000 respectively (Wallace, 1990, p. 88). On the north-eastern and south-
eastern stretch the banks would have run along the same line as the later
defences, which enclosed the castle. As we stated earlier, archaeologists found
a section of the eastern bank of the Viking-age town along the Poddle estuary.
For the location of the western stretch of the first enclosing walls it is town-
plan analysis that comes to the rescue. The property boundaries south of
Skinner's Row along Ross Lane follow a curve. Most likely it was the existence
of the first enclosing wall that had this long lasting effect on the shape of
property boundaries in this section of the town. We can therefore suggest that
on the south-western section the banks of the Viking-age town would have
followed a line along Little Ship Street just above the Poddle, passing north of
Ross Lane across to Skinner's Row. According to personal communication
with Patrick Healy rescue excavations south of High Street (Skinner Row)

have produced evidence of an earthen bank of 3 metres, which might very well have been part of the enclosing banks. The large scale Ordnance Survey map of Dublin (1866, 1:1056), shows that Ross Lane actually crosses the Poddle and it must be assumed that the ditch ran just inside the Poddle in order to protect the settlement from flooding and simultaneously to maximize the protective element of the small river. The bank would then have continued under the west end of Christ Church cathedral and across to the Wood Quay–Fishamble Street site. Taking into account the alignment of plot-patterns on Rocque's map it must be assumed that the banks extended along Smock Alley and continued in such a way that their most northerly end rested on hard ground, which comes closest to the Liffey on the eastern side of the ridge. The banks would then have turned towards Cork Hill in the direction of the tenth-century stronghold. Had the tenth-century Viking settlement not developed in the area of the present-day castle, but rather on the site of Christ Church cathedral, the highest elevation inside the walled town, then the street pattern would probably have evolved in a concentric fashion around the church, which it clearly did not.

Archaeological evidence gives the impression that Viking-age Dublin was a very busy place. Its exports included hides, woollens, pelts, combs and probably decorated objects used as jewellery. Charles Doherty (1998, p. 304) has suggested that late-tenth-century Dublin owed a great deal to the Norse king Amlaíb Cúarán whom he believed encouraged the development of a formal layout for the town and was responsible for civic sites such as the Thingmount and the Long Stone. It has been suggested that the Thingmount was probably an inauguration site for Irish kings before the coming of the Vikings and that Amlaíb himself was inaugurated in an Irish fashion. This symbolizes the complexity of tenth-century Dublin, where the inhabitants spoke Norse and Irish, where Christianity and pagan traditions existed next to each other, where Norse kings took the daughters of Irish kings as wives, and where the slave trade was still economically important.

It is not surprising that the assimilation process between the two ethnic groups should also have found expression in the built environment. Patrick Wallace (1992a) has classified Viking-age houses in Ireland on the basis of the remains of 200 foundations. The dominant type was broadly rectangular in shape and measured about 8 metres by 5 metres. It was built of post and wattle and had a thatched roof that rested on interior posts. The house was divided into three aisles, with raised beds on each side. An open fireplace was located in the centre of the house. Some of the houses were probably used as workshops by combmakers, shoemakers, metalworkers and jewellers. Patrick Wallace has suggested that the dominant house type in Dublin was an adaptation to an urban environment of an Irish rural house but influenced in form and layout by Norse prototypes. The post and wattle walls of these houses followed the native tradition and so did the thatched roofs. But the layout closely resembles the design of Nordic houses and we are drawn to the conclusion that the Irish and Norse traditions of building houses merged in the Viking-age buildings of Dublin.

Hiberno-Norse Dublin

From the end of the tenth century onwards Dublin lost its political independence, when Irish overlordship was extended over the town at intervals until 1052, when it became incorporated into the Irish political scene. The settlement entered the next phase, the Hiberno-Norse phase, which we dated from c.980 to 1170. A tangible outcome of this was the fact that the Vikings were converted to Christianity by the beginning of the eleventh century. They built two churches of their own in Dublin. The first was erected on the site of the later Christ Church cathedral; the second was the church of St Olav's near the lower end of Fishamble Street. The latter church underlines the importance of Fishamble Street in Viking-age Dublin and it continued in use until 1538, when the parish was united with that of St John's, a later parish church at the upper end of Fishamble Street (see Figure 2). St John's is shown on Rocque's map on the western side of Fishamble Street just north of Christ Church cathedral. St Olav's was demolished some time in the sixteenth century and has left no trace above ground. It has been suggested that it stood nearly opposite the western end of Smock Alley, today's Essex Street West.

Excavations at High Street and Fishamble Street (Ó Ríordáin, 1971) dating to the eleventh century have shown that the growth of Dublin was due primarily to the activities of merchants and craftsmen in an economically and politically advantageous climate. The craftsmen relied on the immediate hinterland for much of their raw material – antlers for carving combs and hides to produce shoes. In the High Street excavations some 600 combs were found and a very large number of shoes. However, what could not be obtained locally was imported such as amber from the Baltic for producing jewellery.

Dublin remained a trading port, and commercial life seemed little affected by political change. The town began to mint its own coins by the end of the tenth century (Dolley, 1966). The recent excavations in Castle Street have uncovered three major coin hoards, which were dated to the 990s. As a result of the growing population the built-up area expanded westward along the ridge (Unit B). Present-day High Street was its main axis and Back Lane ran almost parallel to it. A number of lanes connected High Street with Cook Street. We can still follow one of them when we walk down St Audoen's Lane winding its way past the old St Audoen's Church in order to reach St Audoen's Gate, the only still extant medieval gate in the northern side of the wall. On the southern side of the ridge, Nicholas Street descends to present-day St Patrick's cathedral, a church that most likely predates the expansion of the enclosed settlement, as its early-Christian crosses would suggest. High Street like Castle Street and Skinners Row followed closely the edge of the ridge. Archaeological excavations along High Street (Ó Ríordáin, 1971) have revealed the remains of wattle houses with workshops and wooden pathways constructed of planks dating to the late tenth and eleventh centuries. The focus of the western end of High Street was the corn market immediately inside the town gate. It was here that the main road from the countryside to the west of the town reached its terminus and cartloads full of corn, the staple item of diet, were unloaded. Standing on the site today you will see that the place-name 'Cornmarket' has been preserved. Turning westward you will notice the last remnants of the medieval stone wall as it joined the New Gate at Cornmarket. Clearly, the area around High Street constitutes the second plan unit of Viking-age Dublin.

Based on our analysis so far, we can confirm that Dublin consisted of the two units (A and B) as indicated in Figure 7 by the end of the Hiberno-Norse period. Archaeological evidence shows that in the late Hiberno-Norse period both units were enclosed by a stone wall. The western extension of this wall still stands along Cook Street and the excavations on Christ Church Place that predated the building of Jury's Inn have uncovered Genevel's Tower, an Anglo-Norman defensive tower on the alignment of the former Hiberno-Norse wall just west of Werburgh Street.

The walled enclosure of Hiberno-Norse Dublin was small, a mere 12 ha. There was, of course, a substantial part of the town outside the walls. Contemporary trading places in the Baltic and in East Central Europe were more or less in the same league, if not smaller, but contemporary trading settlements on the Rhine were much larger. Nevertheless, Dublin represented one of the most important Viking-age settlements. Its strength did not come from serving a vast hinterland but rather from its key position in a far-reaching trading network. A sense of this network can be obtained from the fact that one of the Viking ships found in Roskilde, Denmark, was made in

Dublin from oak in about 1060. This was a slender warship, about 30 metres long with a crew of between 60 and 100 warriors. Its construction would have been a substantial undertaking requiring a skilled workforce.

Finally we must mention the significant fact that the Dublin Vikings after they converted to Christianity did not accept the spiritual authority of the see of Armagh but opted for Canterbury instead. This decision might very well have contributed to the political interest of Anglo-Norman barons in Ireland.

Anglo-Norman Dublin: institutional changes

After the Anglo-Normans captured Dublin in 1171 the town lost in importance on the European scene. Dublin was no longer an independent city state with trading connections reaching as far as Iceland and the Black Sea. Instead, it became the focus of a lordship dependent on England, where the exchequer was located and from where the justiciar and his court would leave on their itineraries through the colony. It was only in the late-medieval period, when the colony was much reduced in size, that Dublin itself became the main focus of administration.

The greatest innovation that the Anglo-Normans brought to Dublin was a reliance on the institutions which successfully supported urban life in continental Europe at the time. These included an independent municipal government as well as a strong ecclesiastical presence in the form of parish churches and great monastic houses. Of course, the latter two had existed from the Hiberno-Norse period but now received new emphasis. The great monastic houses played an active role in education and health care, but they were also powerful landholders and acted as developers in the suburbs outside the medieval walls. These institutional changes transformed the fabric of medieval Dublin.

By issuing the appropriate charter in 1171, Henry II handed the town over to the men of Bristol, and granted them the same privileges as English townspeople enjoyed at the time, namely immunity from tolls and customs. According to tradition, the new townsmen expelled the remaining Hiberno-Norse population across the river to Oxmantown. From now on the people who lived and worked within the medieval walls of Dublin were deemed to be of English blood. They would have spoken some form of Middle English or Old French interspersed with some Irish and Norse as spoken by a few craftsmen who stayed behind or by people who visited the town.

In some ways we can regard the charter that John issued in 1192 as the beginning of municipal administration in Dublin as it referred to 'the will of the citizens' and it gave legal recognition to the merchant guild. But it was not until 1229 that Dublin was to have a town council with an elected mayor and two provosts. By the late-medieval period the council also consisted of aldermen. The town council met in the Tholsel on Skinner's Row opposite Christ Church cathedral on the site of the present Peace Garden. This building stood as a symbol of municipal self-government. Speed names the building but does not afford it any extra space on his map.

An important element in the internal self-government of medieval towns was the guilds, corporations of merchants and craftsmen, which were not controlled by the king. The origins of the Dublin guilds most likely go back to the Hiberno-Norse town. In 1192 the Lord John issued a licence for guilds in Dublin and this document may have contributed to the safekeeping of the Dublin guild merchant roll, which has recently been published. The record shows that a large number of well-to-do merchants were members. Many of them came from Cardiff, others from Bristol, Gloucester and Worcester, but also from continental towns like Bordeaux, Cordoba, St Omer and Ypres (Connolly and Martin, 1992).

The Anglo-Normans not only changed the institutional picture of Dublin but they also set about land reclamation. Speed's map of Dublin for 1610 shows the town at the end of the medieval period. It is immediately obvious from Speed's map that, in contrast, to Viking-age Dublin, the width of the Liffey had been narrowed by land reclamation on the southern banks of the river above the confluence with the Poddle. The land on the northern bank of the river around St Mary's abbey remained marshy. In early-medieval times the waters of the Liffey reached the Hiberno-Norse town wall where it ran parallel to the river and the river itself was broader and became shallow towards its banks. This posed a real problem to the Anglo-Normans whose ships, built for the transport of bulk goods such as wool or grain, could not navigate the shallows. The solution was to reclaim land and thus gain access to the deeper channel.

The charter of liberties of Dublin issued by the Lord John in 1192 gives helpful topographical information (Gilbert, 1889, 1, pp 2–6). The document refers to a built-up area outside the walls. It encourages the inhabitants to reach common consent and lay out land in messuages. A messuage was a burgage plot – a parcel of building land and garden that a citizen would hold within or without the walls. Provision was made for some messuages to be laid out over the water, which looks like a suggestion that land should be reclaimed. This, of course, happened with the reclamation of the land between the city wall and

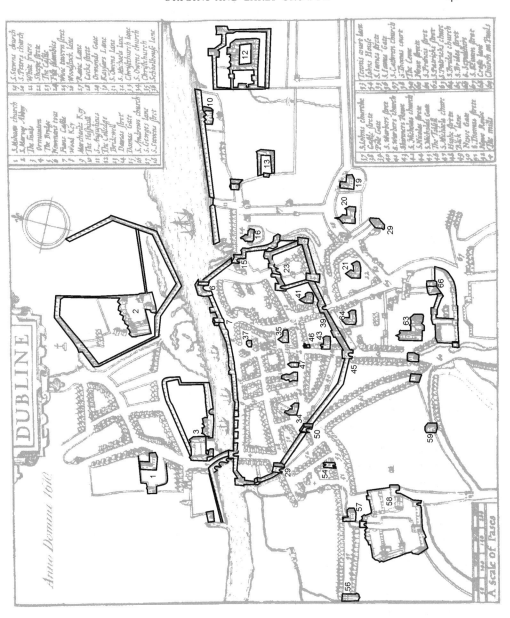

9 Dublin in 1610, using as a background John Speed's map in his *Theatre of the Empire of Great Britain* (1611), London. This map was re-issued in various editions and copied by others until well into the eighteenth century. Speed's numbering of buildings and his spelling (except for variations in spelling *church*) have been maintained. Modern identification is shown in brackets. The walls, churches, religious houses and major secular buildings have been highlighted.

Churches and religious houses
Within the walls

34 S. Owen's church (St Audeon's, extant, parish church)
35 Christ Church (extant, cathedral; former Holy Trinity, Augustinian's)
37 S. John's church (demolished)
42 S. Warber's church (extant; St Werburgh's church)
43 S. Nicolas church (Within; only some of the façade remains)
47 S. Michael's church (only tower extant, incorporated into Dublinia (heritage centre)

Outside the walls

1   S. Mihan's church (St Michan's, extant, parish church)
2   S. Mary's abbey (demolished with the exception of the crypt, Cistercian's)
16 S. Andrew's church (rebuilt; Dublin Tourism)
19 S. Steven's church (demolished)
20 S. Peter's church (demolished)
21 White Friars (rebuilt, parish church)
54 John's House (extant, St John's parish church; former St John the Baptist's hospital, Augustinian's)
57 S. Cathren church (extant; St Catherine's church)

58 S. Thomas Court (St Thomas Abbey, demolished, Augustinian's)
63 S. Patrick's church (extant cathedral)
64 S. Bride's church (demolished)
66 S. Sepulchres (the former archbishop's palace; foundations incorporated in Kevin St police station)
69 Church on Pauls (demolished)

Secular buildings

1   The Inns (present-day's Four Courts; former St Saviour priory (Dominicans)
6   Newman's tour (demolished)
7   Fian's Castle (demolished)
10 The Hospitall (former St James's Hospital; demolished)
12 The Colledge (present-day Trinity College; former Augustinian monastery of All Hallows)
13 Bridewell (demolished)
15 Damas Gate (demolished)
23 Castle (extant; Dublin Castle, Government functions)
29 Ormond's Gate (demolished)
39 Pole Gate (demolished)
45 S. Nicholas' Gate (demolished)
46 The Tolsell (demolished) New Gate (demolished)
56 S. James' Gate (demolished)

Speed did not name all street gates. He also omitted a number of churches – St Nicholas Without (on Nicholas St), St Francis friary on Francis Street, Holy Trinity friary and St Mary de Hogges' abbey between the walled town and present-day Trinity College Dublin. (Clarke, 1998, pp. 51, 53, 55.)

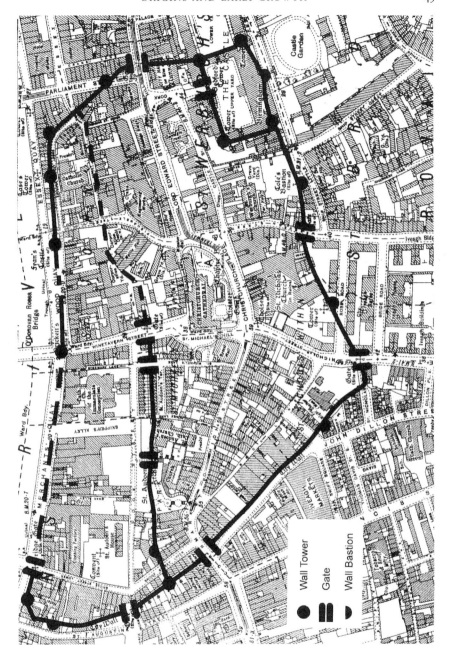

10 Location of the medieval walls in the modern city. (Superimposed on OS sheet 18, 1939 revision, by Paul Ferguson, based on Healy, 1973.) The only continuous section of the wall remaining lies to the west of St Audeon's Gate and between the Castle and Cole's Bastion.

the river. In 1202 King John issued a document in which he confirmed Holy Trinity (Christ Church) in its numerous possessions and he ended his text with the following statement – 'He grants all these with their appurtenances in churches and chapels, in sands and mudbanks' (McNeill, 1950, p. 29).

The thirteenth-century wooden revetments, which provided the framework for this massive land reclamation were excavated by Patrick Wallace at Wood Quay (Wallace, 1985). The regular street-pattern in this reclaimed part of the medieval town, which was walled in the fourteenth century against the threat of the Bruce Invasion, constitutes the last plan-unit (C) of the walled medieval town.

The layout of medieval Dublin

The clear image from Speed's map is of a walled town south of the river with substantial suburban growth, focused around the great monastic houses. The walled town encloses the area of the Hiberno-Norse town enlarged by the land reclamations along the Liffey by the Anglo-Normans. Speed does not give any clear indication of the harbour but it may be assumed that Merchant's Quay fulfilled this function.

An important feature of Speed's map is the bridge across the Liffey. As one of the first concerns for any colonial society is good communications and safety, the Anglo-Normans rebuilt the old bridge in stone in *c.*1215. This bridge was the forerunner of the one shown on Speed's map. The Anglo-Normans presumably repaired and strengthened the walls for reasons of safety soon after their arrival. Information on details comes incidentally from contemporary documents. For example, the hospital that had been founded in early Anglo-Norman times by Ailred le Palmer and his wife was referred to in early charters as the hospital of St John without the Western Gate, whereas in deeds from about 1200 onwards it is referred to as the hospital at the New Gate (Brooks, 1936). The obverse of the common seal of Dublin portrays a gate that resembles Newgate (Clarke, 1998). Speed shows the hospital with a church symbol.

The walls needed an extension down to the river in the early thirteenth century, because in 1221 Henry III issued a murage grant – 'in aid of enclosing that city, and for the security and protection of it, as well as the adjacent parts' (Gilbert, 1889, I, p. 7). On the basis of title deeds referring to the 'old city wall', Linzi Simpson (1994) has narrowed the date of the building of the city wall along the quays to *c.*1250. A rescue excavation carried out to the west of Bridge Street (Cotter, 1989) before the present offices were built showed the

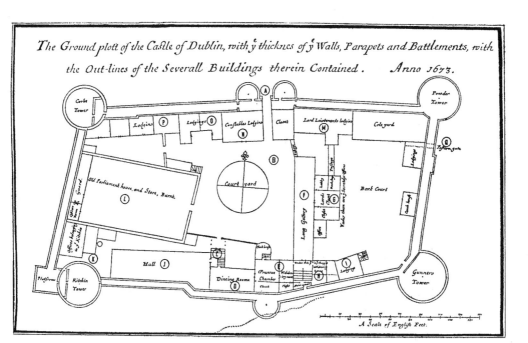

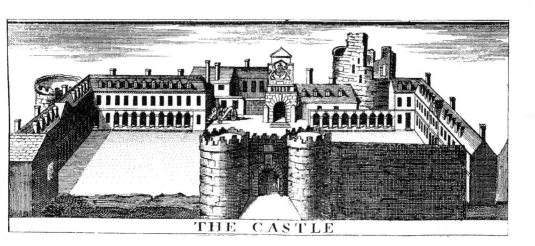

11 Dublin Castle. The upper image is from a ground plan dated to 1673 (Maguire, 1974). The lower image shows how the Castle appeared in the eighteenth century as a vignette on Brooking's map of Dublin for 1728. The orientation of Brooking's image is the opposite to Maguire's.

foundation of the extended town wall in this area reclaimed from the Liffey flood plain. The new fortifications made the wall along Cook Street obsolete. At the exposed north-eastern eastern end of the quay wall Linzi Simpson discovered Isolde's Tower, which was built in the late-thirteenth century to protect that end of the city's defences from any attack from the river. During the excavations on Christchurch Place in 1989 the remains of the medieval town wall were revealed by Margaret Gowen at a depth of 6.5 metres below present street level as well as the foundation of one of the mural towers on the southern section of the town wall. The superimposition of the medieval walls on the modern map of the city helps us to relate the alignment of the medieval walls to the modern city (Figure 10). This map, drawn by Paul Ferguson, is based on the first accurate map of the medieval walls of Dublin produced by Patrick Healy in 1968 who used Perrot's survey of 1585. The only substantial part of these walls still standing, though with partial reconstruction, are to be found in Cook Street and Ship Street Little.

The largest building on Speed's map is the castle, strategically located on the eastern side of the ridge in the south-eastern corner of the town. However, Maguire has noted that as a depiction of the castle, 'Speed's map was ... worse than useless ... because it was totally inaccurate and led many astray' (1974, p. 5). The building of this stone castle in 1204, some 30 years after the arrival of the Anglo-Normans, was a concrete expression of Dublin's new role as a colony. It was a constant reminder of the presence of royal power in the town.

The first century after the Anglo-Normans took over Dublin was a period of considerable economic growth in Europe. Trade flourished on the basis of local markets and international fairs. Dublin joined in this upsurge of development mainly through its trading connections with Bristol. The rebuilding of Christ Church cathedral as a large stone church in late Romanesque style, starting in c.1186, and the establishment in 1220 of a second cathedral, St Patrick's, south of the walled town, are vivid expressions of the new prosperity (Clarke, 1999). The extensive crypt under Christ Church cathedral, the oldest medieval building-fabric in Dublin, preserves the atmosphere of the original building. In the nineteenth century the two cathedrals, both by then in very poor condition, were reconstructed so that their fabric is now largely modern. Figure 4 shows Christ Church in 1779, prior to this reconstruction, and Figure 12 shows St Patrick's in 1797. The Anglo-Normans also built two churches that had distinctly Norman patronal names. These were St Audeon's in High Street on the site of an earlier church and St Werburgh's in Werburgh Street. On the other hand, as Howard Clarke

12 St Patrick's cathedral as drawn by Francis Grose (1797).
(*The antiquities of Ireland*, vol. 1, plate 20.)

has suggested to me, these churches could predate the invasion by the Anglo-Normans and reflect trading connections with Normandy and England. Both of these churches are shown on Speed's map along with many other medieval churches south of the river. In contrast, on the north side of the river the Dominican friary on the site of the present Four Courts was the only newcomer in the Anglo-Norman period. Howard Clarke's map of 1978 depicting the medieval town in the modern city provides a classification of the large number of former medieval sites in Dublin.

Unlike most medieval continental towns which were focused on a big central market place and a town hall as the expression of the cultural and economic power of their merchant communities, Dublin's medieval markets, following the English example, were divided between different streets. Fishamble Street catered for fish, the open space within the Newgate was preserved for the corn market, as the later placename indicates, and meat was sold along High Street.

The symbolic centre of the town was the high cross just south west of Christ Church cathedral. The municipal administration was located in the hall of the merchants' guild. According to Howard Clarke (1999, p. 116) the first one was located between Christ Church cathedral and the river Liffey but in the early-fourteenth century a new one was erected on the opposite side of the cathedral, called (the) Tholsel, a name common in Bristol. The development of urban land was clearly based on the granting of burgage plots, meaning a plot of land and garden that a citizen would hold within or without the walls. Unfortunately the archaeologists have not been able to trace in general the topographical continuity from the Hiberno-Norse town to the Anglo-Norman town because the building of the cellars of Georgian houses must have destroyed the layout of the Anglo-Norman town. Contemporary land grants recorded in the land registries of great landowners as, for example, cathedrals or monasteries in medieval Dublin, provide some information as to the size of these burgage plots and show their arrangement in contiguous rows. In Archbishop Alen's Register referring to the possessions of Christ Church cathedral, an entry between 1228 and 1255 refers to 'land with buildings in New Street which was formerly Bartholomew the baker's, lying between the lands of Arnulph Marecall and William Wulf, and containing in front thirty feet' (McNeill, 1950, p. 83). For the year 1336 the same register records – 'Peter de Willeby, clerk, grants to Walter le Gret, clockmaker, a piece of ground in St Patrick's Street, Dublin … containing in front fifty four feet, in rear sixty six feet, and extending in length from the High street (*alto vico*) on the west as far as Peter's land on the east, containing in that length five score and nineteen feet' (MacNeill, 1950, p. 203). This was obviously a plot of land that would later be subdivided. From the early-fourteenth century onwards, economic life in Dublin and the fabric of the town were described in terms of decline. Archbishop Alen's Register recorded in 1326 that 'the burgages of New Street used to pay 57s. a year for their burgages … now they pay only 32s. 8d. because the rest of the burgages lie waste. Certain burgages in St Patrick's Street hold houses and tenements, and they used to pay 45s. 2d. … they now pay only 36s. 2d. because the rest of the tenements lie waste' (McNeill, 1950, p. 171). It would be of great importance for our understanding of the

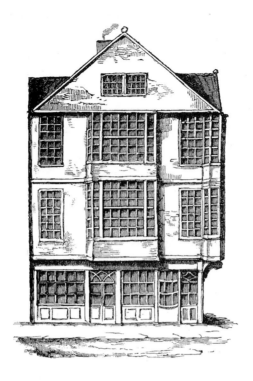

13 A late-medieval timber-framed house in Castle Street. Described in the *Dublin Penny Journal* (1833, p. 268) as having been the last remaining in Dublin.

topographical development of the town to find remnants of these medieval plot patterns on Rocque's eighteenth-century map, the earliest map we have for showing individual property boundaries.

As far as the houses are concerned, there is evidence for a change from the Viking-age post and wattle houses to heavier timber-framed buildings (Figure 13) under the Anglo-Normans in the early-thirteenth century and of the increased use of stone (Wallace, 1985, p. 390; Coughlan, 2000, p. 232). The change in building techniques was accompanied by a change in raw materials. While the post-and-wattle houses were built of hazel and birch, the timber-framed houses were constructed of oak by experienced carpenters.

Cage-work houses were still extant in the city when Walter Harris completed his *History and antiquities of the city of Dublin* (1766) but they were of sufficient rarity even then to merit detailed discussion of the survivors. He describes such houses in Castle Street, High Street, Wood Quay, Bishop Street and Patrick Street and he argues that the 'oldest house of this sort now subsisting, is (for what appears, there being no date to aid an inquiry) that in Skinner Row near the Tholsel' (p. 79). This house had been built prior to 1570. Harris concludes this section of his book with the observation that he doubts that any of the new houses then being built would last as long as these cage-work houses!

One of the interesting results of the Wood Quay excavations was the realization that some craft traditions changed little after the take-over by the Anglo-Normans (Wallace, 1985). This would suggest that Hiberno-Norse craftsmen remained within the city. Specialization in craftwork led to distinct quarters in the town, a trend traceable to the Hiberno-Norse town. At Christ Church and Skinner's Row (now Christchurch Place), where the combmakers and metalworkers had been concentrated during the Hiberno-Norse period, leather workers were busy in the twelfth and thirteenth centuries. At the upper end of Winetavern Street wood-turners and coopers produced wooden bowls, platters and barrel staves (Wallace, 1985). Manufacturers of spurs and other small iron objects were active in Castle Street. Wine was served in the taverns in Winetavern Street. Bakeries were presumably banished to just outside the old walls at Cook Street.

Extra-mural development in medieval Dublin

More than some other European cities at the time, medieval Dublin extended into the suburbs around the nucleus of ecclesiastical sites, which are shown on Speed's map. The transpontine suburb to the north of the river was focused on two pre-Anglo-Norman religious institutions, the Cistercian abbey of St Mary's and the parish church of St Michan's, which still functions as such. As already mentioned, the Dominican priory of St Saviour, on the site of the present Four Courts, was founded after the arrival of the Anglo-Normans. St Mary's abbey maintained its own harbour on the river and a marketplace to the west of its enclosed space (Clarke, 1998, p. 50).

In the western suburb the two most important religious houses were the hospital of St John the Baptist, founded very soon after the arrival of the Anglo-Normans, and the Augustinian abbey of St Thomas, also an Anglo-Norman foundation, both on Speed's map. His map also shows a medieval ribbon development along the old road from the west, called Thomas Street after the monastery, which entered the town at Newgate. By the fifteenth century, Thomas Street and its western extension James Street were built up and a street gate protected the western entrance. As Clarke (1998, p. 51) shows, a cistern for the all-important water supply in the city was built just south of the gate and the water ran through an aqueduct along High Street into the city. This suburb had two parish churches, St Catherine's which was rebuilt on the same site in the eighteenth century, and St James' outside the western street gate which was rebuilt in the nineteenth century.

To the south of the walled town, the major focus was St Patrick's cathedral, the biggest medieval church in Ireland. The Celtic cross at the back of the cathedral reminds us that this is the site of an early Irish church. This was recreated as a collegiate church in 1192, with the archbishop's palace of St Sepulchre nearby (Gwynn and Hadcock, 1988, p. 72). The massive eighteenth-century granite gate posts on Kevin Street leading into the enclosed area once demarcating the archbishop's palace are the only reminders of the earlier grandeur of this place, which now serves as a police station. Five parish churches have been identified in this suburb, as well as two friaries and a leper house, St Stephen's, the predecessor of what was later to become Mercer's Hospital (Clarke, 1988). By the late fifteenth century, Francis Street and Patrick Street were defended by street gates that are shown on Speed's map. Clarke (1998, p. 53) also identified three markets on the southern periphery of this suburb.

The eastern suburb was centred around two monastic houses, both founded in the pre-Anglo-Norman period. One was the Augustinian priory of All Saints on the site of present-day Trinity College Dublin, and the other was St Mary de Hogges', sited not far from where St Andrew's church (Dublin Tourism) stands today. The Houses of the Exchequer stood on the east side of St George's Lane, the predecessor of today's South Great George's Street. They were solid stone houses, which were later demolished (Clarke, 1998, p. 55).

One important function that applied to all suburbs was the provision of public greens for the grazing of animals. Horses were needed for transport and cattle for the supply of milk and meat. An entry in Archbishop Alan's Register in c.1192 confirms that the archbishop's 'men of the city and suburbs shall have the freedom of the city in common pasture and in all else' (McNeill, 1950, p. 22). The biggest of these commons was St Stephen's Green, to the south-east of the area depicted by Speed, which was common ground for all citizens and as such was built-up only along the fringes. The fair green outside Newgate, shown by Speed as open space, preserved some of its communal function when it became the location for the Iveagh Markets, which have only recently been closed down. Oxmantown Green, again just open space on Speed's map, was shown on Rocque's map just west of Smithfield. Hoggen Green in the area of today's College Green is also represented on Speed's map as open space. It was already built over in 1756 and is recalled on Rocque's map only by the street name Hog Hill.

The big monasteries built their own enclosing walls, as Speed's map shows. Unlike many continental towns it is surprising that these suburbs were never incorporated into a larger Dublin by an enclosing wall. Instead, once the extra-mural streets were built up, at the latest by the middle of the fifteenth century, they were protected by street gates. For example, south of the Liffey important streets such as Thomas Street, The Coombe, Francis Street and Nicholas Street ended at their far ends in street gates. One possible explanation for the lack of incorporation of the Dublin suburbs was the landholding system, which carried more of the feudal paradigm into urban living than would have been the case in most continental towns at the time. The archbishop and the major monastic houses in Dublin held large tracts of land under their own jurisdiction called liberties. This is how ecclesiastical authority came to compete with municipal authority in some suburban areas. The last section of John's charter of 1192 is interesting in this context, as it assures those who held land outside the walls that their tenures were not to be interfered with, even if certain individuals or institutions were given large tracts of land, an obvious reference to land granted to the monasteries.

Clarke (1998) has recently drawn attention to the great importance of the suburbs for medieval Dublin by referring to the fact that before the great fire in 1317, with which the citizens frightened off the Bruce siege, more tax was collected from the four suburbs than from the citizens within the walls. He suggests that in the early-fourteenth century some 80 per cent of Dubliners lived outside the town walls. In the light of this it is not surprising that these suburbs had their own market places.

Religious houses as urban developers

The most interesting aspect of the growth of Dublin's medieval suburbs is the role played by the great monastic houses as urban developers. It appears that just as the Anglo-Norman lords used the establishment of manors to strengthen their colony in rural areas, so they used the great monastic houses to develop and stabilize their colonial towns. In the eighteenth century the pattern repeated itself, when great landowners in Dublin played an important role in the transformation of the city.

Mark Hennessy (1988) has used the example of the Augustinian hospital of St John the Baptist just outside Newgate to illustrate the role of monastic houses in an urban context. The hospital was founded between 1185 and 1188, primarily to assist the poor. Speed showed the hospital with a church symbol and called it 'John's House'. The buildings of the old hospital were replaced by the nineteenth-century Augustinian church of St John's, which remains a landmark for present-day Dubliners. An analysis of the register of the hospital shows that between the 1280s and the 1350s the income of the hospital from landed estates, particularly those in Tipperary, was greatly enhanced by revenue in the form of urban rent. The hospital acted as an urban landlord in its own right, but it also received money from people who granted the rent due to them from their urban property to the hospital (Hennessy, 1988, p. 45). The charters of the hospital mention payments from a potter, a goldsmith, a weaver, a locksmith, a clerk and a carpenter. After the 1350s the income of the hospital from urban rents was greatly reduced because of the economic depression brought about by plague and local wars. At the time of the dissolution in 1539, during the reign of Henry VIII, the number of beds available for the sick had dropped from a much larger medieval figure to 50 (McNeill, 1925, pp 62–4). Spiritually the monastery must also have been in decline as in the early-sixteenth century one of the priors got involved with a woman of low reputation. In those circumstances the dissolution of the monastic house was probably less of a trauma than it would otherwise have been.

Using the example of St Thomas' abbey in the western suburb of Dublin, Cathal Duddy (1990) has shown how these ecclesiastical institutions integrated into the overall structure of society. It was Henry II who founded this abbey in 1176 and later provided it with a large private liberty. When this monastery was dissolved in 1539, it was granted with its substantial lands to the Brabazon family, whose descendants now live in Kilruddery House outside Bray, County Wicklow. Nothing remains of this once important institution save the streetnames – Thomas Street and Thomas Court. While the hospital of St John the Baptist at New Gate served the medical needs of the poor, the abbey of St Thomas provided parochial care. Simultaneously, the abbey acted as a developer in the western suburb. It received rent from its urban possessions and also received extra income from the donation of rents on other properties. The abbey was actively involved in laying out new burgage plots and in the transfer of existing burgage plots.

The charters of St Thomas' abbey, written in medieval Latin, record the early grants of land or rent to the abbey. My quotations from the various twelfth- and thirteenth-century grants to the abbey are given here in translation as provided by Cathal Duddy. The concept of a suburb must have been well known as the grants refer to land *in suburbia*, in the suburbs. The very first grant is dated between 1177 and 1189 and mentions 'one stone-house as a gift'. This was an important gift as in late-twelfth-century Dublin stone houses were the exception rather than the rule. Most buildings in medieval towns consisted of wood and were always in danger from fire. One of the grants, dated between 1190 and 1240, refers to 'houses of his land burnt down'. In another grant there is a reference to *domos ipsas reficient*, meaning that houses were rebuilt.

Grants that record the transfer of land make reference to burgage plots, in Latin *unum plenum burgagium*, meaning a full burgage. In a grant dated pre-1230 the proportions of such a plot of land are given – 20 feet frontage, 15 feet at the rear and 60 feet depth. The plots mentioned along Thomas Street have a frontage of 32 feet, 30 feet, 27 feet, 21 feet and 16 feet. Some burgage plots are subdivided into halves, thirds or quarters, indicating as Cathal Duddy suggests pressure on urban land. The grants imply that some plots were contiguous, but not all. The grants also demonstrate how topographical features acquired local names. The street that in the late-twelfth-century grant is described as 'extending towards Kilmaynan' becomes Thomas Street, *vico Sancti Thome*, in the thirteenth century (Duddy, 1990, p. 69). The 'great bridge', *pons magnus* becomes 'Dublin bridge', *pons Dubliniensis* or 'bridge of the Ostmen', *pons Ostmannorum*. The grants also throw light on the craftsmen who worked in the quarter. There were millers and bakers along the northern edge of Thomas Street, potters near Crokers' Street. There were two weavers on Thomas Street, a tailor and a carpenter and there were tanners on James' Street. This short exploration has shown that both monasteries acted as agents of organized urban expansion, based on a policy of accepting grants of land and grants of urban rent. The income was used for charitable purposes and for further investment in the expansion of the suburbs.

Dublin in the sixteenth to mid-seventeenth century

In common with English towns, but made much worse by the turbulent political situation as Irish chieftains reasserted themselves, Irish towns went through a period of contraction in the fifteenth century. Dublin suffered from a poor harbour and the neglect of its public buildings, for example the town-walls, the stone bridge and the castle. Dublin was also at the mercy of continuous attacks by Irish clansmen on the southern suburbs of the city. In addition the city felt the impact of the plague and other epidemics which

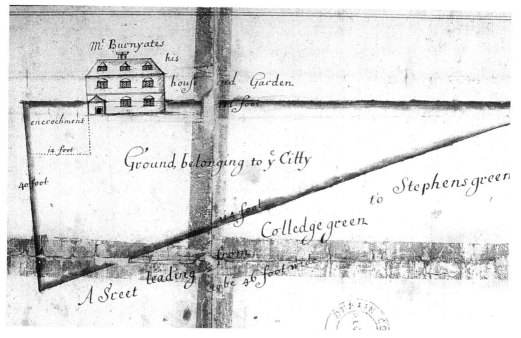

14 Lease of a house and ground near St Stephen's Green dated 17 January 1680.
Reprinted by kind permission of Dublin City Archive.

occurred regularly through the fifteenth and sixteenth centuries. The most important change which Dublin experienced in the first half of the sixteenth century was the dissolution of its medieval monasteries during the reign of Henry VIII. In 1536, Henry VIII was acknowledged by a Dublin parliament as supreme head of the Church of Ireland. The Suppression Bill issued in the same year supplanted papal by royal supremacy, and Protestantism was established as the official State religion. The dissolution provided the Government with more revenue, which allowed them to increase the pay of the army and provided Dublin Corporation with new property and income that was spent, in part, on establishing charitable institutions.

The fortunes of the city changed in the second half of the sixteenth century after the city had been incorporated as a county borough in 1548. This Act provided the Corporation with enhanced legal standing and with more power to regulate social and economic affairs. In the aftermath of the dissolution of the monasteries, many former monastic properties were conferred on the city, including the lands of St Thomas' and St Mary's, which provided the city with much needed revenue. On the basis of Speed's map John Andrews (1983) calculated that there were 254 houses within the walled city in 1610, which would suggest a population of 3800 people but perhaps 10,000 people if the suburbs were included.

In the second half of the sixteenth century under the influence of the lord deputy, Henry Sidney, the city benefited from good relations between the civic and state administration. Under his reign a major reconstruction of the castle was carried out, which became the viceregal residence. The optimistic view prevailing in the city at the time, must have inspired Richard Stanihurst, an Elizabethan chronicler and commentator, when he described Dublin in 1577 in glowing terms. He wrote of a city where the municipal institutions were in full control and trade, both internal and external, flourished. Among the 'gorgeous buildings' in Dublin which he singled out for praise were the Tholsel, the archbishop's palace of St Sepulchres and the market cross, all now gone, the old bridge, the quays and Christ Church cathedral. According to a contemporary English soldier, the city had been 'replenished with a thousand chimneys and beautified with as many glass windows' in around 1600 (Lennon, 1989, p. 29). Citizens were granted leases with the direction to build houses of oak wood with slated roofs. A lease of 17 January 1680 shows such a house with glass windows and a chimney in the proximity of St Stephen's Green (Figure 14).

During all this time, up to 1605 when the proclamation was issued that ordered priests to quit the realm, Catholics were able to hold senior positions on the city-council and practise their religion without threat to their position. In 1606, of the 26 aldermen on the Dublin Council 11 were Protestants and 15 were Catholics (Lennon, 1989, p. 179). It appears that in the sixteenth century the division between Catholics and Protestants was not very clear-cut, but certain churches in Dublin associated more with the new order than others. Christ Church became a place of worship for the State officials and their families and St John's and St Werburgh's became predominantly Protestant, as indicated by the tombs erected there after 1560. On the other hand, St Andrew's was the parish church for civic leaders, of whom the majority were Catholics at the end of the sixteenth century. With the encouragement of the crown, which was interested to see a stable government in the city, an élite of 26 aldermen, most of them wealthy merchants, played an increasingly dominant role in the city (Lennon, 1989, p. 37). They operated through the powerful merchant guild of Dublin and it was this group who in the seventeenth century pressed hardest for religious change towards Protestantism in Dublin, as Colm Lennon (1989) has described so well in his book on *The lords of Dublin in the age of reformation.* As a consequence, Catholic patricians withdrew from services in the increasingly Protestant-orientated churches and began to attend mass-houses, which appeared all over the city. The first of these was recorded in 1599 and by 1610 there were three mass houses in the area of High Street alone (Lennon, 1989, p. 145). The religious orders returned to the city in the seventeenth century. The Dominicans were represented by 1622 by the presence of a vicar-provincial with eight friars. They stayed in Cook Street, where the Carmelites and Franciscans also had a base (Gwynn and Hadcock, 1989, p. 225).

The wealth of the Dublin merchants came from the export of agricultural products, for example hides to England, while metal products and coal were imported from England. The number of masons, glaziers and carpenters increased in the later years of the sixteenth century, which indicates that new houses were being built in the city. The wealthier merchants lived on the quays on the southside of the river, for example the Usshers, who gave their name to Usher's Quay. Some of the wealthy merchants lived in fortified residences, which were part of the city's fortification. The leasing of gate-towers was a cheap way for the Corporation to ensure that they were well maintained, repaired and roofed (Lennon, 1989, p. 33). In the medieval period a crane on Merchant's Quay had functioned as a custom house, but in 1620 the Government erected a purpose-built custom house and a new crane and wharf down on the quays at the lower end of Winetavern Street (Bennet, 1991, pp 48–9). In 1707 another custom house was built on the site of the present-day Clarence Hotel and finally in 1781 the foundation stone was laid for the new Custom House downstream on the northern bank of the river.

In spite of Stanihurst's praise of Dublin there must have been latent tensions in the city. As religion and politics became closely associated, the frontiers hardened between colonialism and ethnic nationalism. The dissolution of the religious houses in Dublin may be interpreted as part of a continuing modernization process in the city. But, as Margaret McCurtain (1972, p. 22) has written, the impetus was arrested by the ethnic divisions among the population and by the general unpreparedness of the Church in Ireland for the doctrinal changes then sweeping Europe. Given the importance of the monasteries in the topography of the medieval city, their dissolution had a great spatial impact. The monasteries had been an essential part of the life in the medieval town, although it is difficult to avoid the impression that they were not remotely as active at the time of dissolution as they had been in the late-twelfth and early-thirteenth century. Given their wealth it is surprising that they did not play a more important role in the city by the mid-sixteenth century. This was not true of the mendicant orders, who had undergone reform, in particular the Franciscan friars, who had a strong pastoral orientation and kept theological libraries.

The often repeated contention that the loss of educational and health services previously provided by the monasteries had a disastrous effect on the city has been questioned and it has been suggested that by the early-sixteenth century the torch was already passing from the monks. For example, secular schools were established in Irish towns from the early-sixteenth century onwards. When the lease for such a school in Dublin changed hands in 1540, the new tenant was obliged 'to repair and uphold the school house and reserve the nether part quit and clear for all scholars thereto coming to learn grammar or any other science' (Bradshaw, 1974, p. 223). The evidence indicates that the monasteries were in decline economically and spiritually from the second half of the fifteenth century. Secular priests set up corporate bodies, for example a large almshouse for the poor and sick in 1497 at St Patrick's (Bradshaw, 1974, p. 221). A grammar school was later established in St Patrick's from monies that became available from the dissolution of the monasteries.

Those who were granted the religious properties in most instances did not have the wish or the necessary capital to redevelop the buildings. Some were used as residences or store-houses and many of the sites fell temporarily into ruins. The dissolution records show that most monastic houses had a functioning farm within their precinct and these buildings were preserved by the king's commissioners. We will now briefly investigate the transformation of the major monastic houses in the aftermath of the dissolution.

Figure 15 shows the location of these monastic houses, all of which with the exception of the Augustinian canons attached to Christ Church stood outside the walled town. The first monastery to be dissolved in Dublin was the old Augustinian priory of All Saints, which had been in existence for more than four hundred years. It was Dublin Corporation itself who petitioned the Crown to receive a grant of this property in return for their loyalty when Lord (Silken) Thomas Fitzgerald tried to storm the castle in 1534. The citizens wanted to be compensated for the 'ruin and decay that the said city sustained in breaking their towers, bridges, houses, leads of the conduits of the water in the siege thereof' (Bradshaw, 1974, p. 79). The prior with the sub-prior and four canons, having received a pension, signed the deed of surrender in 1538. The Corporation used the site as a pest house during the plague of 1575–6 but the buildings were in ruins when Queen Elizabeth erected the College of the

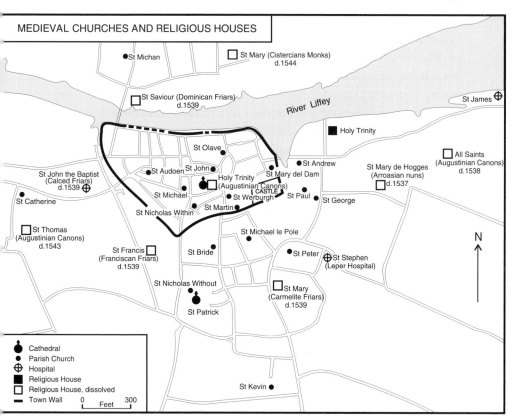

MEDIEVAL CHURCHES AND RELIGIOUS HOUSES

- St Michan
- St Mary (Cistercians Monks) d.1544
- St Saviour (Dominican Friars) d.1539
- River Liffey
- St James
- Holy Trinity
- St Olave
- St Andrew
- All Saints (Augustinian Canons) d.1538
- St Mary de Hogges (Arroasian nuns) d.1537
- St John the Baptist (Calced Friars) d.1539
- St Audoen
- St John
- Holy Trinity (Augustinian Canons)
- CASTLE
- St Mary del Dam
- St Catherine
- St Michael
- St Werburgh
- St Paul
- St George
- St Nicholas Within
- St Martin
- St Thomas (Augustinian Canons) d.1543
- St Michael le Pole
- N
- St Francis (Franciscan Friars) d.1539
- St Bride
- St Peter
- St Stephen (Leper Hospital)
- St Nicholas Without
- St Mary (Carmelite Friars) d.1539
- St Patrick
- St Kevin

Key:
- Cathedral
- Parish Church
- Hospital
- Religious House
- Religious House, dissolved
- Town Wall
- 0 — Feet — 300

15 The dissolution of medieval monastic houses in Dublin. (The base map is from Andrews, 1983, and the dates from Gwynn and Hadcock, 1988.)

Holy Trinity on the site of the former priory in 1592 (Gwynn and Hadcock, 1988, p. 172). Nothing is left of the original college but we know from contemporary drawings that the area occupied by the Elizabethan foundation was small. The houses were two storeys high and were constructed of red Dutch brick and wood with large dormer windows beneath the roof. The college, located on what was then a green site, was completely walled in. A street was built from the college to connect with the castle, which had become the seat of government. The new street was called Dame Street, after the former medieval parish church of St Mary del Dam, which stood just north of the castle.

Immediately to the west of the former priory of All Saints stood the nunnery of St Mary de Hogges for Arrouasien nuns, which was suppressed in 1537. The last abbess was granted a pension. The church and monastic buildings were demolished by William Brabazon, then under-treasurer of Ireland, who used the stones for the repair of the king's castle in Dublin. The site and possessions were granted in 1537 to Francis Cosby, who tried to set up a cloth-weaving project on the site of the Hogges nunnery. In 1542 this and other religious houses were granted to James Sedgrave (Gwynn and Hadcock, 1988, pp 316–7). The property was then sold to the Elizabethan commander, Sir George Carew, who constructed a large building on Dame Street which he proposed to use as a hospital for 'poor, sick and maimed soldiers'. In the event the place was never used for this purpose and passed through various hands until purchased by Sir Arthur Chichester, who in 1604 was appointed lord deputy. After his death the house was completely renovated and following the restoration of the English monarchy was used as the Parliament House between 1661 and 1666. The house was demolished in 1728 and the foundation stone for the new parliament house was laid in 1729.

It is interesting, that the same mayor who had gladly received the Augustinian house of All Saints for the benefit of Dublin Corporation strongly opposed the dissolution of Christ Church cathedral and its community of Augustinian canons, when it was threatened a few months later. In their petition the citizens condemned the intended suppression as 'a great desolation and a foul waste and deformity.' The citizens made it clear that Christ Church was the St Paul's of Dublin, a civic, religious and popular centre. The public outcry in favour of Christ Church was so strong, that the commissioners appointed by King Henry VIII were authorized to constitute Christ Church as a secular cathedral, thereby saving it, but not the Augustinians in it, from suppression. This was a most unusual step to take as there was another secular cathedral in Dublin already, St Patrick's cathedral. St Patrick's in turn was reduced to the functions and endowments of a parish church in 1546. Bradshaw (1974) comments that given the developments at Christ Church, the suppression of the monasteries did not touch the religious susceptibilities of the citizens of Dublin. The acquisition of All Saints and the preservation of Christ Church were both matters of civic pride at the time.

The other site on which the citizens of Dublin had their eye, when they were granted the property of All Saints, was the priory and hospital of St John the Baptist just outside New Gate on the western end of the walled town. According to Gwynn and Hadcock (1988, p. 350) it was probably the largest hospital for the sick under the care of brethren and sisters in Ireland. The income of the hospital came from more than 1700 acres (c.690 ha) of good agricultural land and from messuages, cottages, tenements and shops in the town. The hospital had a turbulent history in the fifteenth century and in 1536 the commissioners reported that St John's 'serveth to no purpose'. The house was surrendered under its last prior in 1539 with the consent of his community and he and two other religious were granted a pension. Surprisingly the prior agreed to assist with the confiscation of the land formerly belonging to his monastery in Tipperary. The church was demolished and the stones were sold to William Brabazon. This site is a good example of how lay-people took over the care of the sick. At the dissolution Edmund Redmond got a 21-year lease of the house. Redmond was a surgeon and when the crown surveyors visited the site a year later they found that he lived there and maintained the hospital with 50 beds (Bradshaw, 1974, pp 220–1). In 1544 the monastery was granted to Maurice, earl of Thomond and when it went to James Sedgrave in 1552 a house with 50 beds for sick men was still operating.

There were two monastic houses in the southern suburbs of the city. One was the Carmelite priory of St Mary's which was founded in 1274. When it surrendered in 1539 it consisted of a half-acre site, nine messuages, seven gardens and two meadows. In 1541 the property was granted to Nicholas Stanyhurst. By 1541 the jurors, appointed by the county sheriff, found that the church and other buildings had been destroyed, except for a small hall, a room and a stable with two cellars. The roofs of the demolished buildings had been sold by the enterprising William Brabazon. Queen Elizabeth later granted the property to Francis Aungier, who became baron of Longford. He developed that part of the city with Aungier Street and Longford Street bearing his name. During Elizabeth's reign the calced friars (Carmelites) returned to Dublin. As we already know they set up a house in Cook Street in 1627, where they were still active in the first part of the eighteenth century. The medieval site of the Carmelite friary is now occupied by the modern Carmelite priory of Whitefriar Street (Gwynn and Hadcock, 1989, p. 289).

The other monastic house in the southern suburb was St Francis' for Friars Minor of Dublin. Before November 1538 there were twenty friars in this house, but the number was reduced to four by persecution and the removal of all support. At the time of dissolution it consisted of a church and belfry, dormitory, hall, three chambers, a cemetery and garden in the precinct, four messuages and three gardens in Francis Street. In 1541 the monastery was granted to Thomas Stephens and the friars had to abandon the place. In 1615, a house was built for them close to Merchant's Quay, where the present friary stands (Gwynn and Hadcock, 1989, pp 248–9).

The most substantial monastic house on the southside of the river to be dissolved was the abbey of St Thomas the Martyr (Thomas Court). The monastery was surrendered by Henry Duff, the last abbot, who, together with seven other canons, was paid a pension. In 1540 the jurors, reported that the hall, with a tower, a chamber and an upper room and other buildings, called the King's Lodgings, were unsuitable for the king's deputy and commissioners, while the remaining buildings were needed for the farmer (Gwynn and Hadcock, 1989, pp 172–3). The monastery had owned over 2300 acres (930 ha) of land in the best agricultural counties, three castles, many messuages, cottages, shops and five mills. The site of the monastery with the lands around it was granted to William Brabazon in 1545 whose family name is commemorated in Brabazon Square in the Liberties.

The oldest and most substantial monastic house on the northside of the river was the Cistercian abbey of St Mary's, which had been founded in 1139. It was dissolved in 1539, when the abbot and five monks received pensions. In 1540 the church was occupied by John Travers who as master of the King's Ordnance used the buildings for artillery and munitions. Lord Leonard Grey used the abbot's lodging as a mansion but all other monastic buildings were used as farm buildings. Fortunately, the twelfth-century chapter house has survived under the present street-level (Mary's Abbey) and is once again open to the public. The possessions of St Mary's had consisted of 5870 acres (2375 ha) of land in the best agricultural counties, two mansions, five castles, twelve mills and many messuages, cottages, shops and five mills (Gwynn and Hadcock, 1988, p. 131).

The Dominican priory of St Saviour's at the northern end of the stone bridge crossing the river from the walled town was surrendered in 1539. In 1541 the jurors suggested that the priory church should be pulled down and the stones sold as building material. The monastery owned *c.*93 acres (38 ha), two messuages, 21 tenements or cottages. In 1542 the priory was granted to Sir Thomas Cusack but in 1578, the priory, church and site of three acres became the possession of the earl of Ormond. About four years later the 'King's Inns' was established there on the site of the present Four Courts (Gwynn, 1989, p. 225). On Speed's map the site is called the 'Inns'.

Even after the dissolution of the monasteries the influence of these medieval institutions lives on in the urban landscape of Dublin. Street names, as for example Thomas Street on the southside and Mary Street on the northside of the river, remind us of the former existence of these monastic houses, which once dominated their quarter of the town. Trinity College sitting astride Dame Street at its eastern end echoes the topographical importance of the former priory of All Saints on that site.

It appears from the contemporary documentation that in the fifteenth and sixteenth century, at a time of Gaelic revival, the fords across the Liffey still caused a problem to the citizens of Dublin. Gaelic clansmen had long used these passages at low tide in order to carry out hit-and-run raids. In 1455 a Great Council had been held before Thomas, earl of Kildare which decided that all the fords on the Liffey between the bridge of Lucan and the City of Dublin and all fords and shallow places between the bridge of Dublin and the island of Clontarf should be discontinued. The ford that caused particular concern was the one near St Mary's abbey by which Gaelic clansmen entered Fingal by night and raided the king's servants. The Act written in French had referred to 'la vade par le pier de Saint Mary Abbay'. To ensure that the pier was no longer used a wall 20 perches long, 6 feet high and a tower had been built at St Mary's abbey to prevent people using the ford. But, these measures were not effective because over 100 years later in 1534 when Silken Thomas rebelled, he rode through Dublin with armed men and went over the ford to St Mary's abbey, where at a council of state he renounced his allegiance to the king and returned across the river in the same way (Haliday, 1882, p. 205).

On Speed's map of 1610 there is only one bridge which crosses the river and that is the successor to the oldest stone-bridge from the early-thirteenth century, which connected the walled city with St Mary's abbey on the northern banks of the river. This Old Bridge or Dublin Bridge, as it was called alternatively, stood on the alignment of today's Fr Mathew Bridge. It remained the only bridge across the river until a wooden bridge was built upstream in 1670 to make a crossing from the riverfront at Usher's Island in the direction of Oxmantown. In 1704 the wooden bridge on this site was replaced by a stone bridge, which became known as Barrack Bridge, because the Royal Barracks, later to be called Collins Barracks, were constructed at the time. In 1858 this bridge was replaced by an iron bridge, renamed Rory O'Moore Bridge in 1922, that is still in use today (de Courcy, 1996, p. 336). A third bridge was built in the later-seventeenth century by Jervis at Essex Quay.

Dublin had had a difficult time up to the early part of the seventeenth century. Its population had barely recovered from the losses caused by the Black Death in the mid-fourteenth century and other epidemics in the fifteenth and sixteenth centuries (Lennon, 1993, p. 30). For example, the plague of 1575 killed one third of Dublin's inhabitants. The lack of growth contributed to the problems of maintaining the urban fabric. Up to the

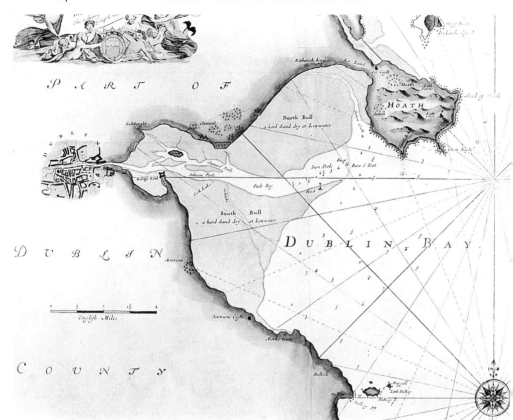

16 The bay and harbour of Dublin. (Surveyed by Captain Greenville Collins, 1686.)

middle of the sixteenth century the city revenue was small in comparison to the income of the big monasteries. At the time of the dissolution St Mary's abbey had a yearly income of £1000 whereas the treasurer of Dublin had only £195 at his disposal in 1543 (Lennon, 1983, p. 33). At the same time public buildings were in bad repair. A dramatic demonstration of this situation was the collapse of the south wall and roof of Christ Church cathedral in 1562 and the collapse of the nave vaulting in St Patrick's in 1544 (Gwynn and Hadcock, 1988, p. 72). The state of the Tholsel was an embarrassment to the Corporation. In 1597 an accidental explosion of gunpowder on Merchant's Quay caused far reaching damage to the medieval fabric of the town but the chronic shortage of resources meant that complete rebuilding was achieved only later in the seventeenth century.

Shipping in Dublin Bay remained hazardous for larger ships because of the sandbar which stretched across the mouth of the Liffey estuary (Figure 16).

The problem of silting caused continual problems for the export trade. Richard Stanihurst recorded that Archbishop Alen's vessel went aground on these sandbanks in 1534 and a shallow sea covered the area north of today's Merrion Square, Townsend Street and College Green. Only smaller boats could come up the river and berth at the quays. This required that bigger boats anchor in the Bay and smaller boats, called lighters, sailed back and forth in order to unload the freight on Merchant's Quay or Wood Quay.

While the physical fabric of the town deteriorated the social fabric of the town became strained under the impact of the arrival of new English families, who, with the support of the crown, attempted to introduce the Protestant religion into a society that largely refused to change religious allegiance. In a cultural sense Dublin became a contested space. By 1613 religion had become the major bone of contention between the royal administration and the majority of the Dublin civic leaders. English state officials seemed to have been convinced that adherence to Catholicism would necessarily lead to civil disobedience.

Civil life steadily improved in the first half of the seventeenth century. A new mint was set up, a prison, an armoury, an office for the registry of deeds and a court. But in essence Dublin was still a medieval city with narrow streets and overcrowded houses. Charles II was restored to the English crown in 1660 and this event had momentous implications for Dublin. The duke of Ormonde returned as viceroy in 1666 and a new atmosphere of peace and prosperity facilitated a dramatic expansion of the town influenced by new European ideals of town planning. Dublin soon became one of the most gracious cities of Europe and the process is discussed in the next chapter.

Designing the capital city

Dublin c.1660–1810

EDEL SHERIDAN

Introduction

The medieval walled town of Dublin with suburbs as shown by Speed in 1610 (see Chapter 1), grew dramatically in spatial extent from the late 1600s onwards.

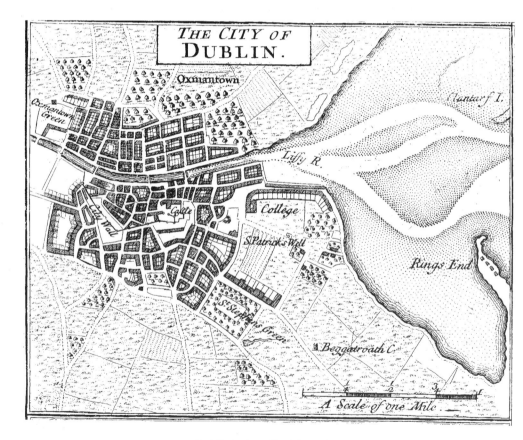

17 Dublin in the early-eighteenth century.
(*Tindal's Continuation of Rapin's History of England*, 1740.)

The new urban quarters, in particular in the eastern half of the city, differed quite considerably from the earlier extensions beyond the city walls in layout, scale and architecture. Dublin's rapid development in the period was related both to economic recovery and development after an unsettled period in the first half of the seventeenth century and also to the city's recovered capital status.

Seventeenth-century Ireland had suffered unrest and rebellion against the English Government, and brutal retaliation under Cromwell. In Dublin, high taxes levied to pay for the war and for military action against rebels, together with the ravages of plague and famine, had led to population decline and a decrease in the value of civic property. Many houses had been demolished or were in a semi-ruined condition, and manufacturers and traders had suffered greatly (Gilbert, 1894, 4, pp v and 256–7). A petition to the English crown submitted by Dublin Corporation in 1664 asking for more money to improve the security of Dublin as well as its representative function ('dignity'), reflects the unfavourable situation:

> Whereas certaine of the commons preferred their petition unto the said assembly, shewing that whereas this citty had beene under many and greate sufferings by reason of the severall calamities of warrs, pestilence and famine, together with oppressions of the usurpers for the space of about twenty yeares now last past, whereby the citty hath bin soe impoverished, and the revenue thereof soe exhausted, as that there is not sufficient to support and maintaine the dignity and safety of this citty in such a manner as is necessary and becomeing.
>
> (14 September 1664)

With the restoration of royal English power in 1660 and the return to Dublin of the viceroy, at that time the duke of Ormonde, a degree of political stability was established that made economic expansion possible. The reinstatement of the Irish Parliament in Dublin in 1661 and Ormonde's arrival as viceroy in 1662 are often regarded as prime events in paving the way for the recovery of the city and its emergence as a monumental capital (see Craig, 1969, pp 3–4; McCullough, 1989, p. 32). The Corporation had already been making efforts, however, to improve the city's economy and building fabric. As early as 1651 the Corporation had publicly invited Protestant English manufacturers, traders and artisans to settle in Dublin, offering them admission to the city franchise 'on favourable terms'. By 1661 the Corporation had forbidden the use of thatch in the city or its suburbs in order to avert the danger of further

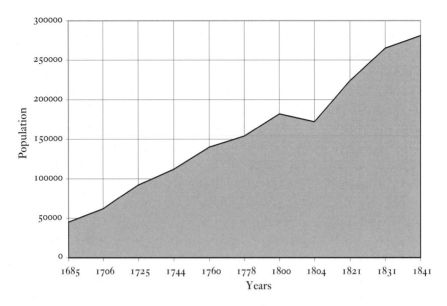

18 Dublin 1685–1841 population estimates.

destruction by fire as 'the inconvenience of any such buildeinges hath of late beene a wofull spectacle unto this cittie by the late fire in Saint James streete' (Gilbert, 1894, 4, pp 197–8).

As the city grew beyond its walls, its centre and focus shifted northwards and eastwards. For a time the northside of the city flourished and places such as Henrietta Street and Sackville Mall became highly desirable locations. Later the focus shifted southwards again but this time to the south-eastern sector of the city which has retained its up-market character to the present day. Private individuals became very important agents of development during this period. Great estates were assembled and their owners created much of the urban streetscape in the period from the early-eighteenth century onwards. Dublin Corporation was not idle and was an important developer until the demands of the city required a more focused development agency, the Wide Streets Commission.

After the first new quays were built in the late 1600s and a custom house erected outside the walled city in 1707 immediately east of the later site of Parliament Street (not to be confused with Gandon's late-eighteenth-century Custom House much farther downriver), the eastward drift began. Castle Street, High Street and Fishamble Street in the historic city centre continued to be important shopping and trading streets, but higher quality retailing moved towards Capel Street to the north-east.

Rapid growth produced a fragmented urban landscape, ill equipped to accommodate the increase in private and commercial traffic. There was a visible difference between the walled medieval core with its narrow, irregular streets and lanes and the newer suburban developments, and the movement of traffic between the core and the suburbs was made difficult by the lack of adequate points of access. Throughout the latter part of the seventeenth century the Corporation of Dublin exerted itself to overcome these disadvantages and invested considerable energies in the general improvement of the city. While the Corporation was responsible for the innovative open spaces of St Stephen's Green and Smithfield, as well as Dublin's extensive quays, developed from the late 1600s on, it was not, however, the only significant group involved in developing the city.

Along the arterial routes to the city core much uncoordinated development took place, with individuals building single houses or at most small groups of houses with no overall vision or plan, as for example in Dorset Street or Thomas Street. A pattern emerged where piecemeal development dominated the area to the west of the medieval core, while large and more coherently developed private estates characterized the city east of the walled city. This highly significant group of Dublin developers – the private landlords and entrepreneurs who shaped so much of the city's eighteenth-century residential areas – had begun to make their influence felt by the latter years of the seventeenth century. The overall pattern of development, though strongly dominated by the two largest estates, the Gardiner estate in the north-east and the Fitzwilliam estate in the south-east of the city, reflects also the fragmentary nature of the many private estates. The Dublin landlords were instrumental in introducing the type of uniform layout common in continental cities at this time. Lord Aungier to the south of the medieval city (Burke, 1972) and Sir Humphrey Jervis on the opposite bank of the Liffey (Craig, 1969, pp 25–7) brought new types of urban design to Dublin, emphasizing straight streets forming rational and often symmetrical or geometrical patterns.

Neither the new suburban developments initiated by Dublin Corporation nor the private estates were spatially integrated with the medieval core nor particularly well-connected one to the other. After decades of complaints by citizens regarding the appalling traffic congestion of the streets accessing the town centre, a body was established to intervene in urban development. The Commissioners for the Making of Wide and Convenient Streets and Passages, otherwise known as the Wide Streets Commissioners, were set up by an Act of Parliament of 1757. The commission was financed largely by taxes and grants of money made by the Parliament, and is one of the earliest examples of a State-sponsored urban planning authority.

After the widening and rebuilding of parts of Dame Street by the Wide Streets Commission in the mid-eighteenth century, this street achieved fashionable pre-eminence. While the Castle and Tholsel remained as political nodes in the old walled town, the new Houses of Parliament on College Green (1727, extended 1787–1789) provided a focus for the capital city well to the east, complemented by the imposing extent of Trinity College. Mosse's Lying-in Hospital (1742) with its pleasure gardens and concert rooms in the Rotunda on Rutland Square (now Parnell Square) on the Gardiner estate to the north-east, as well as St Stephen's Green (1664) and Merrion Square (1762) to the south-east were popular haunts resorted to by the fashionable classes. The building of a new custom house from 1781 to 1791 at what was then the eastern limit of the city beyond Lower Abbey Street, as well as the southward extension and commercialization of Sackville Street (O'Connell Street), Carlisle Bridge and the erection of the new axes of Westmoreland Street and D'Olier Street south of the river reinforced the movement of Dublin's economic centre eastwards. A multi-centred city developed, with a scattering of political, social and economic centres to the east of the old core, a trend reflected by the concentration of upper and middle class residential use in the eastern half of the city (see following chapter).

Three aspects of Dublin's spatial development in this period are of particular importance:

- rapid population and economic growth and uncontrolled physical expansion, leading to –
- congestion within the city walls and a lack of continuity between the centre and the various new suburban developments, resulting in –
- attempts to give the city an overall unity and coherence in accordance with its representative role as capital city and to facilitate its better economic functioning, culminating in the large-scale developments of the Wide Streets Commission.

Thus Dublin gradually emerged into a form that was to become part of a new common European urban heritage. In this chapter we will look in some detail at the contribution of the three agents of development mentioned above – Dublin Corporation, selected private landlords and the Wide Streets Commission – in shaping the modern city.

The capital city

> If however court, fortification, merchant town and university are in the one place, so it is certain, that a large city lends the country greater recognition, brings it into better repute, and attracts more people, than several mediocre ones; every foreigner is more curious to see it, every craftsman prefers to work there, every wealthy man prefers to live there, where he finds either continuation of his sustenance, should he practise a particular trade, or all sorts of intercourse, pleasure and air, if he lives on his income …
>
> (translated from Leibniz, 1669, p. 106)

Towns, as well as possessing identifiable physical forms and particular patterns of social activity, have an important symbolic dimension. Thus the eighteenth-century streetscapes of Dublin are a monument to the aesthetic ideals of the upper classes of that time, ideals that sprang from Ireland's openness to continental European influences and trends. The writings of notable European architects were available in Dublin, and were to be found in the libraries of those actively involved in shaping the urban landscape. Educated citizens participated in the intellectual debates and movements of the times through publications not only in English, but also in French, Italian and German. What emerges from this is a realization that the city needed to assert its dominance not just in the economic or administrative sphere but also in the grandeur of its architecture. This is a theme which has persisted to the present-day and underlies the debate about the Millennium Spire or 'spike' for Dublin.

Public buildings were of particular significance, next in architectural rank to churches, and they were the principal means for a ruler to achieve immortality in the fabric of the capital city, announcing 'the opulence of cities, the splendour of nations, and the beneficiency of princes' (Diderot and d'Alembert, 1762, p. 9). The authors of an illustrated description of Dublin published in 1780 echo this sentiment, remarking that public buildings 'must be considered as the most certain means of transmitting to posterity an idea of the wealth and power of Nations' (Pool and Cash, 1780, p. ix). They argue that even when empires have fallen, the ruins they leave behind attest to their glory.

City building may be a means of consolidating power by giving a physical expression to a ruler's control over the State; it is a way to immortalize oneself in stone. This is as true for the twentieth century as it was for the seventeenth and eighteenth centuries – a fact borne witness to by, for example, the determination of Dublin's Corporation in the late 1970s to carry through its plans for new monumental civic offices on an archaeologically sensitive site at Wood Quay despite public pressure to abort these designs; likewise the costly restoration (at the expense of the Irish taxpayer) of Government Buildings in Merrion Street in the late 1980s. Though relatively modest in scale these examples show that there is a continuing pressing desire on the part of governments, whether municipal or national, to erect monuments to themselves.

Dublin, c.1660–1760: Corporations are the creatures of the monarchy

Corporations are the creatures of the monarchy, and therefore, they have a particular obligation beyond other subjects at large to depend upon the monarchy and to uphold it … The character, humour, and passion of this city seems to be loyalty … how chearfull and how ready an obedience they gave to the king's late proclamation and the act of council … So that, in a word, this city may be an example to the greatest cities of the world, of a most submissive and implicit loyalty … if any body could finde out a shape of government, or devise any rules that would make you more subject to the will and personal power of the prince, you would petition the king for that model and those rules …

> Extracts from a speech of Sir Ellis Leighton, recorder of
> the city of Dublin, on 4 April 1672, at the Tholsel
> (Gilbert, 1895, 5, appendix IV, pp 559, 560–1)

In April 1662, Dublin Corporation granted its Lord Mayor an extra allowance of £100 sterling 'to enable him henceforth the better to support the creditt of the government of this cittie', perhaps the first example of an expense account. The inspiration for this lay in the imminent arrival of the new lord lieutenant of Ireland, the duke of Ormonde, and the desire of the city to put on a good show. The Corporation, recovering from the exigencies of several decades of rebellion, wars and uncertain government, was anxious to maintain its status and public image as governing body of the now firmly established capital of Ireland. During the remainder of the seventeenth century and the whole of the eighteenth century, there are repeated references in the assembly rolls to keeping up the 'dignity' of the city. Early in 1740, for example, the Corporation was debating means to finance 'a sufficient number of officers to attend the sword' at the appearances of the chief magistrates, to maintain the 'grandeur' of the city. There are annual references to the lord mayor's representative obligations towards the city, and an allowance was paid to the lord mayor towards this end. Thus, in 1741 William Scriven, clerk to the lord mayor, applied for and was granted £500 for this purpose, as 'his Lordship hath been at great expense in supporting the dignity of the city' (16 October 1741). The efforts probably paid off. After the Restoration, King Charles II 'desirous to put a marke of ... royal favour upon the said city' presented the lord mayor with the first Cap of Maintenance, a ceremonial chapeau.

In the 1660s Dublin Corporation governed by means of two chambers or houses. The upper house was formed by the lord mayor and 24 aldermen, the lower house being made up of the sheriff's peers (not more than 48) and 96 representatives of the guilds of the city. The lower house, generally known as 'the sheriffs and commons' or simply 'the commons', was presided over by two sheriffs. The Corporation met in the Tholsel in Skinner's Row four times annually at assemblies – at Christmas, Easter, Midsummer and Michaelmas. Any other business arising was dealt with at 'post assemblies', of which there were many. The decisions made at these gatherings were known as 'acts of assembly' and were recorded by the town clerk. These are the assembly rolls transcribed by Gilbert (and later by his wife) in his *Calendar of ancient records of Dublin*. These volumes provide ready access to documentation of the most significant decisions affecting the urban landscape taken by the Corporation. The weekly meetings of the lord mayor and aldermen were recorded in the 'Monday Books'. From 1742 onwards, the proceedings of the lower house were recorded in the journals of the sheriffs and commons.

The mayor and aldermen were self-elected. Throughout the Restoration period, attempts were made by the English crown to reduce the power of both English and Irish corporations. In 1671 Lord Berkeley, then viceroy of Ireland, introduced a set of rules, known simply as 'Berkeley's Rules', to restructure some aspects of Dublin's municipal government. Public opinion had been expressed in a tumultuous manner on several occasions in the preceding years. 'For the better preventing of disorders', Berkeley demanded that all assemblies 'be held with due respect to the lord mayor and aldermen of the said city for the time being, in peaceable manner, without clamour, disturbance or contention' (24 November 1671, in Gilbert, 1895, 5, appendix II, p. 549). The superior position of the lord mayor and aldermen over the commons was reinforced, as was the self-electing nature of this upper house of the Corporation. The lord mayor, recorder and sheriffs were to be 'such persons as shall be approved by the chiefe governour or governours' of the kingdom (24 November 1671). The lord mayor, recorder, sheriffs, aldermen and commons were to take the oath of supremacy and an oath of allegiance. The commons were to be chosen from the guilds of the city, with the Trinity (merchants) Guild in a privileged position.

No Corporation or guild offices could be taken by persons unwilling to take the oaths of supremacy, allegiance and non-resistance to Royal authority. By early 1673, however, some members of the commons refused to be sworn. In 1686 the oath of supremacy was dispensed with in response to Royal pressure so that Catholics could be admitted to the freedom of the city. However, a ruling of 1653 stated that only Protestants could enter the guilds or become apprentices. The same year the Irish urban charters were declared invalid, and in 1687 Dublin was reincorporated and the Corporation reconstituted. The new structure consisted of a mayor, 24 aldermen, a chamberlain and 48 free burgesses, who formed the Common Council. All appointments made by the Corporation were subject to viceregal approval. The members of the Corporation could all be removed at will by the lord lieutenant and the privy council, thus giving the Government vital control over municipal affairs. However, the lord mayor could also be removed by the Common Council, and the two sheriffs (appointed by the lord mayor) could be removed from office by the Common Council and the lord mayor. The structure of the Corporation remained unchanged until 1760, when an Act of Parliament (33 Geo. II, c.16) liberalized the election procedures, with the commons being entitled to participate in the choice of the lord mayor, aldermen and sheriffs. For the entire period from 1660 to 1800, however, the Corporation was very much under the thumb of the representatives of royal power in Ireland.

Gilbert's transcriptions of the assembly rolls of Dublin Corporation give evidence for the duties and responsibilities of that body. It was the task of the Corporation to direct the maintenance, lighting and cleansing of the streets within its jurisdiction (city scavengers were employed for this purpose). The Corporation also supervised water provision for the city. It controlled those properties and buildings in its ownership and was answerable for the upkeep of the city walls, gates and fortifications, as well as of municipal buildings such as parish schools, civic charities and prisons. The Corporation had the right to impose fines for the neglect of civic duties on the part of citizens or employees of the Corporation. Many of its activities were financed by taxes levied on the citizens, and by the Corporation's income from plots and properties that it let out. The Corporation also regulated the markets and fairs within the city and was entitled to exact tolls and customs for all goods sold within the city, these providing an important source of municipal income. The Corporation was furthermore required to provide for the security of the city and for manning and maintaining the watch houses.

Early city-wide planning measures of the Corporation include a ruling of 1661 forbidding the construction of thatched buildings within the city franchises, so as to prevent the danger of widespread destruction by fire. Their only response to the Great Fire of London in 1666 was to 'testify their compassionate sence of the misery of the said people of London, and render some relief to theire necessities' by organizing a subscription for their benefit (Gilbert, 1894, 4, p. 386). No debate ever seems to have taken place on the implications of such a disaster for a city largely built of wood and perishable materials. During the final decades of the seventeenth century, however, the building stock of the city was upgraded and many timber-framed houses were replaced by more solid constructions of brick and stone (Malton, 1799, p. 13).

The ban on thatch of 1661 does not seem to have been entirely effective; in 1739 one suggestion for laws necessary for the city read – 'That no house, cabin, or shade thereafter to be built within the city, or Liberties of Dublin, shall be roofed or covered with any other covering than slates or tiles.' The city expanded rapidly towards the end of the seventeenth century, and by the 1680s it was noted that the area outside the walls was greater than that enclosed by the walls. The Corporation was somewhat uneasy by the extent of the suburban development because it left the city exposed to attack. It would have liked to fortify the suburbs as the increased security so provided would encourage many foreign Protestants to come and settle in Dublin.

As early as 1673, plans for a citadel to the south-east of the walled town had been submitted by Bernard de Gomme, together with a detailed estimate for its erection. De Gomme calculated that the entire citadel, with fortifications and buildings, would cost £131,227 5s. 9d. The Corporation did in 1681 petition the lord lieutenant and privy council to consider fortifying Dublin, but no action seems to have resulted. Dublin was thus saved by inertia from the ruinous cost of soon-to-be obsolete fortifications on the continental scale. Many continental cities expended huge amounts on the creation of complex fortifications, designed to negate the destructive power of artillery, only to find that the technology of artillery soon made redundant anything that could be built. Most cities removed these fortifications in the nineteenth century, often retaining their line as parkland but Vienna used the land to create the Ringstrasse.

Street trading and traffic problems in Restoration Dublin

Mid-seventeenth-century Dublin had much to do if it was to assert itself in architectural terms as the representative capital of a kingdom. The walled town was narrow and confined, and inadequate access was provided from the new more regular streets to the east in Temple Bar and the bustling business area to the north of the river in the district from Smithfield through the busy thoroughfare of Capel Street to Drogheda Street (the latter occupied part of what is now Lower O'Connell Street).

There are many examples of the Corporation's late seventeenth-century attempts to deal with the traffic problems caused by increasing wheeled traffic in the narrow winding streets within its jurisdiction. In the sixteenth century the old-fashioned solid wooden wheel had been replaced by a modern version made of separate parts, and a fifth wheel was developed for many vehicles to facilitate turning. As a result, carts and wagons came into more general use in European cities (Mumford, 1966, p. 421), and by the Restoration period severe traffic problems were manifest in Dublin. The struggle to adapt urban design to deal with these traffic problems was to be one of the factors ultimately leading to the establishment of the Wide Streets Commission in 1757, but in the late seventeenth century rather different measures were being taken to combat this difficulty.

In 1667 measures were introduced by the Corporation to control hackney coaches in Dublin. Numerous complaints of traffic congestion had been voiced by concerned citizens; how little has changed in 300 years. The Corporation responded by restricting the number of hackney coaches permitted to 30. Fixed fares were established. The coachmen were to have their names and numbers painted on the backs of their vehicles, as in London. Both the owners and drivers of the coaches had to have licences, for which an annual payment was necessary. Coach stands were restricted to fixed locations, outside the city walls, ten coaches in Thomas Street, six in Castle Street, four in Saint Werburgh's Street and a further ten in College Green.

The coachmen were, it seems, somewhat tardy in acknowledging and observing these new regulations. In December 1667 there was a further complaint to the Corporation, that 'through the perverseness and disobedience of severall coachmen useing the said hackney coaches, none of the said rules, orders and constitutions hath been hitherto observed, to the greate contempte of the good government of this citty' (Gilbert, 1894, 4, p. 426). The Corporation responded by appointing one René Mezandiére, a 'gentleman belonging to

19 The area around Christ Church cathedral as shown on Rocque's map of 1756.

His Grace, James, Duke of Ormonde' and holding a 'pattent' from the king to licence and oversee hackney coaches and coachmen in the corporate towns of Ireland to be the seventeenth-century equivalent of the Carriage Office. There was but one complaint of congestion in Dublin's streets over the following two years, in January 1668, and this complaint does not refer to the hackney coaches, so the Corporation's regulations must have operated relatively smoothly for some time at least. By March 1669 the problem had reared up once again. There were too many unlicenced hackneys and they were clogging up the streets. Regulating the number of coaches was nevertheless not a sufficient measure to tackle the congestion of the streets.

Casual trading was also blocking the streets. In December 1667, it was complained that both freemen and others were setting out stalls on the streets both on market days and other occasions and that this was causing problems for shopkeepers as well as blocking the streets. Presumably the shopkeepers saw this as unfair competition. Orders were given by the Corporation to limit and control such street trading. Early in 1670 complaints were made to the Corporation concerning the nuisances caused by the lack of a market place or building for the sale of poultry, wild fowl and rabbits etc. The narrow streets were 'much pestred with hucksters sitting under bulks and stalls in the streete, whereby the streetes are made soe narrow that coaches or cartts cannott well passe or turne, which is a greate annoyance to the inhabitants of this citty ... ' (Gilbert, 1884, 4, p. 489).

Later that year further measures were taken to alleviate traffic problems. This time there were complaints that thirty coaches were 'too few for the necessary use of the inhabitants and others', accordingly the number of licensed coaches was increased to 50. The citizens complained, however, that there was no suitable rank for these additional hackneys. The obstreperous coachmen reappear once more in this period, fines being imposed on them late in 1670 for non-observance of new regulations. The money was to be used for the repairs of the city pavements. In 1703 a limit of 150 was imposed on the numbers of hackney coaches, but in practice the numbers continued to increase throughout the eighteenth century. In 1732 there were 200 hackney coaches in the city, according to one visitor (Anon., 1732, p. 520). The English clergyman, the Revd Campbell remarked on the excessive numbers of hackney coaches and sedan chairs in Dublin in 1777, finding them to be 'everywhere as common as about St James'. The rather particular Campbell was 'hurt by the nastiness of these streets, and by the squalid appearance of the *canaille*', and concluded that so many vehicles were necessary because of the poor condition of the 'abominably dirty' older streets, which made them unsuitable for walking (Campbell, 1777, p. 29, 48). By the 1840s the streets were congested by about 1500 licensed cars (Walsh, 1847, pp 64–5).

So, just as today, the city streets in this period were unsuited to the traffic requirements of the day. They had been built in an earlier era and could not cope with new means of transportation and the lack of proper infrastructure. The Corporation then, as now, struggled to find the appropriate solution. In the early 1680s the Corporation began to tackle the congestion and health problems caused by the presence of street markets in the old city. The matter went as far as the king in England, who responded with a letter to Lord Arran, then Irish viceroy, stating that the sale of meat, fish and other goods in the streets 'very much disturbs and annoyes the common passages of our said cittie'. Arran was instructed to see to it that the markets be removed to an appropriate location and that 'noe persons whatsoever may be permitted to incumber the streets of the said cities with any marketts whatsoever'. The Corporation promised to deal with this matter, and in March of the same year detailed regulations were approved by it, dealing quite exhaustively with all manner of obstructions to the streets (Table 1).

Table 1 Dublin Corporation's regulations on street sales, 16 March 1683.

First	That noe person be permitted to incumber the streets with any stalls, formes, stooles, or otherwise to stop the passages of the streets; but all the streets shall be free for common passage for all people and for horses, coaches, carts, carrs, etc., to pass to and froe without interruption.
Secondly	That noe pease or beanes be suffered to be shelled in Fishamble street, Warburg street or Skinner row, nor any annoyance suffered there or in any other streets of the cittie, to indanger by their stench the health of the cittizens.
Thirdly	That all butchers be removed from Fishamble street, St Johns lane, St Patrick street, except such as have taken or shall take shops there, which shall constantly be kept cleane and sweet.
Fourthly	That the bakers doe remove their stalls from the middle of High street, and noe bread be suffered to be sould there but such as shall be putt in shops, under pent houses, or along the side of St Michaells church, on markett dayes.
Fifthly	That all formes be removed from the Ould Crane markett, except such as may stand there without annoyance of the passages, for the selling of stockins and linnen and woollen cloth, and that all the butter, cheese, bacon, and other things to be removed.
Sixthly	That the Crane markett and markett for coales, carrs, timber and hay, be continued in St Thomas street, St Francis street, and St James street, and the shoes and brogues in New Row, so that the passages are left clear, and that all other things be removed.
Seventhly	That herbes and rootes, green pease and beanes and garden stuffe be sould in shops and bulkes in Fishamble street.

→

Eighthly   That persons be permitted to sell linnen and woollen cloth in
            High street, soe they make noe stalls or stoppage in the streets, but
            carry the same in their armes.

Lastly   For all other things that are hereby ordered to be removed from
            the marketts, we conceive Ormonde Markett in Oxmantowne to
            be the most convenient place for the same to be removed for to
            answere the present occasion of that part of the cittie.

Gilbert (1895), 5, appendix XIV, pp 606–7

These regulations throw some light on the patterns of trading in late
seventeenth-century Dublin, and also reflect two concerns that were to be
repeatedly expressed by urban commentators into the eighteenth century – the
unimpeded flow of traffic and the cleanliness and healthfulness, or otherwise, of
city air. The listing of street markets allowed to continue in operation clearly
demonstrates the initiation by the late-seventeenth century of the east–west social
and functional gradient so characteristic of Dublin by the late 1700s. All of the
streets mentioned in the regulations as having street markets are in the walled
town or to the west and south-west in the Liberties; none are farther east than
the old Custom House at Essex Bridge (now Grattan Bridge).

By the second quarter of the eighteenth century, the Corporation was
contemplating taking more radical initiatives to tackle the problems of traffic
congestion. In 1734, when recommending the demolition of the building over
St James' Gate, presented as a nuisance, the Corporation wondered if it should
use the opportunity to widen the passageway. One Captain Paul Espinasse
proposed that he pull down the gate and give a foot of ground on its south
side to enlarge the passage, a proposal promptly accepted by the Corporation.

In 1739 the Corporation suggested regulations on projections in a further
attempt to lessen congestion. Shop windows and cellar stairs frequently jutted
into the narrow streets making them more unsafe and difficult to negotiate
and such projections were forthwith forbidden in any streets less than 20 feet
(6 metres) wide. The Corporation did undertake some small street-widening
projects, ordering the widening of the passage from Cooke Street to New Row
in 1764. The following year a small section of the street leading past the Little
Green in the parish of St Michan was widened slightly.

However, these were piecemeal efforts and fated to be ineffectual. Either
the regulations were ignored or the problems simply outgrew the solutions. It
took the Act of Parliament setting up the Wide Streets Commissioners in 1757
to tackle the large-scale problems faced by the city.

New departures from the old town: St Stephen's Green and Smithfield

These various measures taken to relieve congestion on the streets did not involve any far-reaching intervention in urban form. It took financial necessity to drive the Corporation to one of the most significant initiatives in urban design in Dublin. In May 1663 members of the Commons of Dublin petitioned the Corporation, expressing their awareness of the imminent danger of bankruptcy of the city as a result of the poor economic and political climate consequent on years of rebellion. The Commons suggested three remedies for the city's financial difficulties:

- 'that the out skerts of Saint Stephens Greene and other wast lands about this cittie, that now addeth nothing att all to pleasure or profitt, may be set for ninetie nine yeares, or to fee farme, and a considerable rent reserved;
- that there may be a course laid downe that the incroachments in and about this cittie may be removed, other than such as will yeild to pay a rent to the citty;
- thirdly, that a course may be laid downe how that the water may yeild a constant revenue to this citty ...'

A committee of six aldermen and twelve of the Commons was appointed to consider these proposals, and within six months had reached a decision on the development of St Stephen's Green. The development of the Green as a residential square was perhaps the single most important decision of the Corporation in the late-seventeenth century. This development introduced to Dublin the neo-classical square that was to become such an important element of the capital's upper-class quarters. For Palladio (1736), a prime influence on the architecture of the period, squares were an integral and essential part of a city, for purposes of commerce, recreation and adornment. They were places of resort where people might meet and conduct both economic and social business. Palladio, in common with other Renaissance theorists, held that squares should be designed in the classical style. This meant that they should be enclosed and that the lower stories of the buildings should have porticos wherein people could walk and do business. This would protect them from the vagaries of the weather. The use of porticos had continued throughout the Middle Ages but received new emphasis during the Renaissance and could be found across the continent of Europe providing uniformity and continuity in Turin, St Mark's Square in Venice or in the Piazza Real in Madrid. The Dublin squares fulfilled Palladian conditions in the point of location as well as social and ornamental function but lacked arcaded walks. It may be that Dubliners shared an alternative view of porticos based on the tendency for shop and house owners to clutter them with refuse while night vice thrived in their dark recesses. However, these considerations, though part of the background to the St Stephen's Green project, were secondary to the prime aim of making some profit from the development of building plots in an attractive area.

St Stephen's Green was at this time a large common to the south-east of the walled city and its extra-mural suburbs, used by the citizens for grazing their animals. By October 1663 the 'committee for advance of the citty revenue' was able to report to the Corporation that its members had inspected and surveyed the Green, and found that 17 acres (c.7 ha) might 'be sett for a yearely rent for the advance of the citty revenue, without any prejudice to the citty of Dublin'. By July of the following year these plans had been formalized and the process of letting was put into motion, the plots being divided among the commoners and aldermen by lot. The edges of the Green were divided into plots with a frontage of 60 feet (c.18 metres), their depths ranging from 80 feet (c.24 metres) to 525 feet (160 metres). A rent of one penny per square foot per annum was to be charged for the plots on the east, north and west sides of the Green, and a lower rent of one halfpenny per square foot per annum for the south side of the Green, more remote from the urban centre. Each lessee was to pay 10d. for every 12s. of rent in order to wall-in the Green and for paving the roads and streets in an appropriate manner. Should these funds prove to be insufficient for the walling and paving of the Green, more was to be raised in the same manner though if too much money was raised it was to be redistributed equally among the lessees.

The Corporation made provisions for the aesthetic appearance of the Green, showing an admirable ability to go beyond their primary and pressing pecuniary motives in this development. It was decreed that each person should plant six sycamore trees near the wall. They were careful to impose conditions requiring a reasonable standard of building from any lessees who wanted to build on their plots, but building was not compulsory. Lessees who were 'disposed to build towards the front of all or anie parte of their severall proportions' were 'engaged to build of brick, stone and timber, to be covered with tiles or slates, with at least two floores or lofts and a cellar, if they please to digge it' (Gilbert, 1894, 4, p. 298). By 1739 three sides of the square, the west, north and east sides, were said to be complete with a range of handsome buildings, the fourth side being then under construction.

A Prospect of S.ᵗ Stephens Green

20 St Stephen's Green in 1728. (Charles Brooking, *The city of Dublin.*)

A London visitor to Dublin in 1732 placed the Green among the four most fashionable promenades of the city at that time, the other three being the 'waterworks in St James' street' (the City Basin), the 'deer park' or Phoenix Park, and the Strand. The same visitor found the walks 'wide and smooth', and notes that 'in good weather the quality of both sexes make a gay appearance' (Anon., 1732, p. 528). A few years later, another writer refers to 'one of the finest squares in Europe' as 'the common resort of the beau monde' (Anon., 1739, p. 26).

In 1753 plans were also afoot to give the Green a focal point by erecting a statue of King George II; the statue was designed by Van Nost and erected in the Green in 1756. Rocque's detailed survey of 1756 shows the Green almost completely built up. The north side (Beaux Walk) was completely developed, except for the section on the road leading to Ballsbridge. The west side (French Walk) was also occupied with houses, apart from the Quaker Burying Ground on the corner of York Street. The south side of the Green (Leeson's Walk) showed several empty or partially vacant plots, as did the least developed east side (Monk's Walk).

In 1792 the Corporation resolved to improve and beautify the Green, making a street 100 feet wide (*c.*30 metres) around the Green, of which 12 feet

21 The Green set for the fireworks display to celebrate the treaty of Aix La Chapelle in
1748 (*Universal Magazine*, London, 1749). In the enlarged extract (lower image),
the trees lining the edge of the Green can be seen and some impression
can be gleaned of the different housing styles.

(3.7 metres) were to be made into a flagged footpath in front of the houses. An enclosed gravel walk 40 feet (*c*.12 metres) wide was to be made inside the Green. This area was to be given up 'for public accommodation and recreation' and no further revenue claims made on it by the Corporation. The residents of the Green were to be responsible for maintaining these 152 feet (*c*.46 metres) of path, street and gravel walk, and to pay for the same. The Corporation retained the central area of the Green and even mentioned a plan for a new Mansion House here 'with four beautiful fronts', an interesting concept that never materialized (Gilbert, 1909, 14, p. 277).

St Stephen's Green is favourably mentioned in virtually every eighteenth-century account of Dublin. It is indeed the only feature in Dublin to receive a detailed description in all of these works. Even that lugubrious and critical Englishman, the Revd Campbell, finds praise for Europe's largest urban square, where 'genteel company walk in the evenings, and on Sundays, after two o'clock, as with us in St James' Park'. Campbell found that among the fast multiplying buildings, 'the great inequality of the houses, instead of diminishing, does, in my opinion, add to its beauty' and admired the cheerful situation (Campbell, 1777, p. 6).

The Green became a fashionable place to live, and the social position of its inhabitants was reflected in its architecture, with 'some grand houses and … in general well built and inhabited by people of distinction' (Pool and Cash, 1780, p. 14). Although in Wilson's eyes it could not compete with the more uniform developments of the late-eighteenth century, he saw in it much grandeur and elegance (Wilson, 1786, p. 25). The Green receives one of the longer descriptions accorded to individual features in Dublin in Lewis' *Dublin Guide* as a 'scene of elegance and taste' (Lewis, 1787, pp 239–40). Malton also greatly admired the Green for its scale as much as for anything else, but regretted the simplicity of design of even the largest houses 'in the modern plain taste'. He showed a hankering for the type of stucco ornamentation so favoured in continental cities, as he found that the lack of 'noble Grecian ornaments of architecture' in the simple stone façades gave an impression of 'flatness and insipidity' (Malton, 1799, text accompanying Plate 29). Malton's engraving of the Green executed in 1797 shows the grassy enclosure surrounded by the plain redbrick Georgian façades typical of Dublin streetscapes (Figure 22).

The Green continued for some time to receive much admiration but gradually it lost its grandeur. An anonymous visitor to Ireland, writing in the English periodical, the *Monthly Magazine,* in 1798, reported that cattle grazed on the Green in winter (Loeber and Stouthamer-Loeber, 1994). The semi-rural

22 St Stephen's Green in 1799. (James Malton, *A picturesque and descriptive view of the city of Dublin.*)

picture evoked here sits rather uneasily with Malton's very urbane image but echoes Ferrar's dictum of 1796 that the Green 'is extremely rural and pleasant in the summer' (Ferrar, 1796, p. 28). The Revd Whitelaw, writing in 1818, does not seem to like the square much, saying that it 'has, in its present neglected state, little else but its magnitude to recommend it', and complains of the irregularity and 'mean appearance' of many of the houses. Whitelaw also laments the passing fashionability of the gravel walks in the early-nineteenth century, now frequented at best by the 'middle-class', and describes the unpleasant practice of throwing animal corpses 'in a disgusting state of putrefaction' into the ditch along Beaux Walk (Warburton, Whitelaw and Walsh, 1818, 1, pp 459–61). G.N. Wright, however, in 1821 found the Green a 'magnificent area' but complained that the tall old lime trees 'cast a gloominess on the surrounding houses and rendered the atmosphere unwholesome' (Wright, 1821, p. 258). Malton had, 22 years earlier, admired the young lime trees 'which, when in leaf, diffuse an effect and chearfulness, the square without, could not impart' (Malton, 1799, text accompanying Plate 29). Shaw's *Pictorial Directory* shows a square in 1850 very much the province of tradesmen, merchants and the professions, with a small sprinkling of aristocracy. Soon it was to be given a comprehensive redevelopment which gave it the form it has today.

Smithfield is a product of the same initiative to make profitable use of common spaces as St Stephen's Green but never became as fashionable. The earl of Bective did build a town house there, but by the late-eighteenth century even this was dismissed by most chroniclers of Dublin as good only in a very old fashioned way (Wilson, 1786, p. 37). Smithfield was Dublin's main wholesale market for cattle and hay, 'forming a fine, airy, spacious place, of not an unpleasing aspect' (Warburton, Whitelaw and Walsh, 1818, 2, p. 1123).

There is no evidence for controls over the form of the buildings erected on the new market place, unlike the grants for St Stephen's Green, though trees were to be planted. Smithfield became both architecturally and socially more varied and less exclusive than the Green. Possibly the use of Smithfield's open space as a market discouraged non-commercial residents, and the approaches were found to be too narrow and the market too confined for the volume of business transacted there.

Other Corporation initiatives showed concern for the aesthetic detail of the urban landscape. When the City Basin was being made in 1721–2 for the city water supply, walks were levelled and laid out beside the basin and trees planted; the place became a popular promenade.

Looking to the river: early quay initiatives

The Anglo-Normans had out of practical necessity begun to modify the course of the Liffey. In the seventeenth century, the city authorities turned their attention to the development of the quaysides. Since the 1670s the Corporation had been consciously promoting the development of quayside streetscapes. The Amory grant of 1675 of land on the north bank of the Liffey close to Oxmantown Green, specified that 60 feet (c.18 metres) be left for a 'highway' along the river bank while the assembly rolls from the 1710s to the 1740s are largely concerned with accounts of the works to reclaim large tracts of land from the Liffey estuary.

In the early 1680s one William Ellis 'laid out considerable sums of money in purchaseing ground in Oxmantowne, with design to make a quay along the river to the Parke wall, and to make a considerable addition of building there, to the honor, beauty and profitt of the citty' (Gilbert, 1895, 5, p. 237). Ellis was bound to leave unbuilt the 40-foot highway (c.12 metres) along the river and to build a quay 'all along the river, six and thirty foot wide'. He offered, and was bound, to build a new stone bridge over the river Liffey, at the end of Queene Street, and another wooden bridge, where the wooden bridge had previously been. He was to pay for this bridge himself and maintain it for seven years, but the Corporation was to raise £700 from the citizens towards the cost. The completed quays can be seen on Brooking's map of 1728.

In 1684 the Commons petitioned to have Blind Quay (east of Wood Quay) widened, as it was narrow and inconvenient for the large numbers of coaches and carts using it daily. The problem was that it was so narrow that two coaches could barely pass and there were frequent accidents and stoppages. The committee appointed to review this proposal 'did conceive it would be a very necessary, commodious and ornamental work if a quay were made not exceeding thirtie foot wide unto the river', and work was commenced carrying Wood Quay eastwards, the finished work 'to be continued an open key or street for ever'. The inhabitants of the city carried the main costs of the project; city expenditure was not to exceed £40 (Gilbert, 1895, 5, p. 323).

Small alterations were carried out along the existing quays before the creation of the Wide Streets Commission. In 1752, for example, it is reported that in 1735 one William Coates, holding a plot on Blind Quay since 1723, had complied with an order to rebuild his premises and widen the quay fronting the river. In 1757 a new, 40 foot wide (c.12 metres) quay was ordered to be made running from Aston Quay eastwards. On the same day, an order was given to widen Aston Quay to 40 feet, showing the combination of aesthetic and commercial considerations typical of the Corporation, who expected that 'this enlargement will not only add to the beauty of the quay, but also tend greatly to the benefit and advantage of trade' (Gilbert, 1903, 10, p. 293).

In summary, the Corporation's chief contribution to innovation in the urban design of Dublin in this period was the transformation of the great open space of St Stephen's Green at the fringes of the walled town. Their attempts to channel and control the flow of traffic were not sufficient to solve the problems of communication between the old narrow streets of the walled town and the developing areas beyond the walls. It was not until the mid-eighteenth century that a body was created that had the power and the resources to tackle this issue.

Developments on private estates, 1729–1810: spacious and regular streets

Private individuals became important agents of urban development from the 1660s and were particularly important during the eighteenth century.

Landlords, such as the Viscounts Fitzwilliam and the earls of Meath, held large areas as parts of great estates, some of these holdings also providentially close to the growing city. Many of these estates had been given to those loyal to the English crown as a means of colonization and to maintain stability. Others saw the opportunities offered by property speculation and over time built up holdings of land with an eye to profit. From the late-seventeenth century onwards, these wealthy and ambitious citizens of Dublin, such as Humphrey Jervis and Luke Gardiner, set about acquiring the leases of large tracts of land bounding on the old walled city. This pattern of urban landholding has great similarities to the private estates of London (see Summerson, 1945). The new streets on the estates of Lord Aungier (Aungier Street, Longford Street), Humphrey Jervis (Jervis Street, Mary Street, Capel Street) and in the early-eighteenth century, the Moore family, earls of Drogheda (Henry Street, Moore Street, Earl Street, Off Lane, Drogheda Street) were in marked contrast to the narrow and winding streets of the old town (Bush, 1765, p. 10). The greatest contribution by private landlords to Dublin's monumental streetscape came in the eighteenth century, particularly in the second half of that century, when the Gardiner family (later Barons and Viscounts Mountjoy) and the Viscounts Fitzwilliam of Merrion developed large tracts of land to the north-east and south-east of the old city respectively (see Figure 23). It is to private developers that we owe the four of the city's neo-classical squares – Rutland Square, Mountjoy Square, Merrion Square and Fitzwilliam Square. The practice in planning these squares was for the owner to provide a plan of the layout as a guideline, and then to lease plots for development to architects, builders, speculators or private individuals, whose buildings were controlled by clauses in their leases and sometimes by the Wide Streets Commission, as for instance in Merrion Square. In this way, one agent maintained a considerable degree of control over the appearance of the development without having to provide all the money necessary for such large projects; in general this system worked to produce a startlingly uniform streetscape. However this control was by no means as tight as in some continental European developments. Louis XIV's Place Vendôme in Paris had its façade finished first and only then, in 1701, were the plots behind it sold. The Commission for the Building of St Petersburg in the 1760s proposed that the Government build the façades on the squares and then let the houses behind them be built as the owners wanted (Kostof, 1991, p. 260).

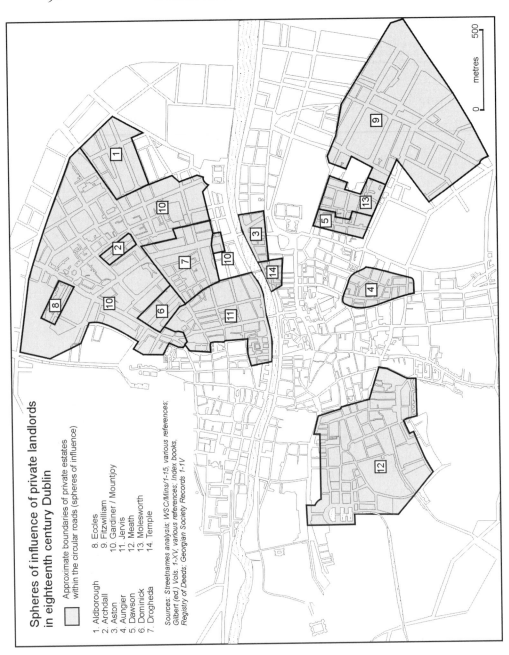

Spheres of influence of private landlords in eighteenth century Dublin

Approximate boundaries of private estates
within the circular roads (spheres of influence)

1. Aldborough
2. Archdall
3. Aston
4. Aungier
5. Dawson
6. Dominick
7. Drogheda
8. Eccles
9. Fitzwilliam
10. Gardiner / Mountjoy
11. Jervis
12. Meath
13. Molesworth
14. Temple

Sources: Streetnames analysis; WSC/Mins/1-15, various references; Gilbert (ed.) Vols. 1-XV, various references; Index books, Registry of Deeds; Georgian Society Records 1-1V

23 Spheres of influence of private landlords in eighteenth-century Dublin.
(Compiled by Edel Sheridan.)

The Gardiner/Mountjoy estate

Much of the north-east of Dublin within the Royal Canal was developed by the Gardiner family over a period of about one hundred years from *c.*1720 onwards. There were two Luke Gardiners. The first was a banker (in partnership with Arthur Hill, brother of Viscount Hillsborough) with a premises in Castle Street until the bank was voluntarily liquidated in 1739 (Fraser, 1964, pp 127–8). He was also a member of Parliament from 1725 to his death in 1755, and became a member of the privy council as well (McCready, 1892). He made a judicious marriage in 1711 to Anne Stewart, niece of the second Viscount Mountjoy, and cousin of William Stewart, third Viscount Mountjoy and first earl of Blessington. When the latter died in 1769, the Right Hon. Charles Gardiner, son of Luke and Anne, inherited the Tyrone estates of the Viscounts Mountjoy and their country house, Mountjoy House, but not the titles. Charles Gardiner's eldest son, the Right Hon. Luke Gardiner (1745–98) was created Baron Mountjoy in 1779, and Viscount Mountjoy in 1795. The son of the second Luke Gardiner, Charles John Gardiner (1782–1829) was created earl of Blessington in 1816, and was the last male Gardiner at his death in Paris in 1829, having outlived his own son.

The first Luke Gardiner acquired property on the south side of the Liffey, along the Strand, and in Fleet Street, in 1713. The scantiness of documentary material due to the dispersal of the estates in the nineteenth century hinders identification of the exact boundaries of the estate built up by the Gardiners on the north side of the Liffey. Streets named after members of the family (Blessington Street, Charles Street, Florinda Place, Gardiner Street, Place and Row, Montgomery Street, Mountjoy Square) can be readily identified as coming under the Gardiner sphere of influence. The Gardiner involvement in Henrietta Street, Rutland Square and Sackville Street is also well known (see Burke, 1972b; Craig, 1969; *Georgian Society records*, 1913; McCullough, 1989). Luke Gardiner was erecting houses in Henrietta Street in the early 1720s, in Sackville Mall in the 1740s and in Rutland Square in the 1750s. He also purchased the Drogheda estate in Dublin in the early-eighteenth century. His will lists his Dublin property. As well as lands near Harold's Cross just south of the city, and estates in County Wicklow and County Meath, by the 1750s the Gardiner estates in Dublin comprised:

Grounds and houses in Great Britain Street, including 10 acres (4 ha) at the back of George's Church

Ground and a house in Bolton Street

Grounds and houses in Henrietta Street and in Cavendish Street

Two holdings in St Stephen's Green

Two holdings in Stephen Street set at the yearly rent of forty three pounds

A holding in Mary's Abbey

A holding in Mary's Street

A holding in Capel Street set at fourteen pounds a year

Holdings in Strand Street

Two houses in Skinner's Row.

Will, 5 November 1755, Right Hon. Luke Gardiner, Esq.

This great city estate was not continuous and this caused problems in execut-ing a grand design. Dominick Steet, Temple Street and Eccles Street commem-orate the families who owned them, the Archdall family owned land where North Great George's Street was erected (Rocque, 1756), and Lord Aldborough had interests in Gloucester Street. The first planned urban expansion directed by the Gardiners was Henrietta Street, on ground bought in 1721 from Sir Thomas Reynell and the earliest leases on this street date from the mid-1720s. A Gardiner lease of 1723 to one Samuel Braithwick, 'cloathier', of a plot of ground on the west side of Bolton Street, states that Braithwick's plot is bounded to the north by 'a Newstreet intended to be called Henrietta Street', and refers to a stable lane providing access to the back of the Henrietta Street plots 'which ye sd. Luke Gardiner did thereby covt. to Leave Twenty Two foot wide from ye East to West for a Passage and Coachway along the Rere of the Premes' (*Books of transcripts*, 40, p. 30, no. 24050, 4 June 1723). The early leases for Henrietta Street show that from the very start a distinguished and wealthy tenantry was aimed at; all plots are occupied by large houses with coach houses, stables and other outoffices (*Books of transcripts*, 63, 71, 76, 77 etc.).

Transcripts of leases for Henrietta Street also provide evidence of development practices on the estate. It seems that long-term leases were not granted until a house was built by the lessee on the plot, a practice similar to that followed by the Fitzwilliams on their estate on the south side of the river. The *Books of Transcripts* also show that plots let by Gardiner to a developer were frequently re-let by the first lessee to a second, once a house and outbuildings were erected on the site. As on the Fitzwilliam estate, peppercorn rent (nominal or minimal rent) was often charged for the first 18 months of a lease (for example *Books of transcripts* 92, pp 255–6, no. 64501, 8 and 9 September 1738) and, as on the Fitzwilliam estate, this may have been to encourage rapid building.

Henrietta Street maintained an aristocratic character to the end of the eighteenth century; from the number of archbishops living there, it became popularly known as Primate's Hill (*Georgian Society records*, 2, 1910, p. 11). Around 1730, Luke Gardiner had a mansion built for himself there (now No. 10) by the German architect Richard Cassel, who also designed the Lying-In Hospital in Rutland Square and Kildare/Leinster House. On 19 September 1740, the gentlemen living in the 'great houses' of Henrietta Street applied to Dublin Corporation for piped water, so by this time the street must have been more or less completely built up. The manuscript returns of Whitelaw's census of 1798 show five peers (automatically members of the House of Lords), two peeresses, one Member of Parliament, one judge, one doctor as well as one gentleman designated 'Hon.' residing in Henrietta Street (*Georgian Society records*, 2, 1910, pp 28–30).

Sackville Street, also known as Gardiner's Mall, was developed on an even grander scale than Henrietta Street; Malton calls it 'the noblest street in Dublin' and says it is 'very well built' and 'inhabited by persons of the first rank and opulence' (Malton, 1799, text accompanying Plates 21 and 22). Sackville Street was planned as a residential mall and promenade by the first Luke Gardiner from the 1740s onwards. By 1752, the street was sufficiently developed for the inhabitants to put in an application to the Corporation for piped water. A Gardiner lease of the central part of the mall to one Carleton Whitlock in 1755 survives in the National Library of Ireland and gives some indication of Gardiner's plans and the state of development by 1755. The lease tells us that 'the said Mall is now and for some years past hath been laid out and used as a Mall or Walking place'. Luke Gardiner obviously intended that the mall remain a promenade and was anxious to prevent any building on the central area:

> In Trust nevertheless and to the Intent and Purpose That the said hereby Granted and Released Ground and Premises shall for Ever hereafter be and remain a Mall or Walking place as well for the use, pleasure and accomodation of the Tenants and Inhabitants of the several Houses on the East and West sides of the said Mall and their Servants and followers as for the use, pleasure and accomodation of all other persons whatsoever who shall think fit to pass and Repass thro' the same And that the said peice of Ground or Mall shall be Remain and Continue unbuilt upon.
>
> (Indenture between Luke Gardiner and Carlton Whitlock, 1755)

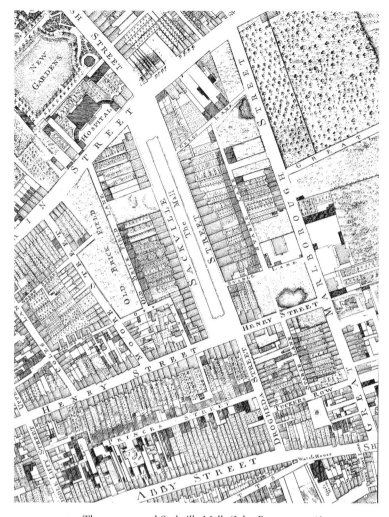

24 The area around Sackville Mall. (John Rocque, 1756.)

This extract shows that by 1755, the street on both sides of the mall was already at least partially built up (Rocque's map confirms this impression); that the tenants and inhabitants had servants and followers indicates their wealth. The lease also shows that the central mall was enclosed by a wall and lit with lanterns, and that the inhabitants of the street had contributed towards the cost of this wall and other expenses. Large residences were erected and a chronicler of Dublin in 1766 declared that 'for elegance of plan and architecture [Sackville Mall] exceeds any street in London' (Harris, 1766, p. 101). It seems that Gardiner originally planned to extend the street southwards to the river, and terminate the vista with a public building on the south bank. This plan was later partially fulfilled by the extension of Sackville Street, the building of Carlisle Bridge (O'Connell Bridge) and the creation of Westmoreland Street with a view of Parliament and Trinity College by the Wide Streets Commissioners. However, this extension contributed to the transformation of the Mall to a business street.

Rutland Square (now Parnell Square), on the northern edge of the Gardiner estate, was by the end of the eighteenth century one of the most aristocratic residential areas in the city and 'an elegant square' (Malton, 1799, text accompanying Plates 21 and 22). In 1798, Cavendish Row alone boasted among its residents two peers, two peeresses, two bishops and one MP (*Georgian Society records*, 1909, I, pp 28–9). Its physical plan and elevations matched this exalted social composition. The square (which, as was common, is not square, but an irregular polygon) has its origins in the 1750s. Dr Bartholomew Mosse (1712–59), an educated and innovative man, much travelled and very interested in the arts, had in 1745 opened the first maternity hospital in these islands in a house in what was then George's Lane (later South Great George's Street) on the south side of the city, close to the old medieval centre and the Castle (Pool and Cash, 1780, p. 62). In 1748 Mosse leased five acres (2 ha) north of the newly-developed Sackville Street, and commissioned the German architect Richard Cassel to design a new hospital. The hospital was built between 1751 and 1757 (Malton, 1799). The building was much admired – 'As a building, it is magnificent, and, being the most faultless I ever beheld, is a lasting monument of the abilities of Mr Castels [*sic*]' (Campbell, 1777, p. 25).

To fund his charitable venture, Mosse had an area north of the lying-in hospital planned and laid out as pleasure gardens for which an entrance fee was charged. Concerts were also held out of doors in the gardens and in a circular building erected in 1784 for that purpose to the east of the hospital, the Rotunda that gave the hospital its popular twentieth-century name. These gardens became a tremendously popular and fashionable promenade. Campbell, whom we have seen frequently to be a reluctant praiser of Dublin, waxes almost lyrical, declaring that 'this is the Vauxhall, Ranelagh and Pantheon of Dublin. Nay, it is something more than all these, it is a polite place of public resort on Sunday evenings ... On these nights, the rotunda and gardens are prodigiously crowded, and the price of admission being only sixpence, every body goes' (Campbell, 1777, pp 26–7). Certainly the 'really romantic' walks in the gardens afforded 'delightful recreation' for the inhabitants of the neighbourhood and the hospital became the 'vortex of all the fashion of that part of the town' (Malton, 1799, text accompanying Plates 21 and 22). The Rotunda became the location for a form of entertainment known as a promenade; the participants paid for a ticket, and for this sum they could show themselves in the promenade and partake of tea:

> They have devised in Dublin a rather singular form of entertainment, the proceeds of which are applied to the maintenance of a Maternity Hospital. It is called a Promenade, and the name made me wish to go and see one. The visitors walk in a circular hall called the Rotunda, and while there is somewhat more freedom than that which obtains at private entertainments, people only mix with, and speak to, members of their own circle … everywhere there reigned a kind of quiet enjoyment which gave me much more pleasure than I expected to find. The good mammas were not very numerous, and those who were present appeared to be absent-minded. The young folk, on the other hand, were very numerous and making good use of their time – I think, perhaps, the Promenade attained its object along more lines than one. The cash result is nearly all the hospital has to depend on for maintenance.
>
> (La Tocnaye, 1796–7, p. 24)

Around the hospital residential streets were developed, their course partly determined by the presence of the pleasure gardens and partly by the existence of an old laneway to the west of the gardens. In the early 1750s Luke Gardiner opened up Cavendish Row leading from the Mall northwards to one of the principal northern approaches to the city, the road to Drumcondra, later Dorset Street. Granby Row and Palace Row, with the town palace of Lord Charlemont (now the Municipal Gallery), followed in the 1760s. The square's appearance was given a final neo-classical polish by the Wide Streets Commissioners, who in 1786 erected new buildings on its south-eastern corner, replacing less regular older development. More imposing access from the north was provided when the same body opened up North Frederick Street after 1790.

The form of this square is not entirely regular, and it incorporates several inconsistencies of design that originated through the involvement of more than one agent in its development. In this respect it is different from the other great squares of Georgian Dublin, which were all initiated and carried through by one principal agent – St Stephen's Green by the Corporation, Mountjoy Square by the second Luke Gardiner, Lord Mountjoy, and Merrion and Fitzwilliam Squares by Lord Fitzwilliam. One of the peculiarities of Rutland Square is the position of the hospital. The location of the Rotunda to the east of the hospital eventually provided, in 1784, a fitting termination for the Mall and rescued the 'grand perspective of Sackville Street (one of the noblest in Europe)' (Cromwell, 1820, p. 49). Rutland Square is a good example of the evolution of a reasonably unified urban ensemble through the actions of several agents, and speaks for the strength of the prevailing fashions in urban design.

Mountjoy Square was the last large-scale project of the Gardiners, begun in the 1790s and completed early in the nineteenth century. The initial plan for the square was one of the grandest in Dublin. Gardiner planned to erect buildings with unified palatial façades on all four sides; the buildings would have entrances to separate dwellings at regular intervals. A new church for the parish of St George was planned for the centre of the square. This plan proved too expensive to implement and uniform four-storey brick houses were built around the square (Warburton, Whitelaw and Walsh, 1818, 1, pp 466–7). Faden's Dublin map of 1797 shows all four sides of the square built up, but Whitelaw's census of 1798 shows the east side empty of inhabitants. There were residents on the east side by 1799, for in that year they petitioned the Corporation for pipe water.

In 1802 a Commission for Enclosing and Improving Mountjoy Square was set up by Act of Parliament (Ashe, 1941, p. 100), and by the second decade of the nineteenth century the square was completed in all respects. The 72 houses were well built, regularly arranged, roomy and convenient. The central part of the square was enclosed by a neat iron railings on a granite base, and was well lit by 82 lamps on the railings and lamps at the fronts of the houses. The houses were amply proportioned and well built, and the green space at the centre had been 'laid out with taste and judgement' by the Enclosing Commissioners, with flowering shrubs, gravel walks and lawns (Warburton, Whitelaw and Walsh, 1818, 1, p. 467).

It was a neat and elegant square and it became a node of attraction for the prosperous in Dublin in an area which was still quite fashionable. It was well situated, with good views of the mountains in Wicklow from its elevated and airy location. McGregor (1821, p. 295) was moved to superlatives and declared that with the 'general splendour of the adjoining streets, all combine to render it one of the most agreeable city residences in the British Empire'. It is hard to imagine this from the perspective of the late-twentieth century when the square has only lately been saved from ruin and when no more than 60 per cent of the original fabric remains. The decline of Mountjoy Square to decay and dereliction is an excellent example of the dynamic nature of cities and its changing geography (see Murnane, 1988).

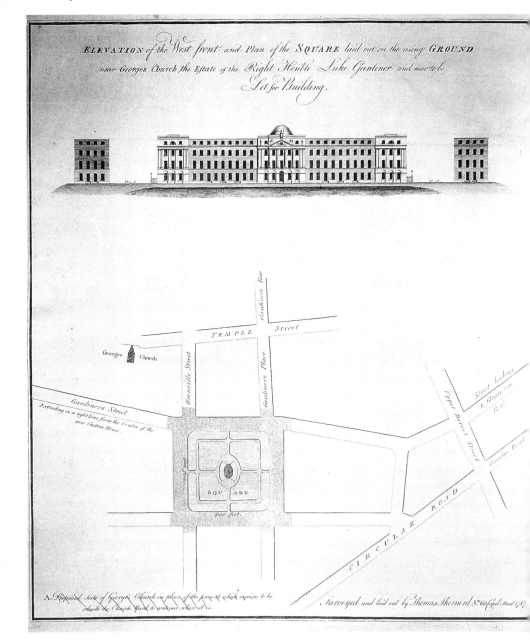

25 Proposed elevation and plan for Mountjoy Square, Dublin, in the
late-eighteenth century. (Wide Streets Commissioners, 1787.)
Reprinted by kind permission of Dublin City Archive.

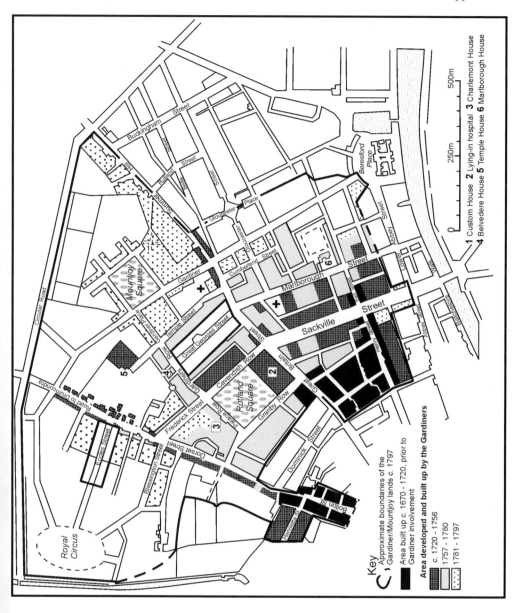

26 The Gardiner estate, Dublin, in the late-eighteenth century.
(Compiled by E. Sheridan.)

From 1790 onwards, the Wide Streets Commission, discussed below, played a role in the development of parts of the Gardiner estate (Figure 23). Initially set up as a development agency with significant powers to solve the intractable problems of Dublin's planning, it had become crucial to the redevelopment of the city along European lines. An Act of 1782 had legislated for the commission's extension of Sackville Street to form what later became Lower Sackville Street. Likewise, the commission took over the development of Lower Abbey Street from the Gardiners (24 February 1797, WSC/Mins/14, pp 100–5). An Act of Parliament of 1790 extended its remit and empowered them to control new development in private estates and authorized the development of North Frederick Street. Thereafter, the approval of the Wide Streets Commission was necessary for any new streets laid out on the Gardiner estate. The Commissioners intervened in, and watched over, the development of streets such as Gardiner Street and Blessington Street, insisting on the maintenance of straight lines and uniformity.

In some cases, the commission's intervention in the streetscape led to the development of a social profile markedly different from that of the streets planned solely by the landlord. The commission's house designs incorporated shops on the ground floor, unlike the purely residential buildings erected under the Gardiner direction. Thus, although the physical scale of Sackville Street and its continuation made it 'one of the grandest [streets] in Europe', the mixture of gentry and tradesmen introduced by the Wide Streets Commission diminished its 'importance of appearance', the houses being occupied by 'Peers, Pastrycooks, and Perfumers; Bishops, Butchers, and Brokers in old furniture, together with Hotels of the most superb description, and a tolerable sprinkling of gin and whiskey shops' (Jefferys, 1810, pp 85–6). The intervention of the commissioners probably suited the Gardiners well; the second Luke Gardiner (grandson of the first) was a commissioner and could therefore exert some influence on the activities of the commission, and also save money by availing of the commission's plans for continuing Sackville Street, for instance, a project that his grandfather may originally have contemplated when laying out the street (Bush, 1769, p. 11). There seems to have been a strong coincidence of interest between commission and landlord in the case of the Gardiner estate.

The Fitzwilliam/Pembroke estate

The Viscounts Fitzwilliam of Merrion held a huge wedge of land in Dublin, extending eastwards from near St Stephen's Green to Ringsend and southwards

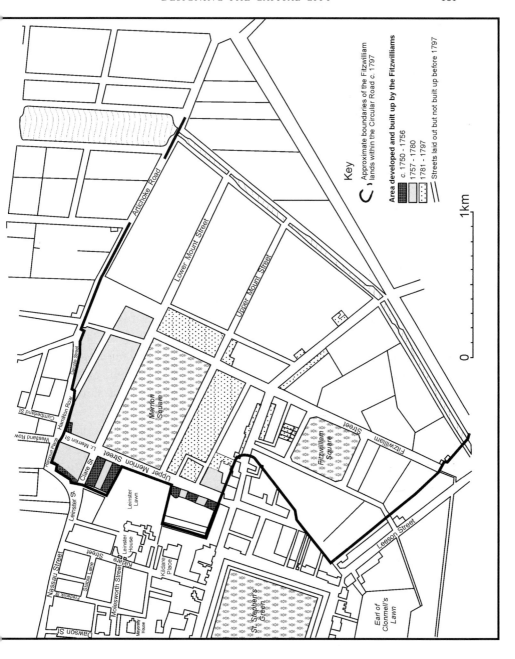

27 The formation of the Fitzwilliam estate, Dublin, in the late-eighteenth century.
(Compiled by Edel Sheridan.)

as far as Bray. The minutes of the Wide Streets Commission for the 1790s throw some useful light on the concerns and ideals of its agents acting in developing Merrion Square. (Figure 27.)

A volume of estate rentals from 1773–84 lists the following streets as being in the estate up to the 1780s – Merrion Street, Clare Street, Merrion Square, Holles Street, Denzil Street and Baggot Street (Fitzwilliam Square and Fitzwilliam Street had not then been developed)(excerpts by Malcomson, n.d.). The Fitzwilliam estates brought in £3067 in 1743, £5068 in 1773 and £8020 in 1784. The Fitzwilliams resided for the most part in London, and employed (Catholic) agents to run their Dublin estates. Bryan Fagan was the agent from 1751 to 1761, his wife Elizabeth took over at his death and continued as agent until 1777, when their daughter Barbara became the agent. Barbara Fagan later married Richard Verschoyle, and together they continued as agents until 1821. The seventh Viscount Fitzwilliam was lord lieutenant of Ireland in 1795.

In 1745 the earl of Kildare (later duke of Leinster) built his town house in Kildare Street, the lawns of which faced onto the western edge of the Fitzwilliam property. By the 1750s Fitzwilliam had leased plots at this western end of his estate for buildings, and Rocque's map of 1756 shows these early beginnings of Merrion Street. In 1762 Lord Fitzwilliam caused a square to be laid out on his land, using Merrion Street as the west side. Ralph Ward Esq. and Mr John Ensor 'who built considerably', laid out the square; Ensor also laid out Holles Street, and built Antrim House on the north side of the square. In 1780 Mr Samuel Sproule (who also worked for the Wide Streets Commission) finished Holles Street and laid out the east side of the square and both Mount Streets (Ferrar, 1796, p. 73). Fitzwilliam Square and Fitzwilliam Street were laid out in the 1790s, and not completed until the 1820s.

There seems to have been some disagreement between Lord Fitzwilliam and Lord Kildare concerning the line of a street planned by Fitzwilliam in the 1750s, presumably Merrion Street. This disagreement led Fitzwilliam's brother, William Fitzwilliam, then assisting Bryan Fagan as agent, to advise Lord Fitzwilliam to the following effect:

> One caution let me give leave to give you: let him [Lord Kildare] have no lease from you until the passage to your buildings is actually put into the shape wherein it is to remain. I am for doing business like a man of business and trusting to no one, especially in a place where there is no virtue.
>
> (Letter from William Fitzwilliam to Lord Fitzwilliam, 21 July 1753)

It may have been this incident that gave rise to the apparent Fitzwilliam policy of not signing leases until there was some evidence of building on the plot taken by the lessee; in 1769 one Robert Price had to prevail upon Elizabeth Fagan to intervene for him and get Lord Fitzwilliam to sign his lease so that he could dispose of the two houses he had built in Merrion Street. It would be reasonable to assume that this was a conscious policy, given that it seems to have been the practice on the Gardiner estate as well. In comparison to the transcripts of the Gardiner leases available in the Registry of Deeds, Fitzwilliam leases offer quite detailed building specifications. One Columbine Lee Carre (also sometimes spelt Caree or Carée) was given a lease of a plot on the north side of Merrion Square on 16 August 1763; he was required to build, within three years of the start of the lease, a slated house of no more than three and a half storeys with a cellar and paved area, and to flag the foot passage in front of the house and pave the street to the wall around the central green ('Lease of a plot … to Columbine Lee Carre', 16 August 1763). The terms of this lease in fact closely echo the original St Stephen's Green leases granted by Dublin Corporation in 1664. A lease granted to John Gibson of a plot in Fitzwilliam Square in 1791, requires him to build, within four years, a house of 'redstone bricks', with no bow windows or projections, and with a basement enclosed by a stone kerb with iron railings ('Lease of a plot … to John Gibson', 1791). The Fitzwilliam leases often contain periods of peppercorn rent (nominal or minimal rent) of from eighteen months to seven years – as on the Gardiner estate, this may have been to encourage building in the early years of leases. There is also evidence in the leases, and in letters from Elizabeth Fagan to her employer, that Lord Fitzwilliam would not tolerate any plans for buildings that would encroach upon or interrupt Merrion Square, no matter how elevated the social position of the prospective lessees.

A 1762 estate map by Jonathan Barker shows an early plan for the square. The square is shown surrounded by red brick gabled houses, and is somewhat longer than the finished square. A long street running from north to south along the eastern end of the square is shown; this indicates that the idea for Fitzwilliam Street (not developed until the 1790s) was already being considered.

The first houses in the square were built in 1762 and 1763 (*Georgian Society records*, 1912, 4, pp 79–81), and by the late 1770s or 1780, most of the west side of the square was finished. Campbell records in 1777 that 'they have finished one side of a square called Merryon's Square, in a very elegant style' (p. 6). Pool and Cash comment a few years later that 'there is an elegant and spacious square laid out, and partly erected, situated near St Stephen's Green, called

Merrion-square, where the houses are lofty and uniform' (Pool and Cash, 1780, p. 15). Many of the houses on the north side of the square have a rusticated stone finish to the ground floor. The stone finish of the first floor gave the buildings 'an air of magnificence, inferior to nothing of the kind, if we except Bath' (Lewis, 1787, p. 39). The landlord's role in encouraging this type of high quality development was appreciated by contemporaries (Wilson, 1786, pp 25–6).

In 1791 building on the square was quite advanced, and the residents were beginning to express concern about the state of the central green area, up till then quite unadorned, which was 'become, and must continue to be a very great nuisance to the inhabitants surrounding it, unless a proper inclosure round the same be made and supported'. An Act of Parliament entitled 'An Act for inclosing and improving Merrion-Square, in the City of Dublin' was passed in 1791, setting up a Commission for Inclosing and Improving Merrion Square, as many inhabitants and proprietors had 'signified their earnest wish and desire that the said square shall be properly inclosed, and the inside thereof improved and ornamented for the convenience and comfort of the several inhabitants' (*Statutes at large*, 31 Geo. III, c.45, clause I).

The 21 Inclosing Commissioners (all being lessees of plots on the square), or any five of them, were empowered to 'contract for the making, finishing, compleating, improving, ornamenting and inclosing the said square … in such manner as they shall think most proper' (clause I), and were to set an annual charge on the residents to this end, payable twice yearly for 147 years from 1 November 1791 (clause II). The Commissioners were given legal powers to enforce the payment of this subscription (clauses VII, VII), to fine anyone caught damaging anything in the square, or climbing over the railings (clause IX) and to purchase any leases existing on the central area (clause XI). They were also given powers to enforce the purchase of any such leases by appointing a jury, as with the Wide Streets Commissioners (clause XII). Conditions of design similar to those followed by the Wide Streets Commission were to be adhered to, and no projections into the street tolerated (clauses XVII, XVIII).

A schedule of occupants and proprietors of the houses and plots around Merrion Square is appended to the act, and facilitates analysis of the development of the square. It is apparent from this list, that the north and west sides of the square were completely built up by 1791, while the other two sides contained a mixture of houses and building sites. The latter two sides were partly let in very large lots with frontages of over 100 feet (*c.*30 metres) for development. Of the 61 lessees in 1791, 18 were members of titled families.

The Inclosing Commissioners seem to have executed their work well and speedily. Ferrar says of the square in 1796, that it was superior to any in London in its scale, building and symmetry and that it had been recently improved by the laying out of the green area in the centre of the square. The Inclosing Commissioners laid out the square 'with much taste and good sense'; the decoration was planned to suit the natural form of the surface and 'thus at once produced a pleasing variety, and avoided a very considerable expence'. The square was well lit, and the green area was the 'exclusive property' of the residents, 'who thus may be said to possess Rhus in urbe' (Warburton, Whitelaw and Walsh, 1818, 1, pp 463–4).

Some writers wax lyrical about the square, great indeed was its popularity, enclosed as it was on three sides:

> … by lofty houses, all built in the modern style, and though not perfectly uniform, yet so nearly so, in their form, elevation and decorations, as not only not to hurt the eye, but, in the opinion of some, to please it by this small variety.
>
> In short, when we consider its seven spacious approaches, formed by so many modern streets, its magnificent extent, its elegance, neatness, and convenience, its remoteness from the hurry and bustle of business, the salubrity of the air, with the additional circumstance that the lawn of Leinster-house is really an extension of the same noble area, we may rate it among the finest squares, not only in the British empire, but in Europe.
> (Warburton, Whitelaw and Walsh, 1818, 1, p. 463, 466)

The northern footway of Merrion Square became a popular promenade and the estate agent Barbara (Fagan) Verschoyle was pleased with the result: 'Merrion Square looks so handsome it is so fashionable a walk and drive … you have nothing in London so handsome as Merrion Square – the irregularity of the ground forms a first part of its beauty and I think you will say it is well laid out' (letter from Barbara Verschoyle to Lord Fitzwilliam, 18 May 1797). The stylish buildings attracted a high status tenantry: 'the houses in this square being built in the most elegant modern style, it is inhabited in general by persons of the first rank' (McGregor, 1821, p. 293).

One clause in the Act of 1791 led to a misunderstanding between one tenant (and commissioner for the square), Robert Day, and his landlord, in 1792. This rather petty case provides a telling example of the lengths to which the Wide Streets Commissioners *and* private landlords were prepared to go to

realize their urban ideals. Clause XVII of the 1791 Act of Parliament had authorized Day to build a sunken area before his basement. He, however, understood
it as permission to build a porch, and proceeded to do this. Richard Verschoyle,
husband of Barbara Fagan, and acting for Lord Fitzwilliam, took the matter
before the Wide Streets Commission, thus making use of the Act of 1790,
which had made the Wide Streets Commission responsible for ensuring that
no projections be built into the streets of Dublin.

A series of meetings of the Wide Streets Commission followed, which must
have been heated to judge from the language of the minutes. The commission
demanded to know 'by what authority [Day was] proceeding' in the
'encroachments' he was alleged to be making on Merrion Street (8 May 1792,
WSC/Mins/11, p. 12). Day declared his belief that he was acting 'under the
inspection and controul of the Paving Board strictly to the provisions of the
Act' and was firmly instructed that 'any Building other than a Porch shall be
prostrated' and told only to build 'so as not to encroach upon the foot path'
(28 May 1792, WSC/Mins/11, pp 22–4). Mr Verschoyle, however, held Mr
Day's porch to be 'so very great a nuisance' (4 June 1792, WSC/Mins/11, p. 33),
and 'very prejudicial to Lord Fitzwilliam's Estate in that Neighbourhood'
(8 June 1792, WSC/Mins/11, p. 35). The Paving Board was dragged into the
debate. A letter to Mr Day was drafted, desiring him to 'desist from proceeding any further with said Building' (8 June 1792, WSC/Mins/11, p. 35).

Eventually, on 8 June 1792, Robert Day agreed to stop building on condition
that he would be reimbursed for any expenses incurred in building, an arrangement with which the commission duly concurred (18 June 1792, WSC/Mins/11,
p. 50). A few weeks later, Mr Day reappeared before the Commission with
a proposal to cover and enclose the area he had opened up 'with an Iron
palasadoes', provided that the commission paid his expenses and removed the
building materials he had accumulated on the site (6 July 1792, WSC/Mins/11,
p. 64). The commissioners agreed to this proposal. The case of Robert Day is a
good example of the extent to which Fitzwilliam was prepared to go to maintain
the regularity of Merrion Square and the adjacent streets; it also illustrates the
extent of co-operation between the landlord and the Wide Streets Commission.

Fitzwilliam Square was the last and smallest formal residential square to be
erected in Dublin in the eighteenth century. Unlike Merrion Square, the
Fitzwilliam Square project from its very inception was subject to the veto of
the Wide Streets Commission. By 1793, all of the plots were committed with
a stipulation that building be completed within three years. It was not,
however, completed until well into the nineteenth century. Fitzwilliam Square

I.—Mountjoy House, Henrietta-street.

II.—Charlemont House, Rutland square.

III.—Tyrone House, Marlborough-street.

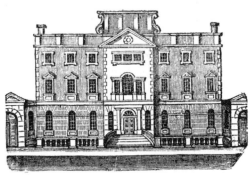

IV.—Powerscourt House, William-street.

V.—Aldborough House, Circular Road.

28 Town mansions of the Irish nobility and gentry in eighteenth-century Dublin.
(*Dublin Penny Journal*, 1836, p. 257.)

was disregarded by some because of its small extent, 'possessing little to recommend it beyond its air of cheerful neatness' (Cromwell, 1820, p. 92), though some
critics were more generous to the 'beautiful little square' (Wright, 1821, p. 262),
which 'though much smaller, promises, when completed, to vie with Merrion
Square in neatness and elegance' (McGregor, 1821, p. 294).

The Fitzwilliam estate, like the Gardiner estate, demonstrates the very great
influence that private individuals could have over the streetscape of eighteenth-
century Dublin. These landlords can be seen to have had architectural aspirations
similar to those of the Wide Streets Commissioners, ideals informed by Vitruvian
and Palladian literature on neo-classical building. Both the Gardiners and the
Fitzwilliams were prepared to co-operate with the Wide Streets Commission,
after that body was granted city-wide planning powers, and also to use the
commission to help them further their own ends.

Interspersed with these developments were the town houses (Figure 28) of the
very rich and influential, though perhaps palace is the more appropriate word.
Despite the freedom of these people to build as they desired, the stone mansions
of Dublin all show certain similarities of form. These include the Provost's House
(Trinity College/Grafton Street), Charlemont House (Palace Row, Rutland
Square), Powerscourt House (South William Street), Kildare House (Kildare
Street, Merrion Street), Tyrone House (Marlborough Street), and Aldborough
House on the Strand near the Royal Canal. They face onto the street, and are in
this sense part of the urban streetscape, but they are larger than their neighbours
and possess in many cases more spacious grounds. Their size and location, some
with gardens extensive by urban standards (for example, the Provost's House and
Kildare House), together with their architectural form, link them with country
residences. In this respect they correspond to the Parisian *hôtels*, which
represented an urban house form with a strong resemblance and connection to a
country seat. In form they differ from the narrower houses surrounding them by
having not merely a large number of bays (five to nine bays in Dublin, as
opposed to the terrace norm of two to four bays in that city), but also in the
organization of the façade into at least a symbolic central block with attenuated
wings.

The Wide Streets Commission, 1758–1802: order, uniformity and convenience

The city was transformed under the operations of the Wide Streets
Commission (Figure 29). Today's planners must be envious of the sweeping

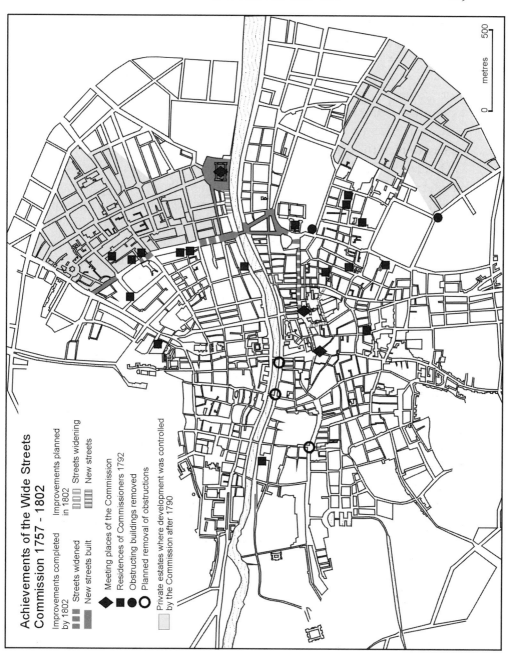

29 Achievements of the Wide Streets Commission, 1757–1802.
(Compiled by Edel Sheridan.)

powers that this organization enjoyed and of its ability to see its will in action. McGregor writing in 1821, noted that 'it must be admitted that no other city in Europe can boast of greater improvements in the short space of half a century' (p. 175). In a similar vein, Lewis, some fifteen years later (1837) wrote, 'the city may be said to have been new-moulded since the year 1760, through the instrumentality of this board, as there is no portion of it which does not exhibit in a greater or small degree the results of its labours in improvements tending to augment its beauty or to add to its salubrity' (p. 532)

The importance of the Wide Streets Commission for Dublin's evolution as a capital in a European context is unique. The Commissioners regulated spatially extensive and significant developments for nearly a hundred years and represent an important shift from independent municipal control to State involvement in planning the capital city. At the start of their activity, the growing city lacked coherence. In the last four decades of the eighteenth century, the haphazard conjunctions of old and new were moulded to a more unified whole as Dublin was prodigiously enlarged and improved. New large-scale developments linked the more impressive of the older schemes, and private developments were subjected to more centralized control. The far-reaching activity of these decades was generally well received, the ever patriotic Messrs Pool and Cash declaring warmly that 'which way soever a stranger turns himself, he will perceive an increasing spirit for elegance, and improvement' (Pool and Cash, 1780, p. 23).

On examining a map of the city at the end of the eighteenth century and contemporaneous drawings and engravings, or indeed on walking through late twentieth-century Dublin, the visitor cannot fail to appreciate the scale and grandeur of the principal streets linking the chief public buildings in the city centre. The great length and width of the axis from Sackville Street (formally renamed O'Connell Street in 1924) through D'Olier Street and Westmoreland Street to Dame Street and Dublin Castle via College Green provided in the eighteenth century a sharp contrast to the narrowness of the streets of the walled city. Some two hundred years later the same contrast is evident between these great representative streets and the sadly few streets of the walled city still untouched by twentieth-century widening. Moreover that the city functions at all at the end of the twentieth century is due in no small measure to the creation of these streets. It would be hard to imagine the traffic circulation of Dublin functioning without the wide thoroughfares of D'Olier and Westmoreland streets.

The upper image in Figure 30 is from Wilson's *New Plan of Dublin*, published in the *Dublin Magazine* (1762) and shows the area of Sackville

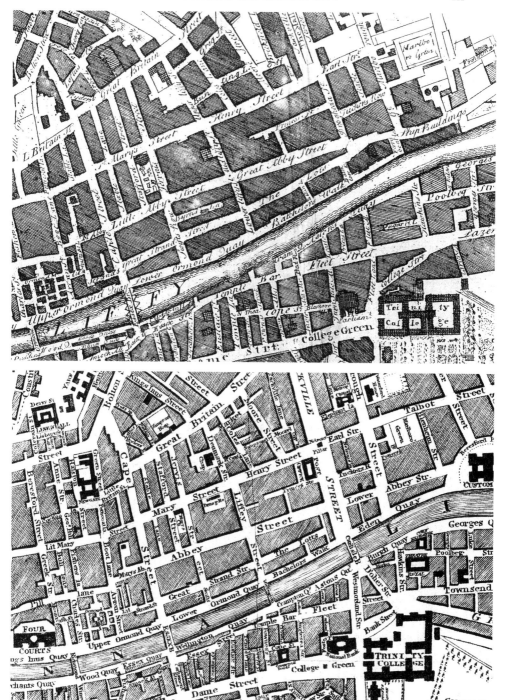

30 The development of Sackville Street – College Green axis.

Street/College Green before development by the Wide Street Commission. The lower image from Corbet's *New map of the city of Dublin* (1832) shows the completed axis. Sackville Street has been completed and the new Carlisle Bridge leads into Westmoreland and D'Olier streets.

Origins of the Wide Streets Commission

The Commissioners for making Wide and Convenient Ways, Streets, and Passages, as they were entitled, were established by Act of Parliament in 1757, which was given royal assent in 1758 (*Statutes at large*, 31 Geo. II, c.19), and were active until the commission was dissolved in 1851 following the adoption of an Act for the 'Improvement of the city of Dublin' in 1849 (Gough, 1991, p. 11). When the Wide Streets Commission was initiated the climate was ripe for major change in the way in which Dublin was planned. For almost a century, Dublin Corporation had been grappling with the traffic problems arising from the ever-increasing number of vehicles and pedestrians on the narrow and winding streets of the old city.

There had been much discussion arising from the severe congestion along the quays and in the streets around Essex Bridge, with traffic from the main northern routes into the city leading down the important and fashionable thoroughfare of Capel Street, and across Essex Bridge coming to a virtual dead end at the narrow and convoluted windings of the small streets leading past the bustling old custom house and on into the medieval urban core or outwards to the Parliament House and Trinity College. Rocque's 1756 survey of Dublin gives valuable insights into the city's pre-Wide Streets Commission morphology.

In 1749 a Parliamentary committee had been set up to inquire into the causes of this traffic congestion, yielding the recommendation that the bridge be replaced by a larger one further downstream. This would have necessitated the removal of the custom house to a more easterly location. Two members of this committee, Nicholas Archdall, recent purchaser of the Eccles estate in the north-east of the city, and Charles Gardiner, son of Luke Gardiner senior (who owned the large Gardiner estate, also in the north-east of the city), must have been anything but disinterested in making this suggestion. The Corporation gave voice to strong opposition to this scheme.

The widening of the streets leading onto Essex Bridge and of the bridge itself to accommodate the 'great concourse of passengers, coaches and other carriages' was proposed to the Corporation by interested citizens in 1751. It is in the context of this proposal that the first moves were made to apply for Parliamentary aid to purchase the buildings concerned. The old Essex Bridge was demolished in 1753 and replaced in 1755 by a new wider one in the same position, built by George Semple. In 1755 Semple published a plan for opening an approach to the Castle from Essex Bridge, and a Parliamentary committee was set up to examine the best method for putting this scheme into effect (McParland, 1986, pp 97–8). In 1756 the Corporation petitioned Parliament regarding 'opening the avenues leading to Essex Bridge' and requested that 'so necessary a work' be speedily done. This resulted in an Act to provide a street leading from Essex Bridge to the Castle.

> Whereas the ways, streets, avenues, and passages leading from Essex-Bridge to the Royal Palace or Castle of Dublin, and several other ways, streets, and passages within the city of Dublin and liberties adjoining thereto, are at present narrow, close, and crooked; and the making a wide and convenient way, street, and passage from the said bridge to the said castle will contribute to the ease and safety of passengers, the adorning those parts of the city, and will be of use and benefit to the publick.
>
> (*Statutes at large*, 31 Geo. II, c.19, clause I)

Commissions were a normal means of effecting urban change as in the development of Mountjoy Square and Merrion Square, discussed above. When citizens petitioned Parliament (generally via the municipal authority) for assistance in development, a bill could be drawn up establishing a commission to achieve the desired result. In the case of the Wide Streets Commission, decades of petitioning regarding the catastrophic conditions at the eastern end of the walled town had preceded the Act. This Act combined a solution to some of Dublin's traffic problems with measures to add to the city's image as a capital. The Wide Streets Commission, in cooperation with the Corporation, commenced the activities that were to reshape Dublin and leave a heritage of urban design comparable to that of many European capitals. The Corporation had to provide juries for the valuation of property affected by the new streets, rather like the present-day compulsory purchase process. By July 1758 the Corporation had issued a notice to the proprietors of the houses and grounds in the area to 'send an account of their interest' and was preparing to treat with the commission regarding Corporation plots there. This Act was not an isolated incident in the legislation for Irish urban development. In the same year another Act was passed, setting up a commission to 'widen, repair, or rebuild' Baal's Bridge in Limerick (*Statutes at large*, 31 Geo. II, c.20). This Act refers to the importance of the bridge as the only communication route between Limerick barracks and 'the principal fortifications' of the city, and as 'the only convenient passage between most parts of the two great provinces of Munster and Connaught'. It is pointed out that the same bridge 'is now in a most ruinous and dangerous condition' and that its improvement would contribute much to the safety and ease of passengers, and accommodation of the forces in the garrison. Cork also had its own Wide Streets Commission (McParland, 1972, p. 27). In 1790 Waterford Corporation appointed a 'Committee for laying out and widening streets and Avenues in this City' (McParland, 1985, p. 146).

The members of the Commission

The members of the Wide Streets Commission named in the Act of 1757 were, with the single exception of the lord mayor, members of Parliament. Many of the commissioners' names have been perpetuated in the streets that they designed in this role and also in other parts of the city where they held private estates – Arran, Beresford, Burgh, Clanbrassil, Conyngham, Gardiner, Kildare, Leinster, Mountjoy. Several of the commissioners named in the 1757 Act held positions of responsibility and authority in the Government of Ireland, with justice, revenue and the military represented, among others. Of the first set of commissioners, none was particularly renowned for devotion to the arts or architecture. By the early 1760s, however, new commissioners with a very real involvement in the promotion of architecture were beginning to be appointed to the commission.

David La Touche, of Huguenot extraction, is well known as a successful banker, and his interest in the arts is indicated by his presentation of a cast of Laocoön to the Dublin Society in 1790. William Burton Conyngham, appointed to the commission in the 1760s but not particularly active until the 1770s, together with one Redmond Morres, who was appointed some few years later, had been appointed trustees for building an academy of painting, sculpture and architecture for the Society of Artists in Ireland in 1767. The Society faded out by the 1770s, but the idea of such an academy must have been an important influence on the two men and their activities in the Wide Streets Commission (Trench, 1985, p. 53). William Burton Conyngham also welcomed Gandon, the architect of many of Dublin's most important buildings, to Ireland in 1783 and encouraged him to stay, with the support of

Lord Carlow (Trench, 1985, p. 48; McParland, 1972, p. 15). In the 1770s
Theophilus Thompson and William Colvill were commissioners, and these
two were also trustees of the Royal Exchange and had been involved in the
organization of the competition for a design for that building, a competition
that had a great influence on the course of development of Irish architecture
(WSC/Mins/1, 2, 3; McParland, 1972, p. 3).

John Foster, a prominent architectural patron, Luke Gardiner, who had
become a commissioner in the late 1760s, together with John Beresford, also
a patron of architects, and Travers Hartly, both joining in the 1770s, and the
architectural critic Andrew Caldwell, who joined the commission in the mid-
1780s, must have been familiar with current thinking on new and ideal towns
as well as on architectural design. Three commissioners appointed in the mid-
1780s had a special interest in architecture. Lord Carlow was a patron of
architecture, and both Samuel Hayes and Frederick Trench were amateur
architects. Thus the commission was remarkable not merely for the aggregate of
power embodied in its combined membership but also in the members' varied
and sometimes deep involvement in architecture and the encouragement thereof.
The responsibility for what were to become some of the most significant
developments ever undertaken in Dublin seems therefore to have been in most
able hands.

It can be safely assumed that most members of the Wide Streets Commission
had in their private libraries some of the architectural treatises so popular in the
eighteenth century and they must have been familiar with Vitruvius, Alberti and
Palladio, and also with Campbell's *Vitruvius Britannicus*, especially in the light
of the direct involvement of many of them in matters architectural. Sale
catalogues of the libraries of John Claudius Beresford, Burton Conyngham
and Andrew Caldwell contain listings of large collections of travel and
architectural books, and works describing antiquities.

Some of the Commissioners, notably Luke Gardiner, had considerable landed
interests in large areas of Dublin and these men were, naturally enough, not
above using their position to further private interests. The intrigues surrounding
the planning and building of Carlisle Bridge (O'Connell Bridge), the new
Custom House, Lower Abbey Street and Beresford Place in the 1780s and
1790s bear witness to this. It was no accident that Beresford and Gardiner, two
commissioners related by marriage and both holding land in this area,
strongly supported the new plans, which would certainly not be to their
financial disadvantage (Burke, 1972b and McParland, 1972, p. 4, pp 9–10).
Volume eight of the commission's minutes lists the streets in which the

commissioners lived and in the ninth volume of the minutes this is supplemented by the actual house numbers (WSC/Mins/8, p. 9). The residences of the commissioners were largely concentrated in the areas that benefited most from the building of a new bridge and relocation of the Custom House – namely in the new fashionable suburbs to the north-east and south-east of the medieval city core.

The commissioners were, however, anxious to disclaim personal interest in the schemes with which they were entrusted, declaring that 'it must be observed, that in endeavouring to promote these useful Objects of general Concern, the Commissioners have not, nor can they have, any Interest but the public Good' (Wide Streets Commission, 1802, p. 30). Whatever their disinterestedness or lack thereof, their contribution to Dublin's urban design is certainly very great. It can be demonstrated that the Wide Streets Commissioners brought a truly European vision of urban design to Dublin.

A new vision of the city

The work of the Wide Streets Commission was very much a product of Enlightenment Europe, attempting to impose order on the city through the application of rational aesthetic principles. The commissioners themselves were not afraid of overestimating their importance in applying the ideals typical of the European Enlightenment to the planning of Dublin's streets and buildings. In a memorial to the lord lieutenant in the *Extracts from the minutes of the Commissioners ... for making wide and convenient ways, streets, and passages ...* , published in 1802, they 'humbly' write 'that your Memorialists have faithfully applied the several Sums appropriated by Parliament to special Purposes and vested in them' (Wide Streets Commission, 1802, p. vi). They refer repeatedly to the 'Utility and Usefulness' of their projects and describe their schemes as 'great plans of Public Utility' and 'great and munificent Improvements ... which have considerably contributed to the Healthfulness, Ornament and Convenience of the Metropolis' (Wide Streets Commission, 1802, p. 1, 18). They proudly list the many projects over which they presided in the years from 1758 to 1802 and remark that the commission's role as controlling body for the design of all new privately-developed streets in the metropolis 'has successfully promoted Order, Uniformity and Convenience' (Wide Streets Commission, 1802, p. 16).

The commissioners were consciously concerned to avail of the most modern ideas on the European scene, and their place in a rapidly internationalizing arena is clear. From the late-seventeenth century onwards, Irish art in general had come under the same influences as the art of the rest of northern Europe – inspiration stemming initially from Holland and later from Italy and France. Eighteenth-century Irish art and, by extension, architecture, can be seen as more truly European than merely colonial, with England acting as a 'neutral conduit' for European influences (Turpin, 1987, p. 50). McParland claims a conscious political motivation for the work of the commissioners in the late-eighteenth century, remarking that support for Irish Free Trade and legislative independence from the 1780s onwards can be seen to be reinforced by a desire that in all cultural matters Dublin should not be inferior to London (McParland, 1972, p. 4). The commissioners were eager to learn from foreign example, in order better to adorn their capital city. Their indebtedness to French prototypes can be seen in a comment on their introduction of apartment-type buildings with residences over shops on the corner of Cavendish Row and Great Britain Street, where it is noted that 'the Style of Building proposed here, has long been in use on the Continent, and found uncommonly convenient in procuring Bed Chambers contiguous to shops or the Apartments of Persons in Trade, unconnected with the Upper Floors' (WSC/Maps/206). The commissioners were anxious to produce designs for terraces of individual dwellings built so as to look like one palatial façade (20 March 1789, WSC/Mins/9, p. 4), as was the pattern in many continental cities.

They were keen to be up-to-date on what was happening in London and in April 1792 they ordered copies of the 'elevations of such range Buildings or others in London … as will be of advantage towards furnishing designs for the new Streets and Places in this City' (WSC/Mins/9, p. 316). In 1796 Thomas Sherrard, surveyor to the commissioners, was ordered to subscribe on behalf of the commission for two copies of a new plan of London, and to organize the hanging of one in the Board Room, that is, in the room in the Exchange where the commission met. There is evidence that members of the commission had plans of London and Paris, as well as of other cities, in their private libraries.

The achievements of the Wide Streets Commission are an expression of Dublin's growing confidence as a capital, and reflect wider changes in urban design taking place all over Europe. It has been claimed that baroque urban fortification theories and changing military technology transformed the patchwork space of the medieval city, opening up vistas and reflecting an increasing desire to conquer space. This new approach to politics and military control had a deep influence on the structure of the city, leading to the building of *viae triumphales*, great streets where 'both symbolically and practically, the design established that everything was "under control"' (Mumford, 1966, p. 413, 417). The Wide Streets Commission's planning of the axes linking Dublin's most important buildings can be seen as an expression of this European trend in spatial design. Their vision was certainly anything but provincial, as their conscious choice of English and continental models reveals. They did not hesitate to adopt new house forms, as evidenced in their readiness to accept the integrated shop and house designs proposed by Sproule, Gandon and Baker among others. Nor did they limit their activities to single or piecemeal interventions, but had a broader city-wide impact. The scale of their interventions in the streetscape made it possible for Dublin's great eighteenth-century delineator, James Malton, admiring 'so vast a display of utility, taste and spirit' to write of the city in 1799 that, 'when reference is made to the grand plans that have been executed within these last ten or fifteen years, Dublin will be found not only deserving to be mentioned with respect, but worthy to rank among the first capitals of Europe' (Malton, 1799, pp 14–15).

The executive powers of the Commissioners

The twenty-one powerful and influential men appointed to the Wide Streets Commission were given considerable, though not absolute powers, their efficiency depending on pragmatism, discussion and compromise. Those affected by their operations were given various legal safeguards. All details of the design and layout of the new streets, together with the disposal of the building lots, were left to their discretion. Designs were provided by the Commissioners to the buyers of the publicly auctioned plots, with recommendations that all builders adhere to these plans. The commissioners were empowered to buy all buildings, grounds and properties necessary to their design. If owners refused to sell their property, or could not establish a clear title, the commissioners could fall back on the sheriffs of the city to raise a jury of twelve to establish the title and deliver an appropriate estimate of a fair price. Conveyances of the property in question were to be made to the commissioners on payment to the owner of the sums decided by the jury. In the case of any disputes of uncertainties as to the recipient, the money could be deposited in Chancery until such time as the claim was settled. In the meantime, the property was to be considered as legally belonging to the commission, which could proceed with its plans. Materials from old buildings pulled down at the orders of the commissioners were to be removed from the site as fast as possible. Those suitable for the purpose were to be re-used in the new buildings and the remainder were to be sold as advantageously as possible and the proceeds used for the purposes of the Act.

There were safeguards built into the Act for tenants-at-will or yearly tenants, who were to be given due compensation for having to leave their dwellings. The commissioners could fine the sheriffs, jurors or witnesses up to £10 for neglect of duty or failure to attend. All expenditure was to come from a £7000 grant made to the commission by Parliament. A treasurer and clerks were to be appointed, and these were to be answerable for the expenditure of the commission. There were also provisions made should legal actions be taken against persons acting under the Act. If any money was granted by Parliament for widening other streets, the Wide Streets Commission and any persons appointed by the lord lieutenant or chief governors were to have similar powers.

The powers of the Wide Streets Commission were refined and extended in further Acts of Parliament in 1759, 1781/82, 1790 and 1792. The Act of 1759 was 'for removing of such doubts and difficulties' as had arisen in the execution of the original Act. The most important change was the empowerment of the commission 'to make one *or more* wide and convenient way or ways, street or streets, passage or passages, from the said bridge to the castle' (*Statutes at large*, 33 Geo. II, c.15, clause V). Thus, almost from the start of their activity, the potential for city-wide intervention began to creep into the brief of the Wide Streets Commission.

In 1781/82 an 'Act for the Improvement of the city of Dublin ...' (*Statutes at large*, 21, 22 Geo. III, c.17) entitled the commission to a tax of one shilling per ton of coals imported into Ireland; the commission financed its activities with the proceeds of this and other taxes, and by using Parliamentary and Royal grants (Wide Streets Commissioners, 1802, p. 2). The commissioners were to widen Dame Street and to make or widen other ways through the city and to widen the various roads within 2 miles (*c.*3 km) to not less than 100 feet (*c.*30 metres). The Act of 1790 (*Statutes at large*, 30 Geo. III, c.19) extended their powers still further. They were now entitled to borrow up to £100,000 at an interest rate of not more than 4 per cent per annum. The same Act also empowered them to open up what was to become North Frederick Street and 'a passage from Summer-Hill to the great northern road'. Clause XV underlined the rights of the Commissioners to alter existing streets or build new ones 'when and as often as it shall appear to the said Commissioners, or any nine or more of them, to be necessary or expedient'. Their responsibilities as overseers of new development in Dublin were extended to cover the design of privately developed streets (clause XIX).

The commissioners were not slow to implement these new powers, and evidence of their involvement in the planning of the new streets laid out in the Fitzwilliam and Gardiner estates in the 1790s can be found in their minutes (WSC/Mins/10, pp 212–3; 244–5). The 1790 Act also contained a clause regulating the architectural style of all new buildings on Dame Street and Lower Sackville Street (then still known as Drogheda Street, now Lower O'Connell Street), which were to be built 'in a style or manner correspondent with the style and manner of the fronts of the new buildings already erected'. Interestingly, the difference of expense entailed in providing more elaborate matching façades, as opposed to plain brick ones, was to be met by the commission. Any houses newly-built or refronted between Trinity Street and Church Lane (that is, on College Green) were to be in a line with the new buildings already erected on the newly widened Dame Street, otherwise a fine of £200 could be imposed and the commission could empower the city sheriffs to have any buildings or parts thereof that encroached on these lines 'prostrated and abated, without the said Commissioners, or the said sheriffs, or any persons employed by them, being liable to answer any damages for the same' (*Statutes at large*, 30 Geo. III, c.19, clause XVIII).

As well as being given wider powers in specific instances of their own scheme, and the role of a sort of planning authority for private development, the commission was given a general mandate to involve itself in large-scale improvement of Dublin's streets. The Act recommended the commission to take the initiative in any areas needing development, as:

> … there are many narrow streets, lanes, and passages in the city of Dublin, and the liberties thereof, where there are waste and unbuilt grounds, or where houses and buildings have been heretofore made, and such houses or buildings have fallen or are going into decay, and the opening and widening of such narrow streets, lanes, and passages would be of great benefit to all and every the inhabitants of such narrow lanes, streets, and passages, and also to the owners and proprietors thereof, and of such waste or unbuilt grounds or houses, and would be a great improvement to the said city …
>
> (*Statutes at large*, 30 Geo. III, c.19, clause XXVII)

The influence of this Act can be seen in the many small-scale modifications of the streetscape and the more ambitious plans for opening up and modernizing many parts of the city's medieval core, projected by the Commission from the last decade of the eighteenth century onwards (Wide Streets Commission, 1802).

In an Act of 1792 the jurisdiction of the Wide Streets Commission was extended to half a mile (*c*.1 km) beyond the Circular Road. Since this encompassed the city, the two Acts of 1790 and 1792 created what was in effect a metropolitan planning authority. This was the first and only time that the development of Dublin could be said to be under the jurisdiction of a single unified authority. Thus in the course of three and a half decades, a body emerged with wide-ranging powers to supervise, plan and initiate the development in Dublin of a specific type of streetscape – long, straight, wide streets. Care and attention was to be given to the three-dimensional form of these streets, and these new developments took place, not as haphazard geometric lines imposed at will on the city, but as part of the integration of new and old, commercial, governmental and residential quarters in the city.

Activities and achievements, 1757–1802

In the second half of the eighteenth century, large parts of Dublin east of the city walls were transformed by the Wide Streets Commissioners' interventions. New streets were built and old ones altered and widened, and the resulting thoroughfares were lined with imposing buildings of a uniformity and harmony of architectural composition never before seen in Dublin on such a scale.

The schemes of the Wide Streets Commission were not always merely autocratically imposed from above, many of them having their origin in petitions and memorials presented to the commission by Dublin Corporation or other interested groups. Some projects were responses to traffic or communication problems affecting the community at large, while others directly expressed the desire to furnish Dublin with a streetscape worthy of its status as a capital city. However, while the commissioners had to obtain Parliamentary approval for any plan not previously legislated for, the Corporation had little say in what was undertaken. Only the mayor sat on the commission, though it must be noted that gradually the composition of the commission came to reflect the business community rather than the aristocracy.

From 1782 onwards, the post of secretary and clerk to the Commission was combined with that of surveyor, a position occupied by Thomas Sherrard well into the nineteenth century. Designs for the new houses were supplied by independent architects, who were paid for their drawings. McParland (1972) points out that though many of the drawings are signed by Sherrard, these were mostly copies of the originals, and it is uncertain whether or not Sherrard ever made any designs of his own. When a proposal was finally accepted, it was displayed in the coffee room of the Royal Exchange for public viewing, much as Dublin corporation's plans are displayed today.

The commissioners then set about acquiring the lands necessary for the execution of their plans. The sheriffs of Dublin were required to provide the makings of a jury to inquire into the value of the properties involved. The juries often spent many months establishing title and value, interviewing the owners and inhabitants of every house. Thus the jury records provide a valuable, if complicated, source for aspects of social geography, giving insights into the actual use and subdivision of Dublin houses before the commission's intervention and replanning.

Once a price was fixed for each property, the commission applied its powers of compulsory purchase and the house-dwellers affected by the plans were given due notice to quit their tenancies. The new streets and levels were laid out by workers paid by the commission and overseen by the author of the plans and maps or by other persons appointed and paid by the commissioners. The lots were sold at public auction to the highest bidder. The terms of auction for the sale of lots on the south side of Dame Street are fairly typical of the conditions imposed on the purchaser:

> All the Lots to be sold at 25 Years Purchase. An Uniform Front to be made by the several Purchasers and Builders according to the Levels and after the Manner which the Commissioners shall direct with Posts and Flags before the Houses as in Parliament Street – the Buildings to be carried out according to the Lines of the Map, the Materials on and opposite to each Lot to go with it, No projecting Windows or signs to be to any of the Houses to be built – One fourth of the Purchase Money to be deposited with the Treasurer at the Time of the Purchase of each Lot, and the Rem.r at the time each Purchaser shall begin to pull down, or shall be at Liberty to do so.
>
> (17 April 1766, WSC/Mins/2, pp 22–3)

Thereafter, the responsibility for building lay in the hands of the new owner of the lot. That the commissioners were interested that their plans be executed to the letter is obvious from the following instance of correction of irregularities in the execution of buildings on Dame Street. In 1783 the commission complained of an 'Irregularity now conspicuous' on the south side of Dame Street, where one Mr Todderick had placed his windows a few inches too low and his neighbour Mr Colles had his some four and a half inches too high. The commissisoners expected these gentlemen to 'forthwith alter their Windows agreeable to the Plan laid down for them' (26 September 1783, WSC/Mins/5, p. 75). A lack of symmetry and order in the composition of a building was abhorrent to neo-classical architecture, 'for Lights being thus disorderly posited, makes it look all a squint, and as deformed (almost) as to see a Man have an Eye in his Temples' (Neve, 1703, p. 88). The commissioners were also concerned to provide a footpath along the new street, clearly divided from the carriageway by posts, as the auction terms for the leases for new plots on Dame Street show.

The major projects of the commission carried out in the first forty-five years of their existence provided Dublin with a coherent system of major axes linking the buildings symbolic of power and government with the residences of the powerful and wealthy and with the chief commercial areas of the city. They shaped an ensemble of monumental streets linking the Castle and the Parliament Building via Dame Street to the stylish residential quarters on Gardiner's estate and to the centre of fashionable social activity associated with the Lying-in Hospital and its gardens and assembly rooms. To do this, modification of Dame Street was necessary as well as the carving out of new streets through the network of small grid systems that had grown up along the river on the Temple and Jervis estates to the south and north of the Liffey respectively.

Parliament Street and Dame Street
The thrust of the early large-scale interventions of the commissioners was concentrated on providing suitable approaches to, and improving the communications between, the Castle, the Houses of Parliament and the Viceregal Lodge in the Phoenix Park. The very first project was Parliament Street which was opened in 1762. Initially there was some resistance on the part of the tenants of the area to be cleared to vacate their homes. The commissioners, irritated by delays, sent the city sheriffs with some men to remove the roofs from the old houses on one night in 1759. The hint was taken. The plan to leave an open square at the top of Parliament Street, at the north entrance to the Castle, never materialized, but, by the 1770s and 1780s, the street was being lauded in accounts of Dublin. Campbell described it in his grudging fashion as 'a new and exceedingly neat trading street' (Campbell, 1777, p. 8), while the more enthusiastic and patriotic Dubliners, Pool and

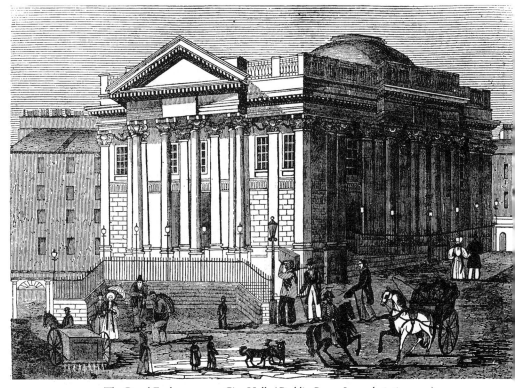

31 The Royal Exchange, now City Hall. (*Dublin Penny Journal*, 1836, p. 145.)

Cash, declared that 'for the uniformity of its buildings and grandeur of its shops, [it] is no way inferior to the best trading streets in London' (Pool and Cash, 1780, p. 9).

It was, however, necessary to do something with the area planned for the square, and ultimately a new city Exchange, today's City Hall, was built there. Part of this plan necessitated the demolition of some houses which confined the street at this point, as 'the scite of the Exchange was formerly occupied by a range of old houses, and a particular one, called Lucas' Coffee-house, which so narrowed the passage to the Castle, that two carriages could scarcely pass abreast, there being not more than twenty feet space from house to house' (Malton, 1799, text accompanying Plate 14).

A competition was held for a design for the Exchange. Work on the winning entry, by Cooley, was begun in 1769, and once again, Pool and Cash enthuse on its architectural merits, pronouncing it to be 'a most magnificent edifice, and justly claims the admiration of Foreigners, being perhaps the most elegant structure of its kind in Europe' (Pool and Cash, 1780, p. 43). The

32 Dame Street/College Green (Pool and Cash, 1780). Note the Flemish gables.

replanning of Dame Street complemented Parliament Street. This latter was built along the line of an old route that led to the monastery of All Hallows, later the site of Trinity College. Rocque's survey of 1756 shows it as an irregular and at times very narrow street and at this time it presented to the stroller a series of modest gabled façades (some remaining houses in this style can be seen on the title page of Pool and Cash (1780). (Figure 32.)

Throughout the 1770s, the inhabitants of the street complained to the Wide Streets Commission, asking for improvements:

> Dame Street which is the only Passage from his Majestys … Castle to the Parliament House is a most narrow and inconvenient Street, and, as it is a Street of the greatest Trade and the greatest Thoroughfare in the said City, is become by means of the vast Number of different Carriages and the great Crowds continually passing thro' it, not only very inconvenient and injurious to the Trade and Intercourse, but also extremely dangerous to the Limbs and Lives of the several Inhabitants of Dublin, especially during the Sitting of Parliament.
>
> (16 June 1772, WSC/Mins/2, p. 93)

By 1778 the commission was ready to take action. The street was to be expanded 'to open a convenient Street, from his Majesty's Castle of Dublin to the Parliament'. In 1772 a plan had been developed to open a new direct approach to the Castle from the east, cutting through Castle Market (which was to be moved) and running parallel to the existing line of Dame Street. The new street was to have a semi-circular public space east of the castle, echoing European baroque designs, but this plan was never put into effect. Instead the widening of Dame Street to a planned width of 80 feet (*c.*24 metres) (12 February 1782, WSC/Mins/4, p. 47) was commenced in 1778 and the south side of the street was largely completed by 1784, although the street was by then but 65 feet (20 metres) wide and the widening and rebuilding of the north side proceeded somewhat desultorily for over a decade longer.

A drawing of 1785 shows an elevation of new buildings on the south side of Dame Street (WSC/Maps/342). The block is 38 bays wide, the four bays at each end and the central six bays projecting slightly into the street, giving the plain façade emphasis and rhythm. These projecting blocks are further emphasized by corner quoins and the whole four-storey block is linked by a continuous cornice above the upper storey. The house designs for the north side of Dame Street were provided by the architect Samuel Sproule (WSC/Maps/115). The five-storey houses had shops with a unified design of arched entrances and windows on the ground floor, almost identical to those on the south side, and the whole block was given some coherence with the first and second floor end windows framed by a high shallow relieving arch. The end buildings of the block were further distinguished by being only one bay wide with tripartite windows on the first floor.

In widening Dame Street the commission was responsible for a dramatic change in the appearance of one of Dublin's main commercial streets, the representative importance of which was very great, as it linked the medieval core and Dublin Castle with the Houses of Parliament and Trinity College. Before the commission's intervention, Dame Street was an unassuming and rather haphazard routeway. There was no unified street front, some houses abutted many feet beyond their neighbours, and houses were of varying heights and appearance, many with gabled façades. By the late-eighteenth century this image had changed completely. Gone were the irregular gabled houses, replaced with long palatial façades of a level of uniformity never seen in Dublin before the Wide Streets Commission was established. The new Dame Street offered vistas from Trinity and the Houses of Parliament, past regular and harmoniously planned shops and residences to the imposing bulk of the Royal Exchange, and on to the entrance to Dublin Castle.

Cromwell (1820) wrote that the street 'from its width and the splendour of its shops, (inferior only to the best in London) has an air of considerable importance' (p. 66). There was, however, some criticism of the commission's failure sufficiently to widen the western end of the street, where some felt that the vista from Trinity College could have been expanded to include a full view of the Royal Exchange (Warburton, Whitelaw and Walsh, 1818, 2, p. 1079).

From Sackville Mall to College Green

The 1780s saw the birth of several important projects, which, when completed, would give further coherence and grandeur to Dublin's central streets. In 1782 a plan was submitted to and approved by Parliament (Wide Streets Commission, 1802, p. 5). This would continue the line of the widened Dame Street and College Green, cutting through the blocks of houses along Fleet Street to provide a link with a new bridge across the Liffey and joining up with a new continuation of Sackville Mall beyond Drogheda Street to the river. This was the genesis of Westmoreland and D'Olier Streets and Carlisle Bridge. Two years later a plan to widen and straighten Lower Abbey Street and to build a new quay front 'absolutely necessary for the Accommodation of the Trade of this Port, in consequence of the building of Carlisle Bridge' from Bachelor's Walk to Gandon's Custom House, then under construction, was also approved. In 1786 the commission was empowered to improve Rutland Square, widening the south end of Cavendish Row, and to improve the road westwards from the city to the Phoenix Park. Their scope continued to increase when in 1790 the commission was authorized to improve the northern approaches to the city and, among other acts, open the street that became North Frederick Street. These 'useful and desirable Improvements' were not all immediately executed, partly for lack of finance; the perennial problem in planning for Dublin. The commission's plan to complete the great complex of representative axes, which they had started by opening Parliament Street and widening Dame Street, by opening new streets to the river and linking them to an extended Sackville Mall, was not in fact completed until shortly after the Act of Union in 1801.

In their published report of 1802, the commissioners outline the reasons why they chose to develop Westmoreland Street and D'Olier Street as they did. Firstly, the plan as executed provided a good 'perspective view' of the portico of the House of Lords and Trinity College, a vista that they felt

33 Proposed elevation for Dame Street. (Wide Streets Commissioners, 1791.)
Reprinted by kind permission of Dublin City Archive.

of College Green and *DAME STREET*

necessary to the aesthetic quality of Westmoreland Street, giving it a sense of
direction and artistic purpose. Secondly, they felt the direct communication
to the Parliament and Grafton Street afforded by the new streets to be important.
They also thought that the width of the streets would be more suitable to
shopping than another version that suggested greater width; an interesting
early insight into the relationship between the physical form of streets and their
function. Finally they favoured the greater regularity of form and appearance in
the approved plan. Their concern with regularity and uniformity of physical
form has already been noted. The pragmatism expressed in their views on the
relationship of the preferred forms to functions very real and important,
however mundane, is an interesting feature of their approach to planning.
Monumental planning need not be blind to less 'elevated' aspects of city life.

Sherrard's 1792 designs for Westmoreland Street did not lead to any immediate
building on the site, and by 1799 the commissioners were discussing the notion
of a new type of continental-inspired design for the buildings on this street,
incorporating colonnades into the ground-floor shop façades. Henry A.
Baker's designs for such buildings (WSC/Maps/195/1A) were, however, not
executed. Several sets of designs seem to have been submitted, until in 1800
very much plainer elevations than any previously suggested were accepted
(WSC/Maps/195/2). These designs, which partially survive in a somewhat
clumsy restoration of the *Irish Times* offices on D'Olier Street, were quite
austere but nonetheless elegant, the arched shopfronts of Dame Street and
Lower Sackville Street replaced by almost unadorned straight lines. This
austerity is counterbalanced by fine working of granite shopfronts, lintels and
moulding over the windows and in the smooth sweep of the façade of the west
side of D'Olier Street round onto Fleet Street.

The linking of Dame Street to Sackville Mall is a project that Bush
indicates was proposed to Gardiner when first building the Mall:

> Sackville-street, about 70 feet wide or nearly, with a mall enclosed with
> a low wall, which, but for the execrable stupidity of the builder, would
> have been one of the most noble streets in the three kingdoms, had it
> been carried, as it might have been, and was proposed to him at the
> time of laying it out, directly up to the front of the lying-in hospital,
> the most elegant and the best finished piece of architecture in Dublin,
> and I believe in Ireland: and if besides this, the projected addition of
> a street from the bottom of it, on the same plan, directly on to the
> Liffy, to which the present street directs, and terminated, as was

34 Proposed Elevation for the west side of Westmoreland Street.
(Wide Streets Commissioners, 1800.) Reprinted by
kind permission of Dublin City Archive.

intended, on the opposite side of the river by a view of some public
building that was there to have been erected in front of the street, it
would have been one of the grandest and most beautiful streets perhaps
in Europe. But as the first absurdity of carrying up the present street
just by the end of the hospital has taken place, this projected
improvement will hardly ever be carried into execution, and the
obstinate fool of a builder will deservedly be damned by every stranger,
of common sense and taste, that shall ever walk up Sackville-street.

(Bush, 1765, pp 10–11)

This 'execrable stupidity' was remedied by the plans of the commission.
There is some indication that Mosse had planned to build the hospital facing
directly onto Sackville Mall, but that Gardiner refused to exchange some
ground that would have been necessary for this purpose (Warburton,
Whitelaw and Walsh, 1818, 2, p. 671). A suitably dignified architectural style
was ensured for the new part of Sackville Street by Act of Parliament. The
original designs submitted to the Wide Streets Commission were prepared by

35 View of the Irish Parliament House (*Dublin Penny Journal,* 1835) Double Supplement – *Views in Dublin.* From an original drawing made by Henry A. Baker in the year 1787, before the alterations took place.

Gandon in 1786, with ground-floor shops and palatial façades unifying the whole block of what were, in fact, separate houses. These designs were not executed, however, and were abandoned in favour of Thomas Sherrard's elevations of 1789 (McParland, 1972, pp 17–18). Sherrard's designs were similar to Sproule's for Dame Street, as indeed had been Gandon's. The gracefully arched ground-floor shops were virtually identical to those on Dame Street. The single-bay end houses of the blocks were distinguished with elegant tripartite windows on the first floor – one still survives today on the corner of Lower O'Connell Street and Bachelor's Walk – plaster moulding over the second floor window and quoins decorating the outer corners. However, elegant though the new developments were, they changed the character of Sackville Mall. It was now a thoroughfare and it never recovered its former air of grandeur as a place of resort for those who wished to see and be seen.

The buildings on Lower Abbey Street were never very remarkable, but those on Beresford Place, designed in 1790 by Gandon, might have been. This was intended to be a crescent but only five houses were built, though they have a unified architectural style. Today, they sit rather uneasily in decayed grandeur between the loop line bridge and Busarus.

Thus by the end of the eighteenth century a person wishing to travel from Dublin Castle to Rutland Square could proceed through an urban landscape that in scale and architectural uniformity rivalled many a Continental city. The aspect of Dame Street had been entirely altered, by 1801 the new buildings on Westmoreland and D'Olier Streets were complete, and the new bridge (Carlisle Bridge) across the Liffey afforded a prospect eastwards of the Custom House, the emerging quays and a view north all the way along Sackville Street to a vista closed by the Rotunda. To the west, the dome of the Four Courts could be glimpsed upriver, so that the prospect from the bridge presented to the pedestrian 'such a cluster of architectural beauties grouped together, or scattered in every direction which he turns, as are not to be seen from any other spot in any other city ... Strangers who visit Dublin are particularly struck with the beauty of this assemblage of objects' (Warburton, Whitelaw and Walsh, 1818, 2, p. 1081).

The new axis was well received. Wilson considered the depth of the plots in Sackville Street and the street's proximity to the new Custom House a great advantage for trade, 'when the new custom-house is completed, this street will be then a most desirable situation for wholesale merchants' (Wilson, 1786, p. 24). The perspective of the street, terminated by the Rotunda, was praised by many, and one writer even goes so far as to declare the Dame Street–Sackville Street ensemble 'one of the finest avenues in Europe' (McGregor, 1821, p. 175). Dame Street, 'the greatest thoroughfare in Dublin for the carriages of the nobility' and 'filled with elegant shops', provided 'one of the most accustomed and amusing lounges in the city of Dublin', and apparently bore a strong resemblance to Bond Street in London, with 'numbers of elegant women continually passing and repassing, and the numerous parties of military officers from the barracks (foraging in the fruit shops)' (Jefferys, 1810, pp 54–5).

All of the new buildings erected under the auspices of the Wide Streets Commissioners had provided for shops at ground-floor level with residences on the upper floors; commercial functions of the city were thereby linked with the provision of living space and the servicing of some of the most affluent residential areas. Such strategies in planning ensured that Dublin's chief monumental axes became more than just representative façades of officialdom. The integration of varied facilities into the monumental streetscape ensured that the streets would have a life of their own not entirely dependent on activity centred on the Castle and the Parliament, though visually and socially strongly influenced by it. The Castle and the Parliament provided foci of State activity, balanced by the Gardens and the Rotunda in Rutland Square, and punctuated by regular activity in the shops in the Wide Streets Commissioners' buildings.

Other projects

The quays had been the focus of attention before the activities of the Wide Streets Commissioners. Details have been given above of various projects to produce pleasing and functional quaysides and the Corporation had encouraged the construction of broad highways since the 1680s. Therefore, as early as the 1730s, one writer, describing the view from Essex Bridge, had commented on the aesthetic contribution of the river to the cityscape, describing the 'noble view down the river, which is always full of vessels; and in winter evenings, when all the lamps are lighted, you have three long Vistos [sic], resembling fire works, both up and down the river, and before your face [along Capel Street], as you pass the bridge from the old town' (Anon., 1739, p. 24). So by the 1770s, the quays already presented quite a uniform appearance and were the city's 'principal beauty ... at the breadth of a wide street from the river on each side, the houses are built fronting each other, which has a grand effect' (Campbell, 1777, p. 7). Much of the quays (Bachelor's Walk, Ormond Quay(s), Inns Quay, Arran Quay and Ellis Quay) contained by this time quite handsome merchants' houses and it fell to the Wide Streets Commission to put only the finishing touches to Dublin's riverside streetscapes. This involved, amongst other things, the removal of projecting buildings along the quays to ensure that 'communication between His Majesty's Castle and the Vice-Regal Lodge in the Park, the Barracks, the Royal Hospital, and the access to the High Courts of Justice, would be rendered commodious and safe' (Wide Streets Commission, 1802, p. 35).

The commissioners were also active on smaller projects at this time. They opened up St James' Gate to facilitate the movement of traffic along one of Dublin's principal westerly axes and removed some houses that projected from Nassau Street into Grafton Street and from St Stephen's Green into Leeson Street, as well as 'many other obstructions of less import'. In addition they widened and improved part of Baggot Street (Wide Streets Commission, 1802, p. 16).

While all these improvements were being carried out, several Government-sponsored projects were providing foci for the commission's new streets. The new Four Courts and Custom House, both designed by Gandon, and

36 The Four Courts and the quays looking towards Phoenix Park (after Virtue).

extensions to the Parliament were being executed, giving Dublin its three most famous and architecturally significant buildings. These, together with the new Royal Exchange on Cork Hill, gave the commission's plans the necessary focal points for overall coherence, being 'superb Edifices' and reflecting 'honor on all concerned, and to the age in which they were raised' (Malton, 1799, p. 18).

Living in the capital city

Dublin in the eighteenth century

EDEL SHERIDAN

Introduction

The splendid carriages and the apparent wealth of the principal houses
render the more displeasing the sight of the beggars.

(La Tocnaye, 1796–7, p. 17)

By the late-eighteenth century Dublin had developed a very marked social
gradient from west to east. The haphazard physical character of the western
suburbs corresponded with their mixed social status, housing chiefly 'merchants
and mechanicks', while the more regular and ordered streetscapes of the suburbs
to the east were home to the 'gentry' (Pool and Cash, 1780, p. 14). The development processes which resulted in this marked spatial skew in the provision of
residential space have been discussed in the preceding chapter; this chapter
presents an analysis of contemporary material to give a more detailed picture
of the different 'lifeworlds' of the eighteenth-century capital, that is, areas of
residence and spheres of commercial, professional and leisure activity.

The social order of early modern cities and towns was a complex one. In
the larger towns there was a very wide variety of occupations and a fine gradation
of social class. The more rigid order of medieval society was breaking down and
adjusting under the pressure of commercial and economic as well as social and
philosophical or intellectual change. The social structure of capital cities was
further complicated by the co-existence of State and municipal hierarchies, as
well as of both hereditary and nouveau riche 'upper classes'.

On one level, citizens of the municipality could be designated by their legal
status, a carry-over from the strictly defined hierarchical order of medieval
towns. Dublin's Corporation mirrored civic social hierarchies, with an upper
level of mayor, recorder and aldermen, many of whom were titled, and a lower
level of freemen drawn from the ranks of masters of the guilds. Only freemen
could vote for members of the Corporation or become candidates, thus this

37 College Green looking towards Westmoreland Street. (From an engraving of 1816.)

status was an important access to political power in the civic arena. The granting of freeman status, as well as the use of disenfranchisement as a punishment, continued throughout the eighteenth century. Likewise the municipal guilds had an established order, with a distinct and clearly defined status accorded to master craftsmen, journeymen and apprentices or servants.

Existing beside, or intertwined with the municipal order, common to every incorporated town, was the hierarchy of residents directly or indirectly connected with Dublin's role as capital – civil servants or state employees in administrative jobs, and members of Parliament. The additional presence of courtiers and/or government officials also gave a special character to the economy of a capital city, giving it a class of people who were not wealth producers, but solely consumers, with particular demands. This class of people was important for the market for luxury textiles, quality household goods such as fine porcelain, silver and gold, jewellery etc. A large portion of tradesmen and guild crafts in the capital city owed their prosperity to the high demand created by the presence of State bureaucrats, and many merchants and traders profited from this state of affairs to work their way up the social scale. The city was a place where the traditional social order could be challenged and broken, social mobility was at its greatest here.

For the period under discussion, it is difficult to find a logically consistent method for defining social class – wealth alone is not a sufficient indicator, nor are birth or heredity. On the one hand the town embodied the forces of market, enterprise, freedom and cultural development; on the other hand it was dominated by oligarchic groups, restrictive guild structures and myriad rules and regulations. Thus the power wielded by any one social group in urban affairs is of great importance. Potential influence over state and municipal affairs is an indicator that may overcome the difficulties inherent in measuring social status by either hereditary status or more recently acquired wealth or prestige. In Dublin the municipal powers of the Corporation were overridden by those of the Wide Streets Commission where the development of new streets was concerned. Thus the power to control physical expression of Dublin's urban role as a state capital moved into the hands of government officials and representatives, individuals not necessarily traditionally occupying a prominent place in the municipal hierarchy of the Corporation.

Several contemporary sources give clear expression to the social hierarchy of eighteenth-century Dublin. Whitelaw, in his essay on the population of Dublin, published in 1805, and based on a survey of the city's population in 1798, divides the population into four groups. These are, the upper and middle classes (calculated together in all his tables), their servants, and the lower classes. He does not give an explicit account of the criteria he applied in thus subdividing the population, but the two surviving detailed house-by-house tables for The Poddle and York Street give some indication of his standards (Table 2).

Whitelaw seems to have used two main indicators of social status, type of occupation and employment of servants, as reflecting relative wealth. In Whitelaw's judgement, traders and artisans with no servants are relegated to the lower classes, while those tradespeople with some servants join the ranks of the upper and middle classes, whereby it may be assumed that they would have been classified as 'middle class' unless extremely rich or influential. The very poor, and unskilled workers also belonged to the lower classes – seven of the houses enumerated for The Poddle were let out in tenements and populated entirely by 'lower class' inhabitants.

Belonging to the upper and middle classes are persons of leisure (no occupation given) with servants, members of Parliament, councillors, the professions
(clergy, jurists and medical doctors) and prosperous merchants with servants.
Again, considerable material differences, as reflected in the numbers of
servants employed, can be observed between various representatives of this
very broad grouping.

Walsh, writing in the mid-nineteenth century about the late-eighteenth
century, gives an indication of the distinction between middle and upper class
in the eyes of Dubliners of the latter period, when 'any approach to the habits
of the industrious classes by an application to trade or business, even a
profession, was considered a degradation to a gentleman, and the upper orders
of society affected a most rigid exclusiveness' (Walsh, 1847, p. 10). This passage,
therefore, indicates that those inhabitants of York Street with no given occupation or who were members of Parliament would probably have been regarded
as belonging to the upper class by contemporaries, while the members of the
professions, merchants and better traders may have been designated 'middle
class'. Senior members of the professions, judges, bishops etc. had their place
in the upper classes. The boundary of the upper class with the upper middle
class must have been fluid as, for instance, some merchants became members
of Parliament or of influential public bodies (for example several members of
the Wide Streets Commission in the 1780s were also members of the
mercantile Chamber of Commerce (Lewis, 1787, pp 97–8)). At this boundary,
the acquisition of power in the wider public arena, beyond the confines of the
person's own business circle, was a decisive factor in signifying the individual's
arrival in society, and was presumably a passport to the 'right' social circles.

The hasty assumption of the lifestyles, manners and fashions of the
hereditary upper classes by newly wealthy members of the mercantile class was
condemned as folly by one visitor to Dublin in 1797; the very fact that a
visitor noticed such a process is a good indicator that it was fairly widespread
or at least obvious:

> ... the middle order too much (I fear) imitate their superiors, as to
> luxury of the table, cards, balls and routs [crowded house parties]; the
> wives and children of persons in business, shop keepers, &c. assume
> and affect all the airs of the beau monde; and when a man in business
> has accumulated a very few thousand pounds, he is induced by the
> influence of this baneful example, and the additional entreaties of his
> wife and children, to set up his carriage, take a more expensive house

in town, a country lodge and demesne, and become a private gentleman
retired from business, just at the time when wisdom would say, begin, and
with your present stock arrive at wealth.

(Loeber and Stouthamer-Loeber, 1994)

Table 2 Social class in Dublin 1798 as extracted from Whitelaw's
tables for The Poddle and York Street.

Street	Lower class	Upper and middle class	No. of servants per upper or middle class household
The Poddle	5 Publicans	1 Starch manufacturer	1
	2 Huxters	1 Distiller	3
	1 Toyshop keeper	1 No occupation	1
	1 Pawnbroker		
	1 Linendraper		
	1 Chandler		
	1 China-shop keeper		
	1 Tin-man		
	1 Grocer and dram-shop keeper		
	1 Old iron shop keeper		
	1 Baker		
	1 Haberdasher	14 Attorneys	4
York Street	1 Porter-house keeper	13 No occupations	2–3
	1 Hair-dresser	8 Counsellors	4
	1 Law-scrivener	4 Merchants	3–4
	1 Tailor	2 Nobility	8–9
	1 Publican	2 Doctors of law	6
		2 Surgeons	4
		2 Members of Parliament	3
		1 Master in Chancery	7
		1 Medical doctor	5
		1 Doctor of Divinity	4
		1 Brewer	6
		1 Haberdasher	1
		1 Grocer and dramshopkeeper	3

(Whitelaw, 1805)

Dublin had a significant Huguenot population in the eighteenth century. No author seems confident to estimate the number of Huguenots living in Dublin at any one time (Caldicott, Gough and Pittion, 1987) and by the time of Whitelaw's census they seem to have been well integrated into Dublin society, as he does not list them separately at all. The Huguenots were invited to Dublin, partly as a charitable move and partly to encourage Dublin manu- acturing. In 1681, Dublin Corporation had ordered a collection to be made in the city for persecuted French Protestants, and offered favourable conditions (particularly for 'artizans and handicraftsmen') for their admission to the franchise, allowing freeman status *gratis* and relief from city taxes for five years (Gilbert, 1895, 5, p. 229).

One group important in the eighteenth-century city, though of the 'lower class', provides an indicator of wealth in the city. Servants formed a large proportion of urban populations in the eighteenth century. London (22 per cent) and Hamburg (18–22 per cent) seem to have been exceptional, with one in five of their inhabitants working as servants in 1796, and Dublin's figure of 10 per cent seems to have been more the norm for a city of its type. The dis- tribution of servants throughout the city is a revealing measure of social topography.

Social control through urban form

An important aspect of neo-classical planning was the notion of social control through urban form. This found a particular application in a capital city, where control over the city carried the representational weight of control over the kingdom. 'Improvements' not only provided new vistas and a wider overview of the city but also facilitated surveillance or supervision of people on the streets. Upper-class and aspiring middle-class residents of cities were at least subconsciously aware of these implications, as evidenced by their pleas to planning authorities to alter or replan the physical environment in the interest of maintaining certain social standards.

Some illuminating examples of public perception of the role of urban design in this respect are afforded in the minutes of the Wide Streets Commission. For instance, in 1792 one Henry Attivell, holding some of the plots where new houses were being erected along Lower Sackville Street and trying to make money by attracting sub-tenants to his property, wrote to the Commission expressing his own and his tenants' concern at the inclusion of a narrow laneway in the original plans for the terrace:

The line from Sackville Street to the New Bridge being divided by a
Lane of six feet which is taken off the rere of my Ground appears to
me, and to those whom I have Let to as a very great Nuisance tending
to create dirt, and probably will be resorted to by Thieves, and Night
Walkers, that may very much anoy [sic] the Neighbourhood – the
Tenantry have therefore devised of me to represent it, that it may be
shut up for the Public accommodation.

(15 June 1792, WSC/Mins/11, p. 43)

Later that year, the tenants of the northern section of South Great George's
Street, around the corner from the already improved and widened Dame
Street, requested the intervention of the Commission to control activities on
the street perceived by the residents as anti-social and undesirable. These
tenants were occupying new houses built by the commissioners as part of the
Dame Street project (for which they paid rents of £80 to £100 per annum,
which they considered very high). Eight years previously, when the new
buildings were first occupied, the commissioners had promised that the George's
Street phase of the plans would be quickly implemented. The commission lacked
funds for what was considered a less important improvement than the
opening up of more representative and monumental axes such as those linking
the houses of Parliament with the fashionable residential areas in Gardiner's
estate on the north side of the Liffey, and the tenants of South Great George's
Street felt that this unfinished planning was contributing to social as well as
economic problems.

Two plots not yet built on were walled-in for the use of one of the 'city
scavengers' (rubbish collectors) and this led to a heartfelt protest. It was noted
that these plots were, 'a most intolerable and offensive nuisance not only
destructive to your Memorialists' property in depriving them of Lodgers, but
injurious to their health, the proprietors of those houses in particular, that are
contiguous, and opposite to those Lots, cannot get any respectable person to
live in them'. Behind the scavenger's yard, vagabonds and robbers were said to
congregate to play ball, pitch and toss, have boxing matches all of which were
accompanied by foul language, blasphemy and 'every immorality'. This was a
clear threat to the morals of their children and apprentices (WSC/Mins/11,
pp 134–6). This document clearly expresses the feeling that physical environment strongly affects the viability and profitability of an enterprise, in this case
various unspecified 'businesses' and the subletting of rooms to lodgers. Also,
physical form and design as well as the use to which space is put (here referring

to the 'nuisance' of the city scavenger's yard) plays a part in determining the type of social (or anti-social) activity that takes place within this space.

Lord Aldborough in 1794 attempted to use his influence with the Wide Streets Commission to direct the planning of Gloucester Street in such a way as to attract residents from the ranks of the gentry as opposed to the trade classes. He feared that the commission's plans to continue Gloucester Street at a width of 80 feet (c.24m) would encroach upon plots he had laid out to be 70 feet (c.21m) deep, which 'if narrowed to 50 feet [c.15m] by making the Street 20 feet [6m] [wider] will convert Lots intended for the Residence of Gentlemen into Shops which would be a disgrace instead of an ornament to the continuation of Gloucester Street' (WSC/Mins/12, pp 184–6). A similar consciousness of the need for control over physical space in order to control the activities of persons using that space is expressed in a memorial to the Wide Streets Commission from the residents of part of the Gardiner estate in 1798. The residents asked that gates be erected on several lanes and other routes so that control could be exercised over the use of these routeways at night. Compare this with the current proposals for gates on North Great George's Street.

Today's households might be surprised that concern about the dangers, social and otherwise, of areas of low visibility (such as narrow back lanes) in the city was being expressed in Dublin in the eighteenth century. Indeed such concerns had been voiced long before. It is, however, in the eighteenth century that this awareness finds concrete expression in the planning of the streetscape to discourage illicit or undesirable activities in public spaces. Municipal records of the seventeenth century show a concern to maintain a form of civic order by keeping the streets tidy and clean; in the eighteenth century this concern goes beyond 'cosmetic' maintenance to active planning for order, for representation of the power of the ruling class and to declare the city 'under control' (Mumford, 1966, p. 415).

Patterns of social topography

It is here necessary to remark, that the eastern side of the City, contiguous to the sea, is almost entirely laid out in elegant streets, for the residence of the gentry: and the western side, though more remote from the sea, and consequently not so conveniently situated for the purposes of commerce, is chiefly inhabited by merchants and mechanicks.

(Pool and Cash, 1780, p. 14)

To read Pool and Cash one would think there were no poor in the Dublin, they are scarcely referred to. But there were poor there, and in large numbers. The development of the city, however, served to remove the wealthy from close contact with the great mass of the poor, save when the latter came out to beg. Contemporary accounts as well as statistical evidence point to the rapid development and firm establishment of an east–west social gradient in eighteenth-century Dublin, the only exception to this pattern being the dockland parish of St Mark on the south side of the Liffey at the eastern edge of the town. The focusing of fashionable new urban developments on the eastern part of the city was very evident by mid-century – all of the streets named by Bush in *Hibernia curiosa* (1769) as fashionable or elegant are to the east of the old town. In the 1750s and 1760s this pattern was still emerging, and the early editions of Wilson's *Dublin Directory* still show a concentration of shops catering for an upper class clientele (perfumers, wig-makers, gold and silversmiths, jewellers) with premises in the walled medieval core.

By the last decades of the eighteenth century the east–west gradient was firmly established (Figure 38). Indeed, it persisted well into the nineteenth century, becoming if anything more marked. The south-eastern part of the city, containing St Stephen's Green, Merrion Square and Fitzwilliam Square, was dominated by the nobility, gentry and members of the 'liberal professions'; the north-eastern district, including Mountjoy and Rutland Squares, was 'principally inhabited by the mercantile and official classes'; the south-western area outside the medieval walled city was 'in a state of lamentable dilapidation, bordering on ruin' while the north-western section containing the royal barracks and Smithfield presented 'striking indications of poverty' (Lewis, 1837, p. 533).

In the light of Dublin's topography, and the obvious attractions of the Liffey estuary for the mercantile classes, the favouring of the eastern quarters by the upper and middle classes seems somewhat unusual. This was commented on by Campbell in the 1770s. Campbell visited Kilmainham hospital (for retired soldiers) to the west of the city, and was as much taken by the location as by the building, where, 'as the winds on this coast are mostly westerly, they are but little annoyed by smoke from the city, or fogs from the sea; the air is so pure, that one would have thought it might have invited the gentry to extend this way, instead of intercepting the merchants from the sea' (Campbell, 1777, p. 23). In a passage by the same author describing parts of the north-east of Dublin city, some factors emerge that may have influenced the upper classes to locate here:

Yesterday I went down the North Strand, catching the sea-breezes as I rode along. Summerhill, the suburb leading to it, affords one of the most charming prospects in the world. Before you is the sea, covered with ships; on the left of the bay, is a country beautifully varied and sufficiently dressed by art, to enrich the landskip; to the right, the conical mountains of Wicklow terminate your view. The river Liffy, and part of the city compose the foreground of this exquisite piece.

Summerhill, as well for the beauty of the situation, as purity of the air, is become the residence of several persons of fortune.

(Campbell, 1777, pp 32–3)

The varied and panoramic coastal views of the higher ground to the north-east could not be rivalled by the land-bound prospects available to the west of the city; the benefits of sea air were also obviously appreciated. Beautiful views alone can hardly have been the grounds for the development of fashionable streets eastwards. It is possible that the westerly location of unattractive public buildings such as the workhouse, hospitals, barracks and asylums, blocked off expansion to the west. The Phoenix Park, however, could have acted as an attraction for high status urban development – the positive perception of green spaces in Dublin is evidenced by the development of the squares, and their popularity among the middle and upper classes. The Park did not encroach so closely on the seventeenth-century extent of the town as to preclude the possibility of growth north-westwards on a grand scale. The Phoenix Park was praised as an excellent amenity by many but nevertheless no upper class eighteenth-century development is to be found bounding on this green area.

It seems more likely that the pull of existing buildings and functions may have influenced the eastwards drift of the upper classes from the early to mid-eighteenth century onwards. Firstly the Castle, representative of the vice-royalty and symbol of the State served by the ascendancy, was located to the east of the walled town. In 1592 Trinity College had been established on the site of All Hallows monastery, at the eastern end of what was then Damas Street (Dame Street). When the site of Lord Chichester's house on College Green became the location for the Irish Parliament in 1729, the advantages of the sector east of the city on the south bank were greatly enhanced.

The social contrast between the eastern and western ends of the city was not as absolute as many contemporary accounts might indicate. Whitelaw's census of 1798, summarized in his 1805 *Essay on the population of Dublin*, is the most accurate remaining account of Dublin's population in the late-eighteenth century (unfortunately the original census has not survived; it consisted of detailed returns for every street in the city along the lines of the extant sheets for The Poddle and York Street). Whitelaw concentrates in the essay on portraying the wretchedness of some of the poorest parts of the city, as it is his aim to awaken an awareness of the need for assistance for the inhabitants of these slums. However, a careful analysis of Whitelaw's data shows a more subtle pattern emerging than the more sensational contemporary accounts might lead one to suppose existed.

Whitelaw gives both numbers of people and numbers of inhabited houses for every street and lane in the city, but these data are difficult to interpret in the absence of corresponding data on house size. In the city as a whole, the average number of persons to a house was 11. On the fringes of the city, on the main routes, some remarkably low figures appear; these may be attributed to wealth and spacious housing, as observed by Lewis in the picturesquely named Paradise Row in 1787, which he described as being:

> A most agreeable and pleasant place, at the upper end of Dorset-street, that has a greater resemblance to a sweet country village, than an appurtenance of Dublin ... on account of its rural appearance, and the purity of its air, is the residence of many persons of easy fortunes, and wealthy citizens, whose houses and villas are here remarkably neat and elegant, and rendered more commodious by having good gardens belonging to them.
>
> (Lewis, 1787, p. 202)

On the other hand, such low levels of occupancy might also result from extreme poverty, very small house size and the wretchedness of dwellings on semi-rural city fringes. Twiss made a journey through Ireland and published his views in 1776. The book was regarded as scandalous, chiefly because of his unflattering comments on Irish women but he noted the peasant dwellings on the outskirts of Dublin which consisted 'chiefly of huts, which are termed cabbins. They are made of mud dried, and mostly without either chimney or window; and in these miserable dwellings far the greater part of the inhabitants of Ireland linger out a wretched existence. There is generally a small piece of ground attached to each cabbin, which produces a few potatoes ... Shoes and stockings are seldom worn by these beings, who seem to form a race distinct from that of the rest of mankind' (Twiss, 1776, pp 29–30).

Two detailed tables for The Poddle and York Street are printed in Whitelaw's census and have been referred to on page 140. These show the numbers and

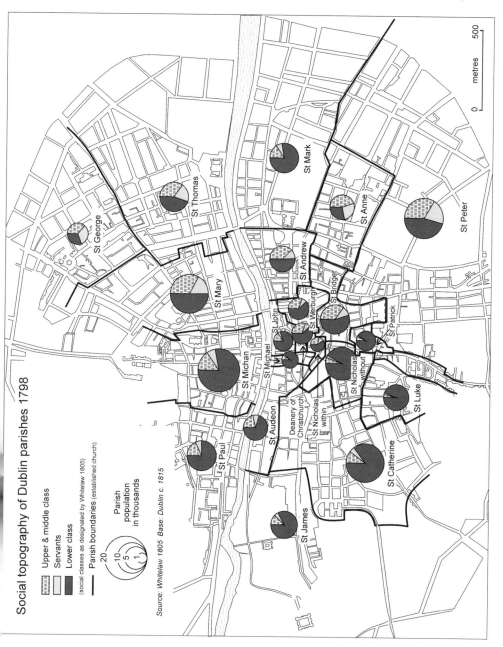

38 Social topography of Dublin parishes in 1798. (Compiled by Edel Sheridan.)

social class of persons in each individual house on these two streets; they give some idea of the type of socially differentiated house occupation prevalent in late-eighteenth-century Dublin. Seven of the twenty three houses enumerated for The Poddle were let out in tenements and populated entirely by 'lower class' inhabitants. These tenement houses had an average of 16 to 17 people dwelling in them; two of them were owned by publicans, one by a chandler, one by a huxter, and three 'back houses' in a yard were owned by a baker. These back houses had an average of seven people in each; the tenements fronting the street had on average 24 persons in each house. The remaining 12 houses occupied by lower-class residents had an average of six to seven inhabitants each. Thus considerable variation in the fortunes of Dublin's eighteenth-century lower classes can be deduced from even this small sample.

The middle-class councillors, merchants and attorneys in York Street lived with averages of eight to nine people to a house, those with no occupation given (presumably persons of private means, and therefore at least minor gentlemen) with six to seven people to a house. The higher numbers per house of the two doctors of law and the two members of the nobility (13 and 14, and 13 and 16 respectively) reflects these households' greater numbers of servants (see Table 2).

More useful on a city-wide scale are Whitelaw's data summarizing class distributions within the Dublin parishes (Table 3). As already pointed out, Whitelaw does not reveal his criteria for defining social class. Nevertheless, it can safely be assumed that Whitelaw's perception of social distinction was representative for his time and place. If these figures are mapped and compared with the data for persons per house, more light can be shed on Dublin's late-eighteenth-century social geography. The parishes containing and adjoining the important representative buildings of the capital, such as the Castle, Parliament and Custom House, have a higher than average percentage of upper- and middle-class inhabitants, with in some cases up to 44.6 per cent of their population (in St Anne's) falling into this category. Some historically fashionable quarters farther to the west, such as St Nicholas Within, St Audeon's, St Werburgh's and St Bridget's, managed to maintain upper- and middle-class populations of 20–34 per cent of the parish total. The remaining western parishes on both sides of the river have well below the city average of 21.7 per cent upper- and middle-class residents.

A further refinement of this measure can be obtained if the numbers of servants per hundred individuals belonging to the upper and middle classes are calculated; this makes possible an estimation of the relative wealth of this upper grouping in the different parishes. Thus it can be observed that all the parishes west of the castle on the south side with average or above average proportions of upper- and middle-class residents, have less than the city average of 49.1 servants per hundred upper- and middle-class residents. The southside parishes of St Catharine, St Peter and St Anne and the northside parishes of St Mary, St Thomas and St George are the only ones that exceed this average, and with the exception of St Catharine's, are all in the eastern quarters. The anomalous figure for St Catharine's may reflect the relative wealth of the small number of upper- and middle-class residents of this parish (only 9.1 per cent of the total). The very high figure of 93.2 servants per 100 upper- and middle-class residents in St George's parish on the north side of Dublin indicates a concentration of the wealthiest citizens in this parish, where 69.3 per cent of the population consisted of upper- and middle-class households and their servants in 1798 (compared to a city average of 32.5 per cent). St Anne's and St George's were the richest parishes in 1798.

The 1798 *Gentleman's and Citizen's Almanack*, also known as *Watson's Dublin Almanack*, is the first issue of this publication to list all peers of Ireland and members of the Irish Parliament with their names and country and city addresses, making it possible to map their Dublin residences. The pattern that emerges is consistent with the evidence of Whitelaw's census of the same year. The streets and areas north of the Liffey most dominated by peers and members of Parliament were Rutland Square, Upper Sackville Street, Gardiner's Row, Henrietta Street and Beresford Place; on the south side St Stephen's Green, Ely Place, Hume Street, Merrion Square, Merrion Street, Kildare Street, Dawson Street and the beginnings of Westland Row (with only a handful of houses) had high proportions of houses occupied by Parliamentarians (Figure 39). There is a concentration of members of Parliament in the areas also favoured for representative or monumental schemes by the Wide Streets Commission and private landlords, especially. In particular, areas close to the buildings and streets that give expression to the city's role as capital were preferred.

Another measure of riches was the possession of a private sedan chair; the licences for which were controlled by the Lying-in Hospital, and the fees paid went towards the support of the hospital. The distribution of the sedan chair licensees through Dublin in 1785 corresponds closely with the patterns of residence of members of Parliament and peers of Ireland just over ten years later (Figures 39, 40). Over two-thirds of the owners of sedan chair licenses were members of the titled nobility.

Table 3 Whitelaw's 1798 census of Dublin. Social class data in percentages.

Parishes	Upper/ middle	Servants	Servants per 100 upper/middle	Lower Class	Total
St James	11.6	4.8	42.0	83.5	6104
St Catharine	9.1	5.1	56.5	85.7	20176
St Luke	4.1	1.5	35.9	94.4	7241
St Nicholas Without	5.6	1.8	31.6	92.6	12306
St Nicholas Within	28.2	12.2	43.4	59.6	1121
St Audeon	21.2	8.8	41.7	70.0	5191
St Michael	8.9	2.3	25.9	88.8	2599
St John	15.7	4.0	25.3	80.4	4142
St Werburgh	32.0	9.7	30.3	58.4	3629
Deanery of Christ Church	15.0	3.0	20.0	82.0	233
Deanery of St Patrick	6.7	2.1	31.4	91.2	2081
St Bridget	34.1	9.7	28.4	56.2	8009
St Peter	33.0	20.3	61.6	46.7	16063
St Anne	44.6	27.7	62.1	27.5	7228
St Andrew	37.3	12.4	33.2	50.4	7682
St Mark	14.8	5.5	37.0	79.7	8692
St Paul	18.0	6.4	35.3	75.6	9904
St Michan	15.0	6.3	42.1	78.6	18092
St Mary	32.8	16.5	50.3	50.6	16654
St Thomas	34.3	20.3	59.1	45.4	8562
St George	35.9	33.4	93.2	30.7	5096
Total	**21.8**	**10.7**	**49.1**	**67.4**	**170794**

(Whitelaw, 1805)

Traders with a restricted and prosperous clientele, such as wigmakers, perfumers, jewellers and workers in fine metals, as well as print- and book-sellers were to be found in the shopping streets in close proximity to the fashionable Gardiner and Fitzwilliam estates, as well as in the central area within and close to the old city (Figure 41). Textile production had a very different distribution, with a weighting towards the Liberties in the south-west of the city and a sprinkling in Oxmantown and in a few smaller less significant streets in the eastern and central parts of the city (Figure 41).

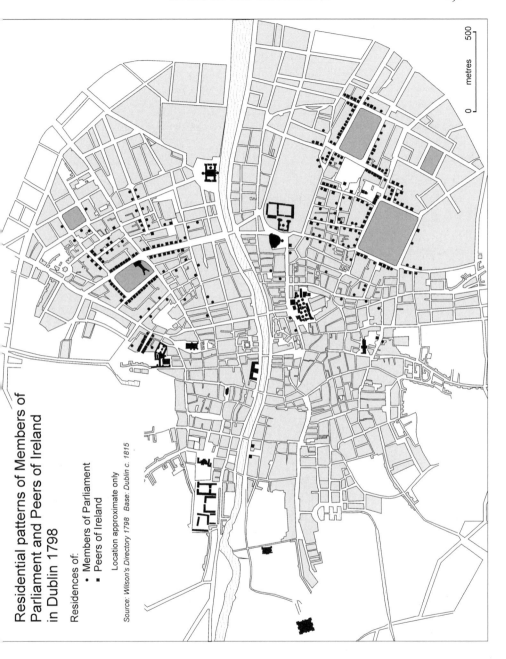

39 Residential patterns of members of Parliament and peers of Ireland in 1798. (Compiled by Edel Sheridan.)

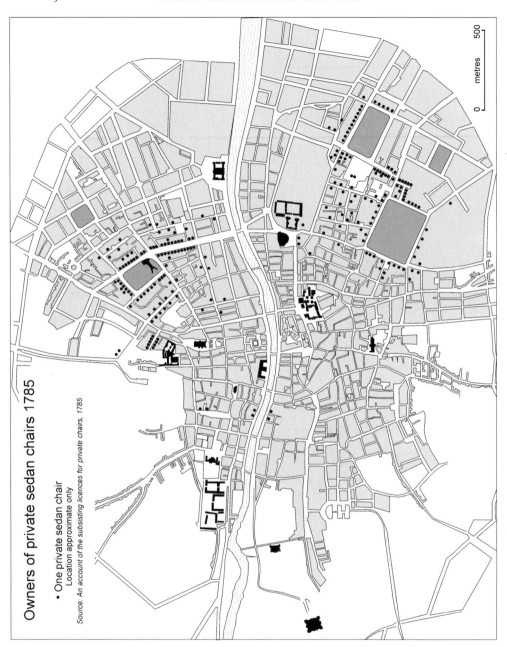

Owners of private sedan chairs 1785

• One private sedan chair
  Location approximate only
Source: An account of the subsisting licences for private chairs, 1785

0   metres   500

40 Location of owners of private sedan chairs in the Dublin of 1785.
(Compiled by Edel Sheridan.)

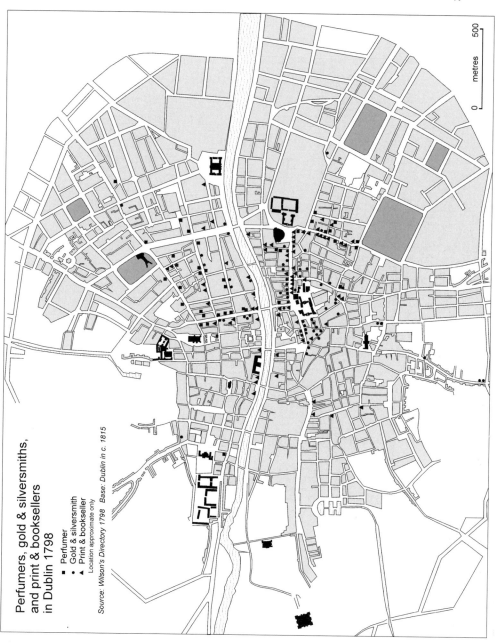

Perfumers, gold & silversmiths,
and print & booksellers
in Dublin 1798

■ Perfumer
● Gold & silversmith
▲ Print & bookseller
   Location approximate only

Source: Wilson's Directory 1798 Base: Dublin in c. 1815

0 metres 500

41 Locations of perfumers, goldsmiths and silversmiths, etc., Dublin, 1798.
(Compiled by Edel Sheridan.)

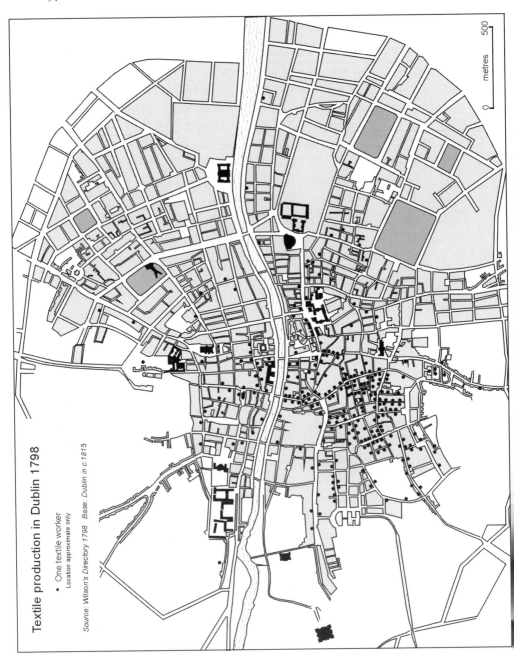

42 Textile production in Dublin, 1798.
(Compiled by Edel Sheridan.)

Whitelaw records a large majority of 'lower class' citizens in Dublin in 1798; it is reasonable to assume that many of these lived in poverty. Campbell comments on 'the painful sensations produced by the general mass' of the population and the numbers of 'wretched harridans who ply for hire … covered with tattered weeds' in the streets of Dublin (Campbell, 1777, pp 31 and 48–9). Contemporary artists rarely illustrated the houses of the less well-off quarters in eighteenth-century cities; much of the information available is of a verbal rather than a visual nature. An impression of the appearance of the poorer housing types can, however, often be gained from such descriptions and backed up by nineteenth-century drawings and photographs of surviving eighteenth-century building stock. The evidence available points to the existence of two basic types of lower-class housing in the eighteenth century – large buildings in multiple occupancy, which had rarely been designed to house the poorer citizens but had declined to this use; and shacks or cabins erected by the poor themselves in back lanes, courtyards and on the urban periphery. The worst houses in multiple occupancy were concentrated in the south-west and north-west of the city, a pattern identified in Whitelaw's census of 1798, and still prevailing in the mid-nineteenth century – 'the neglected portion of the city denominated the Liberty, suffers a daily diminution in the remnants of respectability yet preserved by it' (Cromwell, 1820, p. 49). The poverty of the Liberties in particular horrified visitors to the city, as well as a few conscientious residents. 'In the Liberties were to be found 'many large houses, consisting of a number of rooms; each of these rooms is let to separate tenants, who again re-let them to as many individuals as they can contain, each person paying for that portion of the floor which his extended body can occupy' (Warburton, Whitelaw and Walsh, 1818, 1, p. 7).

Whitelaw evokes in often harrowing detail the misery of the occupants of such dwellings. High rents and the lack of smaller dwellings were the driving factors behind the evolution of such living conditions, where two, three and even four families became joint tenants of a single room in order to be able to meet the weekly rent of one or two shillings for 'truly wretched habitations' (Whitelaw, 1805, p. 50). Up to 30 persons dwelt in some of these houses (Whitelaw, 1805, pp 50–1). The dirt and disorder of these quarters contrasts most harshly with the bright and harmoniously tidy streetscapes portrayed in Malton's engravings for example. Whitelaw records:

> … a degree of filth and stench inconceivable, except by such as have visited those scenes of wretchedness. Into the back-yard of each house,

frequently not ten feet deep, is flung, from the windows of each apartment, the ordure and filth of its numerous inhabitants; from whence it
is so seldom removed, that I have seen it on a level with the windows
of the first floor; and the moisture that, after heavy rains, ouzes from
this heap, having frequently no sewer to carry it off, runs into the
street, by the entry leading to the staircase.

(Whitelaw, 1805, pp 52–3)

Many houses are described by Whitelaw as 'ruinous', and often proximity
to the dirtier industries exacerbated poor conditions. His descriptions indicate
that the state of dilapidation of the Liberties and the north-western parts of
the city as recorded by the lenses of nineteenth-century photographers was not
necessarily of recent origin. Also, a few of Malton's prints contain details that
support the use of such photographs as representative of the poorer class of
large house in eighteenth-century Dublin. Typically, the houses of the poorer
quarters maintained old-fashioned gable fronts for longer than was the case in
the eastern areas. One of Malton's prints (no. 7) shows the west face of the St
Patrick's cathedral, facing onto Patrick Street, a street described by Campbell
as 'so noisome, that it is necessary to stop one's nose in passing through it'
(Campbell, 1777, p. 50). North of the cathedral, Malton portrays a row of
three-storey gabled houses with timber shops projecting into the street (Figure
43). Such gables disappeared very rapidly from the mid-eighteenth century
onwards in those parts of the city that received more attention from the State.

It is interesting to note the very different artistic treatment these poor
buildings receive compared to the better dwellings of Rutland Square or Capel
Street, for example. The dwellings of the poorer classes portrayed by Malton
appear dark, drab and shabby, although they are made of the same red brick
as the better houses. The latter, however, are treated with a lightness of touch
that picks up even the sunlight on the outlines of individual bricks, whereas
the former are blurred and lack individual identity, a treatment perhaps
symbolic of the social anonymity of the poor in the city, and of their
unimportance in the eyes of the planners and portraitists of the city.

The eighteenth-century heritage

The monumental street complexes planned in Dublin up to 1800 combined
many of the main functions of the capital city – the representation of the State
through government and official buildings; trade and commerce; the

43 Patrick Street housing. (Extract from Malton, 1799, plate 7.)

provision of genteel living quarters for the privileged elites who governed both city and State; and a promenade for the public display of finery that was indispensable to a large eighteenth-century city. These roles continue to some extent to be fulfilled by these axes.

Dublin at the period under discussion had a Parliamentary government, subject to a monarch represented but not resident in the city. Dublin was a colonial capital, with a population ethnically different (a higher Protestant proportion, and English-speaking) from the majority population of the smaller towns and the rest of the country. Large private estates were a feature of the city. This system of landholding had been developed by the English as a means of controlling the country in the initial stages of colonization, and later the landlords were responsible for the development of large parts of the countryside as well as important areas within the capital.

Eighteenth-century Dublin was designed as a monument to the State it represented. The representatives of State power sought to leave an imprint that would call them to mind in future generations. The Wide Streets Commission was ultimately answerable to the Irish Parliament, the privy council and the king, and was composed largely of members of Parliament during the eighteenth century. The private landlords enjoyed considerable freedom, and controlled very large holdings, but by the 1790s they too became answerable to the Wide Streets Commission. The efforts of the municipality to perpetuate itself in urban design were overshadowed by greater State-directed projects by the mid-eighteenth century.

The power relations and the representative symbolism of the streetscapes of eighteenth-century Dublin were reflected in patterns of social topography. During this period, Dublin developed a clearly observable spatial gradient of social topography. Wealth and power were concentrated in the eastern quarters of Dublin, closely associated with the location of symbols of power and government.

Dublin in the nineteenth century

An introduction

People often speak of Dublin as being an eighteenth-century city. In so doing they are saying that the city centre derives its character from the elegance of the buildings and urban spaces created during that century which have been discussed and analyzed in the previous chapter. But such areas comprise only a tiny part of the present-day city. In spatial terms the city at the beginning of the nineteenth century scarcely reached as far as the canals, today's inner city. In terms of the totality of the city, Dublin is a creation of the twentieth century when the great suburban expansion occurred and it can be surprising to learn that less than 13 per cent of Dublin's housing pre-dates the 1920s while over half has been built since 1960. Nonetheless, the processes that would control this twentieth-century expansion and give it its character were shaped in the nineteenth century. In the next three chapters we will look at the city from a number of viewpoints but it will first be useful to place the city in a wider political context.

The Act of Union (1801) had a major impact on the city. It lost its status as a capital and this blow was more than psychological. Edel Sheridan has shown in the previous chapter how the ruling classes supported a great variety of luxury trades. These people left the city, preferring or needing to live near London, the only centre of power. This hit at the city's economy which suffered the additional disadvantage of never being able to develop heavy labour intensive industry of the type that made cities such as Manchester, Birmingham or Liverpool wealthy.

It is probably fair to say that if the city has an image from the nineteenth century, it is one of poverty and neglect. Certainly the contrast between that century and the previous one is often remarked upon and as with generalizations there is much truth in it. The nineteenth century offered many challenges to the city in terms of how to meet what we would now see as social obligations and, even by the most generous analysis, the city cannot be said to have responded adequately. The housing of the poor was inadequate and dangerous and remained so into the twentieth century. Mr and Mrs Hall, those tireless early-Victorian travellers, provide a pen-picture of the Liberties that captures the filtering-down process of once great houses in this and other parts of the city.

> The present state of this once flourishing region forms a strong contrast to its former; but it still retains many evidences of what it has been. In passing along its desolate streets, large homes of costly structure everywhere present themselves. Lofty facades adorned with architraves and mouldings to windows, and door cases of stone or marble, grand staircases with carved and gilded balustrades; panelled doors opening into spacious suits of corniced and stuccoed apartments – all attest the opulence of the former inhabitants. They are now the abode of the more miserable. As they were deserted by the rich, they were filled by the poor; and as they decayed, they became the resort of the more abject who could find no other shelter.
>
> (Hall, 1841–3, 4, p. 80)

In the following chapter Jacinta Prunty explains the genesis of the problems that beset the city and analyses how these problems were addressed. However, though it is possible to note a growing engagement with the social problems of the city by the century's end, the judgment of the Commission on the Housing of the Working Classes in Ireland (Housing Inquiry, 1885) is difficult to escape. They noted that 'notwithstanding the energetic action of the Corporation and private persons and of societies, the condition of things in Dublin is very far from satisfactory. It is said that the great improvement that has taken place in some quarters is counterbalanced by the deterioration found in other districts' (Housing Inquiry, 1885, p. 6). This was in contrast to Belfast where the condition of the working classes seemed 'to be on the whole satisfactory' (p. 7).

But there was more to the city than poverty and gloom. The city functioned as a large regional capital. There were industries and commerce, an important banking and insurance sector and there were elegant streets for shopping and enjoyment. Part of the reason that this aspect of the city is less well known lies in the governance of the metropolitan area. The middle classes had moved to independent townships just beyond the borders of the 'city'. The city, as controlled by Dublin Corporation, was left with an unbalanced social and rateable structure. It had the great mass of the poor who could contribute little to the coffers of the city but relatively few of those with money. These lived beyond the reach of Dublin Corporation. But so close were they to the city, that they used the centre for the normal activities of life. They did business in the central area, frequented the shops, attended the theatre and participated in the host of other activities that were provided in a large metropolis. Moreover the quality of the urban environment had improved during the nineteenth century. The water supply had been developed; there were infrastructural improvements to road and rail communications. There had been important civic building, though not on the scale of the previous century. The city had hosted international exhibitions and royal visits. The poor were, of course, largely excluded from this city and these improvements. So we can speak of two urban environments; that occupied by the poor and that used by the better off. These environments overlapped spatially to a large degree but were used in quite different ways with very limited interactions between them. The final two chapters by Joseph Brady look at the city as used by the better-off. They describe the city of business and commerce as it developed during the nineteenth century and present it as it might have been seen by a citizen of the early years of the twentieth century. An important aspect of this examination is an attempt to reconstruct the character of the main commercial and shopping streets.

The governance of the city also underwent radical transformation in the nineteenth century. Some of it was borne of a need to streamline the administration of the city but other changes came about as a reflection of the changing political climate of Ireland. We will not discuss the politics of Ireland here but the reader is directed to a number of texts in the bibliography. Rather we will limit our discussion to the changes that directly affected the city since these give a useful gloss on the changing geography of the city.

Jacinta Prunty notes the fragmented administration of the city in the early decades of the nineteenth century. There were myriad boards and commissions responsible for the various aspects of the life of the city, including the Wide Streets Commission, the Grand Jury (assessing rates) and the Commissioners for Paving, Cleansing and Lighting to name but three. Prunty argues that such fragmentation did little to assist the city in addressing its problems. The Act for the Improvement of the City of Dublin in 1849 was an important landmark in streamlining the process of government within the city. The Act is interesting reading since it lists the legislation by which the Wide Streets Commissioners operated in their hundred-year tenure.

And whereas it is expedient that the said recited Acts, in so far as they
relate to the paving, lighting, cleansing, widening and improving of the
Streets and Thoroughfares within the Borough of Dublin and to
Turnpike Roads therein, should be repealed, and that other and
enlarged Powers and Provisions should be made and granted for these
purposes, and for the sanitary Improvement of the said Borough, and
also that the public Markets within the said Borough should be better
regulated, and that new Markets should be established therein: And
whereas it is expedient that the Fiscal Powers of the Grand Jury of the
County of the City of Dublin and the Sessions Grand Jury of the City
of Dublin so far as they relate to Matters required to be done within
the Borough of Dublin should be transferred to the Right Honourable
the Lord Mayor, Aldermen and the Burgesses of Dublin.

(Dublin Improvement Act, 1849, Clause I)

Dublin Corporation thereby consolidated planning control over the city of
Dublin and the right to regulate the finances of the city. It could raise rates
and could, subject to the Act, 'cause to be paved, drained, lighted, cleansed,
watered and other improved the Borough of Dublin and do all necessary Acts
for promoting the Health and Convenience of the said Borough' (Clause LXIII).
The Act was not a panacea for the problems of the city. It is a matter of regret
that it did not extend the remit of the Corporation to include the townships
or that the port was continued as a separate entity. As time went on, there
were occasions when the relationship with the Port and Docks Board was fraught
and even today it seems strange that such much of the city remains outside the
direct control of the elected representatives of the citizens. Nonetheless over the
next decades the Corporation acquired more powers to plan the city, largely
following similar moves in Britain, for example the Public Health (Ireland)
Act of 1878 followed the Public Health (England) Act of 1875. However, using
these powers to solve the city's problems was quite another matter.

The composition of Dublin Corporation changed as the century progressed.
At the beginning of the century, the Corporation was a largely self-perpetuating
oligarchy which was mainly Protestant. By the end of the century, it was an
elected body, though on a limited franchise, and power had shifted into the
hands of the middle classes, perhaps even the lower middle classes. Daly (1984)
provides a good analysis of this power shift and the consequences it had for
city governance. As Edel Sheridan has described, Dublin in the eighteenth
century was governed by a Common Council which was elected by the

freemen. The freemen were either hereditary members of the guild or elected to that state by the Council – hence the self-perpetuating character. From the Council came the sheriffs and from the sheriffs came the aldermen, one of whom was lord mayor. Catholics were largely absent from the Council and increasingly the Council became less and less representative of the population of the city, but more significantly, of its business and commercial leaders. Reform was inevitable in Dublin and elsewhere and it came in the Municipal Corporations (Ireland) Act of 1840. This introduced a kind of limited democracy to the city. Electors would now be people of property but the property qualification was quite strict and the mass of the population was still excluded from a voice in the control of their city. Towards the end of the century, the electors comprised less than three per cent of the population. Even the parliamentary electorate was only 33,696 in 1892 out of a population of 245,000. Notwithstanding the democratic deficit, the effect on the Corporation was dramatic. The Protestant business elite dwindled as members came to be replaced by a Catholic middle or lower middle class business cadre. It was from the ranks of publicans and grocers that the representatives came, especially from the poorer electoral wards. This was hardly surprising given the structure of the population and the social cleavages that existed; described in detail in previous and following chapters. The wealthy business people and professionals lived outside the city boundaries and though they may have met the property qualifications to be electors within the city, it is easy to see why they might not have sought election from an electorate from which they were increasingly alienated. The extension of the franchise after 1898 to that of the parliamentary elections, but including women of property, set the seal on the nature of the Corporation. Daly (1984, p. 207) noted that 'the professional representation after 1900 [was] virtually confined to the suburban wards of Drumcondra and Clontarf [these having been absorbed into the city after 1900], indicating that the professional class, both Catholic and Protestant, had largely left the central city area'.

While it is interesting to note this social transformation, it is more difficult to assess its impact on the planning of the city. Can it be argued that the new aldermen and councillors, being closer to the great mass of the people, had a more finely tuned social conscience and that therefore the beginnings of social planning evident in Dublin by the latter years of the nineteenth century reflects this? The Housing Inquiry of 1913, published in 1914, has some hard words for at least some of the then members of the Corporation. It noted that 14 members of the Corporation were tenement landlords and it drew particular attention to the property owned by Alderman G. O'Reilly, Alderman Corrigan and Councillor Crozier, whom they described as the principal owners of tenements sitting as members of the Corporation. Of these three the report says – 'We regret to have to report that some of the property owned by the three named gentlemen, and from which they are deriving rents, is classed as third class property by the Sanitary staff, or in other words that it is unfit for human habitation' (p. 13). Moreover they noted that the Corporation had not used effectively the powers at their disposal to improve the quality of housing and they further stated that 'the want of a firm administration has created a number of owners with but little sense of their responsibilities of landlords, and that it has helped much in the demoralization of a number of the working classes and increased the number of inefficient workers in the city' (p. 14). It would suggest that a social conscience was not one of the stronger aspects of the ethos of the Corporation.

The Council became polarized along religious and political lines. This happened almost immediately when Daniel O'Connell became lord mayor and used his position to restart his campaign for the repeal of the Union. There was continuous tension during the remainder of the century between the Catholic majority and the Protestant, and Conservative, minority. Dublin Corporation became the focus of many acrimonious political debates. This had consequences for the planning of the city. Dublin Corporation became estranged from the British administration in Ireland and this proved a serious barrier in its attempts to incorporate the townships within its boundaries. Less militant nationalism might have garnered greater support for such measures among those who had the power to pass the necessary legislation and might have diluted the opposition within the primary targets of such incorporation; the Rathmines and Pembroke townships.

Nationalism found spatial expression in the attempts to rename Sackville Street to O'Connell Street. In 1884, a committee of Dublin Corporation reported on the naming of the city streets. One of their key recommendations was that Sackville Street should be re-named O'Connell Street. The O'Connell Monument was already in place, and the lord mayor had been at its dedication. This was but a step further. However the proposal occasioned a legal challenge that is detailed in Osborough (1996) and makes for fascinating reading as it reveals the relationship between the Corporation and the British establishment. Some traders and householders with property in Sackville Street objected to the change and when the Corporation, having heard their objections, decided to press ahead they went to court. The vice-chancellor of the day, Chatterton, granted an injunction preventing the Corporation from proceeding with the change. He obviously felt that the Corporation was merely following a fad and that they needed to be restrained from such capricious notions. He noted that 'in matters of sentiment there is no certainty or even reasonable probability, of continuance; and that these notions which may be prevalent may – and probably will – in a few years be changed or exploded, and so on from time to time' (quoted, Osborough, 1996, p. 49).

The Corporation were so enraged by such a rebuff to the elected representatives of the city that they considered, for a while, renaming part of Temple Street to Chatterton Street. Such would have been a gross insult given the street's location on the edge of the Monto; the city's notorious red-light district. Chatterton had failed to capture the spirit of the city because the street gradually acquired its new name in popular usage although it was not until 1924 that the change was given legal sanction. The removal of Nelson's Pillar was another failed campaign of the period and this is given attention in chapter 5.

So, without doubt, the political climate was interesting in Dublin during the nineteenth century. It may be that the political environment did little to advance the planning of the capital and may have hindered it. The twentieth century certainly inherited a city with well-defined social and political boundaries and a raft of issues that needed to be sorted out.

Improving the urban environment

Public health and housing in nineteenth-century Dublin

JACINTA PRUNTY

Introduction

It may be fairly said that the Act of Union struck at the heart of Dublin city. During the previous century, while home to an Irish parliament and resident aristocracy, the city had developed according to the best tenets of European design. The grandeur of its squares and malls, its classical public buildings, and widened carriageways had placed it among the finest cities in Europe. It was after all a capital city, and enjoyed the trappings of that status – demand for gracious town residences, luxury textiles and foodstuffs, elegant carriages and evening entertainments, among many other requirements. The transfer of power to Westminster in 1801 reduced Dublin to the status of a regional capital. Many of the leading citizens whose money and political influence had funded the elegant remodelling and extension of the city moved themselves and their entourages to London. The pace and spirit of nineteenth-century urban change was destined to be very different to the grandeur of the preceding century.

The sharp decline in the number of resident nobility, and the economic downturn in trade and building, undermined both city status and income. A further blow was the phenomenon of suburban growth. Suburbs became a feature of most European cities during the first decades of the nineteenth century and were well established by mid-century. The scale and nature of industrialization provided one major impetus towards their creation – wealthy factory owners and other well-to-do persons chose to settle their families away from the noise and dirt of industry, moving to what were presented as idyllic environments on the city fringe. This outward movement was made possible by the willingness of landowners to engage in speculative development of land for housing, and by advances in transport technology, both train and tram, that allowed suburban residents to access the commercial areas of the city as they chose. British cities provide many examples of this phenomenon and the

44 Perspective view of the city of Dublin from Phoenix Park. This view appeared in numerous geography texts during the late-eighteenth and early-nineteenth century. This example is from *Bankes' new and complete system of geography*, *c*.1788. It shows a rather idyllic image of the city.

striking contrasts between city and suburb can be found in Frederick Engels' account of Manchester in 1842.

Suburbanization soon became fashionable in its own right, and not just in industrial cities. The increase in social stratification and class self-consciousness which characterized nineteenth-century urban society produced geographical segregation. Single-class residential areas developed, with each social group anxious to place an indisputable distance between themselves and those beneath them, further enforcing class distinctions. In Dublin the flight to the suburbs was an important factor in the creation of a more socially segregated city. South of the Grand Canal, extensive suburbs developed in Ballsbridge,

Donnybrook, Rathmines and Rathgar. Although only five metres of canal water divided them from the city proper, they were beyond the jurisdiction of Dublin Corporation (Figure 45). This municipal independence, jealously guarded, had grave financial as well as territorial implications. Major city projects such as the provision of mains drainage, as well as the more mundane day-to-day expenses of civic administration, could only be funded by rates on property. But where large numbers of better-off persons settled beyond the municipal boundary the Corporation's financial basis was greatly undermined. As with the flight of the nobility to London, suburbanization deprived the city of the interest and political influence of wealthy residents who might be expected to give a lead in the administration and beautification of the city, as well as their financial backing through rates. Dublin Corporation was left with an impoverished financial basis, just as the scale (and cost) of what was demanded of any city administration was increasing phenomenally. It is not surprising that so much of the nineteenth-century story is dominated by questions of the poor – their health, housing, relief and control.

From the first years of the nineteenth century, with the surveys by Whitelaw and the Cork Street Fever Hospital, through a succession of private and public inquiries into the causes of epidemic disease, the state of the Dublin poor and their wretched homes, through to the Civic Survey of 1925, an ever more depressing picture is drawn of the living conditions endured by the majority of the citizens. Visitors' accounts, diaries and private corre-spondence all add to the catalogue of distress, so that nineteenth-century Dublin very quickly became synonymous with poverty and slum conditions. However, it is important to note that such stories tell only a partial truth. Dublin had large numbers of poor in the eighteenth and preceding centuries; the removal of the upper echelons of society served to make the underlying poverty more visible, while the development of social theory and the science of statistics ensured that the recording, measurement and management of poverty would be a major concern in all nineteenth-century cities. While desperate poverty was certainly the lot of the majority of city residents, the city continued to develop as the centre of business, commerce and culture for suburbanites as well as for those more fortunate residents who continued to live within its boundaries. This chapter will focus on the public health and housing pressures that dominated the lives of a large section of the citizenry, and on the various responses of the Corporation and others to the challenge of improving the urban environment during the nineteenth century.

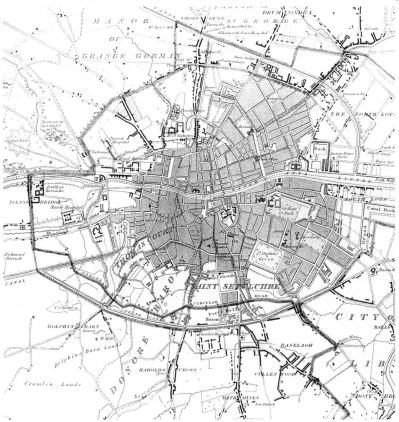

45 The early development of the suburbs. (*The county of the city of Dublin*, by Thomas Larcom, 1831–2.) Note the ribbon development along the main routes from the city.

Geographical extent and administration

In the early-nineteenth century there was no difficulty in identifying where Dublin city officially ended and the suburbs began. The municipal boundary followed, for the most part, the line of the Royal Canal to the north and the Grand Canal to the south, providing a clear-cut administrative area. However, tracing the real extent of the built-up area is a much more complex matter. North of the Liffey from Arbour Hill to Phibsborough were open fields, interrupted only by development around Prussia Street/Stoney Batter, and a complex of institutions around Grangegorman, including the North Dublin Union workhouse, three hospitals, two lunatic asylums, and a prison. To the north-east the aristocratic Gardiner estate stopped short of the canal, leaving a transition zone between it and the wretched cabin dwellings of the North

Strand. While Amiens Street, formerly the Strand, had been laid out since the early-eighteenth century there was little development east of it, bar some chemical works, stores and cabins.

Across the Liffey, the south-eastern Fitzwilliam/Pembroke sector of Merrion Square was well developed, with extensions along Baggot Street indicating the direction that fashion had already determined to follow. There was still much open space on both sides of the South Circular Road, but calico printing mills, cotton manufactories, glue makers and breweries were evident in the oldest and most industrialized part of the city, the Liberties. This south-western district also had its complement of institutions, Steeven's Hospital, Swift's Hospital, and the South Dublin Union Workhouse. Several small and generally very poor villages were also to be found – Ringsend and Irishtown to the east, Dolphin's Barn to the south-west, Old Kilmainham to the west, and Phibsboro to the north, each on the city margins but with its own distinct identity.

From the city fringes to the heart of the built-up area the inherited morphology and built fabric varied immensely, reflecting the complex origins and long history behind early-nineteenth-century Dublin. Street patterns ranged from the closely packed lanes and alleyways of the south city medieval core to the orderly set pieces of eighteenth-century landlord speculation, directly north and south-east of Carlisle (O'Connell) Bridge. The housing fabric was similarly varied, with classical town residences designed for the tastes and finances of a fast-disappearing aristocratic class; Huguenot housing in the Liberties; rows of mud cabins along 'rural' roads leading to Drumcondra, North Strand and Dolphin's Barn, along Blackhorse Lane and Kilmainham; countless other 'rural' cabins behind rows of three- and four-storey town houses filling back gardens and yards; and comfortable terraced housing.

Dublin was a compact city with a relatively small population. In 1800 there was c.182,000 people in the city, but it was destined to grow to 258,369 in 1852. By this date, the suburban population was much smaller, only 59,468, but with a far greater concentration of wealth. Population grew due to migration and not only because of natural increase; indeed the death rate was consistently so high that population would have fallen sharply but for continued new additions, largely from the adjoining counties of Louth, Meath, Kildare and Wicklow. Although most nineteenth-century urban centres relied on in-migration to maintain and increase their population, Dublin as the principal gateway to Britain, and the first port of call for many entering or returning to the country, played a significant but not always welcome role in this movement. The ceaseless influx of destitute poor compounded its notorious health and housing situation throughout the century. The question of coping with the poor by State and voluntary groups was always a matter of grave importance, with claims, that persisted into this century, that Dublin operated as 'the rest house or alms house to which people broken in health, character or fortune come from all over Ireland, to shelter or hide themselves or to take advantage of its numerous hospitals and almost innumerable over-lapping charities' (Cowan, 1918, p. 14).

The long-established tradition among the country poor of resorting to Dublin led to the oft-repeated complaint from the civic authorities that 'this city is become the common receptacle of objects disfigured and frightful, as well as pretending to be miserable, from all parts of the Kingdom' (Gilbert, 1904, ii, pp 523–5). A great number of the 10,329 paupers who in 1815 'forced their way' into the House of Industry, the State-funded warehouse for the elderly destitute, were described as 'adventurers from the Kingdom at large' (*House of Industry Observations*, 1818, p. 24). The city, it was claimed in 1817 by the founders of the Mendicity Institution, 'presented a spectacle at once afflicting and disgusting to the feelings of its inhabitants', with 'crowds of unfortunate and clamorous beggars' frequently carrying about 'in their persons and garments the seeds of contagious disease' (Mendicity Report, 1819, p. 2). The great dearth of alternatives, especially in the period preceding the Poor Law (1838), left many with little option but to head for the capital; it was obvious even to those most critical of the Dublin beggars that there was nowhere else for them to go so that 'nearly the whole tide of wretchedness and want must of necessity pour in upon Dublin'. And there was nothing to prevent this influx. Once arrived 'and actually or apparently in a state of destitution, they of course meet with relief in some way' (p. 89).

Visitors' comments on the poor were often part of their larger pen pictures. John Gamble, writing in 1826, considered Dublin an 'inexpressibly graceful' city, a copy of London, but 'more beautiful, in truth, in miniature than the gigantic original'. However, he regarded the large numbers supported by alms as a testimony to the charity of the citizenry, adding that in London, 'there is much, much suffering, much sorrow, much want in every quarter, in every lane, and in every street – but there are *few* beggars – if there were many they would *starve*' (Gamble, 1826, p. 90). Twenty years later Stirling-Coyne directed the visitor's eye to countless picturesque objects and charming vistas (Stirling-Coyne, 1847, p. 137), focusing especially on the architectural splendour of the various churches, public buildings, and monuments. Even he could not fail to comment on how St Patrick's cathedral was 'surrounded on every side with old narrow streets, of the meanest and filthiest description' (p. 145). He noted also the lack of a resident nobility or gentry and commented dryly that the professors of law and medicine might be said to form the aristocracy (p. 150). Dublin docks, he felt, were in decay and he reckoned that those who crowded the packet steamer left with little regret 'from a country where starvation is the lot of the poor' (p. 156).

Migrants to the city found an administrative structure that can only be described as labyrinthine in the period 1800–1849. There was a multitude of bodies with differing but overlapping functions, operating with varying degrees of competence and commitment, within a myriad of geographical divisions. Local vestries, Grand Juries, the Wide Streets Commissioners, the Paving Board, Pipe Water Board and the city Corporation itself were only some of the bodies with responsibility for the management of the city and the provision of essential public services. A common lethargy and an inability to co-operate with any other body was all pervading.

The 1802 Cork Street Hospital report on contagion includes a lengthy critique (p. 16) of the 'Act for the Improvement of the city of Dublin and the environs thereof, by the better paving, lighting and cleansing the same' (1789) under which the Commissioners for Paving were created. The establishment of special-task 'improvement commissioners' was characteristic of urban government throughout Ireland and Britain during the period 1748–1835; in most cases funded by local taxation. Their aims were clearly specified and limited, such as street paving, lighting, cleansing (scavenging) or widening. The idea that a city Corporation or borough council might itself take on such responsibilities was not common until the municipal reforms of the 1830s to 1850s, and even then it took several decades more before the notion, with all its ramifications, was in practice generally accepted. The powers of the Paving Board included responsibility for ensuring the proper paving, cleansing, and lighting of the streets, the erection of fountains and conduits for the use of the poor and the public, the erection of common sewers and drains. They had also powers to levy rates to fund the prevention or removal of nuisances such as when a private sewer became so blocked as to overflow or become offensive. They could carry out the necessary remedial works and then charge the parties deemed responsible. Inspectors of nuisances under this Act were to be made constables. Further restrictions were imposed under a supplementary Act of 1790 that imposed on owners and occupiers the duty of covering 'with such quantities of lime or earth as shall be sufficient to prevent any stench or annoyance' of waste from slaughter houses, shambles, or privies which might be used as manure on any land within the city boundary (p. 19).

The powers vested in the Paving Commissioners although accepted as 'highly useful and salutary', had proved worthless in the fever dens of the Liberties but this was the legislation under which the city was to labour until the Dublin Improvement Act, 1849. The utter neglect of the backyards was due to the primary responsibility of the Paving Board for transport matters and the safety and accommodation of passengers, so that matters concerning public roads were the principal concern. The penal provisions concerning the removal of filth by country carts, and the impossibility of holding a landlord accountable for the provision of 'dirt holes &c.', where multiple tenancy was the norm, ensured that nothing useful was done.

The landlord controlled Grand Juries, the forerunner in rural areas of the county councils, were limited to ensuring the maintenance of the principal highways. In the case of Dublin's Liberties, the Cork Street Fever Hospital reports criticized the law which, as it stood, facilitated the collection of the 'external filth' of the routeways or free thoroughfares 'by a scavenger who contracts for the purpose with the Grand Jury of the Manor Court of St Thomas Donore' (p. 4). While the performance of this duty left much to be desired, the comparatively free circulation of air in the open streets was welcomed. The real problem was in the backyards and laneways, where the scavengers never ventured, and which were the responsibility of no one. Also in need of immediate attention were the 'dunghills, slaughtering houses, and stagnant pools of the Liberties' (p. 11) which the trustees considered might all be proceeded against as nuisances under the common or statute law as it stood, the principal difficulty being that the sentence would fall on the occupier rather than, more fairly, upon the landlord.

At the beginning of the nineteenth century the vestries of the Established Church parishes in the city exercised a diversity of functions, including the care of deserted children, the relief of paupers, fire-fighting, and the protection of public health; one commentator aptly described them as 'miniature munici-palities' (Cameron, 1914, p. 17). In the areas of scavenging and associated sanitary matters they were spectacularly ineffective; matters of poor relief were similarly mismanaged. However well the ideal of each parish controlling matters within its own borders might apply in a largely Protestant rural context, in nineteenth-century Dublin the levying of local taxes by the vestry was an anachronism and greatly resented, not least because the great majority of the city's population was not of the Established Church and had no voice in the management or disbursement of their taxes. The unfairness of parish-based taxation in a city where wealth was so unevenly spread was identified at the beginning of the century, with Whitelaw (1805) complaining that this antiquated system 'at present universally adopted, of each parish providing for its own poor only, is founded in absurdity itself' (p. 41). Under an Act passed in 1832 at the height of a cholera crisis, Government money could be advanced to the parish officers of health to enable them to distribute nourishment, clothing and other necessaries within their respective parishes (White, 1833, p. 28). This was of little use as the amount so issued had to be repaid by parochial assessment. It was inevitable that the parishes with the greatest need were those least able to pay.

The powers of the Wide Streets Commissioners were transferred to the Corporation following the Dublin Improvement Act (1849). This administrative body had a closely defined purpose, but, more importantly, had in the period before 1800 the political influence, local landlord support and substantial public funding to carry out its functions. The powers it wielded (and the scale of its debts) dwarfs that of the parish vestries while the Commissioners maintained an aloofness from the Corporation. Although the post-Union Wide Streets Commission operated on a smaller scale, with lesser funding and political standing than in the eighteenth century, it nevertheless continued to make significant contributions to the design of the city's street network and the standard of architecture. These objectives were achieved despite the recession and slump in property prices that followed on the Union.

More modestly, the nineteenth-century achievements of the Wide Streets Commission can be seen in the general improvement work in the vicinity of both cathedrals, the Christ Church work being completed by 1821 for the visit of George IV. The work around St Patrick's cathedral in 1821–5 included the widening of Kevin Street and the creation of Dean Street, allowing a direct link-up between the Coombe and Kevin Street, while cut stone walls with capped pillars enclosed the Deanery, Marsh's Library and the former palace of St Sepulchre, used as a horse police barracks (today a garda station). The overall effect was the creation of one of the most striking and intimate city spaces, a fitting approach for the cathedral, following its own restoration (1863).

Other nineteenth-century projects by the Wide Streets Commission were for the purpose of facilitating the canal companies – Great Brunswick (Pearse) Street (1809–11) linking the city with the Grand Canal docks, and a lesser development between Camden Street and the South Circular Road to allow access to the Portobello harbour (1815). Similarly, an avenue, Military Road, was laid out to link the Royal Hospital at Kilmainham with Barrack Bridge, west of Queen's Bridge.

The housing conditions of the poor, 1800–50

A succession of inquiries, prompted by recurrent outbreaks of contagious disease and the perceived threat of vast numbers of vagrants crowding into Dublin, reveal the housing conditions of the poorest strata of Dublin society during the period 1800–50. Field research was undertaken by private individuals, by medical officers and clergymen at the request of institutions and charities, and by the State itself. In many cases astute analysis of the underlying causes of Dublin poverty, and sound suggestions for its reform, was offered alongside distressing accounts of the living conditions and degraded local environment that individual families endured (Prunty, 1998). From the mid-nineteenth-century property valuation records, along with mortality and census data make it possible to construct a city-wide geography of poverty.

The Revd James Whitelaw, whose general report and some sample tables were published in 1805, identified the core problems that were to bedevil the century, namely overcrowding; the tenement system of subdivision of houses and even of individual rooms to meet exorbitant rents and the disgraceful state of the sanitary accommodation (Whitelaw, 1805, p. 64). Human waste was only one part of the problem; private dung yards, dairy-yards, and slaughter houses, overcrowded cemeteries, and noxious activities such as soap-making and lime-burning in the midst of a crowded population all added to the city's problems. Contemporaneous with Whitelaw's surveys, a group of physicians led by a Dr Murray, faced with 'the utter impossibility of effectually checking the ravages of contagion among the poor, while they remain in their own habitations', promoted the establishment of a specialized fever hospital, the House of Recovery, Cork Street (Murray, 1801, p. 4). In their zeal 'to counteract the progress of infection, and to eradicate as far as possible the causes of it' (Cork Street Report, 1802, pp 24–5) the trustees' campaign extended towards purifying and ventilating the houses once the patients had been removed and gradually developing a sense of the importance of cleanliness. However, the best exertions of the House of Recovery personnel indoors were of little worth as long as there was no means of refuse disposal and the back yards of the houses continued to be filled up with heaps of putrid filth. Absentee landlords of these wretched houses took no interest either in removing the nuisances, or assisting the occupiers to do so. The tenants were in a no-win situation. If they went to the trouble of paying to have the filth removed, they were likely to be in breach of the law which expressly forbade any person 'to empty any boghouse or begin to take away any night soil from any house' excepting between the hours of 11 p.m. and 6 a.m. and that the mode of conveyance could only be 'in a cart or car floored and enclosed by a boarded framework' (Cork Street Report, 1802, p. 17). For the very poorest of the city's residents to organize and pay for the services of a driver with a well-constructed country cart to empty cess pits in the dead of night was plainly unreasonable.

The Cork Street Fever Hospital was well supported at its foundation but the larger task, the cleansing of these lanes and backyards, required root and branch reform. The local Grand Jury and Paving Commissioners were exhorted to use existing (if inadequate) powers to the fullest, while reforming legislation in favour of the tenant over the landlord and comprehensive new sanitary legislation were also urged. Taking a radical and well-informed stance, the trustees identified what was to be the kernel of the nineteenth-century Dublin debate – the 'exact point to which public interference must extend and at which private exertion must begin', they themselves having clearly shown 'how inefficient the latter must be, unaided by the former' (p. 34).

The report and observations of Francis White and his colleagues, undertaken at the request of the Mansion House Relief Committee in connection with the cholera epidemic of 1832–3, provide some of the most heart-breaking scenes of life among the poorest residents of Dublin city. Typical was the case of Hamilton's Court off Skinner's Alley in the Coombe, which consisted of three groups of narrow houses containing 182 people, principally mendicant lodgers. They lived in abject misery and want and the houses faced onto an open sewer without any outlet. It was choked up with stagnant and rotting matter and rendered the locality pestilential (White, 1833). In one house in nearby Elbow Lane four cases of malignant cholera occurred within 30 hours in the same room, which was crowded to excess, there 'being eleven straw litters for fifteen individuals who occupied the room at night' (p. 8). In Rowley's Court off Hamilton Row there were two houses containing between 50 and 60 'abandoned females' in the most primitive of conditions. In one room the inspector noted 'three women lying on dung with scarcely a covering, and four more of them sitting opposite to an open hearth without fire, eating some broken potatoes off the earthen floor' (p. 13). In North King Street, the inspector was faced with a maze of overcrowded courts and inner courts behind the main houses, with access possible only through the hallways of these houses or by a narrow winding entry arched over. In the deepest recesses he found three small houses equally filthy and neglected, containing 10 families, comprising 50 individuals, all in the greatest distress. Added to this were countless dark wet cellars into which every kind of filth drained, and which, though the most unhealthy of dwellings, were occupied by hundreds of families.

But, as discussed by Edel Sheridan in chapter 3 for the previous century, the 1833 report confirmed that a dense pauper population was not at all confined to the oldest and most decayed parts of the city, but could be found in the immediate neighbourhood of some of the wealthiest and most respectable districts. In the wealthy north city parish of St George's great numbers were to be found, as in Johnston's court, off Britain street, where one house contained more than 70 poor persons. In the cellars of Lacy's Lane off Merrion Street, south of Trinity College, the situation of the residents, mostly female, was described as 'nothing but one scene of filth, misery and want' (p. 20).

By the mid-nineteenth century the principal characteristics of the housing conditions of Dublin's poorer classes were well publicized, and both legislative and administrative weaknesses identified. But the prevailing political climate of *laissez faire* was heavily in favour of allowing free market forces to prevail, and minimizing State interference in commercial and social realms. Ironically, some instances of the grossest State interference, such as the establishment of the 1838 Poor Law which saw the erection and administration of enormous workhouses, supported by compulsory taxation, were justified by recourse to the political philosophy of *laissez faire*. It was claimed that massive State involvement, in the form of a repulsive indoor relief system, was required to ensure that surplus labour would be forced to move to wherever labour was in demand. But support for increased State interference for the common good, especially in matters of public health, poor relief and mass education, was growing steadily, backed by ever-increasing banks of data illustrating the folly of leaving matters so poorly regulated, allowing selfish interest, lethargy and powerlessness to prevail, with disastrous results.

Griffith Valuation, Dublin 1854

The published reports and inquiries into the state of the Dublin poor that punctuate the early decades of the nineteenth century are largely eye witness accounts, the common aim of which was to expose the dreadful realities behind successive outbreaks of epidemic disease. The large numbers of vagrants and beggars who were prominent on the city streets were suspected, rightly, of contributing to the spread of disease. In the case-study detail these reports provide incontrovertible evidence of the realities endured by individual families locally. To identify areas of poor housing on a city-wide scale, however, it is necessary to move to more inclusive sources, most usefully the General Valuation of Ireland, commonly called the Griffith Valuation, completed for the city of Dublin in 1854. Figure 46 maps the distribution of all low value housing within the city boundary in 1854. The £10 value has been selected as a cut-off point on the basis of the Corporation franchise, that is, to elect members to Dublin Corporation, one had to be the occupier of premises in the borough rated at £10 or upwards, and also have three years' continuous residence in the city. That led to a very small pool of voters, calculated in 1885 as less than three percent of the city's residents (Housing Inquiry, 1885).

While this identifies all premises the occupants of which were excluded from active involvement in civic life, it cannot be considered the only key to areas of low status housing, as the practice of subdivision led to persons having third or fourth class accommodation in houses of the first or second class, as identified in the census (Census of Population, 1841; 1851). The case of houses valued over £10, but in tenements, became an increasingly significant part of the housing market in the second half of the century. Figure 46 also excludes some very poor single-room accommodation that was to be found in commercial streets such as Francis Street, where shoemakers, curled-hair manufacturers, new milk dairy men and rag-and-bone dealers had their businesses. As many such premises were valued at over the £10 limit, and their commercial standing masked whatever tenement accommodation was also present, they cannot be fairly represented either in maps of low-value housing or of tenement distribution. Figure 46 must therefore be regarded as a useful guide to the lowest quality housing rather than a comprehensive map of all low standard accommodation.

The most striking aspect of the city's housing pattern was the widespread distribution of low-value residences. There was practically no part of the built-up area that did not include some low-value housing. However, distinct patterns can be discerned. On the south side the greatest concentrations of housing valued under £10 were found in the oldest parts of the city. In the medieval core, around the Castle, Christ Church cathedral, Cook Street, Back Lane, and behind Fishamble Street were significant clusters of poor housing, while the transitional area between St Stephen's Green and the Liberties proper had pockets of poor housing behind the principal thoroughfares. The

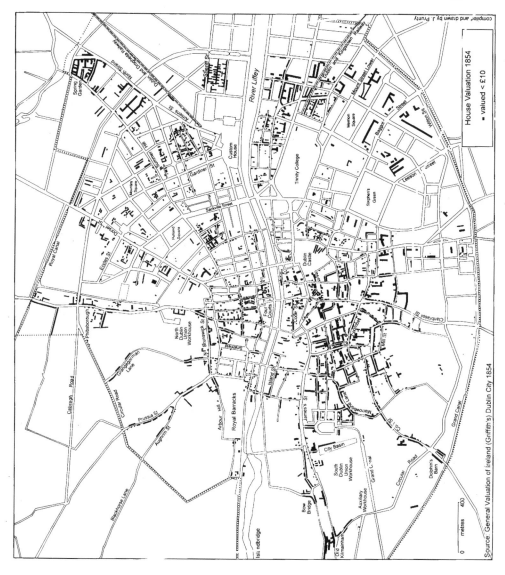

46 Low-value houses in 1854. (Based on the General Valuation of Ireland, Dublin City, 1854.)
(Compiled by Jacinta Prunty.)

Liberties, the extensive south city area west of the medieval core, and the focus of Whitelaw's survey, had the greatest concentration of housing valued under £10 in the entire city. Here decayed eighteenth-century housing such as that in Poole Street (Figure 47) or Chambers Street (Figure 48) was common. The density of housing is remarkable, with literally every square metre of land behind the main thoroughfares commandeered. In Coles Alley off Tripoli, for example, twenty seven houses valued between £2 and £5 10s. were packed tightly together, along with sheds and yards. Along important arteries such as James Street and the Coombe, tenements were intermixed with profitable commercial premises. The south-western sector was dominated by activities for which considerable water supplies were a pre-requisite – breweries and distilleries; assorted mills; tanning and drying lofts; foundries and ironworks; dyehouses and businesses for the manufacture of ropes, cars and coaches, starch, vitriol, glue and lime. This zone had also a significant concentration of institutions – military barracks and military hospitals, other hospitals and asylums, the South Dublin Union Workhouse and its auxiliary, a reformatory and bridewell, and extensive depots for municipal purposes. And throughout the most densely packed and longest settled parts of the city, slaughter-houses, dairy yards and other unsuitable land uses were interspersed with housing.

There was an extensive network of poor courts and alleys off Townsend Street, creating an enclave of slum housing in the wedge between the river and the northern boundary of Trinity College, as in the much larger East End sector in London. A similarly poor area was found on the north bank of the Liffey. The *Illustrated London News* produced a panorama of Dublin in 1846 and this gives an impression of the local morphology of these dockside slum areas (Figures 49 and 50). On the north side between Sheriff Street and Mayor Street West the General Valuation lists at least 34 courts and laneways, each with its own complement of poor cottage dwellings, average valuation £2 15s. This irregular configuration of cottages and small houses hidden behind the quayside warehouses competes for space with vitriol and old vinegar works, coal yards, dairy yards, pig yards, cattle sheds, a railway carriage factory, and open land described as 'waste' or 'building ground'. Insignificant housing straggles out towards the north-east, in association with the railway and with the canal, along Amiens Street into the North Strand, and tracing the line of the Ballybough Road (aptly, the road to Baile Bocht, the settlement of the poor, the 'Irishtown' of the 'English' city). This low-lying area to the north-east of Mountjoy Square (and the associated high-status housing of the

47 Poole Street at the end of the nineteenth century. (Postcard.)

48 Chambers Street at the end of the nineteenth century. (Postcard.)
Notice the large numbers of men in the picture.

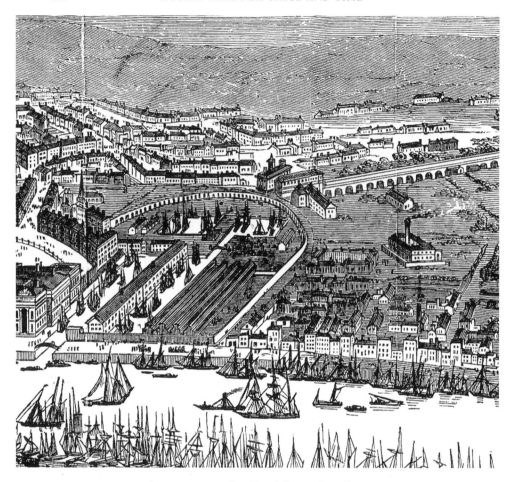

49 North-eastern sector of Dublin. (*Illustrated London News*, 1846.)

Gardiner estate) included Spring Garden and Taaffe's Village, which was appropriately titled 'mud village' on a Campbell/Taylor map of 1811.

On the south dock the intermixing of noxious land uses with residences of low value behind City Quay is also evident. The railway lines and stations on both sides of the city, linking Dublin–Kingstown (Dun Laoghaire) (1834) and Dublin–Drogheda (1844), reinforced rather than created this distinct social geography, further isolating the mixed docks working class housing areas and ensuring their continued environmental unattractiveness. In the vicinity of Westland Row station on the south side were innumerable small pockets of poor housing along Sandwith Street, Hanover Street East, Cumberland Street South and Boyne Street and the lanes and courts associated with them. A

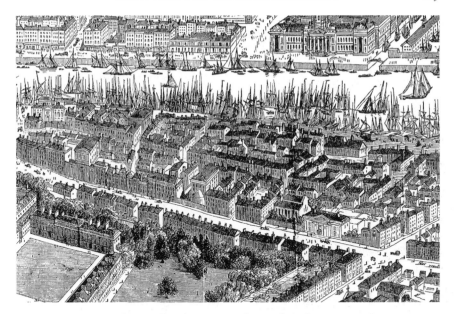

50 South quays from City quay. (*Illustrated London News*, 1846.)

complex courtyard formation characterized this area, with much infilling hidden behind terraces of three- and four-storey houses. The parish priest of St Andrew's, Westland Row, writing to the archbishop in 1861 (Dublin Diocesan Archives, file 1340 no. 78) noted such enclaves of squalid poverty within this 'the richest parish in the city', with two, three, sometimes more families in one small room, 'the bed, straw or shavings, sometimes neither, the clothing, the rags they have on them during the day'. Such scenes could be witnessed any day in 'Bass Place in the rere of Merrion Square, Leeson Place in the rere of St Stephen's Green ... all the lanes off Townsend Street, Temple Bar, the streets between Townsend Street and the Quays, the lanes off the Quays'.

Other north city concentrations of low-value housing focused around the axes of Gloucester, Mecklenburgh and Montgomery Streets (later infamously *The Monto*), in the lanes and alleyways to the north of Dorset Street, and to the west of Sackville Street around the old clothes markets of Moore Street and Cole's Lane (McCullough, 1898, p. 128). There was also an extensive poor area around the old Ormond Market, with its fish, fruit, vegetable, potato and egg markets. Low value housing continued north/north-westwards from Ormond Market until halted by the institutional sector dominated by the South Dublin Union workhouse and associated hospitals, Grangegorman/ Richmond prison and lunatic asylum, and the Royal Canal harbour, subsequently the Broadstone railway station. Figure 51, which shows this area to

51 The city north of the Four Courts. (*Illustrated London News*, 1846.)
Note the institutional landscape in the northern part of the image.

the rear of the Four Courts and crossed by Church Street, illustrates the extent
to which these institutions dominate the geography of this part of the city. The
Royal Barracks further to the west continues this type of domination, its sheer
scale effectively discouraging high class residential developments in this district.
It is not surprising that the routeways that border these institutions are lined
with low-value houses or cabins, along Blackhorse Lane, Grangegorman Lane,
Stonybatter, Phibsborough, and Aughrim and Prussia Streets.

West of the built-up area, there were significant but little discussed areas of
low value housing in conjunction with noxious and industrial land uses. At
Islandbridge, between the cavalry barracks and a lunatic asylum, there was a
cluster of low-value housing in conjunction with woollen and flour mills and
an associated mill race, along the banks of the Liffey. At Kilmainham, where
the Cammock (Camac) river was exploited for power, and literally in the shadow
of the gaol, were found flour and other unspecified mills, in association with low-
value housing. Where Old Kilmainham intersected with Watery Lane were

several tanyards alongside houses of the lowest description (valued at *c*.£1 10*s*.); a similar concentration was found at nearby Mount Brown. Back on the northside, Courtenay Cottages, along Ballybough Road, valued between 15*s*. and £1 10*s*., were 'damp, wretched hovels, utterly unfit for human habitation, and yet have high rents paid for them'.

The colonization of stable lanes (mews) behind the large houses by the poorest was typically associated with the reduction of first class dwellings to tenement status, 'different classes of persons now occupy the houses, and the people in the front houses no longer keep vehicles' (Housing Inquiry, 1885, qs 22,087, p. 13). Typical was Henrietta Place, behind the mansions of Henrietta Street, where barely-converted outhouses were used as dwellings, their former status still unmistakable in the early-twentieth century. This process had been noted by Whitelaw as early as 1805. Even then, the biggest difficulties lay in the enclosed nature of the yards, too many persons reliant on too few privies, and the lack of enforceable regulations – 'The stench of filth in an open street, may be dissipated by an unobstructed current of air; but that arising from human excrement, in narrow yards enclosed by lofty buildings, must operate with unchecked malignity' (p. 55). The houses in the Liberties 'are in general unprovided with necessaries or those necessaries are so choked up and obstructed as not to serve for any purpose of cleanliness'.

Housing types

The poor occupied three major types of housing – the tenement, infill cottages or cabins, and cellars. The extent of tenement housing in the city at mid-century can be judged from Figure 52, where all houses entered as 'tenements' in Thom's and Shaw's commercial street directories have been calculated as a percentage of all premises in each street or lane. Streets where tenements made up over two-thirds (black line) or over one-third (dotted line) have thus been identified. This methodology is subject to all the limitations inherent in commercial street directory information – tenement status is likely to be masked where a business occupies the ground floor, this is most obvious along commercial routes such as Thomas Street, Patrick Street and Bride Street (south city), or Church Street and Dorset Street (north city). A small street such as Hanover Lane, with most of its occupiers grandly titled 'clothes broker' in 1850 therefore does not appear as a tenement street although certainly in multiple occupancy. There is also the likelihood that some back courts and alleys were not listed, while very long streets, which had a large

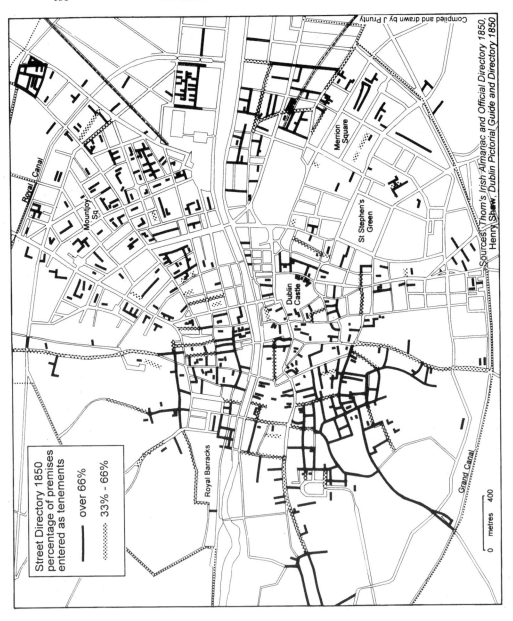

52 Tenements in Dublin in 1850.
(Compiled by Jacinta Prunty.)

number of tenement houses but still too few to reach the 33 per cent or 66 per cent limits, do not feature as prominently as their absolute numbers might warrant. Conversely streets with small numbers of houses might reach the 33 per cent or 66 per cent limits very easily. Despite these and other reservations, this map provides a useful broad brush picture of the geography of tenement housing in the city for 1850.

Tenements were a common housing form in many other cities, especially in Scotland. The name derives from the medieval burgage plot, and came to denote the house built at the head of the plot. It came to be associated with high density high-rise buildings, built to maximize plot use. In Scotland, they were purpose-built by speculators because Scottish law required builders to pay out significant sums before housing could be let and they promised a quick return. Not all were poor quality, however, and Glasgow still boasts many fine streets of tenements where the name does not necessarily carry any connotation of poverty but rather one of multiple occupancy. But the working-class tenement was common also in Glasgow where it was of three basic types – inner city houses following the lines of medieval burgage plots; small units made from sub-dividing unsuccessful middle class developments and the regular hollow squares of the industrial tenement proper (Gibb, 1981). In Dublin, in contrast, there was relatively little speculative tenement building and most comprised the filtered down housing of the rich who had abandoned once favoured areas. In both cities conditions were bad, even by the end of the nineteenth century.

The tenement system was well established in the poorest areas by the beginning of the nineteenth century, and the steady out migration of the wealthiest to the suburbs ensured that a continuous supply of single-family residences could be very profitably converted to tenements for the huge numbers of poor streaming into the city. The most spectacular downturn was in the Gardiner estate to the north-east, where many of the grandest homes were in tenements by the 1880s, but the phenomenon was city-wide. Public debate returned again and again to Dublin's tenement system as the root of all its problems. The Royal Commission appointed to inquire into the sewerage and drainage of Dublin concluded its critical report by affirming:

> That the tenement houses of Dublin appear to be the prime source and cause of the excessively high death rate; that they are not properly classified, registered, and regulated; that they are dilapidated, dirty, ill-ventilated, much over-crowded, and that disease, a craving for stimulants and its consequences – drunkenness and extreme poverty,

are thereby fostered, and that until the condition of these houses shall
have been improved the general health of the city will continue to be
injuriously affected.

(quoted Eason, 1879, p. 383)

This system of housing was also at the heart of the social relations between the
poorest persons, and influenced the dealings of the better off in their regard. The
information networks concerning availability of employment, food and other
necessities, better or cheaper accommodation, medical assistance, schooling
opportunities, religious services, poor relief, and the myriad other areas of human
importance, were all linked up through this housing system. The tenement
system, where generally each family occupied only one room and rent was paid
on a weekly basis without any long term security of tenure, facilitated mobility,
especially if the move was only to another in the same street or district.

The structural arrangements of the tenement houses prevented the
provision of separate sanitary accommodation for each family, and turned
these houses into sanitary nightmares:

> There is no direct means of removing the refuse from the several floors,
> the common stair soon therefore becomes fouled; while the height of
> the houses – seldom less than three, and generally four storeys high – in
> no slight degree operates against cleanliness. Many of these houses
> possess unoccupied cellars, the atmosphere of which cannot fail to
> injuriously affect the health of the occupants of the upper rooms.
>
> (Eason, 1879)

In Dublin, 'as in London and elsewhere, sanitary accommodation used in
common by several families will seldom be properly kept' (*Report on public
health*, 1894, p. 89), particularly when anyone could come in off the street and
use it. Two outdoor closets and a single stand pipe in a yard were the only
conveniences available to the seventy persons who shared a house in Newmarket
Street, in 1913. The Corporation placed a target of twenty persons per sanitary
convenience, a figure that they found repeatedly greatly exceeded throughout the
city. The utter lack of privacy in overcrowded conditions, 'the constantly open
doors and the want of lighting in the hall, passages, and landings at night', were
considered to be the cause of much immorality, so that one witness to the 1913
Housing Inquiry claimed that the children 'acquire a precocious knowledge of
evil from early childhood' (Housing Inquiry, 1914, p. 5).

The biggest difficulty in regulation was to be the legal aspect because it was not uncommon to have as many as five owners to one tenement. F.R. Falkiner detailed the problems in 1882 and noted that 'the existing dilapidation of many city houses is due to the defective title of the owners or representatives of the interests on which the duty of repair should properly fall' (1882, p. 267). Those who endured the privations were without any political influence as they were mainly non-rate payers and thus disenfranchised. So too the destructiveness of some tenants was held accountable for the poor accommodation in some houses, landlords complaining 'of the impracticability of effecting the requisite sanitary reforms owing to the habits of the inmates and the certain destruction which awaited improved appliances'. Further complaints were 'that the more worthless tenants frequently, on falling into arrear, willfully dilapidate or permit dilapidation whilst under notice of eviction, whilst they cannot be dispossessed even by summary order in less than an average of six weeks, and the consequent loss falls, in the shape of increased rent, on the more well-conducted tenants' (p. 269). Living conditions in the tenements were the subject of scrutiny as the century drew to a close. In 1894 Dr Charles Cameron, the city's medical officer, stated the situation very directly:

> The death-rate of Dublin is, unfortunately, high; a fact which I attribute chiefly, if not wholly, to the comparative poverty of the population. One third of the people of Dublin live in single room tenements, in which they eat, drink, cook, sleep, and often carry on their work for a living.
>
> (*Report on public health*, 1894, p. 27)

Along with the tenement housing, attention was continually drawn to the large number of poor cottages or minimally converted stable dwellings that had sprung up throughout the city, particularly as infill developments on small sites, and in the gardens, backyards and rear stable lanes of the larger houses, usually in a court or lane configuration that utilized the existing plot to best advantage (McCullough, 1989, p. 91). Some could be better described as shelters, a number of them erected in narrow areas 'almost surrounded by high buildings or walls, with alleys or passages, which in some cases are scarcely more than nine or ten feet [*c.*3 metres] wide, as a means of approach' (Housing Inquiry, 1914, p. 6). Separate closet accommodation was non-existent, but there was usually a closet and a single tap located in the general vicinity of the housing for use by all and sundry. In comparison to tenements,

these cottages suffered the added disadvantage of being in some cases surrounded by high walls and buildings that shut out light and air. The oft-
repeated complaint against these rows of small cabins built in the gardens of
substantial houses is exemplified in the case of Brady's Cottages, where the yard
space of 16 Francis Street had been completely colonized and entrance secured
through an archway passage. Other classic examples of infill housing could be
found in nearby Burke's Cottages, Binn's Court, Hallahan's Court and
Maguire's Court, while King Street, Church Street and Beresford Street to the
north of the Liffey were infamous for the number and wretchedness of the
cottages their front street houses shielded from public view.

Cellar dwellings were regarded as the worst possible of all poor accommodation. Thomas Willis highlighted the situation of innumerable servants
during the cholera outbreak of 1833 'labouring under disease, sleeping in *turn-up
beds*, in the vitiated atmosphere of these kitchens, or sleeping in small rooms
adjoining, having no light or air except from the kitchen; the ventilation and light
of which were dependent on the gratings in the flagway of the street above'
(Willis, 1845, pp 54–5). On the basis that English law forbade the incarceration
of any prisoner, even if condemned to die, in a dungeon or underground room,
Willis called for the outlawing of all underground storeys as sleeping apartments.
Thomas Jordan recounted the uncivilized situation that still prevailed in 1857
where cellar dwellings, many of which 'can only be entered by a visitor who is a
stranger to them, by descending backwards, as a wild animal descends from the
top of a tree', were still occupied (Jordan, 1857, p. 17). While as many as 2205
cellars had been officially shut up since 1841, some of these were still in use.
Moves to rectify the situation could not keep pace with pressure for accommodation from the mid-century flood of refugees from famine and fever.

In 1873, for example, it was noted that despite the closure of 110 cellar
dwellings, at least 57 were still known to be occupied, and could not be
touched as they did not come within the provisions of the 1848 Public Health
Act. This Act prohibited the occupation as a dwelling of any cellar built or
rebuilt after the passing of the Act, or not occupied as a dwelling at the time
of the Act, and laid down conditions governing the continued occupation of
older cellars. Non-compliance with the law could lead to a fine and, after two
convictions, compulsory closure. In his evidence to the Royal Commission in
1885 (Housing Inquiry, 1885) Dr Cameron argued that there were now no
cellar dwellings that came within the provisions of the Act (qs 22,101, p. 13).
However, others challenged this view. Moreover Dr Cameron complained that

some of those cellars successfully closed had become receptacles for every type of filth, and if anything were more dangerous than when used for shelter.

Corporation action on the slum housing question

The Dublin Improvement Act of 1849, under which the powers of the Wide Streets and Paving Commissioners were transferred to the reformed Corporation, was but the first step towards administrative efficiency. Coinciding with municipal reform, well-intentioned but unwieldy new legislation was introduced in the form of the Nuisances Removal and Diseases Prevention Act, 1848, and the Public Health Act, 1848. There were some efforts made to at least ameliorate the worst aspects of the city's sanitary crisis, with the appointment of the first ever 'inspectors of nuisances' from 1851, who with the assistance of the Dublin Metropolitan Police began to issue innumerable notices to abate nuisances. The adoption of bye-laws for the regulation of lodging houses, also in 1851, looked good on paper, but in practice it was limited to the listing of lodging houses, and a little white-washing, neither of which was going to make any impact on the overwhelming and ever worsening tenement situation. Efforts to inspect and license slaughter houses were also instigated, but were similarly tentative. The appointment of the city's first medical officer of health, Dr Edward Mapother, in 1864 marked the beginning of a serious approach to public health and associated housing matters, while his successor Dr Cameron was, as we have already seen, a tireless and effective campaigner. However, worthwhile progress on health and housing can only be tracked from 1866, with the passing of the Sanitary Act, fittingly, at the height of a cholera epidemic.

The Sanitary Act of 1866, though condemned as a chaotic jumble of sanitary statutes, cobbled together from an English law of 1855 and subsequent statutes (Norwood, 1873, p. 230), led to the formation of one significant body, the Public Health Committee of Dublin Corporation, whose brief encompassed pipe water, markets, weigh houses and sanitary matters. This committee, with an ever expanding staff and regular published reports, was to become the principal forum for debate, policy formation and practical measures to tackle the Dublin tenement crisis.

The enabling legislation for slum clearance and the construction of housing for the working classes was as unwieldy in its own way as the early public health legislation. The Labouring Classes Lodging Houses and Dwellings Act (Ireland), 1866, was copied from the second of Lord Shaftesbury's Acts of 1851,

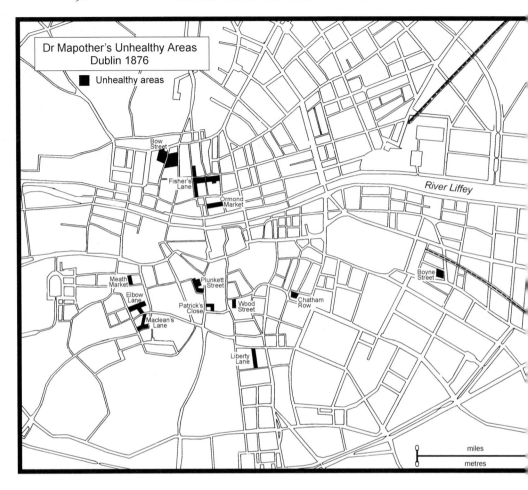

53 Dr Mapother's 'unhealthy areas' in 1876.
(Compiled by Jacinta Prunty.)

and operated to a minimal extent in Cavan, New Ross, Callan and Waterford, and in Dublin through the Dublin Artizans' Dwellings Company (DADC). The Artizans' and Labourers' Dwellings Act 1868, commonly known as Torrens Act, with its amending legislation of 1879 and 1882, was extended to Ireland, but was described as 'an absolute dead letter'. The Cross Act, 1875, as amended in the Labourers' (Ireland) Act, 1883, was utilized in Cork, Belfast and Dublin.

Under the Artizans' Dwellings Act, 1875, all urban sanitary districts in Ireland with a population over 12,000 and authorized by the Local Government Board for Ireland, could apply to the Commissioners of Public Works in Ireland for loans to put the Act of 1875 into practice, that is, to undertake slum clearance.

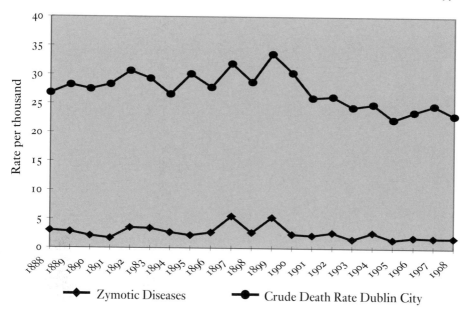

54 Death rates per thousand people in the city, 1888–1908.

The duty of Dublin Corporation, as the sanitary authority for the city, was confined to the acquisition of the property, the removal of the buildings, and the making of the paving, and sewering of the streets within the area.

The powers of the Corporation were therefore limited to facilitating the erection of working-class dwellings; only with the consent of the Local Government Board could it undertake its own building schemes, and even then the Artizans' Dwellings Act provided that they must dispose of them within three years after their erection.

The selection of a modest number of unhealthy areas (Figure 53) by Dr Mapother in his report of 1876 for clearance may be considered the opening move in the municipality's mammoth task of tackling the city's housing and public health problems. Seven of the twelve areas were in the old Liberties – Meath Market, McClean's Lane, Elbow Lane, Plunket Street, Patrick's Close, Wood Street and Liberty Lane. Also on the south side there was Chatham Row, and the Boyne Street area east of Trinity College. On the north side Bow Street, Fisher's Lane and the Ormond Market, three distinct though nearby areas, were chosen.

The characteristics shared by each of these areas illustrate the inclusive under-standing of well-being promoted by the emerging public health movement; all the houses were unfit for human habitation and incapable of repair due to 'dilapidation, closeness of the passages preventing ventilation and lighting, want of decent sanitary accommodation, and the difficulty of affording it owing to absence of yards and soakage of the earth with animal refuse from ashpits, slaughter-houses, etc.'. The resulting conditions included a high death rate, especially among infants; 'a high incidence of zymotic diseases, lung disease and rheumatism, low tone of general health, filthy habits, intemperance, and debased morals' (Harty, 1884, p. 508). The new developments would therefore raise the standard of morals, as well as of physical comfort and cleanliness.

The general pattern proposed in each of the twelve areas was to widen through-ways to permit the free circulation of air, rather than to attempt large scale clearance and rehousing. The contemporary medical obsession with miasmic theory, the spread of disease by noxious but invisible gases, led to the emphasis on broad macadamized streets and open spaces. To the north of Ormond Market, Fisher's Lane and Greek Street were so narrow that there was no circulation of air and little penetration of sunlight. This kept the roadways damp and filthy and thus facilitated the development and spread of zymotic diseases. Parke Neville, the city engineer, supported the clearance of all twelve areas, with further recommendations such as the removal of an entire block from Fisher's Lane to Greek Street. If this was done it would open up an airy space, a lung, in an otherwise miserable district and in this space it would be possible to create a development of artizans' dwellings.

Although Mapother had chosen a very modest number of sites, the Corporation had to decide on the relative badness of many unquestionably bad districts. Of the first twelve areas recommended, official representation was made to the Local Government Board about eight of them, and the Corporation drew up schemes for two – the Coombe and Boyne Street. A provisional order enabling schemes in these two areas was issued and confirmed by Parliament in 1877, at an estimated cost of £20,000. However, the £20,000 borrowed from the Commissioners of Public Works in Ireland was found to be sufficient only for purchasing and clearing the Coombe property, and the Boyne Street plans were shelved; the Coombe scheme required an additional £4,000 for constructing new streets, sewering and lighting, and providing a water supply, so that the possibility of clearing any of the other 'black spots' identified by Mapother was postponed indefinitely (Housing Inquiry, 1885, qs 21,861–70).

In the face of this massive housing problem, many years in the making, the Corporation's strategy, formally adopted in 1879, was to pursue the slow, legalistic, piecemeal process of closing condemned tenement houses throughout the city. Efforts to persuade the city's employers to involve themselves in providing better accommodation for their workers had been made, but to little avail. A report in 1857 overstated the achievements, in an effort to encourage such developments:

> Many of the extensive employers in the city have taken the greater part of a street into their own hands, and have made improvements on it, for their workpeople, or have actually built cottages expressly for their use. This course has been adopted by Messrs Pim at Harold's Cross; the proprietors of the Great Southern and Western Railway; Messrs Jameson and Co., North Anne Street; Messrs Jameson, Bow Street; &c., &c.
>
> (Jordan, 1857, p. 17)

Very few further company projects were undertaken despite pressure on employers to provide housing for their employees (Cameron and Mapother, 1879, pp 344–5).

First steps: two schemes by the Dublin Artizans' Dwellings Company

The first attempts to deal with the housing question required a partnership between public and private interests. The Dublin Artizans' Dwellings Company (DADC) emerged from the Artizans' and Labourers' Dwellings Improvement Acts of 1875 (the Cross Act) and 1877. The DADC was an offshoot of the Dublin Sanitary Association, a voluntary movement of influential citizens concerned to improve health and general living conditions in the city; the DADC has been described as 'a relatively energetic and efficient company, run by Protestant businessmen and paying modest dividends usually not exceeding four per cent to its shareholders' (Aalen, 1990, p. 8). Major investors included the Guinness family and Lady Meath, wife of the 20th earl. The Artizans' Committee of Dublin Corporation had recommended the renting of the Coombe area to the DADC because its objects were akin to those held by the Corporation, and on the basis that they would produce a scheme with a uniformity of design and character. The Coombe was chosen as the site for this first project.

The area outlined in 1876 by the medical officer of health (Figure 53) was extended considerably to improve the roadways and to provide ventilation. This included houses and yards that were in an equally insanitary state (Harty,

1884, p. 504). The network of alleys and back courts were to be cleared (Figure 55). Parke Neville seconded the recommendation for total clearance, with the addition of one extra house, no. 3 Pimlico, to widen the approach to the west. The presence of good main sewers in Pimlico, Meath Street, the Coombe and Great and Little Elbow Lane was advantageous, although to that date the link between the domestic arrangements and these sewers was tenuous. Neville accurately predicted the problem that was to hinder such advancements – 'of any house or yard, a portion of which is wanted, the entire will have to be taken down, and paid for, if so required by the owner, and this he always does'. In a city where practically all houses lined the road in terraced fashion it was almost impossible to remove just the required premises 'without having claims, real or alleged, made by the adjoining owners or occupiers, and the more rotten the property the more loss will be sustained by claims of this sort, as it will be attempted to be proved that buildings are good and sound which are the very reverse' (Neville, 1884, p. 477).

The case for total demolition and rebuilding was earnestly pressed by Dr Grimshaw at the public enquiry held in April 1877. As a physician at Cork Street Fever Hospital he had pointed out on maps of the Coombe district houses where fever prevailed, and others in which cholera had prevailed. Some houses with between 35 and 40 residents, had 'but one necessary accommodation for the entire, and that in the most disgraceful and neglected condition; the yards were also filthy, reeking with most offensive matter' (Harty, 1884, p. 513).

The houses of the Coombe area, with leases dating back to 1691, came under the jurisdiction of the Corporation and were liable for municipal rates only from 1840, being formerly part of the Liberty of the earl of Meath. In the early-nineteenth century the area was the home of manufacturers of cotton, linen, and starch, and many tradesmen, but by 1878, when the land was purchased, there was not a single merchant, manufacturer or trader. Their successors according to Harty were a motley set, some 'in the dog fancying line', others made their living by selling pigs and manufacturing manure, while others were engaged in more 'degraded occupations'. The overall picture is one of near destitution, with persons exploiting every possibility of making a living and at the time of the Corporation purchase determined to capitalize on the opportunity of compensatory payments. There were 110 dwellings, and about 300 separate tenancies, a population of 984 persons giving a density of about 246 persons per acre (608 per hectare). The new scheme resulted in an increase in the local population, consisting of 210 houses, accommodating

1100 persons, at about 275 per acre (680 per hectare). The accommodation of more persons than had been displaced was due only to the large number of premises that were derelict by the time of the redevelopment.

Where families took in lodgers, a widespread Dublin practice, the rent burden on families was reduced somewhat. The weekly rent per Coombe family varied generally between 1s. 6d. and 2s. 9d., far below the lowest rates of 3s. 6d. which were levied by the Dublin Artizans' Dwellings Company for the smallest cottages, rising to 7s. per week for the four-roomed, two-storey houses, in the new scheme.

The cost to the Corporation of acquiring this site, relative to later suburban schemes, was to prove enormous. The area was first valued at £11,134 but increased to £14,421, a figure that resulted in much public disquiet, particularly with regard to nine cases in which the jury recommended increases of nearly 120 per cent. One woman who paid no rent because she had a squatter's title was awarded £600 by the jury. A dairy owner and green grocer were awarded a total of £479 by the arbitrator, which was increased to £1350 by the jury, including compensation for trade disturbance; both business people promptly reopened in superior premises nearby. However, it was accepted that 'the Corporation paid dearly for the property, but not more than all public bodies have to pay whenever property is required to be purchased for public purposes, so that individuals do not always suffer by measures necessary for the benefit of the public' (Harty, 1884, p. 512). The sacredness of private property, even if tumbledown and seriously endangering the health of occupants and neighbours, had to be respected.

The Corporation merely acquired and cleared the four acre (1.6 ha) site, at a total cost of £24,367; it then leased it to the DADC on very favourable terms – for 10,000 years, at a peppercorn rent for the first two years, and afterwards at £200 per annum. The company was bound to erect 199 houses, containing accommodation for at least 984 persons of the artizan or working classes, the houses to be well and substantially built and ventilated, and furnished with water supply, proper drainage, and sanitary appliances and apparatus, to the satisfaction of the Corporation or their architect. The DADC expended £27,600 in buildings. The foundation stone was laid on 20 December 1880, and 120 houses of four different classes were erected – one-storey cottages, containing one living-room and one or two bedrooms; and two-storey houses, containing one or two living rooms and two bedrooms. There were also four houses of three storeys, used as shops.

The sanitary arrangements were advertised as perfect in every way, where 'each tenant has the satisfaction of having his own house and yard reserved to

55 The Dublin Artizans' Dwelling Company development at Gray Street.

56 Dublin Artizans' Dwelling Company housing at Gray Street. (Photograph, J. Brady.)

himself and his family'. Even the smallest cottages had their own scullery, coal-house, privy and yard. The cleansing passages at the rear were all kept strictly private, 'even from the tenants, and are in no case open to the public' (Harty, 1884, p. 517). These passages allowed each house to be provided with its own water supply, and also allowed sewers to be run into each yard, so that no sewers or drains passed under the houses. The yards were surfaced in concrete, so that there could be no percolation of any waste materials into the soil system.

The sanitary arrangements adopted by the DADC were similar in important respects to best practice in Britain in the 1870s. The houses themselves were substantially constructed, the smallest cottages built of portland cement, the larger houses with front and end walls of redbrick and other walls of concrete. Exterior walls were eight inches thick, the interior walls six inches thick, and the houses were acclaimed as 'all very dry, give great satisfaction to the tenants, are eagerly sought after, and are never untenanted' (p. 514). The height of the houses was limited to two storeys (excluding the four shops of three storeys), which it was believed would ensure good sun and air to all the inhabitants and be a great improvement on the cheerless barracks in other locations (Figures 55 and 56).

Artizans' schemes such as those pioneered by the DADC made a huge impact locally on the urban morphology as well as on the social makeup. A comparison of the situation before and after illustrates the very regular layout of the Coombe scheme, with four small squares, contained within the lines of the two major streets, Gray Street and Reginald Street, each street 40 feet (*c*.12 metres) wide from house to house, the streets intersecting at right angles. Both Pimlico and the Coombe itself were widened by 10 feet (*c*.3 metres). DADC housing estates were to be characterized by two house types – single-storey concrete cottages and two-storey redbrick houses, as in this Coombe scheme. Long repetitive lines of parallel streets, conforming to bye-law widths, as laid down under the Public Health (Ireland) Act 1878, which were to characterize several later DADC schemes (such as Oxmanstown) are absent in the Coombe, where a small and compact site facilitated a more pleasing if regular layout.

The effort to provide for the poorest was regarded as a non-starter; the only hope allowed for here was that this new colony with its increased health and strength and a 'very much improved tone of morals' would also 'act indirectly on the conduct of the inhabitants of other houses in the streets adjoining'. It was an interesting aspiration. It was also vaguely claimed that the scheme had given the former inhabitants the chance of improved dwellings in other places in the city by taking up the dwellings vacated by the new DADC tenants, and that 'a sort of levelling-up process has been quietly going on'. How this particular circle could be squared was never spelt out – how could people living in poor conditions better themselves by simply moving? But whatever objections could be made about the scheme there was widespread satisfaction that nothing but good could result from the clearance of such a notorious slum. The condition of those fortunate enough to occupy these bright new dwellings, built to the highest sanitary standards, was, of course, presented as idyllic.

The Plunket Street scheme

The Corporation adopted a resolution on 3 December 1879 directing the Artizans' Dwellings Committee to carry into execution the Plunket Street Area scheme, covering one of the black spots identified by Dr Mapother in 1876 (Figure 53). As with the Coombe scheme, the origins of the project were directly health related. A month previously the consulting sanitary officer had formally submitted that the greater number of the houses within the area delimited were unfit for human habitation, diseases of 'a low type' had prevailed within the area over a long period, and were attributable to the common problem of poor building condition, lack of ventilation and inadequate sanitation.

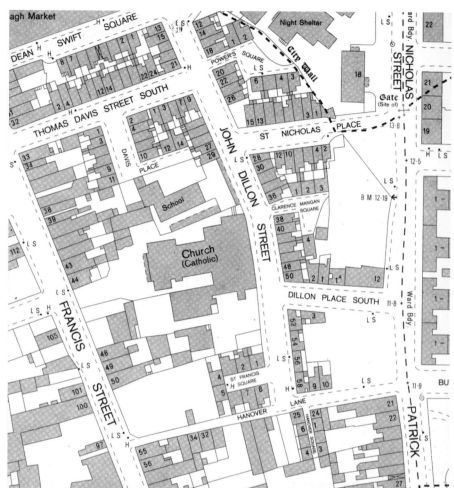

57 The completed scheme at Plunket Street/John Dillon Street). (Ordnance Survey 1:1000. plan, 1971 printing.) Note the Iveagh Trust development to the right of the map.

There was no way of remedying these defects other than by an improvement scheme for the rearrangement of the streets and courts within the entire area.

Despite the unanimity on the need to tackle this particular slum with its 'fever nests and rack rented population', the promoters of the new development faced a succession of obstacles. The original estimate for the purchase of the three acre (*c.*1.2 ha) site was £12,470; the provisional order to enable the Corporation to carry out the scheme was issued and confirmed by Parliament in 1880 and a loan of £15,000 from the Commissioners of Public Works in Ireland was secured; by 1882 it was found that the purchase cost alone of the interests affected by the scheme was £19,115. Application was made to the Local Government

Board to sanction an extension of their borrowing powers by another £12,000. While permission was granted in November 1882, the loan could not be made available (under regulations enforced by the Commissioners of Public Works) until after April 1883. For financial reasons the committee was not able to push forward the scheme as vigorously as they desired, and the local parish priest, Fr James Daniel, who had assisted Mr Gray in clearing the locality six years earlier, complained that the foundation stone had still not been laid. The final cost of clearing the site and making roads, sewers and footpaths was £27,000, well over twice the original estimate (Housing Inquiry, 1885, qs 21,917). The scheme was also greatly delayed by problems in acquiring title to the various properties but it was largely completed by 1887.

The Plunket Street area had featured in Whitelaw's survey of 1805 when he noted that it was more densely populated than the Coombe. He found that 32 contiguous houses contained 917 people, or an average of 28.7 per house. In 1876 Dr Mapother recommended that at least thirty eight of the premises be demolished. A later investigation (Harty, 1884) revealed that some at least of the Plunket Street houses had no sanitary accommodation whatsoever. The first 1:10560 edition of the Ordnance Survey (Figure 58) illustrates the 'narrow and crowded lanes', their 'defective air space, absence of yards and therefore of suitable sanitary accommodation' that made the application of the Artizans' and Labourers' Dwellings Improvement Act to this area 'imperatively necessary' (RPDCD, 1879, 3, pp 616–7). By 1879 there were 1619 persons living in the area, occupying 161 dwelling-houses, of which 28 had been compulsorily detenanted, and not one of which could be regarded as substantial and healthy. The population, with the exception of some butchers, was entirely of the 'humblest class,' and as was the case with the Coombe scheme the best that was hoped was that it would indirectly benefit these poor people:

> There are no manufactories or industries within it, but in its immediate vicinity there are several which afford a considerable amount of employment, and as the dwellings of the artizans and labouring classes in the neighbourhood are of a wretched description, there would be a ready demand for suitable accommodation by an industrious class when erected on this site, and a great social and sanitary improvement would thereby be effected.
>
> (RPDCD, 1879, 3, pp 616–17)

The rehousing clauses of the Act made the developers' task particularly difficult here. It was recognized by the simple process of arithmetic that it would be necessary to build large blocks if the same number of people were to be housed on the same site. Thus people had to be displaced. Some of those displaced had lost their business premises, and the legislation under which the site was cleared precluded any commercial development, despite evidence that the provision of a number of shops and stalls to accommodate the numerous traders who were displaced by the removal of the buildings in Blackhall Market (off Blackhall Row) was greatly needed. This was doubly to be regretted, as the Corporation was thus deprived of a considerable return that might be had if the Corporation was allowed to put the site to the most advantageous purpose.

The Plunket street scheme was confined to a more irregular and broken site than that made available in the earlier Coombe venture. A comparison of the pre-development situation (see Figure 58) with a modern map shows how this site was handled – two-storey (and a few single-storey) houses faced wide, 'healthful' thoroughfares, such as John Dillon Street, Dean Swift Square and Thomas Davis Street, while single-storey cottages faced on to small but open areas, such as Power Square, Dillon Place, and Francis Square. The scheme was bounded in part by the medieval city wall, and set in the midst of very mixed land uses, including a bakery, dairy yards and workshops and the tenement houses of Francis Street and Patrick Street.

The dwellings proposed for the Plunket Street site were to reflect the best sanitary practices, an advance even on the Coombe scheme, as the building conditions spelt out. The whole area of each dwelling and its entire yard space was to be covered with asphalt or waterproof concrete and efficient damp coursing was to be strategically located. Every room had a fireplace and a chimney flue, each ground floor was to be between six and nine inches above the level of the adjoining footway or open space, and each dwelling was provided with a separate water closet. The requirement that the WC be a room separated from all others and with direct ventilation was in line with the most recent advances in 'sanatory [sic] science'. In matters concerning sewers, water pipes, ventilation, and the removal of ashes, all was to be done in accord with the bye-laws and to the satisfaction of the Public Health Committee. Each tenant was to have a key to their house, not as a security concern as might occur today but rather to prevent passers-by from using the sanitary facilities.

The consequence for the poorest of such redevelopment was the loss of affordable, if substandard, accommodation, and their dilemma was repeatedly publicized, to little avail, by medical officers such as Dr Cameron. Even as the first Coombe scheme was under construction he could foresee how slum clearance that resulted in expensive dwellings, all at massive cost to the rate payer, by-passed the poorest citizens, those whom it was plain were in most urgent need of State subsidy. His target group was enormous but readily defined as the thousands who could only manage to pay on average 1s. 6d. per week rent, 'not one in fifty of whom can afford to pay the rents demanded for apartments in the industrial tenement dwellings' (Cameron, 1879, p. 153).

The first occupants of the Coombe scheme represented forty nine different occupations. Among 210 households, the largest single grouping, 61 families, was headed by labourers, fourteen were headed by widows, 8 by carpenters, 7 each by pensioners, bricklayers, tailors, 6 by cutters, 5 each by porters, coopers, 4 each by vanmen, bakers, compositors, brush makers, book binders, boot-makers, bricklayers and soldiers, while the remainder were divided among policemen, cab owners, clerks, engine drivers, plasterers, shoemakers, skinners, travellers, and others. What united this diverse grouping was full-time, reliable employment, allowing each family faithfully to meet a rent of from 3s. 6d. to 7s. each week, for in this scheme it was boasted that the bad debts were practically nil (Harty, 1884, p. 514).

The advantage of control by a single company, in this case the DADC, was that through its tight administration property was kept in excellent repair, subletting was prevented, and a 'better class' of people consequently kept together. The social distance between the residents of the two new schemes and those of the surrounding slums was emphasized; in the Coombe 'the houses also show the improved tone in the people, cleanliness and neatness, windows decorated with flowers, books, neat blinds are everywhere to be seen'. Such efforts were encouraged by the benevolence of Lord and Lady Brabazon who gave prizes for the best kept houses and best window gardening. Being of a 'better class' than the persons displaced, the benefits to traders in the area were also held to be considerable, while the contributions to the municipal and poor law rates had increased tenfold, from an average of £63 per annum collected on the former property, to a total of £611 collected from the new housing.

While excessive claims and valuations made for the old house property required to clear the Coombe and the Plunket Street areas were frequently cited as the major prohibition on further redevelopment, fervent hopes were still expressed that the Corporation might be enabled to persevere in such slum clearance. But the financial and legislative obstacles were such that there was a definite shift towards tackling problems with individual houses; the notion of 'social housing' or building purposely for a loss-making situation was as yet inconceivable (Neville, 1884, p. 477).

Some further distinctions between the Coombe scheme and the Plunket Street schemes were that in the latter the Corporation wrote into the conditions of sale the rents that could be charged, ranging from 2*s.* 6*d.* to 6*s.* per week, so that the cottages might be let at a rent that the people could afford to pay, a curb on strictly commercial considerations that would have allowed the DADC to charge more, and a recognition that the covenant in the Coombe lease to house persons of the 'artizans and working classes' needed to be spelled out. It can be interpreted as another small step in the move on the Corporation's part towards more active regulation of the housing market, at least as it affected the poorer sectors of society. There was also a greater proportion of larger two-storey houses in the Plunket Street scheme than in the Coombe, with 73 two-storey and 44 single-storey cottages and 24 tenements – a recognition that very small houses did not meet the needs of the average Dublin family (Housing Inquiry, 1885, qs 21,919, p. 8).

The cost of clearing 'purlieus' by the compulsory purchase of wretched old houses made city centre schemes prohibitively expensive; Cameron, quoted in an Appendix to the 1885 Housing Inquiry, claimed that all the premises acquired for the Coombe and Plunket Street schemes were unlikely to realize £20,000 if voluntarily disposed of; the Corporation paid almost £52,000 (1885, A(3), pp 102–3). Building for the very poorest could never be recouped in rents, so that without assistance from Central Government it was regarded as impossible, although in 1899 it was noted that the London County Council had adopted the principle of providing dwellings at a loss to the ratepayers, in a special case (Eason, 1899, p. 398). The Coombe and Plunket Street schemes were so expensive that further developments were to be very slow and cheaper suburban schemes increasingly favoured.

Lack of progress in the clearing of the condemned areas identified in 1876 was noted in the Public Health Committee's report for 1879, but even those first small-scale efforts had exposed the very heart of the Dublin slum problem. The residents of the worst slum areas, the citizens most in need of improved accommodation, and least able to procure it by their own unaided efforts, were entirely by-passed by the new developments. In fact, some feared that the DADC schemes by providing for a select number of families of a more 'thrifty' section than the working class in the process were leaving a 'residuum' who are 'by picking out the better people among them even in a more squalid condition on the average than before' (evidence of F.W. Pim,

Housing Inquiry, 1885, qs 22,638, p. 33). The model lodging houses and artizans' dwellings erected in Dublin brought no advantage to the poorest, the very persons whose condition gave, it was noted, employment for the sanitary police. It was they who overcrowded rooms, who had insufficient sanitary accommodation, who lived in the most dilapidated houses, in the narrowest and most crowded courts and lanes, in old stables and in outhouses, more or less ruinous. It was for the thousands of families paying an average of 2s. 6d. per week rent that accommodation was urgently required and not the perhaps two per cent who could afford the rents in the new schemes. One proposal, untried, was to erect quadrangular blocks of cottages, each of which could be let for from 1s. 6d. to 2s. 6d. per week, 'the quadrangular form would admit of the cottages being economically provided with water and gaslight'. 'Until such accommodation as this is provided for the poorest class of the population, it will be very difficult to enforce a proper sanitary state of things among them. So soon as they are forced to leave one place, they go into another equally unfit to live in' (*Report on public health*, 1879, p. 155).

The schemes of the 1870s and 1880s were small scale, experimental and wholly inadequate; however they at least stoked the debate about how to house the poorer people of the city. Though the Corporation eventually began to build on its own behalf, the scale of these developments and the amount of housing provided in the years up to the 1913 Housing Inquiry was insufficient. It was not until the early-1920s that the Corporation had finally accepted that large scale suburban developments were necessary if the housing crisis was to be tackled. However, though it was not a major builder, the Corporation nonetheless did devote greater attention to improving the sanitary state of the existing housing stock.

Block dwellings and tenement refurbishment

While the market for low rent city housing was dominated by one-family houses converted, however unsatisfactorily, to tenement use, and the DADC and similar private companies were building small new houses for a more secure artizan class, there were also attempts to ameliorate the slum situation by building block dwellings. Such apartment complexes accommodated more persons per area cleared, and were thus essential if the requirement to rehouse the number displaced from densely packed slums was to be fulfilled. Despite such an obvious point in their favour, there was much public disquiet attached to the issue. Witnesses to the 1885 Housing Inquiry, such as the Revd James

Daniel, maintained that 'the small houses are preferable, the people themselves prefer them, they give them a sort of homeliness' (qs 22,490), while residents from the DADC blocks in Buckingham Street and Dominick Street reportedly disliked them greatly, abandoning them for small houses whenever possible. However, several flat complexes were built before the end of the nineteenth century; by far the principal and most successful scheme was the Bull Alley project undertaken by the philanthropic Iveagh Trust from 1889 onwards. The Corporation also built blocks at Barrack Street (Benburb Street) and Bride Street. Small-scale blocks were erected on Aston Quay (Crampton Buildings), Echlin Street, Dominick Street, and Stafford Street (McCullough, 1989, p. 94).

The Iveagh Trust scheme

The impact on the Dublin landscape of the Guinness sponsored Iveagh Trust complex between Patrick Street and Bride Street is so striking (Figures 59 and 60) that particular note must be made of it. This complex was by far the single most ambitious philanthropic housing project undertaken in any part of Ireland. Although it must be considered the flagship Iveagh Trust project, it was not the Trust's sole investment, with the earlier Kevin Street block dwellings, shielded from view by later Corporation flats, another ambitious undertaking. Dublin's Iveagh Trust dwellings must also be viewed within an international context; most obviously, as the Guinness family established their trust to operate in both London and Dublin, but also as part of the larger movement towards the construction of 'model' dwellings in large blocks on city centre sites. This was a form of social engineering and architectural experimentation that was unfailingly controversial, as the persons housed were rarely of the poorest classes that most needed the benefit of subsidized good quality housing (Stedman Jones, 1984, pp 183–8).

The Guinness family's role in providing low-rent but good quality housing dates from 1872 when the Belle Vue buildings beside the James' Gate brewery were erected to house the company's own labourers, followed by further such tied housing in Rialto in 1882. These two brewery schemes accommodated a total of 180 families according to the housing inquiry of 1885. Six were three-bedroomed 'cottage class', the others were described as 'separate dwellings', each with its own hall door and key, water supply, water closet, scullery, sharing only a common staircase, variously described as 'exceptionally strongly built' and what some would even consider 'unnecessarily good'. The high standard of this early model housing was claimed to have brought immediate benefits to the health of the occupants, with rickets, so common among those in 'wretched hovels' in the nearby slums, virtually unknown among these children. However, access was limited to Guinness employees only and served only 14 per cent of the 1600 labouring men (as distinct from clerks) that the company employed. Its benefits were very strictly confined. Major investment in the DADC from its inauguration in 1876 extended the family's role in ameliorating poor housing conditions, but it was through the Guinness Trust (1890) funding for the amelioration of the condition of the poorer of the working classes in London and Dublin that the family made the greatest impact on slum geography (Aalen, 1990).

A comparison of the maps pre- and post-development (Figure 58) illustrates the scale of the Trust's accomplishments in the case of the Bull Alley estate. In 1899 Lord Iveagh obtained powers under the Dublin Improvement (Bull Alley Area) Act to acquire and clear the area between Bride Road and Bull Alley and erect new buildings on it, entirely at his own expense. Control and management of the buildings was by 1903 invested in what was renamed the Iveagh Trust. An area of notoriously poor and densely packed housing, along narrow alleys and closed courts, the intermixing of slaughter houses and other noxious land uses did little to improve the ambience. A branch of the River Poddle ran underground through part of the site, complicating the engineering task in a most expensive manner, while the scheme also required the obliteration of an early ecclesiastical site, the church and yard of St Bride's. Wholesale but phased slum clearance led to a fundamental remodelling of the area, with St Patrick's Park (1897) providing a gracious and civilized setting for the national cathedral of the Church of Ireland, and the Bull Alley buildings, incorporating family dwellings and ground floor shops in eight T-shaped blocks each of five storeys, and a lodging house for men facing Bride Road (1905). To complete the complex the Iveagh Baths (1906), including male and female baths as well as a swimming pool, was erected by the Trust on Corporation land facing the men's hostel, while a very large two-storied play centre (1915) with a splendid baroque facade was erected north of the park. Within the scheme high standards of construction and sanitary services were matched by close supervision of the tenantry, facilitated by perimeter gates controlling access and its overall self-contained design. The range of accommodation varied, from single-room tenements (144 square feet or 13.4 square metres), at rents of 2s. 6d. per week, to three-roomed self-contained tenements, with own laundry and toilet facilities at 5s. 9d. per week. Associated with the Bull Alley scheme was the

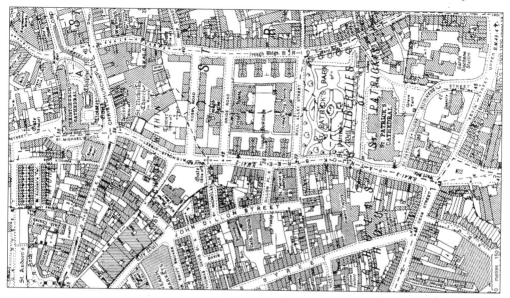

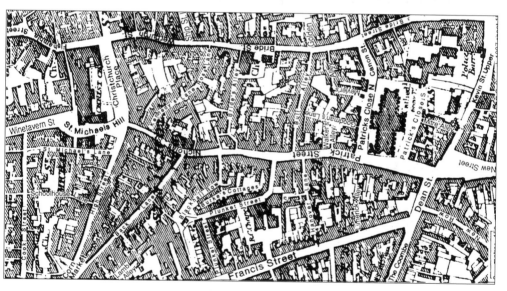

58 The Iveagh Trust (Patrick Street) development. The upper image shows the Iveagh Trust development with the slightly later Corporation development at Ross Road and is taken from the 1:2500 Ordnance Survey plan (1939). The lower image is an extract from the first edition 1:10560 Ordnance Survey map of 1837 and shows the area prior to redevelopment.

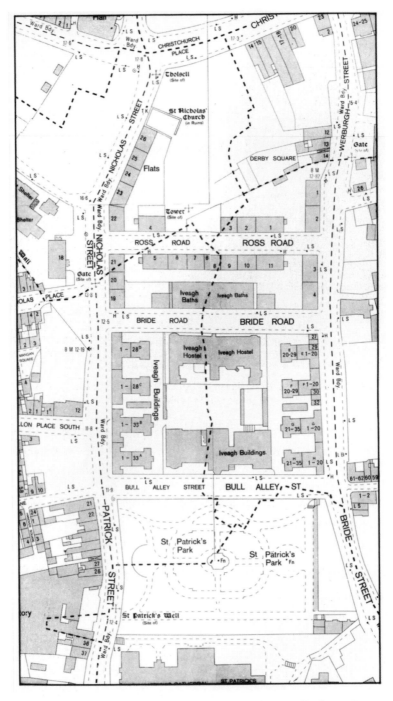

59 The layout of the Iveagh Trust development, Patrick Street. (Ordnance Survey 1:1000 plan, 1971 printing.) Note the Iveagh Baths and the Iveagh Hostel.

60 The Iveagh Trust development on Patrick Street before the road widening programme of the early 1990s. (Photograph by J. Brady.)

Iveagh Market in Francis Street for the sale of vegetables, fish and secondhand clothes, with a disinfecting chamber for old clothes. This was to accommodate the dealers who were dispossessed by the Patrick Street clearance. To the north of Bride Road, the Corporation erected its own less ornate flat blocks, continuing the line of five-storey red-brick dwellings as far as the ruined Church of St Nicholas (Figure 59).

Condemnation and closing of insanitary dwellings, 1879–82

In 1879 the Corporation was for the first time provided with the necessary funds, through the Improvement Rate, to begin a more effective process of sanitary reform under the direction of Dr Cameron. The formulation of this plan of campaign was heavily influenced by the Coombe experience; it was clear that the Corporation could not afford to follow the route of wholesale slum clearance for quite some time, but the crisis demanded effective action immediately. In the face of a task of impossible proportions, the Public Health

Committee formally determined in September 1879 that 'it would be better to prune out here and there throughout the city houses in narrow alleyways and courts than to clear out a whole district'. The Committee judged that there were about twenty courts in Dublin that should be razed, adding that 'some of them are in the best quarters of the city' (RPDCD, 1879, p. 931). The slum geography was more accurately known in 1882 when Cameron directed a 'sanitary survey' of all the inhabited houses in Dublin, resulting in the discovery that 30 per cent of the city's housing stock was occupied by 59 per cent of the city's families, at the rate of 1.5 rooms per family (RPDCD, 1888, 3, p. 778).

A veritable crusade was launched by Dr Cameron and his newly enlarged staff and they had considerable initial success. The total number of houses closed and detenanted as unfit for human habitation from 31 August 1879 to 31 December 1882 was 1345, with 389 cellars and 'several hundreds of rooms' also closed. By 1886 a further 721 houses had been closed. The 1883 report of the Public Health Committee lists a total of 841 addresses of premises recently detenanted, which may be regarded as a good sample of the total number condemned and successfully closed (RPDCD, 1883, pp 873–88).

A block of houses extending from St Michael's Hill to St Michael's Lane and adjoining the Synod Hall of Christ Church cathedral was cleared despite strenuous objections. These houses were regarded as typical of the closures being effected, in this instance being incapable of conversion to healthy dwellings because of their three-storey and quadrangular form; the central yard was only a few square feet in extent and housed the toilet provision for 150 persons, the 'oozings from the filthy so called ashpit permeated through the foundations of the houses, and ascended through their walls, rendering them damp and noisome'. The stairs were dark and the doors of the rooms opened out onto 'dimly lit and ill-ventilated lobbies' (Housing Inquiry, 1885, A(3), p. 102). As there was no proper way of ventilating the building, condemnation was inevitable.

The most striking feature of the closures is the widespread dispersal of such dwellings; apart from the well known high status residential squares and the city centre, there is scarcely a part of Dublin which did not contain at least some substandard dwellings. Cameron's statement at the Housing Inquiry of 1885 was clearly well founded:

> In British cities we usually find good, bad and indifferent quarters, but always distinct, whilst in Dublin there is really no district which is not permeated with purlieus. Some of the poorest and most decayed streets

exist in actual contact with the most fashionable squares and streets. A wretchedly poor population, occupying decayed houses, inhabit the space between St Stephen's Green and Fitzwilliam Square. The stables, in lanes lying in the rear of Merrion Square, have been in great part converted into dwelling-houses. The neighbourhood of Upper and Lower Mount Street teems with a poverty stricken population. Unlike most other great cities, the worst part of Dublin lies to the west. Here there is not a single large street in which tenement houses do not form the major portion of the buildings.

(Housing Inquiry, 1885, A(3), p. 103)

The problems met with by the officers were immense, as rack-renting was a most lucrative and widespread occupation. Members of a Royal Commission in 1880 personally visited a selection of tenement houses, and reported in 'very strong language' on what they found. In one case the rent of a dilapidated house was £10 a year, but the middleman succeeded in extracting £240 from the tenants. Five individuals owned between them 1100 houses; the gross rents of these houses totalled £5,500 a year, resulting in an income of over £1100 per 'house farmer' per year. The house at 36 Upper Mercer Street, rateable value £18, was home to eleven families, totalling thirty seven individuals, yielding an annual rent of over £74. These property owners, who lived by extracting the largest amount of rent possible out of the tenants, were a powerful lobby, and as a number of Corporation members were also tenement landlords the sanitary officials were limited in what they could effect. Confusion surrounding title to land and buildings, where there were sometimes six owners to a house, was a further complication that profited the landlord and middleman. So, too, concern over the lack of alternative accommodation for those evicted could interfere with the processing of orders condemning a house, as in the case of derelict houses 'the magistrates do not feel themselves warranted in giving orders to turn out tenants from such houses when the landlord has failed to evict them and or there is no owner found' (Norwood, 1873, p. 235).

The city engineer, Parke Neville, drew attention to the fate of many of the houses that had been detenanted and closed up by the medical sanitary officer's orders, many of which were 'quickly broken into by the roughs and wreckers, who gut them'. Where houses were taken down by the owners as ruinous, or, in their default, by men employed by the city engineer, there was little prospect of new buildings, and the sites were left as wasteland. In practice the distribution of houses closed under orders prefigured the distribution of long-derelict sites. The very indication of an intention to act against a property was sufficient to ensure that a grossly inflated valuation would be obtained. These valuations, often upheld at law, placed a significant burden on the city and thereby reduced its ability to act.

The number of house closures effected by the sanitary officials was repeatedly upheld as a sign of the Corporation's determination to ameliorate the slum situation. At the Royal Commission in 1880, 2300 houses were reported as unfit for human habitation; at the 1885 Housing Inquiry, it was claimed that 1875 of these had been de-tenanted and closed. However, no mention was made of the number of other houses which had deteriorated in the meantime and were now seriously substandard. The policy also resulted in the creation of widespread wasteland, for example in Wood Street and Boyne Street, where it was claimed at the Housing Enquiry of 1885 by Edward Spenser of the DADC that no rebuilding was possible because of short or uncertain leases and speculation over the Corporation's future plans for the area.

The condemnation and successful closure of individual tenement houses was not the end of the story, for the houses could be reoccupied once the sanitary staff were satisfied with the improvements effected. Only about one third of those de-tenanted were closed permanently, according to the Corporation (RPDCD, 1888, 3, p. 778) and in evidence before the Housing Inquiry of 1885 the chairman of the Dublin Sanitary Association, F.W. Pim, agreed that a large number of houses were surreptitiously reopened without any regard whatsoever for the Corporation's sanitary regulations (qs 22,642–8, p. 33). Thomas Grimshaw, registrar general, could positively list such instances, such as Meath Market off Meath Street, where ten of the twelve houses 'completely closed up' as unfit in every way were fully occupied (qs 23,105–8).

One further stumbling block to the closure of unhealthy dwellings was the unsatisfactory definition of 'overcrowding'. Under the Public Health Act of 1878 (largely the English Act of 1874) local authorities were enabled to enforce their own bye-laws to regulate overcrowding. Dublin Corporation had adopted a widely used standard of 300 cubic feet (8.5 cubic metres) of space per person, a measure that was applicable to the terraces and courts of very small houses built in British industrial cities, but irrelevant in the context of Dublin, where lofty ceilings in even the worst tenement houses ensured that on paper at least each occupant enjoyed plenty of air. In Dublin, where 12 families were found occupying 12 rooms, but each person had more than the standard of air, they could not be moved. And these were the very circumstances where disease was most rapidly communicated. The move to abandon this benchmark was very slow, as it was one of the few measures of 'slumness' that allowed comparison across the board; gradually the separation of the sexes became more significant.

Public health reports

It will be useful at this point to take a more detailed look at the state of public health and the endeavours of Cameron. Much detail is provided in the *Returns of sanitary operations* and the *Reports upon the nature of public health*. The principal endeavours in 1883, for example, were in the areas of inspecting and cleansing sewers, privies, water closets, dwellings, and yards, with some construction of sanitary conveniences. Inspections were also undertaken of bakeries, slaughterhouses and dairy yards, while the disinfecting of articles and the serving of notices and summonses for sanitary offences were also key matters. The commiittee also made public the names of the owners who were fined for the insanitary state of their dwellings, those from whom fines were recovered (131 cases), those who had the fines remitted (12 cases), and those who had failed to pay up and for whom either a warrant of distress was issued (15 cases), or an order committing them to prison had been made (30 cases). One owner, Daniel Connell of Price's Court, was already in prison for defying the magistrate's orders and refusing to pay the fine. The fines in question ranged largely from 5s. to £1, although in a few cases went as high as £6 and £7; the publication of lists of offenders was part of the effort to sway public opinion to regard sanitary crimes as despicable, a shift that would take many decades to achieve.

In his *Report upon the nature of public health* some ten years later (1893), Dr Cameron noted that while the number of sanitary defects had been up to the average, on the whole they were not of as serious a nature as had been the case in previous years. In general, he felt that conditions were improving due, in no small measure, to the activities of his staff. He claimed that during the previous twelve years that '2700 of the 8000 houses in which 60 per cent of the inhabitants of Dublin resided have been de-tenanted' (p. 85). About 350 of these houses had been demolished, never to be rebuilt since their site and situation were unsuitable. Some hundreds more had been demolished but were likely to re-appear. The remainder had been improved sufficiently to permit their use again. He also made the point that, of the remainder, there were very few that were not the subject of orders requiring repairs or alterations. On the whole, he took satisfaction that the tenements of Dublin were in at least as good order as those of London and other large towns. In particular he gave a detailed account of a fieldtrip to London wherein he described conditions as he met them. His conclusion was that he 'did not find that they were in a better state than they are in Dublin, though their rents are nearly twice as great' (p. 86). It would have been a small comfort, however, for those living in these conditions in Dublin to find that they were, on the whole, no worse than elsewhere.

Retrospect

The nineteenth century was a difficult period in Dublin's history. The control of infectious disease and an ever deepening housing crisis dominated the century. By the 1830s the predisposing causes of the recurrent epidemics had been accurately located in damp, overcrowded, poorly ventilated tenement houses packed with families and lodgers from garret to cellar, with no indoor toilets let alone facilities for bathing, and overpoweringly filthy privies in enclosed yards neglected by landlord and tenants alike. Expert analysis of the city's health and housing malaise was not wanting; the real problem lay in the deep seated poverty and political powerlessness that engulfed a large section of the citizenry. The built fabric and urban morphology inherited from preceding generations were pressed into serving this huge demand for city centre housing, close to work opportunities in markets, docks and workshops. From the decaying merchant houses of the medieval core to the mansions of Henrietta Street in the Gardiner district, homes designed for one family were repeatedly subdivided and sublet, while even the most enclosed and airless spaces in backyards and gardens, in courts and alleys, were filled with poorly built and even more poorly serviced cottages. The Royal Commission on the Sewerage and Drainage of Dublin, which sat in the autumn of 1879 and presented its report the following June, had dispelled whatever fond notions still persisted about the slum housing question 'settling itself' with the aid of occasional inspection and fines. 'All that preliminary inquiry can do has been done effectually, and what is now needed is the application of practical and speedy remedies' (Falkiner, 1882, p. 263). The 1870s marked the beginning of effective if very small scale action by the city Corporation – the identification of black spots requiring to be eliminated through (initially) the creation and widening of passageways to allow the dispersal of effluvia-laden air (Mapother, 1876), which in practice became wholesale but expensive clearance of small

61 Housing along Wood Quay in 1878. ('Dublin Illustrated' – *The Graphic*, 1878.)

areas (the Coombe, *c.*1879; Plunket Street, *c.*1887), which were then handed over to a philanthropic company, the DADC, for the erection and management of housing for artizans; in practice, for the most 'respectable' members of the working or lower middle classes who were in regular employment.

The painstaking inspection of unfit houses and the harassment of owners and occupiers to put them in order or face prosecution employed the energies of the Corporation's small sanitary staff to the fullest from 1879. Falkiner, in his presentation to the Social Science Congress in Dublin, October 1881, claimed that the state of the dwellings of the poor is now 'fully recognized as one of the most potent causes of all that is deplorable in the sanitary and social conditions of this city', marking the trend in favour of further state interference in domestic circumstances (Falkiner 1882, p. 263). The only long term solution, the provision of large scale social housing for the urban masses who would never, ever, be able to bear the real cost of constructing and occupying 'sanitary' housing, required such a major shift in public opinion that it could only be achieved gradually. By the end of the century it was becoming just about possible to conceive of the municipality itself investing in loss making housing for the public good, a political stance that would have been inconceivable only a few decades earlier. Progress certainly, but from a rather low base and leaving a great deal to be accomplished in the next century.

But while plans for new urban and, ultimately, suburban estates slowly began to take shape, one of the principal questions that vexed the zealous surveyors at the opening of the nineteenth century continued to break the hearts of sanitary and medical officers alike as the century closed. It is well perhaps to end on this note of realism. Who owned individual tenement houses? Who, if anyone, was in charge? Where shacks continued to be built in back yards without reference to sewers or water supply, and once stately drawing rooms were packed beyond capacity, to whom could neighbours at risk appeal?

Under the Artizans' and Labourers' Dwellings Act, 1868 (Torrens Act), the local authority could, on the report of their medical officer of health that a premises was 'in a state injurious to health, or unfit for human habitation', require the owner to rectify the situation. In default the Corporation could carry out the necessary work itself, and obtain a court order demanding payment from the owner. Such a provision, 'most useful in intention and just in principle' was utterly unworkable in the case of the Dublin tenements. Both the officer of health and the engineer had to prepare reports to determine if the dwelling could be made fit or if demolition was required. Both reports had to be served on the owner, a sitting of the local authority to hear objections had to be held, then the plans had to be prepared, then a second sitting to hear objections to these, and at each stage there was the possibility of appeals to Quarter Session and then to the Queen's Bench, so that each step of the proceedings was separated by weeks if not months of delay. Pending final appeal no work could be done.

The term 'owner' was complicated beyond belief in the case of the Dublin tenements; where there were several owners of a single house they often held fractional undivided shares in common. Where there were several owners the right of carrying out the work had to be offered to each in turn, 'in order of title'. The owner ordered to execute the work had the option of demolishing the premises, but was not to prejudice the operation of existing leases in the covenant! Wherever the ownership could be ascertained, the person had some means, and the premises was of sufficient value so that the outlay could be recouped, there was some possibility of the work being done, eventually. The Dublin system of immediate lessors, 'little removed socially from their lodgers, letting in tenements at the last possible shilling and at the least possible outlay' rendered any such hopes futile. The Amendment Act of 1879 brought some slight improvements, but gave the owner the alternative right of compulsory purchase in every case; wherever an owner was compelled to make improvements he/she could require the local authority to purchase the premises.

While wholesale slum clearance had been tried, and the painstaking closure of individual insanitary rooms, cellars and dwelling houses was continuing apace, there were other possibilities that the Corporation was very loathe to explore. Provisions in the Artizans' and Labourers' Dwellings Acts 1875–1879 allowed the Corporation to 'adapt existing buildings and enlarge, repair, and improve them, and fit them with all requisite furniture, fittings and con-veniences'. The Corporation could then retain management and control or sell the property. As the Corporation was already in possession of considerable house property, and there were many other houses that could be made fit by reasonable expenditure, it was considered that such a wise application of civic property would be much more economical and efficient than the acquisition of large areas under the Acts of 1875–9. However, there was little fear of the Corporation taking on the role of landlord. The Public Health (Ireland) Act 1878, by which Government loans could be made available to the Corporation, at three per cent interest and repayable after fifty years, in combination with the Artizans' Dwellings Acts 'recognize the principle of contributing civic property and State assistance to the supply of homes for the working classes, and of placing these directly under the control of the Corporation, both as to property and maintenance'. At the same time, 'the co-operation of private companies and private persons is invited and encouraged'. However, as legislation stood in 1881 the Corporation could establish a supply of model dwellings, but could not allow them to be managed by any body other than itself. Everyone agreed that houses which in separate ownership could not be improved, when successfully grouped together, 'their adjoining open spaces consolidated and made available for the sanitary and convenient requirements of all' and under effective supervision could be made most acceptable. Private commercial companies, however, working even for moderate profits, could not afford the initial investment, and the Corporation did not see its remit extending to the long term management of such ventures.

In the remodelling and management of nineteenth-century Dublin, exceptional expertise in legal matters, along with endless patience and sheer doggedness were required to see through even minimal improvements in the living conditions of the poorest strata of the city's residents. And at the end of the century, a strong stomach was still a pre-requisite for anyone venturing into the worst of the city's courtyard cottages and tenement rooms.

Dublin at the turn of the century

JOSEPH BRADY

Introduction

Dear dirty Dublin – a city in distress 1899–1916 is the title of a book on the city published some years ago (O'Brien, 1982). Certainly there was much to be distressed about in the city during these years. The preceding chapter has shown that there were many serious social problems, at the root of which was the failure to deal adequately with the housing crisis. The epithet 'dear dirty Dublin' had already been in common currency for many years by the beginning of the twentieth century. It has been attributed to Sydney Owensen (Lady Morgan), the nineteenth-century writer whose salon at 39 Kildare Street was an important part of Dublin's cultural life between 1821 and 1839, and perhaps was meant affectionately. However, its use conveyed but one image of the city; an image that many hoped to dispel.

In the introduction to the *Dictionary of Dublin* (1907), the authors take up this theme. They note that 'it is the custom of those who do not know Dublin, or who have only passed through it on a wet depressing day, to speak of it as "a decayed capital", "a city living on the memory of its past", or even to resuscitate the tempting alliteration –"dear dirty Dublin". It therefore may come as a surprise to the visitor to find a bright cheerful city, with plenty going on, and with streets well filled with well dressed and busy people' (Cosgrave and Strangeways, 1907, p.5). It is on this city – the bright and cheerful city – that this chapter will focus. It will not be possible, however, to deal with all aspects of the geography of the city in a single chapter and so it is necessary to be selective. The chapter will concentrate on the development of the physical fabric of the city and say rather less about its social and economic structure or the political context of the time. This is possible because there are a number of excellent texts dealing with the social life of the city and the reader is directed in particular to Mary Daly's text *Dublin, the deposed capital* (1984) which is still readily available.

The nineteenth century had been eventful for Dublin. Its suburbs had grown and it had developed a class structure with a well-defined spatial pattern. This was facilitated by the introduction of the horse-, and later, electric-trams that linked the suburbs with the commercial centre of the city. Nonetheless the city centre remained the heart and focus of commerce and commuting was even then a fact of life for many people.

Though there had been few grand buildings added to the landscape in the style of the Four Courts or Custom House, except perhaps a number of Catholic churches, the citizens had enjoyed many improvements in the infrastructure of the city. The water supply had been improved, streets and bridges had been straightened and widened and electric light served to keep the city alive after dark. By the end of the nineteenth century, commerce in the city had developed to the extent that problems of traffic congestion, despite the earlier efforts of the Wide Streets Commission, were being discussed and solutions proposed.

The turn of the twentieth century therefore provides an opportunity to look both to the old century and to the new and to try and provide a view of the city as the citizens would have seen it during these first years.

What the visitor saw

The visitor to Dublin in the early years of the twentieth century, using perhaps the popular *Black's Guide* (1908), was encouraged to see the great public buildings such as the Bank of Ireland, Trinity College, the Castle, Christ Church cathedral, the cathedral of St Patrick, and the National Library, taking in what other sights were passed along the way and, of course, visiting St Stephen's Green.

Though more expansive in its treatment, the Corporation's guide to Dublin for 1913 concentrated on much the same features. The visitor was encouraged to visit the Pro-Cathedral and a variety of churches of all denominations. The National University of Ireland on Earlsfort Terrace was suggested in addition to Trinity College. To the Bank of Ireland was added the Four Courts, the King's Inns, the Royal College of Science and the Royal Dublin Society. Interestingly, the list of sights in the city for the visitor was not greatly different to what would have been suggested some fifty years before. If anything the list of attractions is less extensive than that suggested by *Starratt's Guide* in 1849. The city's grandest sites belonged, it appeared, to an earlier age.

The Corporation guide admitted as much. It claims that the visitor could not but be impressed by the magnificent public buildings in the city and asserted that these were the equal of, if not superior to, any city of its size. It noted, however, that practically all of them are in the renaissance style and erected when 'Grattan's Parliament controlled the destiny of Ireland' (Dublin Corporation, 1913, p. 42). Thus most of Dublin's attractions in the early part of the twentieth century harked back to an earlier period in the city's history. The nineteenth century had not been a period of great public building, with perhaps one notable exception to be dealt with later, nor indeed of great commercial building, and the city was fortunate that it had retained the legacy of an earlier period.

The changing civic landscape

It would be incorrect to say that there was no civic building during the nineteenth century nor that there were no fine additions to the urban landscape. In 1818, the opening of the General Post Office (GPO) provided a landmark for Sackville Street. By building in classical form, Francis Johnson carried on the tradition in building of the previous century. It was provided with suitably allegorical statues on its pediment. Hibernia rests on her spear and harped shield while the functions of the building are epitomized by Mercury and Fidelity. The allegories escaped many Dubliners, however, and *Wakeman's Guide to Ireland* (1890) records an apocryphal conversation between a tourist and a jarvey.

> These sculptures are at times somewhat puzzling to the ignorant in allegorical science. It is said that a stranger having asked of the cabby by whom he was being driven the meaning of the figures, was coolly met by the reply that 'they represented the Twelve Apostles'. 'But, man, how can that be when there are only three?' was the next inquiry. The jarvey, unabashed, surveyed his fare with a curious look and immediately exclaimed, 'Faix, thin, it's truth, yer honour, I'm afther tellin' you. You see than in weather like this they only come out three at a time, takin' their turns regular' ... (p. 29)

The GPO was built on the site of a temporary barrack and it was noted that its cost was relatively modest at £50,000. The provision of a post office on this scale was evidence of the continuing and developing commercial life of the city and the country despite the effects of the Act of Union. It replaced the penny post for the Dublin district, founded in 1780 in Fishamble Street, and was the latest of many homes which the post had in the intervening

62 The General Post Office and Sackville Street (Bartlett, 1835).
Note the regular and unified streetscape.

period as increasing business required bigger and better premises. From the GPO the mail-coaches sped nightly with the English mails leaving for Howth each evening at 7.00 p.m.

The city had to wait until close to the end of the century, however, for what was probably the most impressive addition. This was the ensemble of what are now the National Museum, National Library, National Gallery and Natural History Museum. The duke of Leinster had built a fine town palace on Kildare Street where it occupied a large site in keeping with its importance and grandeur. The house was sold to the Royal Dublin Society (RDS) in 1815 for £20,000 and remained their headquarters until they moved to Ballsbridge in the early years of the twentieth century.

The RDS occupied a spacious location as can be seen in the map (Figure 63) and perspective (Figure 64). The map dates from 1836 and was produced by the Society for the Diffusion of Useful Knowledge (SDUK), a London-based organization that, amongst their many activities, produced an atlas of the world including finely engraved plans of major cities. Such atlases are greatly prized today. The perspective is part of the large panorama of the city, viewed from the south-west and was produced by the *Illustrated London News* in 1846

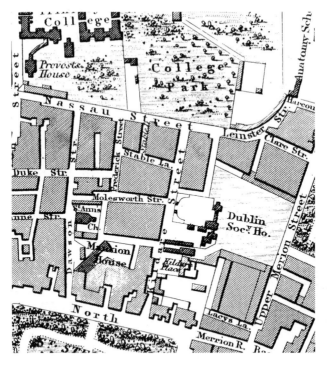

63 The environs of the Royal Dublin Society.
(Society for the Diffusion of Useful Knowledge, 1836.)

as a supplement for their readers, previously introduced in chapter 4. The publishers had intended to produce a series of these panoramas for the main cities of Europe but though a number were produced, no series emerged. Both the map and bird's eye view (Figures 63 and 64) show the considerable space that existed on either side of the house on Kildare Street but more importantly, the great lawn that faced onto Merrion Square. This was to provide a wonderful opportunity for the city of Dublin.

In 1851, London buzzed with the excitement of the Great Exhibition. This was a vast showcase of the industries and manufactures of the Empire and the rest of the world; with a clear aim of showing the superiority of British craftsmanship. The exhibition had its genesis in the French Industrial Exhibition of 1844 and many in Britain demanded that a similar undertaking be held there. The initial official response was lukewarm and it took the endorsement of the prince regent to ensure its success. Albert's plan was for a great collection of works in art and industry which would ultimately encourage British endeavour through competition. It was an opportunity for

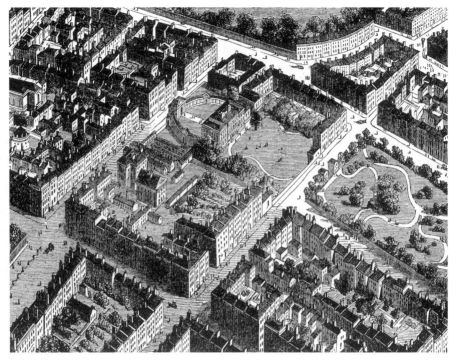

64 The environs of the Royal Dublin Society. (*Illustrated London News*, 1846.)

all humanity to show what they had achieved and a baseline for future progress. A purpose-built exhibition centre provided the opportunity for firms to display their wares to a large and admiring throng of visitors. The illustration below shows the stand of John Henning of Ireland in the south-west nave who displayed 'royal Irish cambric dresses'. What could be done in London, and thereafter in Cork, could be done in Dublin and to the same effect.

Thus it came to pass that an Irish Industrial Exhibition was planned for Dublin for 1853 and the grounds of the RDS provided the perfect location. The RDS was greatly involved in the preparations and it was often described as the 'Great Industrial Exhibition in connexion with the RDS'. It certainly captured the imagination of the commercial world and newspapers such as the *Freeman's Journal* carried references to the forthcoming exhibition for months beforehand from business people anxious to capitalize on the opportunity. For example, in the issue of 16 April, Wright Bros of 58 Dame Street 'respectfully invite an inspection of our new shaped hats such as we intend sending the forthcoming exhibition'. It was also an opportunity for hotel keepers who were addressed in an advertisement on 2 April by S. Frazer of 45 Mary Street

65 Irish exhibits at the International Exhibition, London.
(*Illustrated London News*, 1852, Special Supplement, 23 January.)

and invited to purchase supplies of knives, forks, spoons etc. to cope with the anticipated demand.

The exhibition was housed in a purpose-built building on the site of Leinster Lawn. It owed much to the London exhibition in design terms and was an imposing affair in steel and glass. The main space of the building was like the nave of a cathedral. It was 425 feet (130 m) in length and 100 feet (30m) high covered by a semi-cylindrical roof comprising one span of 100 feet. On either side were the various courts containing the displays of industry and commerce as well as those of other nations. It must have made a great impression on any visitor and it is all the more a pity that the structure was intended to be temporary.

The exhibition opened on 12 May 1853 causing traffic chaos in the city, with complicated diversions and street closures. It was an important occasion for Irish manufactures but it was the inclusion of a picture gallery that was to prove more important in terms of the post-exhibition use of the site. On 9 April previously, in a leader, the *Freeman's Journal* referred to a suggestion that

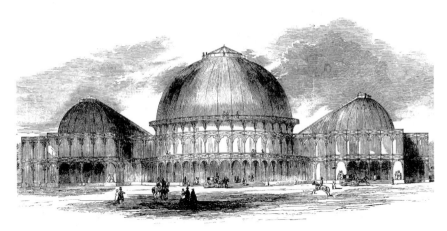

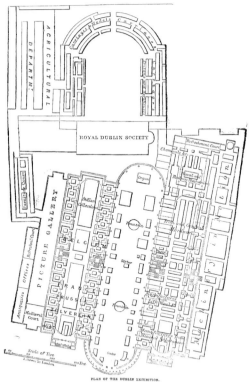

66 The Exhibition building on Merrion Square. The upper image shows the front elevation of the building viewed from Merrion Square (*Illustrated London News*, 23 October 1852), while the ground plan is shown in the lower image (*Illustrated London News*, Special Supplement, 4 June 1853). This plan is oriented so that Merrion Square is at the bottom.

the exhibition should have a gallery devoted to painting, an Irish Gallery. It would be a portrait gallery, not so much for the quality of the art, as for the representation of the great and the good in Irish history. There were, according to the *Journal*, enough portraits around the city and enough people willing to donate them to make the proposal a success. Speaking of the impact of the gallery on a visitor, the writer suggested: 'it would be history teaching [him] by examples – examples of glory achieved in every department of the human intellect. He would learn, perhaps for the first time, Irish greatness in that wide domain, and in learning aspire to imitate'. This was but one straw in the wind but there developed a momentum towards the establishment of a National Gallery.

William Dargan had been the driving force behind the Dublin exhibition. He had made his money from the development of the railways and had contributed some £80,000, perhaps more, to the financing of the Exhibition. He was honoured by a statue in the exhibition but it was decided that a more permanent memorial was needed. As had been agreed, Dargan was given the exhibition hall at the end of its season and for a year or so afterwards it functioned as a tea-house before being dismantled. It was decided to com-memorate Dargan by building a gallery, completed between 1859 and 1864, on the now vacant site. A sum of £5000 was set aside and was augmented by private donations and parliamentary grants. The gallery's holdings were added to over the remaining decades of the century. This was the first of the national institutions to be created around the RDS. The Natural History Museum was placed on the other side of Leinster Lawn. Interestingly, from a geographical point of view, both the gallery and museum were built under the direction of Richard Griffith as chairman of the Board of Works. This was Griffith, the polymath, who produced the very important quarter-inch geological map of Ireland for the Railway Commissioners as well as being responsible for the General Valuation which is such a vital source of information on nineteenth century Ireland.

The map extract below shows this intermediate stage towards the completion of the ensemble. The map from Lett's atlas shows the position in the early 1880s where the gallery and the present Natural History Museum are clearly marked.

The RDS was crucial also in the establishment of the National Library and National Museum. As early as 1836 a Parliamentary Select Committee had recommended that the library of the RDS should broaden its acquisition policy and should function as a national library with improved access to the public. In 1877 the Dublin Science and Art Museum Act established the

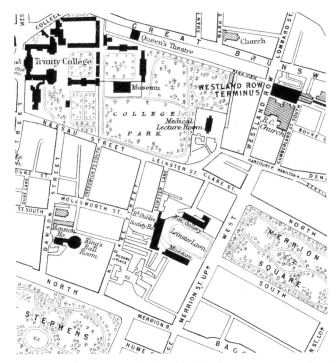

67 The ensemble develops – the Royal Dublin Society environs in the 1880s.
(*Lett's Popular Atlas*, 1881.)

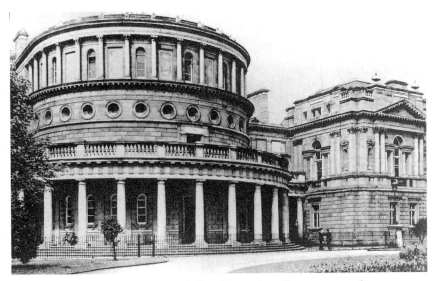

68 The National Library before the security railings were erected
around Leinster House. (Postcard.)

69 The Exhibition Hall, 1865, on Earlsfort Terrace, later demolished.
(*Illustrated London News*, 18 March 1865.)

70 The Exhibition Centre, Herbert Park, 1907, later demolished. (Postcard.)

National Library of Ireland and the National Museum. The RDS provided the nucleus of the library's collection while the Royal Irish Academy donated generously to the museum. The library and museum were designed as a resource for the citizens of Dublin, though not necessarily all of them. It is interesting to note that Fitzpatrick (1907) in his guide to Dublin says that 'an introduction from any respectable resident is generally sufficient to secure the applicant all of the privileges of a reader' (p. 332).

The buildings of the National Library and National Museum were built as a pair to flank Leinster House. They were completed during the period 1883–90 at a cost of £150,000. They are rather tightly fitted into the site and it is not easy to appreciate them, given that Leinster House is inaccessible to the general public. Welcome as this ensemble of buildings might have been to the city, it might be fairly suggested that the contents were more impressive than the architecture.

In turn, both the 1865 and 1907 exhibitions left their mark on the urban landscape. The 1865 exhibition took place in a purpose-built centre that later formed the kernel of the buildings of the Royal University, later University College Dublin. A new façade was given to the buildings in 1915 when it took on the form it retains today. The 1907 Exhibition was suburban, taking place in the Pembroke township. Though none of its buildings remain, the site was redeveloped into Herbert Park through the generosity of the Pembrokes. Another addition, worthy of note, was the South City Markets in South Great George's Street built in 1881 but rebuilt after a fire some eleven years later. More will be said about this development in the later discussion on the geography of this street.

There were more plans than were realized. At the beginning of the nineteenth century the Gardiners (see Chapter 2) had planned a Royal Circus, an impressive housing development, that would have united their various urban properties and provided a focus for the north eastern part of the city. For at least twenty years it appeared on maps of the city of Dublin though it never had any concrete form. Of these virtual projects, perhaps the grandest was that for the Catholic University of Ireland. A foundation stone was laid in 1862 in Drumcondra and the plan was for two quadrangles, one for the university and the other as residences (O'Dwyer, 1981, p. 139). Unfortunately the foundation stone was all that was ever laid of this project and it can be found today in the grounds of the Redemptoristine convent on St Alphonsus Road, Drumcondra, itself soon to be converted to housing. Dublin might have had a theatre to rival the now-lost Theatre Royal had the plans for the

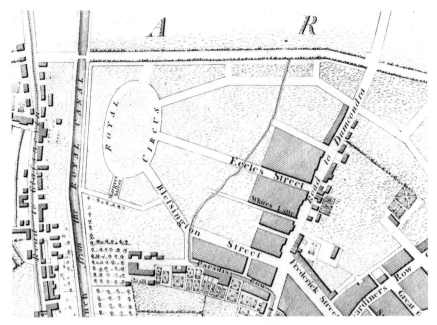

71 The Gardiners' Royal Circus. (Wilson, 1797.)

Lyceum Theatre been realized. This was planned for the junction of Tara Street and Brunswick (Pearse) Street in 1884 and would have held 2500 people.

Changing iconography

These were smaller scale contributions to the urban landscape that were important nonetheless, especially as they mirrored a changing political landscape. The changing political face of the city can be seen in O'Connell Street, still Sackville Street in 1900. The street was given a landmark monument when Nelson's Pillar was placed there in 1808 to commemorate the admiral's victories. The column rose to 134 feet (40.8 metres) with a 13 foot (4 metres) statue of Nelson. It was an imperial monument, with the base proclaiming the location and dates of his victories. It also dominated the street and provided a panoramic view of the city for those prepared to climb the 168 steps. By 1878, increasing nationalism in the city meant that the monument was no longer welcomed by many. In 1891 a Bill was introduced into the House of Commons asking for its removal; it failed. For a number of years previously its removal had been advocated on the grounds that it was a traffic hazard. While this was going on, the street vista was closed at either end by the erection of two equally imposing monuments. Both of these could be seen

72 'Laying the Foundation Stone for the O'Connell Monument'.
(*Illustrated London News*, 20 August 1864). Note the narrowness of Carlisle Bridge.

as traffic hazards, indeed the Parnell Monument is still undoubtedly one, but the key difference was that these were nationalist monuments.

The monument to O'Connell, 'The Liberator', was commended to the early-twentieth-century visitor as one of noblest monuments to be seen anywhere in the city. It was the work of Foley, though completed by Brock, one of his students, who, interestingly, also completed the infamous Gough memorial, which defied numerous attempts at destruction before its final removal. The first stone was laid in 1864 in a great ceremony that brought the city to a standstill and it was unveiled on 15 August 1882. It is a striking monument. The statue of O'Connell is over 12 feet high (3.6 metres) and round the drum on which it stands are almost 50 figures in various stages of relief. In front is an heroic figure of Hibernia trampling her broken fetters with four winged figures at her feet, though every Dubliner refers to them as 'angels', representing Patriotism, Fidelity, Eloquence and Courage. The foundation stone for the Parnell monument was laid in 1899 and was equally impressive. The statue showed Parnell in oratorical pose with arm outstretched: 'no man can put a

stop to the march of a nation' – though
Dublin wags suggested that he was point-
ing to Mooney's pub in Parnell Street or to
the Rotunda maternity hospital.

The street was further augmented by
statues commemorating civic work as well
as national endeavour. Sir John Gray was
commemorated (1879) for his work in
bringing a safe water supply to Dublin
while the statue to Fr Mathew (1893), the
'apostle of temperance' might be seen as an
inducement to Dubliners to drink this
water. The statue to William Smith
O'Brien (1870), now on O'Connell Street,
was originally at the apex of D'Olier Street
and Westmoreland Street until 1929 where
it indeed must have posed a 'hazard to
traffic'.

73 Statue of Sir John Gray,
Sackville Street.

Elsewhere Thomas Moore was honoured by his statue in College Street, a
most infelicitous location given its proximity to a public lavatory and his
association with the 'meeting of the waters'. The statue was not generally
loved. Equally unloved was the memorial to Sir Philip Crampton, the
eminent surgeon, at the D'Olier Street end of College Green (1862), now
removed. Its unusual design earned it the nickname, the 'Cauliflower'.

Wakeman (1890) says, first of the Moore statue, that:

> Of this work a great deal has been written but many think that the less
> said about it the better. It is heavy and commonplace; the drapery
> clumsy and bewildering; and the author of the Irish melodies is
> represented with upraised arm, and pointing finger, as if beckoning for
> a car or cab to 'take him out of that'. It is possibly only not quite so
> displeasing as the neighbouring monument, erected to the memory of
> Sir Philip Crampton, Bart., which stands behind it at the opposite end
> of the street. This very curious structure, was designed as a drinking
> fountain, embowered in lotus leaves, and surmounted by a bust of the
> eminent surgeon. It is now chiefly colonized by a considerable colony
> of sparrows, who are wont to use its numerous crannies as receptacles
> for their nests. (p. 36)

The commemoration of famous Irishmen, particularly in the political field, created an interesting tension with the memorials of imperial Ireland. These additions to the city were the manifestation of a new Dublin or as the 1913 Corporation guide put it 'for many centuries the control of the Dublin Corporation was in the hands of people who had little in sympathy with the great body of the citizens, and it was not till 1841 that a really representative assembly was elected with the great Irish leader, Daniel O'Connell, as the first Lord Mayor' (p. 4). Moreover while there was the 'hope that in a few years [Dublin] will be again the centre of Irish Government' (p. 2), it should be remembered that Dublin 'is at present a prosperous and an attractive place, and one which may be justly termed the second city in the Empire' (p. 3).

Empire could be seen in the other statues that the discerning visitor was directed to view. The statue of William III (1701) still stood in College Green, despite an attempt to blow it up in 1836. George I (1743) held sway in the Mansion House Gardens. George II (1758), for his part, had a place in Stephen's Green. His equestrian statue on a three-tiered plinth was very imposing, though his successors George III and George IV had to be content with an indoor location at City Hall. Victoria reigned in the Kildare Street entrance to Leinster House. This was a quite massive memorial, completed in 1908, showing Victoria in regal pose, flanked by Erin, Peace and Fame. Her late consort, Albert, found it very difficult to secure a place. The Corporation resisted efforts to commemorate him and it was not until 1871 that his monument was completed and took its place in the centre of Leinster Lawn. Their Majesties' tenure was short-lived and one by one they disappeared, sometimes with the aid of explosives. William III and George II were removed in 1928 and 1937, respectively, following explosions. George I was sold in the 1920s to the Barber Institute of Fine Art in Birmingham. Albert was transferred to a quieter location in the Museum of Natural History in 1924, following an unsuccessful attempt to blow him up, where he still languishes. Victoria survived until 1948 when she had to give way to provide car-parking spaces for TDs. She was first transferred to the grounds of the Royal Hospital, Kilmainham and then to Daingen until, on extended loan from the Irish Government, she finally found a home outside the QVB shopping centre in Sydney in the 1990s but without her retinue of Erin, Peace or Fame.

St Stephen's Green was a pleasant place of resort for the population of Dublin at the turn of the century, having been laid out in its present form by Lord Ardilaun, commemorated in turn by a statue in 1880 at a cost of about £20,000. It seemed quite an elegant place in Malton's aquatint view at the end of the eighteenth century. However, Malton comments in the notes on the reverse of this plate that it was only the planting of the lime trees that gave it any real elegance and it was apt to be boggy in the winter. Certainly by the middle of the nineteenth century it was seen by many as rather dreary and unfashionably formal, intersected as it was by walks of mathematical straightness. Ardilaun remodelled the Green with the present ponds and gardens, providing it with a water supply from the Portobello basin, and had it opened to the public. This latter element was very important to the city for though the Phoenix Park on the western edge of the city was accessible and a popular place to visit, the city lacked open green space as neither Merrion Square nor Mountjoy Square were open to the public, both being the prerogative of the property owners of the area.

How the visitor reacted

Dublin, it can be surmised, excited the same range of emotions in visitors then as it does now. Some loved the city and others could not wait to be away from it. Here is one reaction to the city by an anonymous English visitor writing in 1917 in the great tradition of travel writers. He came to Dublin to see the city for himself following the events of Easter week 1916. He was appalled by the way the rebellion had been suppressed and this had heightened his interest in the city. It had made Ireland 'actual' to him and he wanted to build on this feeling.

His initial impression of the inhabitants of the city was that they seemed more at home in an eighteenth-century book than one of the twentieth century. He says that 'they were quite unlike any other English-speaking people with whom I had ever come across. And they appeared altogether lacking in uniformity, tending to go to extremes of ugliness or beauty. No where had I seen so many giants, so many perfectly-formed men and women, and at the same time so many diseased, debased, misshapen, misbegotten or crippled human beings' (Anon., 1917, p. 57).

The anonymous writer took the standard tour. He visited the Four Courts, the Custom House, the King's Inns and the GPO. For him, the Custom House was the loveliest building in Dublin. South of the Liffey, he spent time visiting the two cathedrals, the National Gallery, the Bank of Ireland, the National Library and Trinity College as well as Merrion Square and St Stephen's Green. All of these impressed him and he left the Library declaring it to be 'admirably managed and most clearly of national importance' (p. 67).

His tour was augmented by walks among the Georgian streets both north and south of the Liffey and he found much to admire in North Great George's Street. He noticed, however, the contrast between north and south Dublin and fancied that 'the more elegant Dubliners rarely cross the O'Connell Bridge unless they are on their way to a race meeting in the Phoenix Park or being carried, toes turned up, upon their final journey to Glasnevin' (p. 63).

He was generally positive about the city, something which would have pleased the authors of the guides discussed earlier in this chapter. 'Dublin, despite having acquired a number of unfortunate modern buildings, was still unmistakably a capital city, and not merely a provincial town'. However, the mean streets were not far away as he quite quickly found. He had only to stroll down some of the small streets on either side of Nelson's Pillar on a Saturday night to see scenes quite different to the elegance and ordered life he was used to. He describes scenes of drunkenness, fighting, brawling and intense poverty. In short, this one example would appear to confirm the two views of the city. On the one hand, there is the attractive commercial city with a cosmopolitan air while, never too far away, is the other city so vividly described in the previous chapter in this book.

Infrastructural improvements

Water

Many of the improvements to the city during the nineteenth century would not have been readily apparent to the visitor though s/he would have benefited from them. The city's water supply is nowadays taken for granted but it remains crucial to the life of the city. In fact, probably the single most important limiting factor to development in any city is the availability of a water supply and, by extension, a sewerage system. In the eighteenth century, the city relied on the Poddle as its main source of water and this supply was managed by the building of the City Basin, near James' Street. By the end of that century, this and other sources were no longer adequate and there were constant complaints. Not only was there not enough water, the mains system was heading towards collapse. The records (Gilbert, 1911, 15) for the early years of the nineteenth century contain many references to the efforts of the city authorities to obtain a better water supply, for example the inquiry established in 1799 to examine the adequacy of the system. However, the creation of the canals was a godsend since they were an obvious source of water. The Grand Canal ran close to the City Basin and it was very easy to tap into it while the

74 A prospect of Dublin from the Foster Aqueduct,
Phibsborough, in the early-nineteenth century.

Royal Canal completed the circuit of the city to the north. From the reports,
it appears that the Grand Canal company was easier to deal with whereas
there was considerable discussion with the Royal Canal company before a
satisfactory deal was done on the price to be paid for the canal water.
However, by 17 April 1806 the committee appointed to secure the improved
water supply were able to report that 'the deeds between the Grand Canal and
the Royal Canal, as approved of by both corporations, have been perfected'
(Gilbert, 1911, 15, p. 459). The new supply needed a reservoir and a site was
chosen southward of the Royal Circus for what was to become the Blessington
Basin. On the south side of the city, the supply was assured by the provision
of a third basin at Portobello. The acquisition price for both sites in 1806 was
£1772 9s. 1½d. This was the last occasion on which the reservoirs or basins for

the city's water supply would be within the boundaries of the city. When the
new Corporation took control of the city following the Dublin Improvement
Act (1849), the water supply was one of the issues that they had to deal with.
The supply was intermittent but pressure was also weak. Given the
topography of the canals, there was little or no water pressure beyond that
provided by the natural geography of the city. The reservoirs were only 76–78
feet (c.23m) above OD and this gave a head of only 56–58 feet in the lowest
lying areas of the city and so provided water to ground floors only in many
locations. Supply was improved by the renewal and upgrading of the
distribution system but it was clear that a new supply at high pressure was
needed. The Corporation advertised in 1854 for plans and suggestions and the
evaluation that followed led to the selection of a site on the Vartry river. The
process whereby this decision was reached is outlined by Neville (1874) who
also provides a detailed account of the constuction of the resevoirs and the
piping of the city. It was not an easy process. The canal companies opposed
the move to find a new water supply. They argued that there was no supply like
theirs for quality and cheapness and they managed to defeat a plan that would
have abstracted water from the Liffey near Newbridge by proposing an improved
canal scheme. However, once the Liffey plan was out of the way they reneged
on their plans to improve water pressure. By 1860, plans for a new source of
water were once again under discussion. There were several Liffey plans, one
for the Dodder, another which would have drawn water from the Dargle and
Lough Bray as well as canal projects. A further plan, suggested by Richard
Hassard, was based on the Vartry river but it was the most expensive. The
various proposals were considered by a Royal Commissioner in 1860 who
decided, against expectations, that the Vartry plan was the best. The
Corporation accepted this proposal, and went about seeking the necessary
legislative powers. It was enthusiastically promoted by Sir John Gray, the
chairman of the waterworks committee but they found themselves once more
in conflict with the canal companies and the battle continued to the House of
Lords until the Corporation finally received the royal assent for the Dublin
Corporation Waterworks Act in 1861.

The Vartry scheme had a number of advantages. The fact that the
underlying geology comprised lower Silurian and Cambrian slate meant that
the water was quite pure and soft, the latter providing a distinct advantage
over canal water which was calcareous and furred the piping. The area was
thinly populated and so dislocation was minimized. It was estimated that the
rainfall in the catchment area of the river was sufficient to provide 25 gallons

(114 litres) per day to a population of 400,000 people with an additional 2 million gallons per day (91,000 Hl) for manufacturing. A reservoir was needed and the site chosen was 1.5 miles (2.5 km) south-east of the village of Roundwood and, at a height of 632 feet (192 metres) OD, it was 520 feet (158 metres) above the highest parts of the city of Dublin. Dublin was serviced by distribution reservoirs at Stillorgan and a system of new mains brought modern sanitation to, at least, the prosperous people of the city.

Neville (1874) noted that prior to the introduction of the new supply, people were advised to have their plumbing checked to ensure that it was adequate for the greatly increased pressure. Very few did, with the result that 'rate of pay for plumbers rose to a large premium'. The wastage of water was phenomenal in the early days and even in 1874, people were still using too much; over one-third more than was budgeted for. 'This chiefly [arose] from the carelessness of the public in allowing water taps to remain open (often on purpose with the idea that it flushes the drains), the use of dill closets, and the overflow pipe from the cistern' (p. 30)

The water was also supplied to the townships with the exception of Rathmines which in 1885 was still using canal water. It later decided to source its own supply in the Dublin mountains by building a reservoir at Bohernabreena which was fed by the local watersheds. The other townships paid Dublin Corporation on the basis of the valuation of the township at a rate that varied between 3½d. and 5½d. per £1. In turn, the Corporation guaranteed a supply of 20 gallons (91 litres) per head of population per day. The Vartry scheme continues to supply Dublin but it is now augmented by the more substantial Ballymore-Eustace reservoir.

Railways

The nineteenth century also saw the coming of the railways. Kellett (1969) has argued that 'the Victorian railway was the most important single agency in the transformation of the central area of many of Britain's major cities' (p. 289). This was because it could function only by occupying large tracts of land and so altered the internal geography of many cities, changing their focus and the orientation of their transport routes. Kellett suggests that by 1900 between five and eight per cent of land in the centre of major British cities was occupied by the railways. It was a large and obtrusive land use and once located it often acted as a barrier to future development. Land which was cut off from the remainder of the city by railway yards was often neglected by developers. These locations became the sites of coal and timber yards, warehousing, mixed

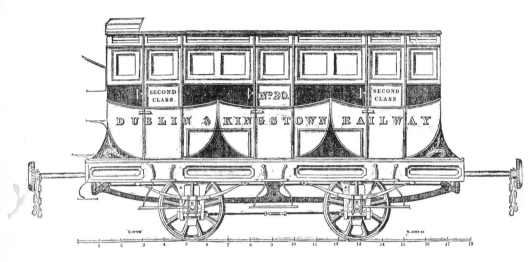

75 One of the first carriages on the Dublin-Kingstown Railway.
(*Dublin Penny Journal*, 1835.)

light and heavy industrial land uses and invariably poor quality housing. The
coming of the railways caused the same problem for Dublin as in other cities.
The railways needed central locations if they were to serve the city and its
population. They also needed large tracts of land, not only for the stations but
for the peripheral works such as machine houses, marshalling yards, storage
and a host of other needs. The track might have to cut through an already
developed area and this was bound to be contentious and expensive. The
result in Dublin was that locations peripheral to the centre were chosen for
the railway termini and circuitous trackways were laid. Thus the Great
Northern Railway (GNR) to the north-east of Ireland had its terminus at
Amiens Street, the Great Southern and Western Railway (GSWR) to the west
terminated at Kingsbridge while the Midland Great Western Railway (MGWR)
to the north was located at Broadstone. The Dublin Wicklow and Wexford
Railway (DWWR) to the south and south-east had discrete termini at
Harcourt Street and Westland Row, the two lines joining beyond Shankill.
The 1849 revision of the first edition Ordnance Survey 6" sheet for Dublin
(1:10,560, Sheet 18) shows the location of these termini quite clearly. The

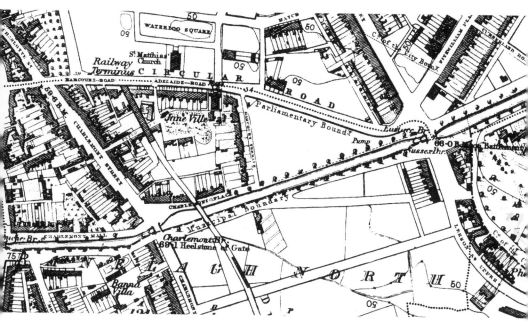

76 The terminus of the Dublin and Wicklow Railway at Harcourt Road.
(Ordnance Survey 1:10,560 plan, Sheet 18 Dublin, 1849 revision.)
Notice the constrained nature of its terminus at Harcourt Road.

Dublin and Wicklow Railway, the 'western' spur of the DWWR, was the most successful at insinuating itself into the urban landscape and managed to do so with a relatively direct route. Only a very basic terminal is shown, though it was later able to expand its site at Harcourt Street. The Dublin and Kingstown Railway, the other component of the DWWR, managed to achieve a central location by taking a quite circuitous route and thus avoided cutting into the expensive housing that blocked its way. The other three termini are quite clearly peripheral at this time. The Broadstone terminus is at the edge of the large institutional complex of the North Dublin Union Workhouse, the Richmond Penitentiary and the Richmond Lunatic asylum. The Kingsbridge terminus is in splendid isolation.

It was a far from ideal system. There were no connections between the stations. This problem was recognized at an early stage and proposals were made as early as 1861 to join up the various termini. There were at least six separate schemes proposed between 1861 and 1865 and in the manner of doing things of the period, each scheme sought the passing of the necessary Act by

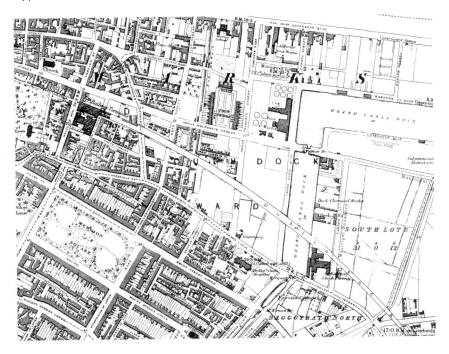

77 The Dublin and Kingstown Line (Ordnance Survey 1:10,560 plan, Sheet 18 Dublin, 1849 revision). Notice the circuitous route from the lower right to avoid the already developed area.

Parliament. However, the Parliament took the view that what was needed was a central station, one that would link all the existing termini; an idea that is still as relevant at the beginning of the twenty-first century. The proposal accepted was for a line from Sandymount to Kingsbridge, via Ringsend, North Wall, Drumcondra, Cabra and the Phoenix Park. The plan was to tunnel under the Liffey and in 1866 work was commenced at the Point Lighthouse but it proved impossible to keep the shafts dry and the project was abandoned. Crossing the Liffey near its mouth proved to be a major obstacle and therefore the first successful linkage of the termini involved an amazingly circuitous route. By tunnelling under the Phoenix Park, the Kingsbridge Line was joined to the MGWR at Glasnevin in 1877. However, the question of linking Westland Row with Amiens Street and, in turn, Amiens Street with the other lines had to be addressed. The pressure came, not from the travelling public, but from the post office. Mails were sent from Kingstown to Westland Row by train where they were transferred to horse-drawn vans and sent to Kingsbridge or Amiens Street. From here they were loaded onto trains again. It was an obvious nonsense.

78 Amiens Street Station showing the Loop Line. (Postcard.)

The DWWR suggested that the simplest answer was an overground line linking Westland Row and Amiens Street which in turn could be linked to the other lines by a circular spur to Newcomen Bridge. Interestingly, it was the Corporation that was most vociferous in its objections. It felt that the line, which would go via Beresford Place, would disfigure the skyline and ruin the prospect of the Custom House. The proposal engendered a hot debate during which a tunnel was ruled out because of the engineering difficulties involved in getting it deep enough below the Liffey in the distances involved. The business case for an over-ground route eventually won out and the Bill was passed in 1882. It took until 1891 before the Loop Line was completed and not without squabbles between the various railway companies but at last the north and south cities were linked by rail. The Loop Line was controversial to begin with and has remained so since. The arguments about its disfiguring nature that were made before its construction have continued to be put during the hundred and more years it has existed. Once again, its removal is on the agenda but it would be a very optimistic person who would envisage seeing its early removal. The system was further developed by extensions to the north wall steamboat connections for passengers and goods. In 1901, the GSW made a branch line for themselves from Kingsbridge to North Wall with stations at Glasnevin and Drumcondra. This explains why there are two proximate and parallel railway lines through Glasnevin and Drumcondra. These stations were joined to the line out of Amiens Street in 1906 but had only a very short existence and were closed soon after though the Drumcondra station was re-opened in 1997. So, a Dubliner in the early years of this century had a more-or-less integrated, if somewhat indirect, rail system and the city was reasonably well served by local stations.

Trams

Perhaps the greatest improvement in connectivity was the development of the tram system and its extension to the suburbs. Trams commenced running in 1872 from Rathgar to College Green and thereafter the line network expanded rapidly. Unlike the rail companies, the individual tram companies were amalgamated into the Dublin United Tramway Company in 1881. By 1886, the basic network had developed. A guide for visitors to the Gresham Hotel in that year drew attention to routes to places as far flung as Dollymount, Rathfarnham or Blackrock. There were fourteen different routes, mostly southside, but it was possible to travel to Drumcondra every twenty minutes from 9 a.m. to 11 p.m. for a fare of 3d. The lines were electrified in 1899 and fifteen or so years later there were twenty one different routes, travelling on the major roadways which included Howth on the northside of the city and Dalkey on the southside. Many of these routes continue to the present-day, utilizing the same numbers for the services. It was essentially a radial system, which suited the city at the time, with its main focus on Nelson's Pillar. This was the terminus for most routes; a role it continued to play until the pillar was unfortunately destroyed in 1966. There was a number of additional termini for specific routes at Hatch Street, College Green and O'Connell Bridge. It is not surprising that it was a radial system since urban expansion in the western world has tended to be radial in form, as expressed in the classic Hoyt model of urban structure (1939); what is surprising is the extent of the lines. Dublin was still a very compact city in the early decades of the twentieth century and the great suburban expansion did not take place until the 1930s. Yet the lines reached far into the countryside. There was a line to Howth and to Rathfarnham, to Clonskeagh, Terenure and Dartry Road. Of course, there was housing development along the route but the system was far ahead of suburban expansion. Interestingly, the existence of public transport routes did not overly influence the location of subsequent suburban developments;

certainly the large local authority developments did not follow the tram lines. For example, the bus still stopped at Rialto Bridge despite the suburban expansion into Kimmage and Crumlin. The playwright Brendan Behan's family were moved from 14 Russell Street to 70 Kildare Road, Kimmage (Crumlin) in 1937. His play for radio *Moving out* (1978) tells the story of a family that moves to Kimmage without telling their father. His brother Dominic (1965) records their own journey there. They came to the end of the line at Dolphin's Barn, on the edge of the inner city, leaving them a considerable distance from their new home. They did not know where they were going:

> We came to a junction of village size and the conductor cried 'Dolphin's Barn! All off here ... ' 'We're tryin' to get to Kimmage please' said Brendan. 'Out there over the bridge', replied the driver. 'But we want to get a bus' said Brendan as the conductor got onto his tram ... The conductor straightened his bag, pulled the bell strap and said 'A bus! To Siberia!'
>
> (Behan, 1965, p. 16)

In addition to the radial routes there were a number of cross-city routes. Thus it was possible to cross from Drumcondra to Terenure, from Donnybrook to the Phoenix Park or Westland Row to Inchicore. Overall, the coverage of the city was quite good, especially when the Lucan Electric Railway, from the Phoenix Park to Lucan along the Liffey valley and the Dublin and Blessington Steam Tramway are taken into account. This latter ran from Terenure to Blessington and onwards to Poulaphouca (Fayle and Newham, 1963). There were gaps in the coverage of the central area, as is clear from the map that follows. The west of the south inner city – the Coombe and the Liberties – was badly served as was the west of the north inner city. In the latter case, there was relatively little housing development in this part of the city and most of it was close to the tram line that ran along the banks of the Liffey. The south city, especially in the Coombe and Liberties, was densely populated and yet there is a marked contrast in the density of the network here with that east of Aungier Street. The simplest explanation is probably found in the social composition of these areas. The western sector was poorer and inhabitants therefore less likely to use the tram service; they walked. It should also be remembered that the terrain in this part of the city is hilly and more difficult for trams to negotiate and would therefore require more justification than other better-served areas.

Table 4 Tram routes and times from and to the city centre (1915).

Route		Weekdays		Sundays	
From	To	First	Last	First	Last
College Green	Drumcondra	8.30	10.30	10.30	10.30
Hatch Street	Kingsbridge	8.00	11.10	10.15	11.15
Nelson's Pillar	Clonskeagh	8.00	11.20	10.25	11.20
Nelson's Pillar	Clontarf	7.50	11.40	10.00	11.40
Nelson's Pillar	Dartry Road	8.27	11.18	10.28	11.15
Nelson's Pillar	Dollymount	7.50	11.40	10.00	11.40
Nelson's Pillar	Dalkey	8.00	11.30	10.00	11.00
Nelson's Pillar	PalmerstonPark	8.00	11.40	10.00	11.40
Nelson's Pillar	Howth	9.00	11.15	10.35	10.30
Nelson's Pillar	Sandymount	8.00	11.30	10.20	11.20
Nelson's Pillar	Terenure	7.30	11.40	10.00	11.40
Nelson's Pillar	Sandymount Green	8.20	11.00	10.25	11.00
O'Connell Bridge	Phoenix Park	8.00	11.30	10.15	11.25
Pembroke Road	Kenilworth Road	8.00	11.00	10.00	11.00
Westland Row	Inchicore	7.57	11.30	10.20	11.25
Ballybough	Parkgate Street	8.00	11.00	10.20	11.00
Rathfarnham	Terenure	8.20	10.52	10.30	10.30
Donnybrook	Pheonix Park	7.30	11.20	9.50	11.10
Drumcondra	Rathfarnham	7.55	11.04	10.06	10.36
Rialto Bridge	Glasnevin	7.30	11.15	10.00	10.50
Terenure	Drumcondra	7.45	11.04	9.30	11.00

From	To	First	Last	First	Last
Drumcondra	College Green	8.05	10.05	10.10	10.00
Kingsbridge	Hatch Street	7.35	10.45	9.50	10.50
Clonskeagh	Nelson's Pillar	7.30	10.50	10.00	10.50
Clontarf	Nelson's Pillar	7.20	11.13	9.30	11.13
Dartry Road	Nelson's Pillar	8.00	10.50	10.00	10.50
Dollymount	Nelson's Pillar	8.07	11.10	10.17	11.10
Dalkey	Nelson's Pillar	7.40	10.30	10.00	11.00
Palmerston Park	Nelson's Pillar	7.33	11.10	9.25	11.10
Howth	Nelson's Pillar	8.10	10.20	10.45	10.20
Sandymount	Nelson's Pillar	7.30	11.00	9.50	10.50
Terenure	Nelson's Pillar	7.00	11.10	9.30	11.10
Sandymount Green	Nelson's Pillar	8.00	10.35	10.00	10.30
Phoenix Park	O'Connell Bridge	7.45	11.15	10.00	11.10
Kenilworth Road	Pembroke Road	8.00	11.00	10.00	11.00
Inchicore	Westland Row	7.30	11.05	9.50	11.00
Parkgate Street	Ballybough	7.35	10.35	9.55	10.35
Phoenix Park	Donnybrook	7.30	11.20	9.50	11.10
Rathfarnham	Drumcondra	8.20	10.52	10.30	10.30
Glasnevin	Rialto Bridge	7.30	11.15	10.10	11.05
Drumcondra	Terenure	7.35	11.20	10.06	11.10

(Source: Dublin United Tramways.)

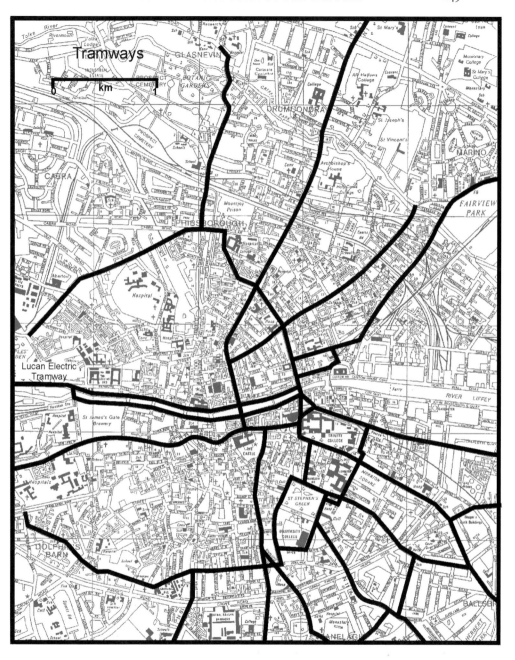

79 Tram routes in central Dublin *c.*1915 superimposed on a modern map of the city. (Compiled by Joseph Brady.)

The times of the service are provided in table 4. On the face of it, it would seem that Dublin was a city which started later than today if the times of the trams are anything to go by. Most services from the city began after 8.00 a.m. and Howth could only be reached after 9.00 a.m. It was possible to get into the city somewhat earlier with services from Clonskeagh and Clontarf close to 7.30 a.m. Daly (1984) noted a similar situation in the 1880s. The Rathmines line offered only four trams leaving Terenure prior to 8.30 a.m. She argued that this suggested that the trams served the middle classes rather than the working classes. However, this was almost inevitable given the spatial distribution of the various classes in the city, the suburbanization of the working classes did not occur in earnest before the mid-1920s, and thus their likelihood of using the service was somewhat less.

However, these times mark the beginning of normal service and there were special cars in the early morning from selected locations. Cars ran from Clontarf at 5.30 a.m., 6.00 a.m. and 6.30 a.m. to Nelson's Pillar, returning at 6.00 a.m., 7.00 a.m. and 7.30 a.m. It was possible to get from Donnybrook to Nelson's Pillar at 5.30 a.m. every morning except Thursdays when the service was 30 minutes earlier because it ran on to the Cattle Market on the North Circular Road. There were special cars from Dalkey (4.45 a.m.) Terenure (5.00 a.m.) and Sandymount (5.30 a.m.). In addition, the early cars from Howth to Nelson's Pillar were 'express' cars with only limited stops on the way and no stop until the tram reached Dollymount.

During the normal day, services were frequent. The service from Rathmines to Terenure ran every three minutes though this was probably the best service. Intervals of between five and ten minutes seemed to be the norm. Cars ran to Clonskeagh every seven or eight minutes, to Palmerston Park or Dalkey every five minutes but those travelling between Drumcondra and Rathfarnham had to wait twelve minutes between trams. However, this journey could still be completed for 4d. in 1915 whereas it cost 5d. to go to Howth but a return ticket to Dalkey could be had for 8d. The shorter lines such as those to Clonskeagh, Palmerston Park or Drumcondra could be travelled for 2d. The trams not only carried people but parcels. Parcels were called for and delivered in Dublin and the suburbs as far as Greystones at a cost of 2d. for a parcel of less than 7 lbs (3.2 kg) while a massive 56 lbs (25.4 kg) could be transported for 6d. We find reference to this in James Joyce's *Ulysses* where Blazes Boylan, preparing for his assignation with Molly Bloom, arranges for a basket of fruit and other items to be sent by the shop (Thornton's) to her by tram.

80 The 'new' King's Bridge in 1831. (Wright, 1831.) Note the visual impact of the barracks.

Daily service ended at times very similar to today. The last trams left the Pillar between 11.00 p.m. and 11.40 p.m. with the last services in the opposite direction leaving their terminus at 10.30 p.m. (Dalkey) and 11.13 p.m. (Clontarf). Sunday was certainly a quieter day. It being a day of rest there was no service into town until 9.25 a.m. and many did not run until 10.00 a.m. This was the start time for most services from Nelson's Pillar and Howth was not accessible until 10.35 a.m. However, it was recognized that people did not necessarily end their day earlier on a Sunday and most services ended at times similar to those of the working week.

Bridges

The trains and the trams had greatly improved the circulation system of the city in the early years of this century. This was in addition to the improvements that were made in the Liffey crossings, then as now, the greatest barrier to the circulation system in the city. This work was undertaken throughout the nineteenth century. Moving downstream, King's Bridge was added in 1827 to commemorate the visit of George IV in 1821 and provided a useful access point for the later railway station.

Victoria Bridge (Rory O'Moore Bridge) replaced in 1863 the earlier Barrack Bridge which had been in decay for a considerable period of time. In 1805, the Dublin Grand Jury had drawn attention to its disrepair. It was also too narrow to allow two vehicles to pass and the footpath was barely 1 foot (0.3m) in width. Despite this, it was patched up and nothing more was done until 1858 when the contract was signed for the single span bridge that is there today. Whitworth (Fr Mathew) bridge was rebuilt between 1816–18 on the site of several much older structures that joined Oxmantown to the south city. Richmond Bridge (O'Donovan Rossa Bridge), its near neighbour, was also constructed during the same period (1813–16) replacing the Ormonde Bridge that had collapsed in 1802. Essex (Grattan) Bridge was an eighteenth-century bridge but, in common with Carlisle (O'Connell) Bridge, had a significant gradient. In the interests of traffic, it was decided to level the bridge and to increase its width. The three centre spans were lowered and the bridge was widened by adding wings of wrought-iron to each side. The work was completed between 1873 and 1874 when it was renamed Grattan Bridge. Treatment of a similar but more extensive nature was given to Carlisle (O'Connell) Bridge in 1878–80. Figure 72 shows that the existing bridge severely constricted north-south movement. It was widened by the addition of spans on either side of the old bridge which then had its arches lowered. This produced a flat bridge of considerable width with the peculiar feature of being as wide as it is long and with a central median which has never been successfully used for anything, having reverted to its present state in recent years following some years as a flower bed. Butt Bridge was a necessary addition downstream of O'Connell Bridge to get traffic across the city. Agitation for such a bridge had begun as early as 1837 but it took until 1879 for it to become reality. When built it was a swivel bridge to permit ships to reach Burgh and Eden quays but this function was short lived when the loopline railway bridge was built since this prevented any ship more substantial than the Guinness barges to pass upstream. It was not long until the swivel bridge was replaced with the current bridge.

So it can be seen that the nineteenth century was a period of substantial improvement in the circulation of the city. By comparison, there has been somewhat less work done on Liffey crossings in the twentieth century. Frank Sherwin bridge, just downstream of Heuston station, was added in 1982 to cope with the increased volume of traffic from the west of the city. The need for crossing points away from the city centre led to the Talbot Memorial bridge downstream of the Custom House in 1978 and ultimately to the East-Link bridge almost at the mouth of the river in 1984. Thus the city continues to rely in great measure on the work undertaken during the nineteenth century.

The question arises whether these improvements in the city were adequate for then-present and projected needs. There are some pointers which may be useful. In 1914, the Civics Institute of Ireland promoted a competition to 'elicit designs and reports of a tentative nature on a plan for 'Greater Dublin', calculated to suggest measures for the development of the City' (1922, p. v). The unanimous choice of the panel of adjudicators, who included Geddes, the well-known town planner, was the plan submitted by Abercrombie, Kelly and Kelly (1922). It was far more than a 'tentative' plan and offered comprehensive suggestions for a thorough re-modelling of the city. The housing dimensions of this plan, perhaps its central concern, will be discussed in a subsequent volume in this series; here the focus will be on the traffic circulation system.

They found that the radial routes into the city centre were quite good and far above the average for a city of the size of Dublin though they needed to be widened in many cases and their interconnectivity improved. For example, the route to Howth had problems. Trams used the narrow Talbot and Earl Streets while it would have been better had they been able to travel down Abbey Street and around by the Custom House. That route was not available; access to Amiens Street from Abbey Street was via Store Street which involved very sharp turns. They also suggested that streets be widened and that Annesley [Bridge] Road and Fairview become 'park highways' of 120 feet (c.36.6 metres) wide. The greatest improvement was to be in altering the focus of the roads in the city centre. Each of the main routes followed its own path into the centre and then was inevitably focused on a single river crossing point. Altering the widths of these crossing points had been part of the work of the Corporation, as discussed above. Abercrombie argued that the process of city development is for these routes to become congested and for an unending cycle of demand for widening of existing crossing points. He proposed that the main routes should join together before they had to cross the river.

They would filter into two short wide avenues, one on either side of the Liffey. These short avenues would be joined by two bridges and one can envisage the massive circulation of traffic around the civic buildings which would have provided a focus in these avenues. He proposed a system of nine routes on the north side of the river and six routes to the south of the city. Thus traffic coming south-to-north would have a choice of nine exits once it had negotiated the traffic centre while that coming in the opposite direction would have six routes to choose from. He argued that such a traffic system would serve Dublin 'so far as can be reasonably foreseen for the next century or more' (p. 9). The traffic centre was to be located in the area of Christ Church, the old heart of the city, leaving the O'Connell Street area to be developed as a civic centre. The plan would have required a bold re-design of the urban landscape with considerable demolition and re-orientation of the street pattern. This would have been part of the wider plan to create a monumental centre in Dublin with broad boulevards and imposing civic buildings and so it should not be dismissed as giving the city over to traffic.

In dealing with public transport, Abercrombie wanted to separate it into two components. The city would be provided with a tram system that focused on the city centre and a complementary system of three concentric routes around the centre, the outermost of which would be the circular roads. The existing routes would be maintained, for obvious cost reasons, in so far as possible but their focus would be taken away from O'Connell Street to the new traffic centre. New bus routes along the north and south docks and other routeways would supplement this system. He argued that it was essential to have what he called 'correspondence tickets' both between radial and circular trams and buses. This would permit travellers to move between the various lines using a single ticket. Almost eighty years later, this is about to happen.

Another suggestion referred to the railways. He suggested that the first thing that needed to be done was to get rid of the loopline which disfigured the city as a whole. Then the railway stations needed to be linked and integrated by an underground system linking a central station. The reader is encouraged to look at the Abercrombie plan in detail, if only for its wonderful maps. It will be seen that though the plan was never adopted in its entirety, individual elements of the plan have been implemented and continue to be discussed to the present day.

Docklands

There was a gradual retreat of shipping activities down the Liffey. The city's circulation system required more fixed bridges and the shipping industry demanded deep berths. The latter could be provided only at the mouth of the river or in purpose-built docks in the bay. So began the expansion of the docklands into the bay, a process that still continues.

Management of the port has always been a priority for the city given the problems with the channel that have been referred to in an earlier chapter. An Act of 1786 created an independent port administration and gave it

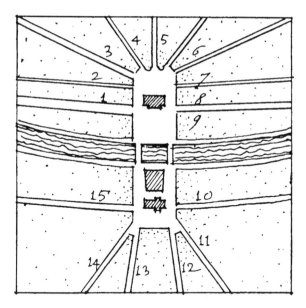

81 Abercrombie's proposals for a traffic centre.
(Abercrombie, Kelly and Kelly, 1922.)

responsibility for keeping the channel free, repairing the banks and taking steps to improve and develop the port and harbour generally. Their remit extended along most of the banks of the Liffey, as far as present-day Rory O'Moore bridge which was reasonable in an age when ships travelled far up the Liffey to berth. Their greatest achievement was undoubtedly the building of the sea walls that were necessary to ensure a deep and navigable channel into the port. By constricting the flow of water in the channel, they created a tidal scour on the ebbing tide that kept under control the sandbanks that had been so long a plague on shipping. The Great South Wall was built first and was designed to provide shelter for shipping entering the harbour. Work on this project occupied most of the eighteenth century. A timber structure was completed in the 1730s but its replacement with the present stone structure began in 1761 and was finished some thirty or so years later. The Great North Wall (Bull Wall) was completed around 1824 having taken five years to complete. Its completion produced the desired scour and deepened the channel and also had the consequential result of accelerating the development of Bull Island. The port authority was reformed under the 1869 Dublin Port and Docks Act which also defined the harbour and port of Dublin as any place between Carlisle (O'Connell) Bridge and the space one mile east of the

Poolbeg lighthouse. Within this space the Port and Docks Board was given responsibility for the quays and walls as well as the bridges, piers and jetties but Kingstown harbour and the Royal Canal docks were excluded. An Act of 1898 amended the nature of the Board so that it then comprised the lord mayor, six members of the Corporation, twelve traders' members and nine shipping members.

In the period up to the end of the century major refurbishment was completed along the southern side of the river along Sir John Rogerson's quay and a total of 4000 feet (*c*.1200 m) of deep berthage was provided. North of the river, the quays were also rebuilt from Commons Street eastwards to facilitate timber imports and for the use of the cross-channel steamship companies (Figure 82). The biggest development was the creation of the Alexandra Basin – an extension eastwards from the site of the present-day East Link Bridge and a detailed description is provided in Gilligan (1988). The basin itself had 2000 feet (*c*.600 m) of berthage with a depth of 22 feet (7 m) on the river side and over 1600 feet (*c*.490 m) of berthage with a depth of 24 feet (7.3m) on the basin side. It was given the name 'Alexandra Basin' to commemorate the inspection of the site by the prince and princess of Wales in 1885. At the northern edge of the port (Figure 83), along the line of the present-day Tolka Quay, was a retaining wall on the port side of which reclamation work was undertaken. The Goulding fertilizer plant was developed there after 1868 and a jetty was built to accommodate the necessary imports. In 1897, the Anglo-American Oil Company sought permission to build petrol storage tanks and this began the tank farm that so much defines the present-day character of this part of the docks. To these were added a rail link from Gouldings to the Midland and Great Western Railway siding at East Wall. The jetties for the factory and the storage tanks developed into the northern edge of the Alexandra Basin – Alexandra Quay – and the docks spread eastwards along Alexandra Road. These combined works gave the city a new harbour and docks but it was effectively cut off from the city and its citizens by the building of a boundary wall along East Road with gates to restrict access. The Port and Docks Board were not the only ones undertaking developments in this area; the railway companies were active. The Midland and Great Western Railway completed their new shipping dock along the north quays at Spencer Dock in 1873. Spencer Dock was at right angles to the quays and was designed to facilitate the easy transfer of people and goods to the railway or the canal boats. The Great Southern Railway built its own terminus and sheds where the Point Depot is today and the London and North Western had their terminus beside the Spencer Dock development.

82 North Liffey quays showing the steamer terminals. (Postcard.)

While the port and surrounding docklands were immensely important to the city of Dublin, the effect of the railway line running into Amiens Street was to cut them off from the city. It is doubtful that many of the people who used the elegant shopping streets would have ventured down to the docks. Figure 83 shows this part of the city at the beginning of the twentieth century. The docklands are a lot more compact than they are today and you will notice that the area north of Sheriff Street is relatively undeveloped. Housing development took place here only in the 1920s and will be discussed by Ruth McManus in the next volume in this series (but see McManus, 1999). Most housing is contained within a zone bounded by the river, the railway and the canal – very effective territorial boundaries. A location as unpromising as this would inevitably be poor. Thom's directory shows streets such as Sheriff Street, Mayor Street and Newfoundland Street with a mixture of local retail provision interspersed with business uses and much of the housing in the form of tenements. Of the 39 individual properties on Newfoundland Street in 1911, a total of 31 was described as tenements (see Kearns, 1994, esp. p. 70 ff.).

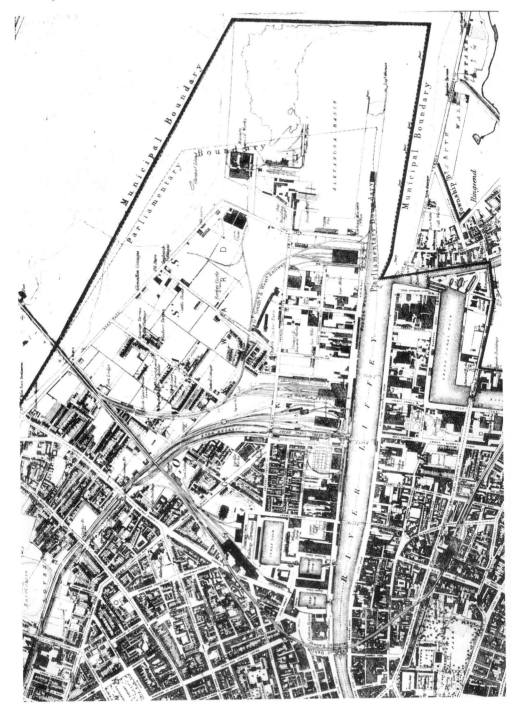

83 Dublin docklands at the beginning of the twentieth century.
(Map to accompany Thom's Directory, 1900 at a scale of 1:10,560.)

Much less obvious, but of greater importance, the city developed a main drainage (sewerage) system focused on Ringsend. The project was begun in 1870, in that an Act to promote this scheme was passed in that year, but it took a long time before the scheme was completed and involved considerable litigation. (Osborough, 1996). The key to this scheme was the location of the treatment works and a small harbour was chosen on the south quays near the south wall. The Pigeon House harbour had once been used for packet ships before they transferred to Howth. It was a small harbour (less than 8 ha) and could be filled in and made waterproof and this is what ultimately occurred. The treatment was quite basic and involved the separation of solids which were finally dumped at sea from the effluent which made its way into the Bay. This has been the preferred location ever since for the city's treatment plant.

The city that might have been

Mention has been made above of Abercrombie's plans to revolutionize the transport network of the city. The plan also offered a radical remodelling of the city centre. Dublin had missed out on much of the civic building that went on in more prosperous industrial cities during the nineteenth century. Moreover the Easter Rising of 1916 reduced much of the central area to rubble and provided an opportunity to re-build the city on a more monumental scale. We, of course, know that it never happened but it is interesting at this point in the discussion of the city to look at what might have been had Dublin decided to re-build in a more monumental style.

The city has always been seen by monarchs and dictators as an opportunity to proclaim their greatness and the greatness of their State. This was as true during the nineteenth and twentieth century as it was in the days of ancient Egypt. Paris was remodelled by Haussmann in the 1850s and 1860s to 'assert in stone the power and permanence of Paris, to show the world that it was the set of an empire of mythic proportions' (Jordan, 1995, p. 12). The Hapsburgs, not to be outdone, demolished the fortifications around the central area of Vienna and created the Ringstrasse with its varied monumental architecture in one of the most charming settings possible. In the twentieth century, both Hitler and Stalin strove to immortalize their leadership in architecture – Hitler in the plans for Germania and Stalin in his concepts for the new Moscow. Democracies find it more difficult to realize ambitions of this kind; though the French have shown in recent times that it is still possible. Usually, there is not enough money. However, the City Beautiful movement in the United

States argued that it was in the interests of urban dwellers to beautify the city. This movement which had its heyday between 1900 to 1910 had a cultural agenda that found expression in urban design. Public buildings, parks, boulevards were all symbols of an improved environment. These additions to the city would persuade 'urban dwellers to become imbued with civic patriotism and better disposed toward community needs. Beautiful surroundings would enhance worker productivity and urban economies' (Wilson, 1989, p. 1). Thus there were many cross-currents in the early twentieth century which might sway the municipal authorities to think about modifying the urban environment in quite fundamental ways.

We have already discussed the fundamental changes to the traffic system that Abercrombie proposed. These would not only have produced a large amount of open space north of the Liffey but they would have removed traffic pressure from other areas and allowed them to be developed in other ways. His proposals focused mainly north of the Liffey because there the greatest opportunities presented themselves.

Abercrombie believed that Dublin should have a grand avenue or mall like the Champs Elysées in Paris. The Phoenix Park Mall would lead from the traffic centre to the Phoenix Park, which could be developed like the Prater Park in Vienna. With a re-orientation of the gates of the Park it would be possible to use the Wellington Memorial as the focus of this route, just as the Arc de Triomphe or the obelisk in the Place de la Concorde functioned in Paris. Leading eastwards, the existing Abbey Street would be improved, though not redeveloped to the same degree, to provide a grand entry to O'Connell Street. The final element of this Mall would lead down Lower Abbey Street to focus on the Custom House, first having removed the blight of the loopline bridge. Under this regime, O'Connell Street would be allowed to come into its own. It would form a perpendicular monumental axis that would lead from a new National Theatre located in present-day Parnell Square across the river towards a new National Parliament complex to be provided in the block between the Bank of Ireland, the quays and Trinity College. The new theatre would provide a focus to the street at its northern point and its location would correspond to that of the Opera in Paris.

An additional vista would be provided along the Mall where it crossed Capel Street with a new cathedral at the head of this street, facing down towards the quays. It would have been an 'interesting' structure; 'a single lofty round tower is placed in the courtyard, its apex is seen rising above the mass of the basilica. This colossal shaft, founded on the traditional Irish Round

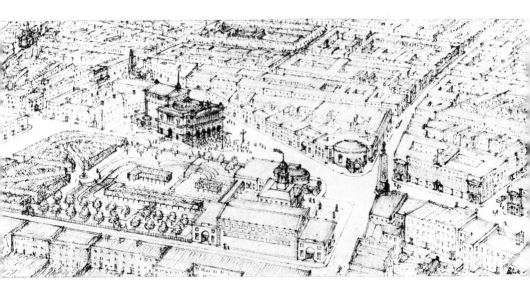

84 Abercrombie's plan for a landmark urban space –
the national theatre. (Abercrombie, Kelly and Kelly, 1922.)
The Parnell monument is in the lower right.

Tower, would serve as the spiritual emblem of the city, as the power citadel [another aspect of the plan] is the sign of its material sanity' (p. 38). Christ Church, on the other side of the river, would be provided with a much more open situation so that it could stand out from its environment.

It is a pity that none of this was ever realized. 'It cannot be denied but that the route from the Custom House (with its restored circus and its true relation to the centre of the town re-established by the destruction of the railway bridge) to Phoenix Park would be of great grandeur' (Abercrombie, 1922, p. 36).

The suburbs

Much reference has been made to the compact nature of the city and to just how much activity there was within its boundaries. But just how compact was it? Looking at the map of Dublin today, it is hard to imagine that it was so small in the early years of the twentieth century. In 1911, almost 88 per cent of the county's urban population lived within four miles (*c.*6.4 km) of the city centre and it is only after 1936 that there was a significant change in this percentage (Horner, 1985). Taking another perspective, over two-thirds of all housing in the city was less than 50 years old at the time of the 1991 census.

In broad terms, the area under the control of Dublin Corporation until 1900 was bounded by a combination of the circular roads and the canals. The boundary line was a little more complicated north of the Liffey, and included the north docks. The revision of 1912 to the 1:10,560 Ordnance Survey map of Dublin (Sheet 18) shows that within this boundary the city was quite built-up. On the northside of the city, only around the docks and the institutional complexes around Grangegorman and Arbour Hill was there any extensive open space. South of the Liffey, the picture was much the same, except in the south-western corner around Dolphin's Barn where there was quite an amount of open space on both sides of the South Circular Road. Within this area, there was a population of 249,602 in 1881 and 245,001 in 1891.

Table 5 Dublin City: occupational structures 1881.

	People	%	Males	%	Females	%
Professional class	15564	12.3	11922	15	3642	7.6
Domestic class	25914	20.4	2842	3.6	23072	48.4
Commercial class	13695	10.8	13398	16.9	297	0.6
Agricultural class	1790	1.4	1705	2.2	85	0.2
Industrial class	69938	55.1	49411	62.3	20527	43.1
Indefinite and Non-productive class	122701		40528		82173	

Percentages are based on the total less the 'indefinite and non-productive class'. This class largely comprised children (73,278 under 15 years) and women outside the paid labour force.

The dominant occupational group was industrial and the single largest occupation within this group was that of labourer (13,251). The large number of servants is interesting, over 20 per cent of the total and almost half of the female labour force. The professional component is probably overstated since it included all those over the age of 15 years in education as well as the military establishment lodged in the various barracks in the city.

The townships of Clontarf, Drumcondra and Kilmainham were incorporated into the city in 1900. However, this still left the Pembroke, Rathmines townships adjacent to the city and, further out, the railway townships of Kingstown, Dalkey and Killiney. That a city the size of Dublin should have such a fragmented system of local government was unfortunate to say the least. That it should have developed in this fragmented way can be explained in terms of the ownership of land around the city proper but that it was allowed to persist into the 1900s was nothing short of scandalous. The existence of townships, each independent, prevented the development of the city being managed in a holistic way. It also denied the city, the Corporation area, much needed revenue because it was in the townships that the middle classes chose to live, leaving the poor to the central areas. This left the city without the money to deal with its myriad social problems, while at the same time it provided a great array of services to the township dwellers because it was they who comprised the clientele of the elegant shops. On the other hand, it must also be noted that Dublin Corporation might not have done much about the social question even if it had the resources. The 1913 housing inquiry did not reveal a well-developed corporate social conscience.

Nonetheless, the city by the time of the 1911 census was over twice the spatial extent of the city in the late-nineteenth century. It occupied 7911 acres (c.3200 hectares) compared to 3733 acres (c.1511 hectares). There were now 304,802 people within its boundary, not a dramatic increase considering the size of land absorbed.

Table 6 Dublin City: occupational structure 1911.

	People	%	Males	%	Females	%
Professional class	18438	13.7	13950	14.8	4488	11
Domestic class	18232	13.5	2636	2.8	15596	38.2
Commercial class	22945	17.0	20910	22.2	2035	5.0
Agricultural class	2276	1.7	2152	2.3	124	0.3
Industrial class	73175	54.2	54579	57.9	18596	45.5
Indefinite and Non-productive class	169736		53429		116307	

Percentages are based on the total less the 'indefinite and non-productive class'. This class largely comprised children (89,029 under 15 years) and women working in the home.

The broad occupational structure of the population had not changed dramatically. The commercial class increased in importance and there were now 1761 women occupied as 'commercial clerks'. The greatest change was in the decline in the domestic class. Not only did it now account for seven

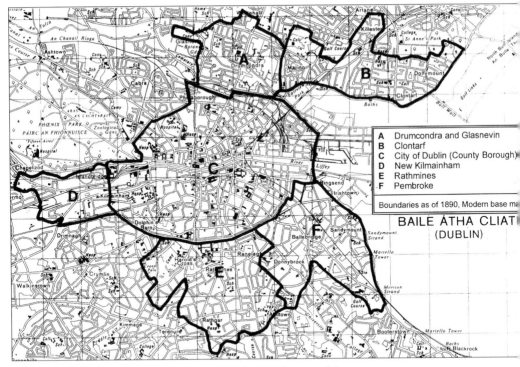

85 Township boundaries at the turn of the century.

percentage points less than it did in 1881, the number of women in this sector had fallen dramatically to 15,596. There were now 11,611 women described as 'indoor servants' compared to 15,360. This undoubtedly had an impact on the large increase in 'unproductive' women to 116,307.

Dublin, in common with many European cities began to experience suburban growth in earnest in the early decades of the nineteenth century. It is a matter of argument as to when the process actually began in Britain and Ireland. Girouard (1985) has argued that suburban development in London began as early as 1794 with the plans for St John's Wood and was well under way by the 1820s. In Manchester the better-off had begun to move to terraces at the edge of the town, such as St George's Street in Hulme, early in the nineteenth century. By the 1830s, the Victoria Park scheme provided villas for the wealthy in a development to the south-east of the city at a distance of two miles (3.2km) though villas closer to the city centre also proved very attractive. They were still far enough away from the dirt and smells so graphically described by Engels (1845). Girouard (1985) noted that those with money in Manchester did not need much encouragement to get them into the suburbs as they were able to sell their original homes for a profit as the city's business core expanded and land values rose. By mid-century the wealthy in Leeds enjoyed suburban life in places like Headingly and Chapeltown that were at a distance of three to four miles (4.8–6.5 km) from the city centre. What was true of Leeds and Manchester was true of other centres such as Oldham, Glasgow, Nottingham and Liverpool (Cannadine, 1977) and suburban life became fashionable.

Exclusive suburbs were in existence in Dublin by the middle of the nineteenth century but were no more than one or two miles (3.2km) from the city centre; their exclusivity protected by the peculiarities of local government boundaries. In the Dublin of the period there was certainly plenty of incentive to move out, since the decline of the city in the years after the Act of Union was characterized by disrepair and physical dereliction as well as a distressed and unhealthy population. By moving to healthier surroundings the middle classes also avoided the financial costs of the city's workhouse, hospitals and police. The increasing demand for suburban housing was also a reflection of the expanding middle class population.

The exodus was such that there was little building of first class housing in the city during the first half of the nineteenth century. Rather, in self-governing townships like Rathmines and Pembroke, developers created fine residential environments, where the 'Protestant and unionist Dublin middle-class could evade the unpleasant reality that they were a minority which was increasingly losing political control in both Ireland and in the city of Dublin' (Daly, 1988, p. 123). The most successful townships were the Pembroke and Rathmines townships that had about half of the suburban population between them. Northside townships never managed to reach critical mass and were absorbed before they could establish an independent identity for themselves. The 'railway' townships of Blackrock, Kingstown, Dalkey and Killiney were truly suburban and too far away to be at any threat of absorption but their relative seclusion also kept population growth low. Details of the growth and development of these areas can be found in Pearson (1999).

Pembroke township

The 1592 acres (644 ha) which formed the Pembroke township lands comprised an area east of Leeson Street to the coast (including Irishtown) and south to include Ballsbridge, Donnybrook and Merrion. The expansion of housing into this area was almost inevitable following the late eighteenth-century growth of the Merrion Square area. As further vacant land in the city proved

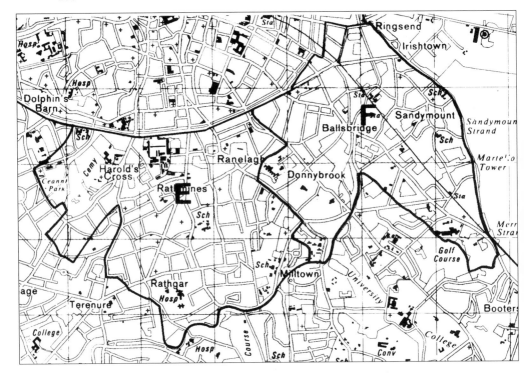

86 The Pembroke and Rathmines townships, 1890, modern base map.

unsuitable, development flowed beyond the canal. The township was created in 1863 and was not incorporated into the city until 1930. Although managed by commissioners it was firmly under the control of the Pembroke family whose agent was an ex-officio commissioner. The founder commissioners included John Hawkins Askins, architect and builder, Sandymount; Edward H. Carson, architect; Patrick Sullivan, builder, Upper Baggot Street; and Patrick Leahy, a major developer in Sandymount, while John E. Vernon, agent of the Pembroke estates was chairman. In all, at least seven of the fifteen commissioners had interests in the building and architectural trades. Both Carson and Michael Murphy, another founder commissioner, also had substantial stakes in Rathmines township.

Pembroke catered for the professional and wealthier classes and prospered during the 1860s. In 1911, it retained its Protestant character with one third of the population declaring themselves Protestant – mainly Church of Ireland. The same census recorded 174 barristers or solicitors among the male population, 303 civil servants, 62 engineers and 114 brokers of various kinds. The township promoted the erection of large houses rather than those within the reach of middle and working class families. The Pembrokes enforced strict planning 'laws', with leases obliging the lessee to keep houses in 'good and substantial repair', as well as limiting the uses of property. The estate kept tight control over what was built with shorter leases, 99 or 150 years rather than the 999 years used in Rathmines, and measures aimed at ensuring that only one dwelling was built per plot. They ensured that substantial houses were built using the best materials and, as a result, the area developed and retained a high status profile. Thus, as at the development of Herne Hill, South London, qualitative control was exercised by estate governors through leases. The protection of the wealthy from contact with the poor did not reach the same levels as in Edgbaston near Birmingham (Cannadine, 1977) nor were there lodges and gates at the main entrances designed to keep the unsavoury out as in Bedford estate in Bloomsbury. Nevertheless the power of Pembrokes was sufficient to ensure that this area became an enclave of large and substantial houses, wide tree lined roads and pleasant vistas, all of which combined to make it one of the most sought after residential districts in the present-day city. The style of house varied but terraces of large houses were the most common as on Raglan Road, Elgin Road or Pembroke Road. These were large houses, three-storey over basement was common, and clearly designed for a staff of live-in servants. Semi-detached villas were also built such as on Clyde Road and villas in their own grounds were constructed on streets such as Ailesbury Road and Shrewsbury Road. These two roads have long claimed to be the most exclusive in Dublin.

The paternalism of the absentee landlord in Pembroke township was in marked contrast to the free enterprise mentality of Rathmines. The Pembroke estate was primarily concerned with safeguarding the long-term value of its property, perhaps at the expense of short-term profits. It virtually controlled the township, owning over seven-ninths of the land (Report of the Municipal Boundaries Commission, 1881), and conveyed generous financial benefits upon it. The estate provided the site and two-thirds of the cost of the town hall; a 20 per cent subsidy towards the cost of the main drainage system; a technical school at Ringsend, and the free gifts of Herbert Park, following the International Exhibition of 1907, and Ringsend Park. The estate also laid out its building ground with paved roads and sewers, thus reducing the burden on the township rates. Nevertheless, Pembroke's rates were higher than those of neighbouring Rathmines, reflecting its higher standards, its expensive Vartry water system, and the implementation of the 1874 Public Health Act from its inception (CDVEC, 1993).

However, with its substantial indigenous working class population, Pembroke was at a disadvantage compared with Rathmines. Poor-quality housing in the villages of Ringsend and Irishtown gave rise to severe overcrowding, sanitation problems, and outbreaks of fever and typhus. In the 1890s, a controversy raged in the newspapers concerning the housing policy in Pembroke, and the contrast between the great houses of the wealthy, and the slums of the poor in Ringsend and Irishtown. Some efforts were made to improve the living conditions of the working-classes from about 1894, when forty artizans dwellings were built in Ringsend. The active policy of working class housing in the Pembroke district was stepped up as Nationalist members gained control of its administration, and by the time of the 1913 Housing Inquiry, six schemes totalling 354 houses had been completed. Since it failed to cater for lower middle-class residents, the growth of Pembroke tailed-off sharply after 1881 though it still had a population of 29,294 at the 1911 census.

Rathmines and Rathgar township
Rathmines, Ranelagh and Rathgar comprised the second major township south of the Liffey. There had been development along the routeways into Dublin in the eighteenth century but Rathmines formally became a township in 1847. It was extended in 1862, 1866 and 1880 by which time it included Rathgar and Milltown in a land area of 1712 acres (700 ha). The township had a population of 37,840 in 1911, up from 32,602 people at the turn of the century.

It was a prosperous place and like the Pembroke estate it appealed to the wealthier section of Dublin society. However, unlike the Pembroke estate, it was not developed by a single controlling landowner but rather along purely speculative lines. Daly (1984) has illustrated the development process in Rathmines in the second half of the nineteenth century, which bears a strong resemblance to the practice in Drumcondra and Glasnevin into the twentieth century. One individual generally laid out roads and prepared sites which were leased in small units, although sometimes the developer would undertake some building in order to generate interest. Business and professional men would buy sites to build their private residences, often building two or more houses as a secure investment. Meanwhile even the full-time builders operated on a small-scale, building just three or four houses at a time. This has echoes of the situation in towns such as Sheffield where Aspinall (1978) has shown the great importance of those building small numbers of houses. More than half of the builders operating in that city constructed three or less houses at a time and 75 per cent built less than eight.

This process produced a varied landscape. A street might take years, even decades, to complete and have quite different styles of housing. It also meant that the development process was often haphazard and depended very much on the zeal and energy of individual landowners. The better quality houses bore comparison with those in the Pembroke Estate. Palmerston Road, for example, was developed in the 1860s with a number of builders involved at various stages. As was common, one of the builders, Patrick Plunkett, lived in one of the houses he constructed. Though there is no single style, typical are the two storey over basement houses which owe a lot to the Georgian period for their design. Plunkett was involved in quite a number of developments and the same names crop up again and again from development to development. He built at Belgrave Road, and lived there too for a while, as well as building in Cowper Road and Palmerston Park.

The development process also skipped about throughout the area as opportunities presented themselves. Developments often took many years to bring to completion as they lacked a single controlling force. Belgrave Square started out as a terrace which was completed around 1851. The residents thought that it would be nice to have a square and suggested to the Commissioners that they organize this. This took some time, there was wrangling over who would pay for the laying out of the square and who would maintain it. It took several years before a builder called Morrison, later a commissioner, built on the south side of the square and it was not until the early 1860s that the north side was complete and the west side was only finally finished in the 1880s.

Dartmouth Square also evolved over a period of time. Its first phase was given the name Uxbridge Terrace and the naming of individual terraces is a clear indication of the relative slowness of the completion of the entire project. The square itself was used for a number of years as a dump before the houses were built (Kelly, 1995). Some schemes never came to fruition. William Pickering, a builder with an address at Richmond Avenue, Palmerston Park, promoted his new development at the International Exhibition of 1907. In an advertisement in the *Irish Times* (3 August 1907) he described the Cowper Garden Building Estate that was to be built at the end of Cowper Road E. It was to be a development of villas in country surroundings with 'all the advantages of both town and country within easy reach of Dublin … Within an unobstructed view of the Dublin mountains, these houses enjoy the advantages of the most advanced civilization, combined with all the scenery and associations of primitive country beauty'. It is tempting to think that the developer had seen Ebenezer Howard's work (1898) on Garden Cities,

87 Ranelagh Road from Charlemont Bridge. (Postcard.)

certainly the sketch of the proposed villas bore more than a passing resemblance to those then recently built at Hampstead Garden Suburb in London. In any event, the estate was only partially realized and most of the land developed during the 1920s and 1930s.

Unlike Pembroke, as the nineteenth century came to an end the township began to build smaller houses at higher densities for the growing clerical population of the city. The shift to smaller houses was in recognition of a growing demand for suburban accommodation from this group, a fact which was also embraced by the commissioners and developers in Drumcondra, and ignored by Pembroke. Beechwood Avenue is one of these more modest, but still 'respectable' developments. It was built in the 1880s but not completed until after 1900 and the housing style changes along it. One house style used here, and in other parts of Dublin, was single-storey to front but two-storey to the back.

Throughout its existence, Rathmines never ceased to grow, and this was achieved without any dramatic decline in the socio-economic status of the district. Although expansion from the late 1870s was mainly due to clerical workers on modest incomes, the area consistently retained a high proportion

88 Rathmines Road showing the tower of the town hall. (Postcard.)

of professional and white collar workers. Of the male population in 1911, some 972 persons (6.1 per cent) were described as professionals while a further 2016 males (12.6 per cent) were described as being engaged in commercial occupations.

The township was important enough to ensure that the city's first tramline in 1872 ran to the township from the city centre; an amenity which undoubtedly helped Rathmines increase its population even further. For all that, there were problems with life in the township. There was almost a religious fervour in keeping rates low, and lower than in neighbouring Pembroke, so that services were kept to a minimum, best exemplified in the refusal to pay the required sum for Vartry water. Nonetheless the township was content to spend money on a town hall and it ran a fire brigade. The town hall was built in the 1890s with its very distinctive clock tower and is a far more imposing building than its equivalent in Pembroke.

Effect on the city
The two townships provided the means whereby middle-class suburbs could develop without significant working-class populations. The operation of the

land market ensured that the very poor were excluded from these areas, except where there was an indigenous population as in the Pembroke area. The Rathmines town commissioners did not build much social housing given their desire to keep the rate down, though in fairness to them it should be noted that they did build 64 artizan dwellings (Gulistan Cottages) in the 1890s and got the Dublin Artizans' Dwellings Company to build for them in Harold's Cross.

Homer Hoyt's (1939) classical model of the residential structure of the city argues that the high status areas of the city do not skip around in a haphazard fashion. Rather once established they tend to move outwards in a sectoral fashion along major transportation routes. The existence of these two townships allowed the high status area of the city to develop in a protected way and thus when the city came to expand, it is not surprising that the high status areas expanded outwards from the townships. In Hoyt's model, the location of the high status areas determined the location of all other social areas. So, in Dublin it was the land to the west of the city that was available for social housing in the 1930s and 1940s, the better-off eastern sector being well developed and established by the time it was absorbed into the city in 1930.

The contemporary social geography of the city shows this east/west cleavage in the south city and it is there that a sectoral pattern can best be seen – the enduring legacy of the townships. The social pattern of the north city is far less well structured and comprises pockets of high and low status rather than well defined areas. This can be explained by the failure of townships on the northside of the city to establish substantial enclaves of better-off people.

Northside townships
The northern side of the city never developed these middle class enclaves to the same extent. There were toll roads in this part of the city until 1855 and these were a major disincentive to development (Ó Gráda, 1982). However, fashion was probably of greater importance. Though Henrietta Street had once been the most desirable residential location of the city, the southside of the city had long been more fashionable and therefore a safer place for the speculative builder to invest. There was also the problem that the northern side of the city had become run down and therefore the aspiring suburbanite had to pass through insalubrious areas before reaching Drumcondra or Clontarf. The latter journey had the additional discomfiture of the Vitriol works at Annesley Bridge and the sloblands on what was to become Fairview Park. Drumcondra, or Fairview as it was then known, was taking on an institutional character. There was the diocesan seminary along Clonliffe Road

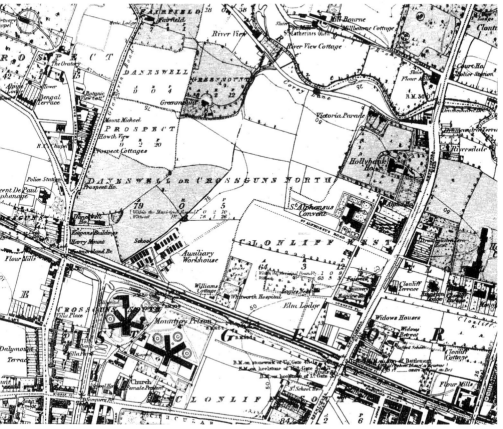

89 Drumcondra, *c*.1878. (Map produced to accompany
British Association Handbook, 1:10,560.)

with the archbishop's residence on Drumcondra Road, the Redemptoristine
convent (the putative site of the Catholic University) on St Alphonsus Road,
the teacher training college on Drumcondra Road, the large complexes of All
Hallows Missionary College, High Park Convent, the Gentlemen's Lunatic
Asylum, Hampton Convent, St Joseph's Catholic Male Blind Asylum all on
Goosegreen Avenue (Grace Park Road). In Glasnevin, the Holy Faith nuns
had a large area of land and there was Drumcondra Hospital on Whitworth
Road. Perhaps the great mass of these institutional uses was a disincentive to
quality residential uses?

Whatever about the reason, Drumcondra never reached the critical mass
necessary to develop into a township. Although it was on the tram routes and
on an important road northwards these were not sufficient to encourage
speculators to develop the area in the same manner as Rathmines and its

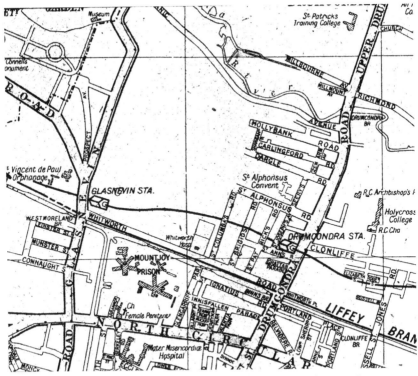

90 Drumcondra, *c.*1900. (*New plan of Dublin*, Alexander Gross.)

population in 1891 was a modest 8,041. It is symptomatic of its failure that there
are no visible reminders of its once-independent existence with the exception of
the roads that the commissioners developed. Glasnevin Road was built to
provide a fine route to the Botanic Gardens and was subsequently renamed
Botanic Road. Corey Lane became Botanic Avenue following its reconstruction.
A court house is marked on the 1912 Ordnance Survey Map at the junction
with Richmond Road. However, on the whole, there was relatively little development within the township and much land remained as greenfields when the
township was incorporated. The map which accompanied the handbook
prepared for the visit to Dublin of the British Association in 1878 shows the
undeveloped nature of the area. There is a smattering of houses along
Drumcondra Road whose main feature is Hollybank House and grounds,
soon to be demolished. There is little development along Whitworth Road,
the boundary with the city, except for the auxiliary workhouse and only on
Glasnevin Road is there any significant housing.

    Figure 90 shows the extent of progress in the twenty five or so years to
1900. A number of roads have been created perpendicular to the main

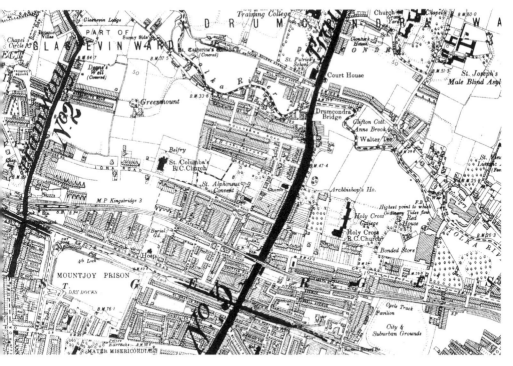

91 Drumcondra, *c.*1912. (Ordnance Survey 1:10,560 plan, Sheet 18 Dublin, 1912 revision.)
Note the well-developed institutional landscape on the right of the map and the
Court House near the centre top of the map.

Drumcondra Road and some cross streets have developed. However these
streets have not yet been continued through to the main road in Glasnevin.
On the other side of the main Drumcondra Road, there has been little
building. A number of streets of small lower-middle class housing have been
developed between Clonliffe Road and the canal. The 1912 Ordnance Survey
1:10,560 plan shows that development continued during the intervening years
with streets appearing along Whitworth Road and there is now a through-
street between Drumcondra and Glasnevin as Iona Road joined up with
St Alphonsus Road. The small houses between the canal and Clonliffe Road
– Elizabeth Street, Bella Street, May Street – had also been completed by this
time. All in all, the maps show that development, if steady, was slow.

The maps, especially the OS 1912 edition, give an indication of how the
development process was undertaken. As in Rathmines, it was individual
builders obtaining sites, building and then moving on that drove the process.
Perhaps the best known of these builders in Drumcondra was Alexander

92 A view of Drumcondra looking towards the city centre. (Postcard.)

Strain. He built in the area over a period of forty years from 1893. His family moved house as each successive scheme was completed and the piece-meal nature of his building is reflected in the fact that he and his family moved sixteen times before his death in 1943. These builders may have had an overall concept in mind but it took many years to realize it. Typical of this is the situation with Iona Road (Figure 91). There are a number of pockets of houses with undeveloped space between them and the trick was to join them up without too much development land being wasted. Lindsay Road is a cul-de-sac at this time. It was eventually completed and joined to Upper St Columba's Road. However, such was the phasing of the development that the cross street which was provided to link Lindsay with Iona Roads could not have any houses on it since the gardens of both roads were back to back. Thus the developer was left with a street with no potential for housing and which was never given a name.

Clontarf township

The Clontarf township had potentially two assets which the Drumcondra township did not. It had a fine coastal location and there was the driving force of a single landowner, the Vernons. However, these were not sufficient to overcome its locational disadvantages and it too was slow to grow. In earlier days, Clontarf had a poor image of being dilapidated, with many ruins and cabins. The land was low-lying and poorly drained, subject to periodic flooding, while long-term plans to deposit sewage from the city nearby proved a further deterrent to development.

A Bill to create a Clontarf township was promoted in 1869, in the hopes of improving public lighting, water supply and poor roads. The Vernon family was the dominant landowner in the area, and the eventual Act constituted John Edward Venables Vernon as chairman for life, with a veto over all policy. Among the original commissioners was Sir Arthur Edward Cecil Guinness (Lord Ardilaun) of St Anne's – property that was later acquired by Dublin Corporation for housing but happily converted to a public park – and local landowner John Calvert Stronge. Three were house agents, including Graham Lemon, an extensive owner of poor quality tenement property in the city, while George Tickell, owner of a furniture warehouse, was also a house-builder over many decades. Another of the commissioners was a pawnbroker, and overall it might be said that they did not have the social or economic status of their counterparts in Rathmines and Pembroke townships.

Despite the creation of a township, the level of amenities did not improve, and in 1880 Clontarf was still without police, fire brigade, public lighting, adequate roads or sewerage (Report of the Municipal Boundaries Commission, 1881).

By 1891, the township had a population of 5105. It was a leafy suburban area. Thom's directory for 1899 notes that 'the High Road skirts the Strand and off it branch many important roads which are lined with villas and houses. Castle Avenue occupies the centre of the township and runs from the High Road to the gate of the castle. The green lanes of Clontarf are justly celebrated for the sylvan beauty, among them are situated many fine residences' (p. 1552). This is certainly the picture shown by the 1912 Ordnance Survey Plan. Most development in the township is concentrated on its western edge in what is now Fairview. There are a number of avenues of substantial houses running perpendicular to the coast – Hollybrook Road, St Lawrence's Road and a cluster around the junction of Vernon Avenue and the coast. These roads were developed in the latter days of the township and Hollybrook Road was finished only after incorporation. Further out along the coast road, the map shows some small terraces at Dollymount, undoubtedly seaside villas from which sea-bathing could be enjoyed on Bull Island. For the rest of the township, the description of 'sylvan beauty' is probably not out of place.

93 Clontarf, *c.*1912. (Ordnance Survey 1:10,560 plan, Sheet 17, revision 1912.)

So though the township had begun to grow by the 1890s, this was not sufficient to avoid incorporation into the city. It badly needed infrastructure and its provision could not await the arrival of a sufficient rateable base. Once in the city, it shrugged off its earlier disadvantages and soon became one of the most rapidly growing areas in the city, providing a narrow strip of wealthier areas along the coast.

The railway townships
The opening of the railway from Dublin to Kingstown facilitated the growth of a number of townships along the coast as far south as Dalkey and Killiney. The railway offered the possibility of true suburban living in picturesque locations and many fine villas were built but growth was slower than might have been expected. The population of Kingstown grew from 1394 to 2119 in the 10 years from 1841 but even this growth rate was not sustained. This was despite the town's development into an increasingly important cross-channel

port. One hindrance was the high railway fares into Dublin. In the beginning a policy of cheap fares had been followed with a service that ran from 6.00 a.m. to 11 p.m. but this changed when the line was taken over by the Dublin Wicklow and Wexford Railway Company who for commercial reasons adopted a much higher fares policy. An overall vision for the township was lacking and development was haphazard. Thackeray described it as 'a town irregularly built with many handsome terraces, some churches and showy-looking hotels ... The better sort of houses are handsome and spacious; but the fashionable quarter is yet in an unfinished state, for enterprising architects are always beginning new roads, rows and terraces' (1843, pp 2–3). Nonetheless because of its unique role as a port, it developed its own distinctive urban structure. It had a considerable working class population who were housed in squalid conditions typical of the rest of the city. These were segregated from the better off so that a patchwork of social areas emerged.

There were other townships along the railway line. Blackrock was an old fishing village that had suffered during the construction of the railway line to Kingstown. It became a township in 1860, its boundaries were extended in 1863, and, as with Kingstown, it contained both a labouring population and a high-class population who inhabited very substantial houses close to the seafront. The Monkstown area, which was acquired in its boundary extension, was one of the most exclusive suburbs in the city.

Dalkey became a township in 1867 but had a population of only 2187 in 1911 while that of Killiney was only 1232. However both places were important as summer residences and much property was occupied on a seasonal basis only.

The triumph of the suburbs
Dublin had its suburbs but only in a locational sense. The system of local government ensured that the city of Dublin was confined within its boundaries with a large population of poor people and most of the better-off across the canal. Yet, Dublin was the centre of shopping, industry and commerce for the entire area and commuting between township and city was very easy; the city centre was within walking distance for most, should they choose to walk.

The suburbanization of the working classes inevitably had to come. There were too many of them in the city centre and too little available building land to provide them with decent housing in the areas in which they lived. The failure to manage the housing of the poor during the nineteenth century meant that radical solutions were required during the twentieth century. The

94 A view of the spacious villas at Dalkey. (Postcard.)

Housing Inquiry of 1913 was a damning indictment of inaction and com-placency. It came to the conclusion that only suburbanisation could meet the need; 'what is required is decentralization' (Housing Inquiry, 1914, p. 31). The Inquiry found that the burden of the housing problem was not in the realm of renovation, but in the building of new units. There were 7967 families living in third-class tenements and small houses requiring new accomodation, while the remodelling of first and second class tenements to meet minimum standards would result in a displacement of 5991 families to be rehoused elsewhere.

The Inquiry strongly favoured the idea of suburban housing. Although some workers employed on the quays would require to be housed within a convenient distance of their work, still 'there are a large number of others all over the old City who could, without much disadvantage to themselves, be housed on the outskirts of the old City. We therefore deprecate much work being undertaken at the start in the heart of the City, and would rather see such houses as may be built erected on virgin soil in suitable sites on the outskirts' (Housing Inquiry, 1914, p. 31, para. 68). This was also the approach of Charles MacCarthy, city architect, who argued strongly for suburbanization and against renovation of existing houses that would 'become ruins in a few years' (para. 955). Thomas O'Dwyer, general secretary of the Dublin Citizens' Association, also stated that the organization's ideal was 'the suburban house for the working man', with self-contained cottages close to tram-lines. Although he emphasized that everything should be done to provide good, healthy housing in the centre city for people 'whose work and means will not allow them to live outside', this was clearly a consolation prize (para. 4200).

The move to the suburbs was not to be an easy path. Trenchant arguments were raised over the next few years against the suburbs, largely on the basis of the transport burden on the displaced and Dublin Corporation never really came to a firm decision either way.

The compact city was soon to spread outwards and grow as it had never grown before. As people moved, so did business and industry. Decentralization was slow at first but it gathered pace and the process of establishing alternative cores to the city centre was well established by the time the first shopping centre was opened in Stillorgan in 1967.

The heart of the city

Commercial Dublin, c.1890–1915

JOSEPH BRADY

Despite all the changes that have taken place in the downtown area of Dublin during the twentieth century, its essential character would be readily appreciated and understood by a citizen from the 1900s. Then, as now, the commercial life of the city revolved around the two shopping districts of Grafton Street and Henry Street and their surrounding areas. The retail area of the city was more extensive than today and streets that have now lost their business role were important shopping locations. Commerce occupied very similar locations to those of today and Dame Street, College Green and Nassau Street were of great importance. But there are differences between the city of today and that of the early 1900s. Dublin was a more compact city and this meant that manufacturing industry was also centrally located; the move to suburban locations is only a feature of the last thirty years. There was also a substantial residential population in the core business areas. This was quickly lost in the great drive to suburbanization after 1925 though the recent upsurge in apartment living in the city centre is reversing this trend.

This chapter will focus on the business and commercial character of the central city area in the quarter-century or so between 1890 and 1916 with a focus on 1911, the year of the census. Others have written about the social life of the city at this time and it was a period of intense political and social ferment which bubbles to the surface in the 1913 strike and lock-out (see Plunkett, 1969 for a literary account). In addition, during the first decade of the century the city experienced two royal visits and the international exhibition of 1907. So there was a lot going on in Dublin, so much that this chapter cannot hope to encompass it all. Therefore it will concentrate on trying to explain the location patterns of the various business enterprises and give a sense of the character of some of its main streets.

At this point it is important to note that land use patterns in cities are rarely haphazard but rather are controlled by the interaction of a number of processes. Central to these processes is the idea of land value whereby the economic return that can be derived from a given location has a strong influence on the type of use that the land will be put to. City centre locations, especially in the pre-car period, were usually the most accessible urban locations. Transport routes tended to be radial and to converge on the city centre. Accessibility was (and is) prized by many urban activities and city centre locations were therefore valuable and competed for. The result of this competition was that the most desirable locations in the city centre were occupied by the kind of land use that could make the most money from them and therefore was prepared to pay more than any other.

In the classic land use model, the most intensively used part of the city centre is the Central Business District (CBD). Retailing and commercial activities dominate this part of the city with retailing occupying the core or best locations within the CBD. Other land uses locate around the CBD, each occupying a particular location depending on their ability to compete for land (see Carter, 1995).

Commercial Dublin

There was an extensive commercial sector in Dublin at this time in which the finance and insurance industries were particularly important. There were 88 stockbrokers licensed to the Dublin Stock Exchange and numerous accountants and solicitors according to Thom's directory (1911). Figure 95 below shows the distribution of larger accountancy practices, members of the various institutes and corporations. In order to keep the map as legible as possible, each dot represents a building housing an accountancy practice; many buildings have multiple occupancy. Dame Street and College Green were the centre of this cluster with a particularly high density on College Green. The distribution spread outwards from there along the main routeways with significant presence in Westmoreland Street and Nassau Street. The northside of the Liffey was relatively unimportant and no particular clusters suggest themselves.

The attractiveness of a city centre location can be understood simply in terms of accessibility. The city was quite compact and the transport routes focused on the city centre. The clustering, however, needs some further explanation. It has long been noted that many functions tend to exhibit spatial clustering because they derive benefits from proximity to similar uses. This is in contrast to the classic model of retail location. Hotelling's (1929) model of ice-cream sellers on the beach suggests that competing ice-cream

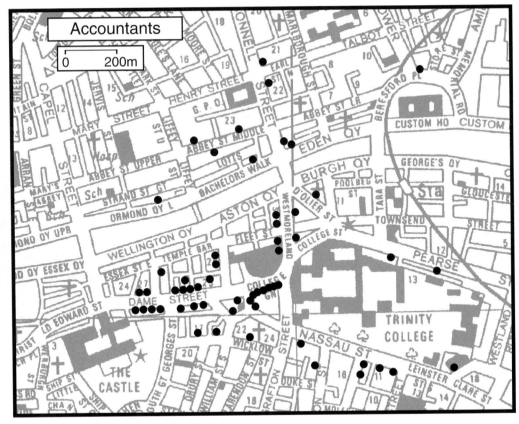

95 The distribution of accountants in central Dublin. The data in this and following maps are taken from the Thom's street directory for 1911 and overlain on a modern map of the city. (Compiled by J. Brady.)

sellers will organize themselves so as to maximize the distance between them and thus maximize the hinterland from which they can draw customers. However in this case, it is useful to be close to one's competitors because of the nature of the business. It must have been beneficial to have the potential for face-to-face meetings and the telephone was a relatively new invention, while proximity also facilitated the exchange of documents and information. The benefits of clustering are greatly augmented when cognate professions occupy similar locations. The similar distributions of insurance companies and their agents demonstrate this point. In addition, there were many solicitors and financial institutions in the same general area.

The street directory for 1911 lists over 125 insurance companies who operated in the city, either with public offices or via agencies. As might be expected, this sector was dominated by British companies. There was strong representation from Scottish companies some of which remain familiar today such as the Scottish Provident Institution and Scottish Widows' Fund. There were branches of insurance companies from Australia (Australian Mutual Provident) and Canada (Canada Life). Who could resist the Patriotic Fire and Life of Ireland or the Hearts of Oak Life and General Insurance Company? Most companies concentrated on life and fire cover and the market was relatively unsophisticated in comparison to today. As well as being important sources of clerical employment, they sometimes made interesting additions to the urban streetscape, though not all survive. The illustration shows the headquarters in Dublin of the

96 The Dublin branch office of the North British and Mercantile Insurance Company at the junction of Dawson Street and Nassau Street.

North British and Mercantile Insurance Company at 1 Dawson Street. Perhaps even more noteworthy is the gothic creation with its turret and gables at the corner of College Green that was built by the Commercial Union Insurance Company.

Figure 97 shows the distribution of the major insurance companies and it is very similar to that of the accountants described above. There are few north of the Liffey and most are concentrated either in the College Green / Dame Street area or in the Dawson Street / Nassau Street area.

Even today, despite the great improvements in technology that have made communication so much easier and the congestion that has made the city centre relatively inaccessible, most commercial companies are reluctant to leave for the suburbs. It is remarkable how many of the insurance companies have remained in the same locations over the years; Dawson Street and Nassau Street are still an important hub for the insurance business. MacLaran (1996) has shown that accessibility for clients, staff and business associates remain of paramount importance for most companies. Despite the development of

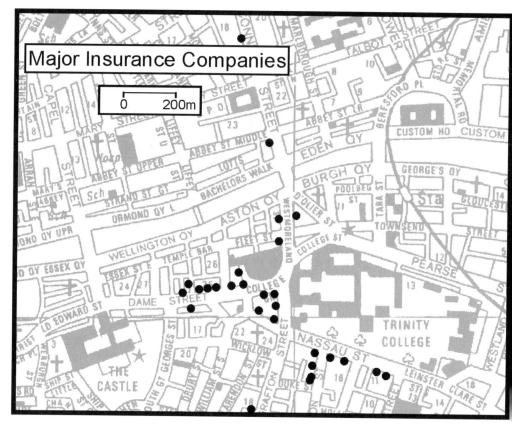

97 The distribution of major insurance companies in central Dublin in 1911.
(Compiled by J. Brady.)

office parks in the suburbs where operational costs are lower, the south inner city remained the preferred location for most; this location being three times more popular than the inner suburbs.

It has been argued above that the city had a commercial core that was concentrated on College Green and Dame Street but no explanation has been offered as to why it should be in this particular location. There are undoubtedly many reasons but the location of the Stock Exchange in Anglesea Street, of the Bank of Ireland and the tradition of banking and financial services in the locality for over a century is doubtless the most important. Successful locations attract more users, adding to its success and then attracting further users in a cumulative process until a major cluster is created. The inertial forces maintaining such a concentration, once established, are very great especially when it is in one of the 'better' areas of the city.

98 A view of Nassau Street towards Suffolk Street. (Postcard.)
Note the ornate nature of the façades, now largely gone.

Retailing

It is usual to divide retailing into two broad categories; convenience shopping and comparison shopping. Convenience retail operations offer those goods and services which are in daily or regular demand and include newsagents, grocery stores and chemists. These kinds of shops need a relatively small hinterland population to survive since they will be used regularly by a large proportion of the population. They offer services that people expect to find in close proximity to them and there is therefore a tendency for them to have a dispersed distribution, reflecting the location of the population. Thus there are newsagents, grocery stores and chemists widespread throughout the city, but they would be expected in the city centre only if there was a local population to sustain them. The advantages of such a location would not otherwise be justified. Proof of this can be seen in the proliferation of convenience goods stores in the city centre in recent years, following the upsurge in apartment building and the attraction of a well-to-do population to these apartments. Comparison goods, on the other hand, like central locations because of their accessibility. They thrive in a location where there are large numbers of people because their goods are purchased relatively infrequently by individual shoppers and people like to compare prices and ranges before making a decision. The city centre is therefore ideal for these activities or such other locations in the city as offer the same level of accessibility. In 1911, there was no real alternative to the city centre. There were town centres in Rathmines and Ranelagh but nothing could compare to the range of goods and services on offer downtown.

Shopping for clothes

Retailing services on offer to the citizens of Dublin were many and varied. Shops were more specialized than today where one-stop shopping – everything under one roof – is very common. Clothing stores were particularly differentiated and formed the dominant retailing sector. There were the boots and shoe shops but the careful dresser could visit his/her dressmaker/tailor followed by calls on favourite hosiers, glovers, hatters, drapers, mantle makers and furriers. The inclemency of the weather might require a trip to the woollen drapers and umbrella and parasol makers or even to one of the waterproof fabric warehouses. All of these purchases might require something from the trunk and portmanteau makers while, on a more personal level, there might be a need for a consultation with the stay and corset makers. However, the effort involved in all of this shopping could be reduced somewhat by a visit to one of the outfitting warehouses, of which there were a number in the city, such as Clery and Co. of Sackville Street or Switzer and Co. of Grafton Street or even to the eponymous Henry Street Warehouse Company.

There were two main areas for clothing shopping in the city. The first was along Grafton Street and the second was across the Liffey in Henry and Mary Streets. This is clearly shown by the distribution of milliners and dressmakers where these two areas emerge strongly. Grafton Street may have been the favoured location but the adjacent streets were also important. Dawson and Nassau and Wicklow streets had significant numbers of units but elsewhere they were very few and far between. The same was true of the northside of the city where there were very few units beyond the main cluster. Since it is likely that these were at the quality end of the clothing market, there was a tendency to cluster in the better areas. There was certainly an attempt by some retailers to present an air of quality. Alfred Manning of 102–103 Grafton Street did not run a clothing store, rather he operated a 'Magasin de Nouveautées' which catered to the quality end of the market. There was no garment which could not be manufactured and the client could be assured at everything was *à la mode*, the costume specialists being 'conversant with every phase of modern fashion and anticipating correctly all its possible and probable permutations' (Stratten and Stratten, 1892, p. 41).

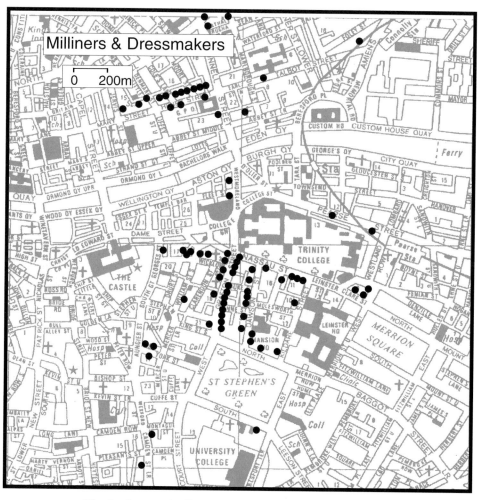

99 The distribution of milliners and dressmakers in central Dublin in 1911.
(Compiled by J. Brady.)

Sellers of boots and shoes had a wider distribution and this is where a number of secondary streets were important. Again, the comparison element was an important factor in the location of shops. As a result there are a number of clusters. One such extended between South Anne Street and Duke Street and onto Grafton Street while another along Capel Street extended the clothing area that was described above. Shoe shops were intermixed with dressmaking on Henry and Grafton Streets.

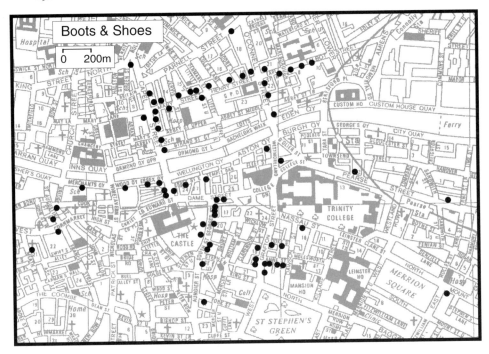

100 Boot and shoe retailing in central Dublin in 1911.
(Compiled by J. Brady.)

What is interesting about this time period is that the shopping area is more extensive than is the case at present. Streets which were in decline until quite recently were more active during this period. There were quite a number of shoe shops around Parliament Street and Essex Street. They are also clustered along George's Street. In later years, this street suffered a decline in its fortunes and retailing contracted into the streets closer to Grafton Street. Until its resurgence over the past five or so years, it had slipped into tertiary retailing with a few restaurants and quite a number of wholesale clothing outlets. Much of what had been previously retail space had been given over to offices. But in the early years of the century, it was newly regenerated after a period of decline. The anchor of the street was the Pim Brothers and Co. Warehouse, a large department store, which had been in operation since 1843.

The linking roads between the two retail cores were also important locations for other forms of clothing stores and there was a cluster of hosiers and glovers around Westmoreland and D'Olier Streets. More specialized shops, then as now, could have a more independent locational existence. That is not to say that they did not enjoy advantages from being in proximity to

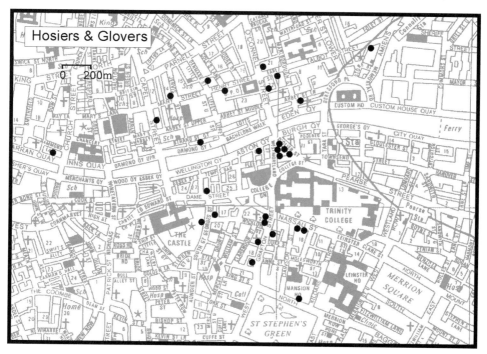

101 The distribution of hosiers and glovers in central Dublin in 1911.
(Compiled by J. Brady.)

other clothing stores but they did not have to be so located if what they offered was such that shoppers were prepared to travel to them. Furriers were centrally located and if they were not located on Grafton or Henry Street, they were on parallel streets such as William or Dawson streets. Hatters had a somewhat more widespread pattern. Certainly they were to be found in the core areas and along Westmoreland and D'Olier streets but there were a small number of outlets beyond these streets, particularly along the quays (proximity to the law courts?) or in Dame Street (meeting the needs of the well-dressed financier?).

In summary, the examination of these maps suggests that there were two distinct functional zones for clothes retailing in Dublin; one north and one south of the Liffey. Although the clothing industry was quite specialized, the different retail types chose, generally, to locate in the same areas. One can point to the maintenance of this pattern today at least in terms of the cores. But in 1911, the linkage between the two centres was stronger with a much greater presence of clothing units in Westmoreland Street and D'Olier Street which bridged the two core areas.

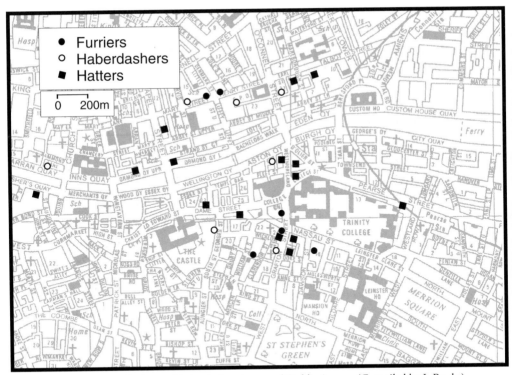

102 Hatters, furriers and haberdashers in central Dublin in 1911. (Compiled by J. Brady.)

Department stores

Department stores or warehouses deserve special mention as then, as today, they provided the anchors for their streets and were the draw that brought people there. It was the presence of such stores on George's Street and Mary Street that improved the business climate of the street. In addition to those that survive today, Clerys, Arnotts, Brown Thomas /Switzers, there were Pims, Todd Burns, the Henry Street Warehouse Company and McBirney's on Aston Quay. The Clery's presence on O'Connell Street was vitally important in giving structure to the varied retailing and services in the vicinity, particularly in Earl Street, and Talbot Street. Without it, these would have been isolated from the main shopping areas and might not have prospered as well. Todd Burns performed a similar function in linking upper and lower Mary Streets to Henry Street. With its demise in the late 1960s, the part of Mary Street closer to Capel Street lost out quite badly and slipped downmarket. Penneys, its replacement, was downmarket in its appeal in its early days and did nothing to halt this. It is only in recent times with the advent of the Jervis Street Centre that this part of the city is beginning to pick up though there

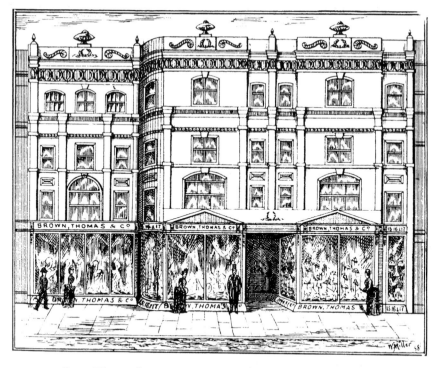

103 Brown Thomas department store on Grafton Street. (Advertising graphic.)

still remains a discernible contrast in the nature of retailing in the parts of Mary Street on either side of Jervis Street. These stores will be looked at in more detail in the discussion of the various shopping streets.

Other retailing

The purchase of fruit and flowers was part of a respectable lifestyle and therefore it is not surprising to find such outlets close to the main streets in 1911. These are the kind of shops which benefit from the passing trade generated by the presence of so many other types of stores nearby and they cater both for planned and impulse purchases. The map shows a cluster of these stores, both fruit shops and fruit and flower shops, in the area between the Corporation Market on George's Street and Dawson Street. There were two outlets on Grafton Street; Knowles and Sons who also had a shop on O'Connell Street and Thornton's, the shop in which Blazes Boylan buys the fruit for Molly Bloom referred to in James Joyce's *Ulysses*. There were stores in other locations too and it is important to realize that there was also a local retailing component in the city centre. There was a significant residential

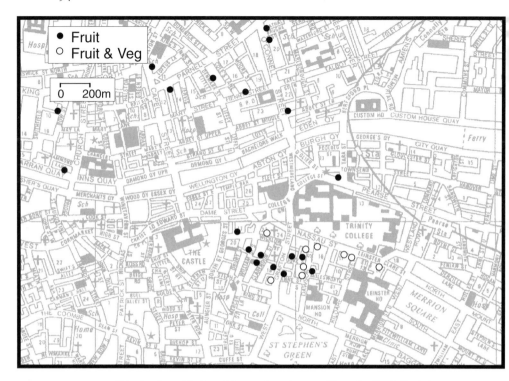

104 Distribution of fruit and flower shops in 1911. (Compiled by J. Brady.)

population, of which a sizeable proportion could be classified as 'poor', which needed these services. Local provision was often interspersed with the more 'up market' shops because of a residential presence very close to the main retail areas.

Other land uses had different needs and therefore different patterns. House furnishers was one such. These uses typically require more space to display their goods than clothing stores. Thus while they would undoubtedly benefit from a large passing trade, the economic return per square metre will not always justify the rents that would have to be paid to occupy a prime site. Therefore they will tend to locate in cheaper areas. In Dublin at this time, there is an amazing example of clustering on the north side of the city. The map shows a great cluster of furnishers, mainly furniture dealers, in Upper and Lower Liffey streets. There are so many that this single use dominates the street. Even at this period, this was quite a dilapidated street with quite a number of derelict and vacant buildings. However, this met the needs of the furniture trade quite well since it provided space in a reasonably central location.

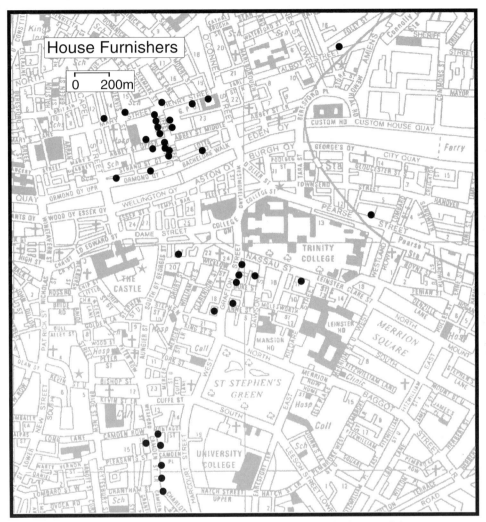

105 Furniture stores in central Dublin in 1911. (Compiled by J. Brady.)

This can be regarded, however, as a somewhat downmarket furniture area, which would have been directed towards the general population of the city.

Those stores appealing to a higher income group were found on the main shopping streets. Robert Strahan and Co. had premises on Henry Street. Millar and Beatty of Grafton and Dawson streets advertised themselves as being the 'leading Irish Furnishing House'. They claimed that their name was a guarantee of good value and fair dealing and that 'their stock is of distinctly superior class to that of most other houses without being any higher in price'. Department (warehouse) stores such as Todd Burns (Mary Street) could offer furniture to their customers without sacrificing valuable locations by having an internal geography to their store which reflected the income generating capacity of the various items on sale. Then and now, it was no accident to find furniture in department stores either at the very top of the shop or deep in the bowels of the store. These locations, being more inaccessible, could more easily be devoted to space demanding facilities. In contrast, make-up and women's clothing would be found on the most accessible locations where there was the greatest flow of people. Men's clothing, interestingly, could often be located in less advantageous positions.

Services

Hotels played an important part in the life of the city. There were over one hundred hotels listed in the 1911 edition of Thom's Directory as well as a large number of private hotels or guest houses. Hotels are a land use that benefit from a central location but they do not need to be in the densest flows of traffic because, in the main, they are not dependent on a passing trade. A central location is needed to facilitate their clients but also to give them easy access to the major transport termini. There is no surprise in finding concentrations of hotels on Gardiner Street and Harcourt Street as well as in adjacent locations. There are eight hotels on Harcourt Street alone with a similar number on Lower Gardiner Street and Store Street. These hotels offered, as one brochure put it: 'ease of access from all stations, trams connecting all parts of the city pass the door and central for city and suburbs'. Sackville Street was another good location as were Marlborough and Kildare streets.

An interesting feature of the time was the number of hotels that advertised themselves as being 'temperance'. The St Stephen's Park (First Class) Temperance Hotel was located on 102 and 103 St Stephen's Green in the 1890s. It was owned by T.W. Russell MP but by 1911 it had become simply the Hotel Russell. Rippingale's Hotel in Harcourt Street produced an advertising booklet in 1907 which tells quite a bit about these hotels. It was a hotel of 50 bedrooms, 'large spotlessly clean and well-aired, all lighted with the electric light … The drawing rooms, the smoke and reading rooms are large, comfortable, airy and luxurious.'

The tariff was as follows:

Apartments and Service and Plain Breakfast	3s. 9d.	4s. 3d.
Apartment and Service and Meat Breakfast	4s. 6d.	5s.

106 Front cover of publicity brochure for Rippingale's Hotel, 1907.

Apartments and Service, Meat Breakfast and Table d'Hôte Dinner	6s. 6d.	7s. 6d.
Apartments and Service, Meat Breakfast, Luncheon, Afternoon Tea and Table d'Hôte Dinner	7s. 6d.	8s. 6d.

For those on a tighter budget a single room could be had for 2s. with an additional 9d. for service and 9d. for a fire in the bedroom in the evening. A hot bath could be had for 9d. but for those of sterner stuff a cold bath was available for 6d.

The temperance nature of the hotel was obviously important and not just a gimmick. It appealed to a particular kind of visitor as can be judged from the testimonials which were included in the booklet. One which catches the eye is from a Mrs McAlery, Hon. Secretary, Inebriate Home, Whitehead, Co. Antrim. That drink was seen in an unfavourable light is attested by one of the advertisers in the booklet. Frederick Johnson of Charlotte Street sold tea and he argued that 'having no connection with the drink trade, we are better able to give our attention to the more legitimate goods'.

These hotels were obviously under pressure to survive without the additional income provided by drink. This point is made obliquely in the booklet where it is noted that the success of Rippingale's shows that a temperance hotel, properly managed, can be successful. Time, however, contradicted the author because Rippingale's Hotel was no more by 1911 having become the Ivanhoe Hotel, without associations of temperance.

There were, of course, more up market hotels than these. The Shelbourne was probably the best hotel in the city but the Hibernian Hotel (Dawson Street), Gresham, Metropole and Imperial hotels (Sackville Street) were available to those with more money to spend; the Imperial offered rooms from 3s. 6d. including attendance.

A glimpse of the services available at the quality end of the market can be obtained from the tariff and guide book issued by the Metropole Hotel in about 1909. It claimed 100 bedrooms, lighted by electricity, and reckoned that it could provide all of the requirements needed by the most fastidious visitor. It was noted that 'the upper floors are reached by a most comfortable and well-appointed Electric Passenger Lift, which is constantly working'. The rate card is summarized below and the comparison with Rippengale's is obvious. Rooms, without breakfast, started at 4s. per night while the simplest breakfast was an additional 1s. 6d. Most indicative, perhaps, of the style of the hotel is the provision for servants. Servants had their own accommodation, from 2s. per night, and were fed in a special dining room on the first floor. However, this would cost the master or mistress the sum of 5s. per day.

The tariff was as follows:

> Single Bedrooms from 4s. per night.
> Double Bedrooms from 6s. 6d. per night.
> Sitting Room, Bedroom and Dressing Room *en suite* from 18s. per day.
> Servant's Bedroom from 2s. per night.
>
> An extra 1s. was added to the accommodation cost when meals were not taken in the Hotel or Restaurant
>
> Hot or cold bath in bedroom   1s.
>
> Fire in sitting or bedroom   2s. per day,
>   evening only   1s. per day
> No charge for electric lights
>
> Table d'Hote Breakfast served from 8.30 a.m. to 10 a.m.
> with Tea, Coffee, or Chocolate, Porridge and a variety of
> Hot and Cold dishes   3s.
>
> Afternoon Tea with Cake etc.   1s.

107 The Metropole Hotel (left-hand side) on Sackville Street. (Postcard.)

Personal services

Dublin was a city where a great variety of personal services were available. Apart from hairdressers, there were masseurs, including K. Lindeberg of Swedish Medical Gymnastics. There was a great variety of professors available who could offer instruction in dancing, music, elocution, languages, drawing and painting as well as in scientific dress cutting. Chimney sweeps and window cleaners might be commissioned. The fact that labour was still cheap is epitomized in the servants' registries. Aside from the newspapers of the day, there were seven registries in the city of Dublin and four, for convenience, were adjacent to the main shopping streets.

Farmar (1995) gives a fascinating account of life in the city for 1911. In this he contrasts the life of the poor with that of the better off. A servant could be employed for a wage of £8 per year, with food and lodgings and was within the reach of many of the middle-classes while some could afford to engage an entire staff. The top employees in Eason's earned £9 per week while the senior partner in Craig Gardner earned £2700 per annum. Teachers did not do so well, though, and might earn only £100 per year. In contrast, an unskilled labourer might earn less than 15s. per week, a sum insufficient to subsist on (pp 19–33).

Dublin Window Cleaning Co.,

ANTIENT CONCERT ROOMS,

42

Gt. Brunswick St.

All our men are insured against accidents.

ESTD. 1897.   TEL. 2690.

108 Advertisement for window cleaners.

Other uses

Comparisons have been drawn from time to time between the present-day city and Dublin at the turn of the century and it has been noted how little has changed in some respects. But it was a different city and one very obvious difference was the importance of the horse. The trams might have been electrified and car showrooms opened on the main streets but the horse was still of immense significance. Stabling was an important land use throughout the city and even in the central areas. Eastman's stables occupied large premises on Drury Street beside the rear entrance to Dockrell's hardware store and there were others on Prince's Street, Mount Street and Dawson Street. The spin-off industries were also centrally located. Where there were horses, there was a need for vets. James McKenny operated a practice from 116 Stephen's Green West that had accommodation for 46 animals in large loose boxes and stalls. The practice of T.D. Lambert in Store Street and Richmond Street was even more extensive. The Store Street buildings covered 2000

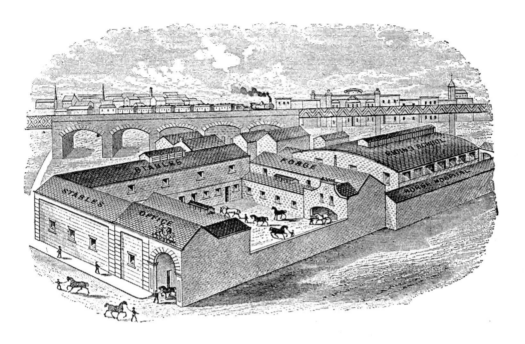

109 The veterinary practice of T.D. Lambert at Store Street.

square yards (*c.*1670 square metres) which not only contained an infirmary for horses and a forge but also a riding school with a gallery for spectators. In similar vein, Mr P.A. Lawlor operated a veterinary infirmary at Westland Row and offered to examine horses 'as to their soundness'. Horses needed to be fed and suppliers of feed were also a notable feature of the city. And when they had passed on to the great stable in the sky, the mattress makers of the city were ready to recycle their hair.

Local retailing

The system of retailing and services described above catered to the entire population of the city and those in the townships beyond. Naturally these were aimed at the middle classes since the services on offer required a degree of disposable income which the labouring classes did not have. Nonetheless the city centre also offered a range of lower-order goods to service the substantial population that lived in the city centre, sometimes above the very shops we have been discussing. Services such as grocery, vegetable and fruit shops, dairies, butchers are found spread throughout the city centre. Interestingly they

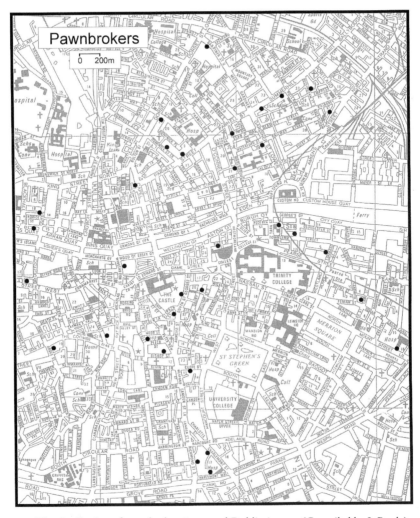

110 The distribution of pawnbrokers in central Dublin in 1911. (Compiled by J. Brady)

are also found close by the more fashionable streets because of the residential population in these streets. There were other services which were aimed specifically at this poorer population and perhaps the distribution of pawnbrokers is one of the better indicators of the pattern of this lower layer of service provision. The pawnbroker was an essential part of the life of the city's underclass. It provided a means of making ends meet and the movement of goods to and from the pawnbroker was part of the essential rhythm of life. Since they were widely availed of, they needed a small threshold population and therefore were found locally. As can be seen from the map, they existed in every part of the city, around Charlemont Street, Bride Street, the Coombe, Smithfield, Dominick Street, Summerhill and Amiens Street. They are also in more central areas and George's Street, Drury Street and Fleet Street all had this service available.

Industry

Ireland, with the exception of the Belfast region, had a relatively underdeveloped industrial base as is typical of most colonies. The country concentrated on the production of food and associated products, as an examination of the exports for the first decade of this century indicates. The total value of exports in 1909 was £61.7 million. Animal exports comprised 24 per cent and a further 17.5 per cent was made up of exports of butter (5.9 per cent), eggs (4.6 per cent) and meat (7 per cent). Industrial exports included ships (3.5 per cent) and linen and yarns (26 per cent) but these industries were concentrated in the northern part of the country and contributed greatly to the importance of Belfast. Dublin never developed a significant heavy industrial base and consequently was deprived of both an outlet for its pool of labour as well as the means of generating wealth for civic projects. That is not to say that there was no manufacturing industry in the city. There was, and it was an important source of stable employment but it was not on the scale of cities of comparable size in Britain and its absence contributed greatly to the poverty that has been so graphically described in an earlier chapter.

Much industry was located outside the city because of its particular locational needs. There was a paper-making industry in Clondalkin where access to water was paramount and there were mills of various kinds; oil, saw, flour etc. An important engineering works had been established in Inchicore, where land was readily available, for the Great Southern and Western Railway company. Within the city, the large industrial complexes tended to concentrate on the food and drink industries. Of these, by far the most important were the brewing and distilling industries with their associated offshoots. These industries were concentrated in the south-western sector of the city but were not confined there. They needed large sites and therefore their impact on the landscape was considerable. The Guinness brewery employed about 1600 people at the turn of the century and occupied a huge block of the city that stretched from the quays to the far side of James' Street. It was not the only brewery in the city. The Anchor brewery was located not far away on Usher Street and as the Figure 112 shows it was also a substantial operation. It covered

III The fermenting house at Guinness. (Postcard.)

a site of seven acres (2.8 ha). While not on the same employment scale as Guinness, it nonetheless employed some 300 people on a regular basis. It too produced stout and ales – 'Dublin' stout and 'O'Connell's' ales. A third major brewery, in the same general vicinity in Ardee Street was that of Watkins, Jameson, Pim and Co. Ltd whose speciality was 'foreign export stout'. This brewery claimed to be older than Guinness with an establishment date of 'early in the 1700s'.

The brewing industry was complemented by the distilling industry. The nineteenth century had been good for the Dublin distillers who considered themselves a cut above those in the remainder of the country. The distilleries in Dublin had a capacity of nearly 10 million gallons (.45 million Hl) and in some years produced one gallon in seven of all the whiskey produced in Britain and Ireland (Townsend, 1997, p. 3).

Indeed Townsend notes that when the Scottish Distillery Company opened the Phoenix Park distillery in 1878, they were quite clear about the competition that they faced. In their prospectus for investors they noted that 'it is a very important fact that the quality and reputation of Dublin-made whiskey is in

112 The Anchor Brewery on Usher Street. (Advertisement.)

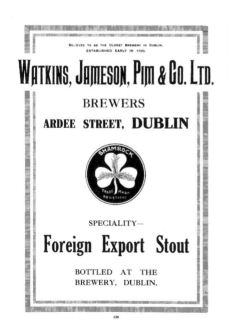

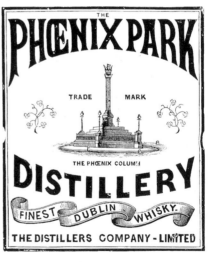

113 Advertisements for Watkins Brewery and the Phoenix Park Distillery.

general equivalent to a premium of one shilling a gallon, or an extra 25 per cent, over whiskey made in other parts of Ireland' (quoted Townsend, p. 3).

Barnard (1887) listed six distilleries in Dublin. There was the 'big four' – John Jameson, William Jameson, John Power and George Roe – as well as the Scottish Distillery Company and a private company that operated a distillery on the River Tolka, near Jones' Road. Their heyday was over by the beginning of the twentieth century and they were soon to lose out to Scottish whiskys. Still, whatever the future might hold for them, in the early years of the last century these companies were a vastly important part of the urban landscape.

As with the breweries, the south-western part of the city was the most important location. William Jameson operated the Marrowbone Lane distillery while the Roe family had their operation at Thomas Street. The Thomas Street distillery was on an immense scale with a site of over 17 acres (6.9 ha) and buildings of up to four storeys in height. It boasted four factory chimneys, the biggest of which was upwards of 40 metres high. It employed about 200 people which was relatively small given the scale of its operation. The Jameson Distillery was not far away and with an employment of the same order as that of Thomas Street, it also occupied a large site of some 15 acres (c.6 ha). It must have been quite a landmark with five chimneys that ranged between 25 metres to 35 metres in height. It was in a good location, close to the Grand Canal terminal basin and the canal may have been used to bring in grain and ship out its whiskey, most of which was for export (Townsend, 1997). The production was considerable and at its height was in the region of 900,000 gallons (41,000 Hl) per year.

John Power provided the fourth element in a large distilling/brewing complex that reached along Thomas Street as far as Steeven's Lane and included the Watkins and Guinness breweries, whose site reached to the quays. The John's Lane distillery employed about 250 people in production and around 25 in clerical posts. The site was also large, about 6 acres (2.4 hectares) and like the others it was a self-contained enterprise with workshops, cooperage, sawmills and, of course, stables. Most of the operation has now disappeared and much of the site is now occupied by the National College of Art and Design but there is still a trace to be seen of it on Thomas Street.

The distillery of John Jameson was located on the north side of the river in Bow Street, near Smithfield on a 5-acre (c.2 hectares) site. There had been a long tradition of whiskey distilling in Bow Street and there are several distilleries listed in the excise returns for the beginning of the nineteenth century. The Jameson operation dated from the first years of the nineteenth

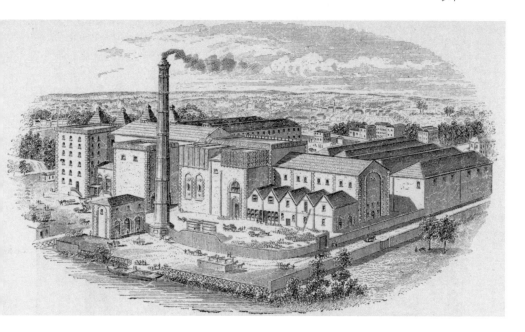

114 The Jones' Road distillery. Only the six storey block to the left of the engraving remains relatively unaltered. (Advertisement.)

century, probably 1805, and there are a number of reasons which would explain its location. Firstly, there was ample space for extensive industries in the locality. There was also good water from wells under the site. Finally the proximity to the Smithfield market gave it ready access to the raw materials it needed, though Jameson soon moved to sourcing his barley directly from farmers and only from those who produced to his specifications.

The city grew around these distilleries, enclosing them in a variety of land uses. When two new operations came on the scene late into the nineteenth century, it was necessary for them to occupy more peripheral locations. The Phoenix Park distillery (1878) was located in Chapelizod on a riverbank site and employed about 60 people. The river provided the added bonus of water power as well as being used to manufacture the whiskey. It could probably be argued that Liffey water was satisfactory this far upstream but in any event the whiskey was made for export. The relative isolation of the location was ameliorated by the tram service that ran to the city centre. The second newcomer to the business was the Jones' Road distillery (1873) on the northside of the city. The name is confusing because it was not located on Jones' Road but a little distance away on the northern bank of the Tolka river; the Richmond Road distillery would have been a more appropriate name. The location was certainly suburban, even rural at the time. The Tolka river was used for power but not for water; rather water was obtained upstream from the Royal Canal though there was also a well on-site. It was similar in scale to the Phoenix Park distillery on a site of 7 acres (2.8 ha). However the process was undertaken in an imposing multi-storey building which still survives, though only as a relic of its former glory.

From this, it can be seen that brewing and distilling occupied a central place in the industrial life of Dublin. Though extensive in spatial scale, most operations were located in the central area of the city and thus proximate to many of their employees, particularly the manual workers. However, the economic climate was not good for the industry, especially the distillers. By the early part of the twentieth century, the Jones' Road, Phoenix Park and Marrowbone Lane distillery had been amalgamated for almost a decade but without the success which it was hoped it would bring. The others also declined during the twentieth century and only brewing remains a significant feature of Dublin's industrial landscape.

The brewing and distilling industries produced both forward and backward linkages. The Irish Glass Bottle company on Charlotte Quay employed over 300 workers who produced some 1300 gross of bottles weekly. Their output was required for the whiskey, wine, porter and ale bottles both for domestic use and export. Warehouses were required for the finished products, especially bonded warehouses. The docklands were a suitable location given the space demands of warehousing but Power's also used the arches under the railway line at Westland Row as a bonded warehouse. Back in Cork Street, close to Marrowbone Lane was the Spence foundry and engineering works. It had a 3-acre (c.1.2 ha) site and produced a great variety of items but it was particularly focussed on the machinery required by the brewing and distilling industries.

The docklands were also the obvious location for other industries such as the fertilizer industry. Much of the raw material, phosphate of lime for example, was imported from Africa and America; some 56,000 tons in 1914, and this made the docklands an ideal location for subsequent processing. The process employed was quite polluting by today's standards and required the application of sulphuric acid to the phosphates. The sulphuric acid was also produced locally from pyrites imported from Spain. Therefore it was normal to find acid producers and fertilizer plants within proximity. Along East Wall

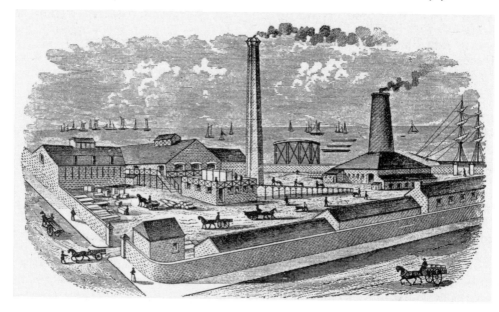

115 The Irish Glass Bottle Company. (Advertisement.)

116 Transhipping Guinness down the Liffey to the quays. (Photograph.)

Road was found the Goulding Fertilizer and Acid Company, the Ulster Manure Co. Ltd, the North-west of Ireland Bone Manure Company, crushed bones were an alternative to phosphate of lime, and Richardsons Chemical Manure Company to name but some. This concentration of activities drew other similar industries to locate close-by and therefore it is no surprise to find other chemical companies such as William Preston and Co., wholesale chemical, varnish, oil and colour merchants nearby.

There were therefore two significant industrial zones in the city. The first, located in the western sector of the south city and the second in the docklands. Both were well within the city's boundaries but were peripheral to the central areas. Neither industrial zone remains in the present-day city, at least not to the same degree. The decline of the distilling industry has been mentioned above while, though the docklands have expanded spatially, they are more a storage facility than a manufacturing one. In recent times, industries had to get out of the city centre; there simply was not the space available to permit new processes to be introduced. The suburbs offered this space, very cheaply, and gave industries the opportunity to have more efficient single storey operations if they so wished; compare the Jacob's biscuits operation today with its old factory in Bishop Street. What permitted industry to move was the arrival of the car and truck age. This changed the centrality of the urban landscape and made it possible to move goods in and out of previously remote locations with ease.

While these two zones were quite distinctive aspects of the landscape of the city, there was more to the industrial component of Dublin than these large-scale industries. Dublin had a variety of other industries, particularly in the food and clothing sectors and a great number of manufacturing units. These were often quite centrally located – sometimes within the core retail areas which is in marked contrast to the city centre of today.

Dublin produced enough whiskey and beer to give the city a perpetual hangover but for the more abstemious there were the mineral waters and cordials. The 1917 Yearbook of the Chamber of Commerce, a fascinating text especially as it came with an index in French, Spanish and Russian, noted that it was the proud boast of one well-known Dublin firm that they were the inventors of soda water. There were about a dozen firms in the city producing drinks still familiar today such as ginger ale, lemonade or soda water as well less familiar items as lithia water, selzer water or Kali. Many of these occupied very central locations. This is particularly so on the northside of the city where Thwaites had a large operation on O'Connell Street and O'Brien and Co.

117 The Cantrell and Cochrane works at Nassau Street.

118 Advertisements for Dublin mineral waters.

were located in Henry Place. The Artesian Mineral Water Company had been located close by off Rutland Square where it occupied a large block that ran from Rutland (Parnell) Square to Rutland Place but it had disappeared by 1911. The Cantrell and Cochrane factory was located in Nassau Place, just off Nassau Street and occupied almost the entire block. The company made great play of the fact that they used water from their own well, St Patrick's Well, which was on the premises. As a result of this and the manufacturing process, it was said, their products were of 'the most absolute purity'. In these days when mineral waters have once again become popular, it is interesting to note that Hayes' Dublin Directory for 1890 lists 25 foreign mineral waters that they could supply to order. William Hayes and Co. were pharmaceutical chemists on Grafton Street and among this list is Apollinaris, St Moritz, described as ferruginous, and Carlsbad which cost 1s. per pint.

Another example of a centrally located industry but which still required large amounts of space was that of the plate glass manufactory in 3–4 Johnson's Place, a stone's throw from Grafton Street. This company was the only such manufacturer in the city and their proud boast was that prior to their establishment in 1900, some 80 per cent of Ireland's needs were imported but that this had since reduced to 10 per cent. Nearby in Upper Stephen's Street was the engineering workshop of Booth's, an extensive operation as can be seen from the graphic.

These are examples of industry with large space requirements but which still found it possible to be located in the central area, close to the main centres of retailing and commerce. Thus there was not quite the functional separation that might appear from an examination of the larger industries. This lack of functional separation between manufacture and retailing is further reinforced when one of Dublin's major industries is examined – that of clothing and footwear. What was notable was the number of retail outlets that had their manufacturing component located in the same premises. This was as true of Grafton Street as of Henry and Mary streets, as will be seen later. Mr James Troy operated a business from 58 Henry Street which offered gentlemen's hosiery, hats, gloves and shirts. The shirt making was carried out on the premises and it was said that Mr Troy employed 'only first-class shirtmakers well skilled in every aspect of the shirt and collar trade'. In fact, he 'enjoyed a high reputation for the accuracy with which shirtmaking orders are completed and in adapting and designing shirts to every condition of gentlemen's wear'. On Suffolk Street at numbers 18 and 19, Messrs Martin and Mumford operated a ladies' tailors and habit makers. While the downstairs

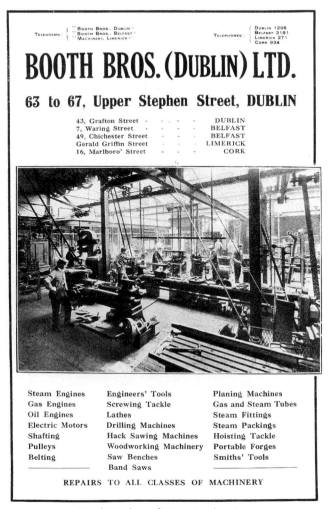

119 Booth Brothers of Upper Stephen Street.

part of the building was devoted to the sales area, the upstairs was where the manufacturing was undertaken. Stratten notes that 'the workrooms, situated on the upper floors, are spacious, healthy and sanitarily perfect apartments, and, as all work is executed on the premises, under careful supervision, clients of the firm can feel secure in their anticipation of the highest quality of workmanship conducted under the most satisfactory hygiene conditions' (p. 75). Presumably the spread of contagion through clothing was a concern which the company sought to address. These industries generated a lot of smoke and engravings of the city centre such as appeared in the supplement to *The Graphic* (1890) show a great number of chimneys belching forth.

Under the right climatic conditions, the air in the city would not have been very healthy.

All this goes to show, how ubiquitous was the manufacturing sector in Dublin and how important the central area was to the life of the city. A great deal of employment was concentrated in the city centre and such commuter flows as existed were directed there. This has been but a brief look at the manufacturing sector in Dublin. The 1917 Dublin Chamber of Commerce guide listed over 300 items made in the city from account books to zinc goods and including such useful items as gunpowder, periscopes and sweeps' machines and who could fail to give a second glance to the Irish Curled Hair Manufacturing Company of South Brown Street.

The character of Dublin streets

We have been looking at the patterns exhibited by various economic activities and it is clear that they are complex. We identified a number of distinct functional zones but these overlapped to varying degrees with the zones of other uses. Certain streets emerged from our discussion as being important for particular functions but this does not adequately convey a sense of the character of the street. This section will take a detailed look at a number of key shopping streets and attempt to reveal more about their nature.

Grafton Street and environs

We have already seen that Grafton Street was home to a number of elegant clothes shops. In fact, looking at the land use map (Figure 20) it is clear Grafton Street was a retail street and that it was dominated by these same clothing stores. Clothes retailing was, by far, the single most important activity and there was a number of large clusters of these stores, especially towards the Stephen's Green end of the street, providing a very clear example of the comparison shopping principle. The street was given its character by the opposition of the two large stores of Brown Thomas (on the present Marks and Spencer site) and Switzer and Co. (drapers; where Brown Thomas now are). As now, Brown Thomas had claims to be the pre-eminent store in the city and Grafton Street thus rose in stature from its reflected light. At the turn of the century, it employed 300 people and offered the complete range of clothing services – they were described as linen drapers, silk mercers, costume and mantle makers, milliners, lacemen, hosiers, glovers and general outfitters. Stratten's guide to commercial Dublin (1892) described their premises as being

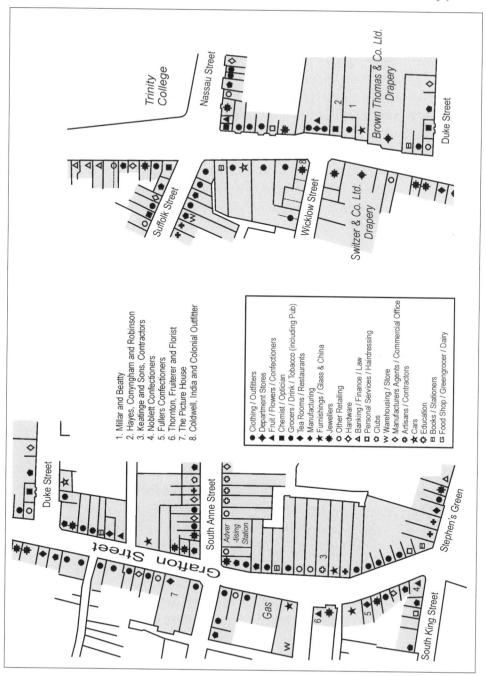

120 Land use in Grafton Street and environs. Based on Goad and
Co. fire insurance plans, various dates.
(Compiled by J. Brady.)

'very extensive and form one of the most striking architectural features of
Grafton Street, the numerous plate glass windows presenting, with their
attractive exhibition of goods, a *recherché* appearance perfectly in harmony with
the high-class character of the establishment' (p. 46). Ignoring the puff in the
description, it is none the less clear that this store and others of its kind were
seen to create the style of shopping on the street on which other uses could
capitalize. Roberts and Co. were located at number 83, just up the street from
Switzers and they offered every conceivable accessory for a lady's outfit, except
boots. Gowns, costumes and blouses were available and every kind of
material, especially lace. They were soon to acquire the neighbouring business
of Taylor and Co. that specialized in linen. Forest and Sons was another high-
class establishment; silk mercers and costumiers who had the added cachet of
a royal warrant. Men were also catered for on Grafton Street, though as is
usual, the provision of men's clothing was on a more modest scale. E. & W.
Seale operated from 97–99 Grafton Street, between Wicklow Street and
Suffolk Street and offered all manner of men's clothing, including military and
court wear. They were shirt makers too and were another of these operations
that kept a manufacturing component on site. Coldwell and Co. had an
equally broad range of offerings further up the street towards Stephen's Green.
What is particularly interesting about them and what says a lot about the
times was that they specialized in 'India and Colonial outfitting'.

To these must be added the impressive premises of Miller and Beatty's
furniture and carpet warehouse, located beside Brown Thomas and, like it,
extending all the way into Duke Lane. Millar and Beatty's presence was
complemented by a number of other home furnishing stores along the street,
the largest of which was probably Cavendish's. Grafton Street, therefore was a
street dominated by personal shopping and shopping for the home and
definitely aimed at the quality end of the market. This facilitated the presence
of a number of jewellers and watch makers, with two very large operations
facing each other across Wicklow Street. Only Weirs survives to the present
day, the other having been absorbed into the block that comprises the Brown
Thomas of today. Louis Wine catered to the antique collector, just across the
road and it is interesting to read in an advertisement of the period for his shop
that 'never was the demand for antiques so great'.

The passing trade sustained a number of stationers, fruit and flower shops,
some of which have been referred to earlier, and tobacconists. Of these, the
best known was probably Kapp and Peterson – 'The Thinking Man Smokes a
Peterson's Pipe' – which had two outlets on Grafton Street, one near Stephen's

121 Advertisement for Millar and Beatty, Grafton Street.

Green and the other at the opposite end of the street near College Green. Here too was located Messrs Ponsonby, booksellers and stationers. They serviced the academic market but with their location at the edge of the commercial core it also made sense for them to have the agency for official publications. With these types of shops, the bulk of the street is accounted for.

Grafton Street had the reputation also as a pleasant place of resort and it had a good selection of cafés and restaurants. They were dotted along the street, often in the upper storeys, with only a limited street frontage. One with an impressive street frontage was Fuller's confectioners with a uniformed doorman to add to the experience. This offered light luncheons and afternoon tea in addition to chocolates, cakes and sweets. Mitchell's Restaurant was another place worthy of visit. This boasted that it was the most popular rendezvous in the capital and 'in its fine rooms one will recognize many of the leaders of the Irish social world'.

There were also novelties on the street, not just the novelty warehouse but also the Grafton Picture House which survived into recent memory. There were a small number of commercial operations and a number of manufacturing units

Grafton Street, Dublin

122 Lower Grafton Street. (Postcard.)

associated with a retail store. Unexpectedly there was a car showroom close to Nassau Street which says much about the relative novelty of the private car.

The character of Grafton Street changed subtly as one crossed over Suffolk Street towards College Green. It gave way quite quickly to commercial uses, especially financial, and there was only a token presence by the clothing industry. This change can be observed equally today where the junction with Suffolk Street is more than the boundary of the pedestrian area. The business and commercial sector became dominant the closer to College Green one walked and only stores such as Kapp and Peterson selling pipes and tobacco broke this pattern.

This kind of change was also exhibited on the streets which led off Grafton Street where a great mix of functions were found. It might seem strange that the change should be so sudden and that there is only one 'core' street but it is simply a question of the level of business that could be sustained. There were only so many stores of a given type that a relatively small city such as Dublin could sustain and these had to occupy the best locations possible if they were to survive. Over time, the sequence of successes and failures produced

123 Switzers and Brown Thomas, Grafton Street. (Postcard.)

the concentrations that have been described above. That said, the streets close to such an important street as Grafton Street were valuable locations. While their character was more varied, there was an important retailing aspect to them that capitalized on the passing trade generated by Grafton Street.

The biggest change seen as one went along South Anne Street or Duke Street was the appearance of ground floor units devoted to contractors of various kinds – electrical, plumbing etc – as well as the offices of commercial agents. Public Houses appeared, there was a hotel, an educational establishment as well as a number of private clubs. There were also grocery stores and tobacconists. All were uses which could benefit from the proximity of Grafton Street but could not possibly afford to be there.

Although Dawson Street is parallel to Grafton Street and only a short distance away, the contrast between them was quite marked. It had a very similar character to the cross streets. There was a number of private clubs, some food halls and pubs, the Hibernian Hotel and commercial offices, some of which were involved in banking, finance and law. There was even a private house. But there was very little retailing with the exception, perhaps, of the

124 Upper Grafton Street. (Postcard.)

block between Duke Street and Nassau Street. Here was located a small number of clothing outlets but the biggest draw must have been the large operation of Drummond and Son, seed merchants. This 'anchor' sustained a small cluster of garden and seed merchants.

Similar mixtures of land uses were seen in Nassau and Suffolk streets. Both streets had a strong commercial presence, particularly on the upper floors in Suffolk Street but retailing was also important. There were clothing and outfitters on Nassau Street as well as florists. We have already mentioned the clothing firm of Martin and Mumford on Suffolk Street and Walpole Brothers had a large outlet at 8–10 which specialized in Irish linen and which had an important international component to their business. Waller and Co. were stationers, lithographers and letterpress printers. It was therefore a mixed street, transitional between the retailing core and the commercial core, not unlike its role today.

Wicklow Street had a stronger retail character than the others, and so it seems today. This may be because of its being a direct route to George's Street, the only one from Grafton Street. It had good flows of people and so could

The demand for

Walpoles' Irish Linen
is significant of its excellence.

The sale of it has steadily increased year after year for 150 years. It is made from high-grade flax yarns, in Walpoles' factories in the Walpole way, which is the cause of its snowy whiteness, silky finish, and wearing qualities. Even in these times of stress the prices are not prohibitive, because Walpoles' are manufacturers.

Patterns and Catalogues will be sent post free, if asked for.

WALPOLE BROTHERS, Ltd.
- - Royal Irish Linen Manufacturers - -
8, 9, & 10, SUFFOLK STREET, DUBLIN

125 Advertisement for Walpole Brothers, Suffolk Street.

sustain retail units that needed passing trade. For example, Forest and Sons who had a shop on Grafton Street also maintained an operation at 4–5 Wicklow Street. But it was a mixed-use landscape and there were hotels and commercial offices. Finally, Chatham Street was given over almost entirely to food and drink. There were nine such shops along one side of the street, quite a number for what is a short road. Since two of the stores boasted Royal Warrants, they were up-market suppliers rather than local shops. On the other side of the street, the uses were more mixed and one would be surprised today to find a car showroom on Wicklow Street. As one moved westwards from Grafton Street the landscape quickly became transitional; number 13 was in tenements while numbers 14 and 15 were vacant.

So, here in the Grafton Street area is shown the operation of the land market in the city. There was a distinct core along Grafton Street which was dominated by high value, high class retailing. This changed in the side streets where other forms of retailing and services located that could benefit from the business generated by Grafton Street before these in turn gave way again to other functions. These were commercial in character towards College Green but less well defined as one moved towards Stephen's Green where specialized food shops soon gave way to local foodshops and warehouses and manufacturing replaced retailing.

George's Street and environs

George's Street shows clearly that the pattern of retailing had a wider distribution in the early nineteen hundreds than is the case today. This street has gone through a renaissance over the past few years but nobody would today call it a major shopping street. Restaurants dominate the present retail landscape and there are still many signs of the decline and decay from which it has only recently recovered. At the beginning of the century, the fortunes of George's Street were much better and the street had a strong retail component. As a parallel street to Grafton Street it could be seen as the western boundary of the retail core in the same manner as Dawson Street was on the east. But there was more going on in George's Street and part of the reason for this must have been the presence of the huge Pims Brothers store which provided the anchor for the rest of the street.

Pim's, alas, is gone and has been replaced by a characterless concrete office complex but in the early years of the last century it occupied almost all of the western side of the street from Exchequer Street northwards. It was not the only large store on the street. Further up, on the same side, there were two large clothing stores, those of Messrs Holmes and Rowan. Holmes, in particular, certainly saw itself as being to the fore in the supply of fashions. An advertisement for 1913 extolled their virtues and noted that 'doing so large a business, the stock is constantly being renewed and patrons are assured that they will at all times be able to secure the latest styles'. The service offered was a complete one; 'for all who desire to achieve success in their dress, it is evident that to obtain the best results for their gowns they must use corsets which are in harmony with the gown of the moment. Messrs Holmes ... have always a fine display of their very latest models.' There was a further opportunity for a clothes shopper across the street in the shape of Kellett's large drapery at numbers 19–21. The store offered every branch of drapery and millinery to the discerning customer in a very pleasant shopping environment. The shop made great play of its lofty 'open roofed' galleries where they displayed their goods.

The street was terminated at its southern end by the presence of Thomas Dockrell and Co. This was a very large enterprise that occupied three sides of the block and could claim to be on three streets at once; South Great George's

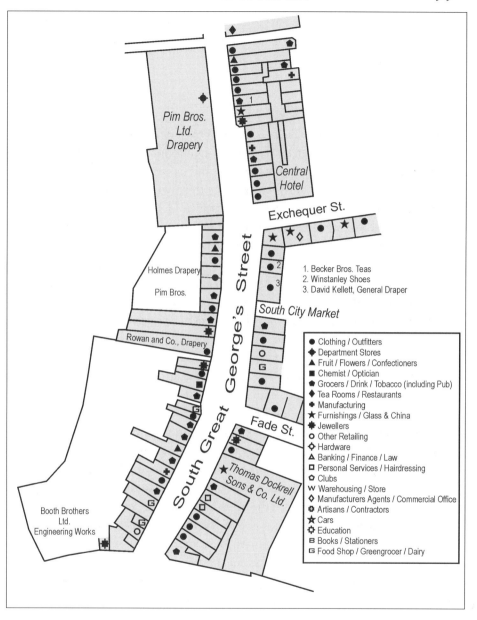

126 Land use in George's Street and environs. Based on Goad and
Co. fire insurance plans, various years.
(Compiled by J. Brady.)

127 Pim's Department Store on George's Street.

Street, Stephen Street and Drury Street. The store offered a wide range of services; they were carpet, linoleum, cement, oil colour and wallpaper merchants, ironmongers, decorators, shop fitters, brass founders, electricians, house, land and estate agents, auctioneers and valuers. It is no wonder that they boasted that their staff numbered several hundreds including 20 lady clerks. In addition to these large premises they had a timber yard and stables at Golden Lane and Chancery Lane. Given the range of services on offer, this store would have been a major draw and its location at the far end of the street to Pims would have ensured good flows of customers for the other stores on the street.

There was considerable variety in the other stores on offer though not surprisingly, most of the stores facing Pims were given over to clothing outfitters of various kinds. There was a hatter, mantle manufacturer and several tailors. The well-known shoe shops of Webb, Winstanley and Tyler each had stores on this part of the street. Exchequer Street had its own attractions in the form of Coghlan's drapery, also a large store. Neither was it all clothing stores. One could enjoy a cup of tea in Bewley's or Fleming's Restaurant and Tea

128 The Markets and retail units, George's Street. (Postcard.)

129 George's Street from the junction with Stephen Street. (Postcard.)

130 Advertisement for Becker Bros. on George's Street.

Rooms. Findlater's had a branch at number 67, beside Pims, where wines, whiskeys, teas and household provisions could be obtained. Becker Bros were not far away and they offered a range of teas for the more abstemious at between 1s. 2d. and 2s. 5d. per pound; china tea was available at 2s. 2s. 4d. and 2s. 6d. per pound. This company also kept a store on the northside of the city at 17 North Earl Street, just off O'Connell Street. Another store to maintain a presence in both shopping districts was McDowell's, the jewellers who had stores both on George's Street and Henry Street.

An additional feature on George's Street that gave it a distinctive character was the south city market and its arcades supplying foodstuffs of all kinds. The market hall was new but there had been a cattle market on the site since the eighteenth century. It had been cleaned-up and renamed the New Cattle Market in 1783 but by the 1870s had gone into decline. The Pim family had spent considerable money over the years modernizing and developing their store so it was to be expected that they would be to the fore in promoting this redevelopment. It was undertaken in the typical manner of the time. A number of businessmen persuaded Parliament to pass legislation that would allow them to acquire the block of property required for the new development. This occurred in 1875 and by 1881, the new Market Hall was complete. Its main feature was a vast iron and glass central market hall, of which only an illustration survives since the building was badly damaged by fire in 1892. It was rebuilt in a less grandiose fashion with two intersecting arcades, only one of which is used today, instead of the central hall. The façade was simplified by the removal of the towering structures over the entrances. This development enhanced the business character to the undoubted relief of the Pim family. Its survival to the present day adds some welcome variety to the street by its red-bricked façade and its interesting architectural features of towers and chimneys.

131 Aungier Street. A secondary shopping street. (Postcard.)

Despite the attractions of the street, its character changed the closer one got to Stephen Street and beyond. There was an increase in foodshops, greengrocers, dairies, fruit shops. These served a local population as well as any passer-by and it did not take long before the signs of a local population began to appear. As one went up George's Street, quite a number of buildings were described as 'tenements' in their upper stories and by the time one had come to Stephen Street, the ground floor of many buildings was given over to housing as well. In short, the commercial heart of the city began to peter out quite quickly and one was in a distinctly different part of the city once Stephen Street had been reached. There were factories located in Upper Stephen Street and all the buildings on the southern side of lower Stephen Street were tenements on the upper floors with foodshops of various kinds occupying the lower floor.

And what of the streets between George's Street and Grafton Street? Of these only the Wicklow/Exchequer Street axis could be called a major retailing street, because as it has been argued above, only it offered a direct passage to Grafton Street. The City Markets between George's Street and Drury Street provided a focus for wholesaling and warehousing and these uses extended

132 The Carlisle Building at the junction of D'Olier Street with the quays. (See Figure 135.)

beyond the market proper. There were wholesale bacon merchants, fish merchants and poulterers as well as warehouses for spirits and tea. Drury Street like South Anne Street had a large presence of contractors of various kinds as well as some manufacturing units.

Westmoreland Street and D'Olier Street

These streets were a transition between the two retail streets of Grafton and Henry Street. The location, particularly of Westmoreland Street was good, since it leads to O'Connell Bridge and thus was passed by trams and a good flow of pedestrians. It was also very close to the business centre of Dame Street and College Green. Both retailing and commerce were found in this area. It had a stronger retail character in 1911 than today and there were large numbers of clothing stores on both sides of Westmoreland Street, especially towards the quays. The street could also support a large piano showrooms. The premises of Cramer, Wood and Co. were quite large and claimed to have the largest

133 Westmoreland Street. (Postcard.)

establishment of its type in the United Kingdom with over an acre (0.4 hectare) of floor space. However, commerce was never far away. The upper floors of the buildings contained a veritable warren of commercial offices with perhaps a preponderance of solicitors. Aston Quay, around the corner might have lacked retailing opportunities were it not for the presence of McBirney's. This store acted as a staging post for those travelling between the two retail cores of Grafton and Henry streets. It saw its location in those terms also and advertised that it was 'situated in the most central position in the city, contiguous to Westmoreland Street, Sackville Street and O'Connell Bridge from any of which leading thoroughfares the establishment is only a few paces removed, and its practically equidistant from all the great railway termini of the city. All street cars stop at Westmoreland Street and those from Kingsbridge and Westland Row pass the door, fare either way 1*d*'. It also made a virtue of the large stock of Irish goods that it carried.

D'Olier Street in contrast, just that little bit further away from the main flows, was dominated by commercial offices, of which the Reformed Priests' Protection Society at number 13 was the most intriguing. The landmark

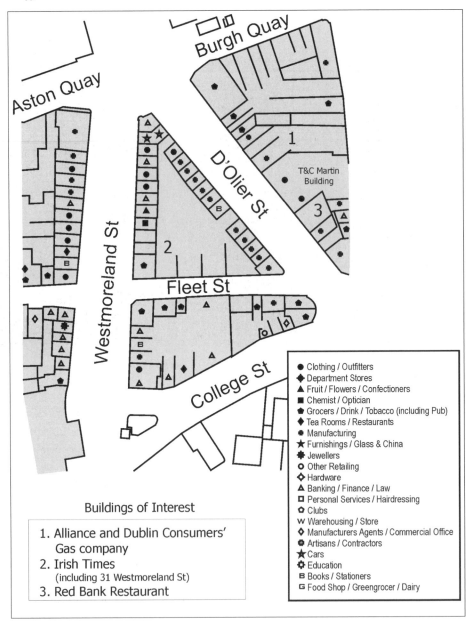

Aston Quay

Burgh Quay

D'Olier St

Westmoreland St

Fleet St

College St

1

T&C Martin
Building

3

2

Buildings of Interest

1. **Alliance and Dublin Consumers'**
   Gas company
2. **Irish Times**
   (including 31 Westmoreland St)
3. **Red Bank Restaurant**

● Clothing / Outfitters
◆ Department Stores
▲ Fruit / Flowers / Confectioners
■ Chemist / Optician
⬟ Grocers / Drink / Tobacco (including Pub)
◆ Tea Rooms / Restaurants
✳ Manufacturing
★ Furnishings / Glass & China
✢ Jewellers
○ Other Retailing
◇ Hardware
▲ Banking / Finance / Law
□ Personal Services / Hairdressing
⚘ Clubs
W Warehousing / Store
◇ Manufacturers Agents / Commercial Office
✿ Artisans / Contractors
★ Cars
✿ Education
B Books / Stationers
G Food Shop / Greengrocer / Dairy

134 Land use in Westmoreland and D'Olier streets. Based on Goad and
Co. fire insurance plans, various years.
(Compiled by J. Brady.)

135 View of D'Olier Street and the apex of Westmoreland Street. (Postcard.)

building at the corner of junction of the street with Burgh Quay was Carlisle Building. By 1913, it was occupied by the Irish Independent Newspapers company who had begun publishing the *Irish Independent* in 1905. It is interesting to read its 'mission statement' as contained in Dublin Corporation's guide to the city for 1913. 'The *Irish Independent* stands for Independence, for the broad true Nationalism. It is the foe of intolerance, the friend of those who strive to promote a more cordial co-operation amongst those holding different political views, in the interests of the common good'.

It was not all commerce though. There were well-known food shops, restaurants (the Red Bank) and public houses on the east side of the street as well as the Junior Army and Navy Stores which had a large store at 21–24. There was a car showroom on the corner of Fleet Street and, of course, the *Irish Times* occupied a large portion of the block, though not as much as today. There was an interesting cluster of heating suppliers on the street. This is where Dubliners came to order their coal or sign up for gas. They could choose from the Diamond Coal Company or Tedcastle McCormick, Wallace Brothers or the Dublin Coal Company to name but four. Gas was an alternative fuel and the Alliance and Dublin Consumers' Gas Co. had its headquarters on D'Olier Street though the consumer was directed to its showrooms on Grafton Street to view the benefits of this means of lighting and heating. It must have been under pressure from electricity as a source of light by this time and its advertising makes a health argument for its use. Gas, they say, is a germicide, reducing the bacterial content of living and other rooms. Moreover it neither tires the eyes nor vitiates the air making it the 'best illuminant'.

Not far away was Brunswick Street Great (Pearse Street). It had a varied character but with significantly more retailing and business concerns than is the case today. There were newsagents, sweet shops, tobacconists, fish shops and butchers all in the portion of the street from College Street to Westland Row. There were drapers, dressmakers and tailors as well as the substantial premises of McKenzie and Son, near College Street, that stocked all manner of farm, garden, domestic and seed merchandise. For example, they provided dining room, drawing room and library furnishings along with repairs to agricultural machinery. There was also quite a number of commercial businesses, particularly on the upper floors, along with the offices of organizations such as the Police-aided Childrens' Clothing society. It gives the impression of a street that was far better integrated into the city centre than it is today and one which must have benefited from the pedestrian flows to and from the railway station at Westland Row.

Sackville Street (O'Connell Street) and environs

Sackville Street was an enigma in the early years of the twentieth century. It was supposed to be the pre-eminent street of the city but it had never really managed to live up to that description. In its earliest incarnation as Sackville Mall, it was *the* place of resort for the well-to-do; a place to see and be seen (Dickson, 1987). It never re-captured that status following its widening and joining to the south city via Sackville Bridge. Even today the problem remains. It has of late been characterized as being somewhat seedy and some effort has been put into improving street frontages and signage so that it does not look like a large fast-food restaurant. It is sometimes suggested that it is its very width – one of its celebrated characteristics – that has militated against its development into a prestigious area. However, the Champs Elysées in Paris is just as wide, if not wider when footpaths are taken into account.

In 1911, Sackville Street was more interesting. The lower part of the street, that closest to the Liffey, was strongly retail with a considerable presence of

136 View down Sackville Street. (Postcard.)

clothing stores with Clery's providing the main draw. Clery's occupied a key location, mid-way up the street and opposite the GPO. The custom it attracted was crucial in sustaining the enterprises in nearby Earl Street and in Henry Street across the street. It was an excellent location. The main terminus for the trams was just outside the door and even in the early years of this century, Clery's clock was an important landmark. Clery's, then as now, was an imposing building with a frontage of 95 feet (29 metres) and neo-classical stucco design. This company also had an extensive manufacturing component present on the site. There were workrooms for mantle-making, millinery and costumes and they boasted that they could undertake at the shortest notice orders of any magnitude for wedding outfits, court costumes or mourning. Typical of all department stores, it offered a complete service; 'it would be impossible to even enumerate the various branches of the company's business; from house furniture to books, and from millinery to shoes; every requirement for the house or person will be found represented by the finest examples in each department'. On Lower Sackville Street, towards the Liffey, there were a number of chemists and opticians, jewellers but not the intensity of retailing exhibited on

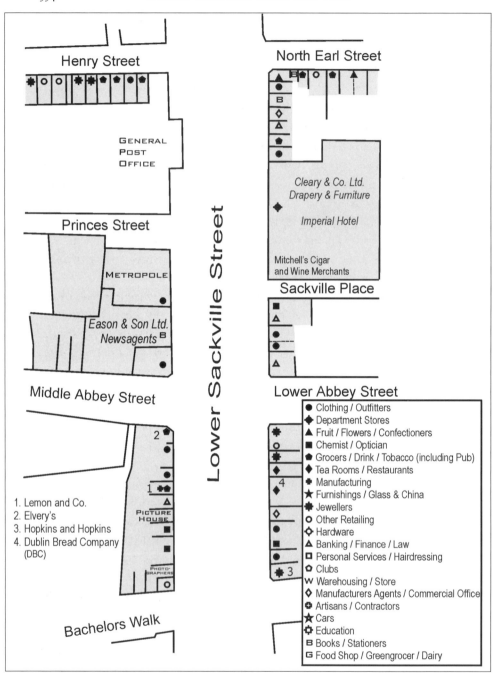

137 Land use in Sackville Street and environs. Based on Goad and
Co. fire insurance plans, various years.
(Compiled by J. Brady.)

Grafton Street. Eason and Co. were at number 40 and Hopkins and Hopkins occupied the key corner site at the junction with Eden quay. This was an up-market company that specialized in making copies of antique celtic ornaments. The brochure that the company produced for the International Exhibition of 1907, boasted of the medal that it was awarded at the 1883 Cork Industrial Exhibition. Quite a number of stores were northside versions of those on Grafton Street or its environs. Hamilton Long and Co. had a pharmacy in number 3 to complement that in Grafton Street while, across the street in numbers 46 and 47 was Elvery's. Elvery's, best known for their waterproof clothing, had a large store on Nassau Street. Close by, Kapp and Peterson had their northside tobacconists as did Noblett's confectioners. There was obviously a belief that the northside of the city attracted a different clientele to the southside of the city notwithstanding the shopping corridor joining the two parts. This being so, it made sense to have stores in both areas just as today stores will maintain presences in the city centre and large suburban shopping centres.

Yet for all this duplication, the street had a distinctive character. There were a number of restaurants of which that of the Metropole hotel was the best known. Lemon's sweets could not be passed-by and across the road was the Dublin Bread Company (DBC) restaurant, believed by many to bake better cakes than Bewley's. But it was the hotels that perhaps made this part of the street distinctive. Between the quays and Clery's there was the Waverley Hotel and the Grand Hotel and then the impressive sight of the opposing buildings of the Hotel Metropole and the Imperial Hotel. The Imperial Hotel was in the same building complex as Clery's. Across the street, the Hotel Metropole claimed to be palatial in its plan and adornment.

The upper part of the street was different in character, as it is today. Tylers shoe shop occupied 1 Upper Sackville Street and the famous Lawrence photographic studio could be found at numbers 5–7. There was little retail activity beyond Henry Street and Earl Street, except towards Great Britain Street (Parnell) Street.

At this end of the street was Findlater's main store, occupying most of the block between Findlater's Place and Great Britain Street. The store also had extensive cellars that ran under Sackville Street. However this was rather the exception, the upper part of Sackville Street had quite a concentration of financial and business concerns and some large hotels. The Northern and Royal Bank had premises as did a number of insurance companies and commercial agents. There was a number of clubs; the Sackville Street club, the

138 Clery's and the Imperial Hotel on Sackville Street.

Catholic Commercial club; the Oxford Billiard rooms as well as the YMCA and the offices of worthy bodies such as the Presbyterian Association, the Catholic Truth Society and the Hibernian Bible Society. The Richmond Institution for the education of the Industrious Blind was yet another land use type. To this mix, must be added a number of hotels, the Hammam, and the Gresham being the best known. While the Gresham remains, little remains of the Hammam which claimed in 1913 to be one of the oldest and most comfortable hotels in the city. The Civil War changed all this when most of this side of the street was destroyed. While the Gresham Hotel was rebuilt, all that remains of the Hammam is the name given to the office building that replaced it. What made the Hammam Hotel particularly interesting is that it had a Turkish bath which they claimed to be the largest and loftiest in the kingdom; 'the hygienic and medical advantages of Turkish Baths are very great, and the advantage of having them in connection with a first-class hotel cannot be over-estimated'.

The upper part of the street, in its mixture of land use, is reminiscent of Dawson Street; not quite a first rank street but sufficiently close to one to be a

139 Henry Street looking towards Sackville Street. (Postcard.)
Notice the distinctive cupola of the Arnotts' Department store.

140 The destruction of Easter Week, 1916 altered the landscape of this part
of the city considerably. This photograph shows the ruins of Clery's
and the Imperial Hotel on Sackville Street.

good place to locate and a sufficiently prestigious address to have. Of note is the presence of large industrial complexes. Thwaites mineral waters had a large site with an office on the street and there was a large printing and book binding operation as well as Gilbey's bottling store. The mix of activities on this street is another example of the overlaying of different functional patterns.

Henry Street and Mary Street were pre-eminently shopping streets and were an important centre for clothes shopping, as would be expected from the alternative pole to Grafton Street. Like Grafton Street, there were jewellers and opticians and a selection of fruit and flower merchants. What was different to Grafton Street is that there were fewer restaurants and tea rooms and more public houses. In fact, Henry Street was 'topped' and 'tailed' by public houses. More shop units were given to hardware and furnishings, more extensive retail operations. As one moved down Mary Street towards Capel Street, the dominance of retailing declined and there were industrial and warehouse units on the street. The Bewley and Draper mineral water company occupied number 23 with an extensive site behind while numbers 48 and 49 were occupied by decorating contractors. Thus Mary Street resembled in character the side streets around Grafton Street; providing a good location for a mixture of retailing, commercial and industrial uses. It also provided local shopping in the form of greengrocers and other foodshops.

This part of the city was almost totally destroyed as a result of either or both of the Easter Rising and the Civil War. Figure 141 below shows the extent of the destruction following the Easter Rising. Produced by the Goad Fire Insurance Company it shows that almost all of Sackville Street Lower was destroyed as was most of the block enclosed by Middle Abbey Street, Henry Street and Liffey Street. Much of the right hand side of Upper Sackville Street, including the Gresham Hotel was destroyed during the Civil War.

The impression given by this group of streets is of a smaller retail core than on the south city. It was one that graded linearly into secondary shopping rather than radiating outwards as Grafton Street does. By the same token, the character of the side streets was quite different. Stafford Street, for example, contained no retail units at all and comprised tenements and warehouse units with an industrial unit interspersed. Jervis Street towards Parnell Street presented a similar picture with tenements and vacant units. Great Britain street ran parallel, almost, to Henry and Mary Street and thus invites comparison with George's Street. However, because there was no large anchor store there, its profile was one of local provision with food shops, tobacconists, a few public houses and some clothing outlets.

141 Goad Fire Insurance Plan showing the destruction of 1916. The darker shading shows buildings destroyed, the lighter shading shows those partially destroyed.

Concluding comments

This tour through some of the main streets of the city shows that there were similarities and differences between the shopping areas of the north and south cities. Both parts of the city had core streets but the northern core was smaller and gave way to residential areas more quickly. The southern core was extensive with a single main shopping street which branched out on both sides to include the parallel streets. Henry Street in contrast did not manage to extend its influence into the side streets and rather the progression was down the street into Mary Street and thus to Capel Street.

The type of shops was not greatly dissimilar between the two areas and it would be difficult to differentiate their 'quality' and grandeur, especially given that many firms were present in both cores. Sackville (O'Connell) Street gave the impression of being two different streets, north and south of Nelson's Pillar. It is as if shoppers would not venture north of Henry Street and thus that part of the street between there and Great Britain Street (Parnell) Street took on a different character. Nowhere was the local population very far away. The tenements extended into the centre of the city with retail uses firstly giving way to tenements above a ground floor store before the tenement use took over completely. Neither was manufacturing industry very far away with many significant operations very close to the centre. For those in the tenements fortunate enough to have employment, the journey to work would not be great and would not have required significant expenditure.

In this compact city, no aspect of city life was far away. There was an urban population, shops, offices, warehouses, clubs and industry all within what is today called the inner-city. The city at the beginning of the twenty-first century may be much larger with extensive suburbs but the legacy of the past exercises a strong influence on today's retail patterns. Dublin continues to have a rather fragmented but compact structure with two cores rather than one. Grafton Street is the major shopping street south of the Liffey with Henry Street being most important north of the river. On a good shopping day, a Saturday close to Christmas for example, around 12,000 people per hour can be expected to pass down these streets. At other times of the year, it might be that Grafton Street probably has an edge of Henry Street in terms of its perceived status and certainly surveys over many years have shown that the shoppers in Grafton Street tended to be of a higher socio-economic group. This is reflected in the higher rents charged on Grafton Street. The gap between the streets is not a large one, however, and is narrowing as Henry Street's attractiveness has been improved by the recent opening of the Jervis Street centre and the remodelling of Arnotts.

The streetscape of the north city was to be dramatically altered by the rebellion of 1916 and later by the Civil War. The combined result of these events was the comprehensive destruction of O'Connell Street and many of the adjoining streets. The opportunity was not taken to rebuild in the grand manner but the reconstruction of this part of the city produced a landscape that was significantly different to what had been there before. The reader is encouraged to follow this story in the next volume in this series.

APPENDIX

A brief guide to maps of Dublin from 1610 to the beginning of the twentieth century

JOSEPH BRADY

This section is to provide the interested user with a brief guide to the maps of Dublin that will assist a study of the development of the city. Access to these maps can sometimes be difficult and the National Library of Ireland, the Dublin City Archive and the Map Library in Trinity College Dublin should be among the first ports of call of any researcher. However, it is possible to obtain copies of many of the maps discussed below at reasonable cost, especially now that the Internet has brought international map dealers within much greater reach than before.

Though the origins of the city of Dublin can be traced back to the ninth century, at least, the first map of the city is dated 1610. This is John Speed's *Dubline* and it was published as an inset to the Leinster folio page in his *Theatre of the Empire of Great Britaine* (1611). The map is approximately 15 x 17 cms and at a scale of approximately 1:10,500. It was one of four maps of Irish cities in the *Theatre*, the others being Cork, Galway and Limerick. While Speed claimed that he had undertaken the surveying work himself, this is a claim that has met with some scepticism (Andrews, 1983a). It is suggested that Speed used an extant map or one that was already in preparation. This, of course, raises the question of whether there were earlier, now lost, maps of the city. The longevity of Speed's map was remarkable. It appeared in many variants until the end of the eighteenth century and since then has been the invariable standard view of the medieval city. Unfortunately, none of the pre-1900 versions of Speed added anything of topographical content to the original. It is Speed's map that appeared in the Braun and Hogenberg *Civitates Orbis Terrarum* (volume 6) as early as 1617. Though the *Civitates Orbis Terrarum* is constantly available as a reasonably priced reprint because of the artistic nature of the maps, the Dublin map never appears in these reprints. Rutger Hermannides produced a version in 1661 (11 x 12 cms) and this is rather more common. Nowadays, to judge from auction offerings on the Internet, the most common variant was that produced by Manesson Malet in his *Description de l'Univers* (1683). This is a rather distorted bird's eye view of the city, approximately 15 x 10 cms, with the Liffey described as the 'Leffer'.

William Petty is famous as the director of the Down Survey undertaken after 1654 (see Andrews, 1997), an unprecedented land survey that followed the Cromwellian confiscations. The barony maps for the outskirts of Dublin provide much useful information on the pattern of landholding and some topographical details.

While Bernard de Gomme surveyed the city and harbour of Dublin in 1673 as part of a plan to improve the city's defences, the resulting map was never published in its own right. It was copied by others and is undoubtedly the source of the map that appears in the margins of Henry Pratt's map of Ireland (1705). The Pratt version in turn inspired the map that appeared in the margins of Henry Moll's map of Ireland (1714) as well as forming the basis for the many variants that appeared in histories and text books. It is worth mentioning that Greenville Collins produced a map of Dublin Bay in his *Great Britain coasting pilot* (1693) that was reprinted many times during the next century. It is interesting because it places Dublin in its spatial context as well as showing the sandbanks around the harbour as they were in the late-seventeenth century (see chapters 1 and 2). However the city itself is shown in no great detail, not surprising since the focus of the chart was on the sea passages.

In 1728 Charles Brooking produced his map of the city. It is a detailed map naming individual streets and showing the built-up area. The south point is at the top of the page providing an interesting, if confusing, upside down view of the city. The value of his plan is augmented by a low-angle perspective of the city from the north and by the vignettes of many public buildings around the edge of his map. Copies of this map are relatively common, having been reprinted in 1983 by the Friends of the Library of TCD. John Rocque's (1756) map of the city of Dublin is special because it was produced at such a large scale (1:2400). He not only outlined the streets of the city but also individual houses, their outbuildings and gardens. It is an essential and versatile research tool as Anngret Simms has shown in chapter 1. It is of additional interest because of its publication date, the year before the establishment of the Wide Streets Commission. The map was split over four large sheets, which are quite rare. Fortunately a same-size reprint was produced in 1977 by Harry Margary who also produced a book version in 1998 – an *A to Z of Georgian Dublin*. Rocque also issued a smaller scale (*c.*1:9750) or pocket version of the map in 1757 which naturally offers less detail. At the same time, he developed a map of the

County of Dublin (1760), in four sheets, also available in reprint. He was a prolific mapmaker and the reader should consult John Andrews (1967) for a list of the maps he produced. Of greatest interest amongst these, perhaps, is the 1757 reduced plan (*c*.1:5000) showing the parishes in the city and suburbs of Dublin. For a variety of reasons, not least of which is the detail in the map, his work was unmatched until the large scale plans of the Ordnance Survey. Thomas Sherrard's map of 1791 would have provided an intermediate stage between Rocque and the Ordnance Survey had not the map been lost. All that apparently survives is one small extract (see Andrews, 1985, pp 280–1). The City Archive contains many of the plans of the Wide Streets Commissioners (see chapter 2) and other developers. These are often large-scale 'neighbourhood' maps and therefore can offer much detail.

Directories contained maps of the city from the middle of the eighteenth century though at a necessarily small scale. The *Treble Almanack*, developed as a compendium of the *Gentleman and Citizen's Almanack* (1729), the *Dublin Directory* (1752) and the English Registry, provided information on communications, lists of Dublin merchants and traders and regularly included a street map of the city from the 1760s. The practice of including a map with a street directory continued with the Thom's Directories of the city until the early years of the twentieth century. The early maps are often crudely printed but provide a useful view of change in the city though care must be taken in using them to date developments. Maps were sometimes revised on a rather irregular basis and sometimes they showed as complete, projects that were still a gleam in the developer's eye. The Gardiners' Royal Circus is a case in point. These days, directory maps tend to be found separately from their almanack and it is all too common to find the volume *sans* plan. William Wilson, the publisher of the *Treble Almanack*, produced a rather nice map of the city in 1798 at a scale of 1:10,560. It provides quite an amount of detail about the city and the date is useful as it comes at the end of the most important phase of the work of the Wide Streets Commission. An interesting, if scarce, map of the city was produced by Thomas Campbell, under the direction of Major Taylor, dated 1811. It is drawn at a scale of 100 Irish perches equals 5 inches (*c*.1:5000) and the plan is some 1.2 x 0.75m in size. Despite this relatively large scale, the detail is no better than the directory maps but it does attempt to show the relief of the city as hachures and the width of the streets would appear to be exact.

Many of the guides to the city of Dublin prepared during the late-eighteenth and nineteenth century contain a plan of the city. Pool and Cash have a map dated 1780 in their guide while Malton's famous volume of views

of the city (1799) also contained three maps of the city. One is a variant of
Speed, the second shows Dublin Bay but the third dated 1797 and produced
by William Faden is comparable to Wilson's map discussed above and owes
much to Rocque, especially in the non built-up areas. The nineteenth-century
guides are too numerous to comment on all but generally speaking the physical
size of the guide determines the scale of the map within. However, Warburton,
Whitelaw and Walsh (1818), Wright (1821; 1825), Curry (1835) and Starratt (1849)
each contain a useful map of the city. Later on in the century, Ward Lock, Black
and Wakeman are among those whose guides contained at least one plan of the
city. Though invariably small, they are useful in tracking change.

   In the years before the Ordnance Survey, John Taylor prepared a map of
the environs of Dublin in 1816. This map covered an area '14 miles from the
Castle' at a scale of 2 inches to the mile (1:31,680). It is a very handsome map
that not only contains a useful plan of the city but provides a great deal of data
on the suburbs. John Dower produced a map of the city in 1832 at about 3
inches to the mile (1:21,000). It contained a small vignette offering a perspective
of the city of Dublin from the Phoenix Park. This perspective, modified to
include the newly built Wellington memorial, was the standard view of
Dublin that appeared in every major geography text for the first 30 years, at
least, of the nineteenth century. At a more useful scale of 4 inches to the mile
(1:15840), the Society for the Diffusion of Useful Knowledge published a map
of the city and a separate map of the environs of Dublin (1836). These maps
are from an atlas of country, regional and town plans produced by the society
after 1829. The SDUK had disappeared by the mid-1840s but the plans
continued to be issued in various editions, with some revisions, for decades
afterwards. SDUK plans are an invaluable source of information on the
topography of American and European cities in the period before the great
burst of urban renewal. The Dublin plan has marginal drawings of important
buildings showing their relative heights.

   Thomas Larcom (Andrews, 1983b), under the directorship of Colonel
Thomas Colby, ran the Dublin office of the Ordnance Survey from 1828 to
1846. Larcom's map (1831–2) of the County of the City of Dublin at a scale of
c.2.25 inches to the mile (c.1:28,000) gives a view of Dublin and its suburbs at
a very manageable size. This map also shows the parliamentary boundaries.
Far more important, however, is the extraordinary series of maps that the OS
began to produce during this period. The OS produced a plan of Dublin at
the standard 6 inches to the mile (1:10,560) in 1837/8 though it was not
actually published until 1843–4 (see Andrews, 1973, pp 579–93). Sheet 18 with

Sheet 19 give a detailed view of the city and its suburbs. The 5–foot to 1 inch plans (1:1056) after 1838, provided astonishing detail for the built-up area, matched only by the modern 1:1000 series. Later editions included the townships. These were complemented in the 1860s by the 25 inch (1:2500) series which allowed the differentiation of individual buildings. The introduction to the OS of the electrotype process allowed very fine engraving to be faithfully reproduced and the quality of the printing of later issues of these plans is extremely good. These represent the standard cartographic research tool for Dublin from this time onwards with the various revisions, particularly 1912 for the 6 inch and 25 inch plans, giving useful temporal snapshots. A contemporary curiosity is the 1847 map of the city of Dublin by Hodges and Smith of Grafton Street at a scale of 1:7200. It shows the ward boundaries and the streets in outline but also the distances between each major intersection.

Mention must be made of the map of Dublin included in the John Tallis *Illustrated Atlas* of 1851. This is perhaps the most decorative map of Dublin of the century. It is at a scale of about 4.5 inches to the mile (*c.*1:14,000) and includes well-engraved vignettes of the city. It is considerably harder to find than the SDUK plan.

Plans of Dublin at 6 inches to the mile (1:10,560) were included in Thom's directory on an annual basis from the 1870s to the early years of the twentieth century. The map was derived from the Ordnance Survey map from 1872–1898 and thereafter it was based on the large-scale Bacon plan of the city. They were regularly revised and by using them it is possible to trace the development of the city, with the usual caveats. The later Victorian period saw the production of atlases for the mass market. Many of these contained a plan of the central area of Dublin, usually in colour and a scale of approximately 6 inches to the mile. Typical of these would be the *Letts' Popular Atlas*, *Bacon's Large Scale Ordnance Atlas of the British Isles with plans of towns* and, from the USA, *Cram's Unrivaled Family Atlas of the World*. While the plans are very generalized, they were revised sufficiently often to allow some changes in the city's topography to be noted.

Finally, there are two additional visual resources that are of interest. The *Illustrated London News* printed a panorama of the city in 1846. This is a bird's eye view of Dublin from the south-east. While one might quibble about the distorted perspective that is apparent in some parts of the city, the size of the plan, *c.*1 m x 36 cm, gives great detail. This is complemented by a similarly-sized (1.2 m) panorama printed by *The Graphic* in December 1890. This views the city from High Street and while it is more impressionistic than the *ILN* engraving, it gives valuable views of the city in the environs of the quays, Christ Church and St Patrick's Cathedral.

Specific References

The reader is directed to the work of John Andrews whose knowledge of Irish maps and mapping is unsurpassed. The following references will be of particular interest.

Andrews, J.H. (1967) The French school of Dublin land surveyors, *Irish Geography*, 5 (4), pp 275–92.

Andrews, J.H. (1973) Medium and message in early six-inch Irish Ordnance maps: the case of Dublin City, *Irish Geography*, 6 (5), pp 579–93.

Andrews, J.H. (1975) *A paper landscape – the Ordnance Survey in nineteenth-century Ireland*. Oxford: Clarendon Press.

Andrews, J.H. (1977) *Two maps of eighteenth-century Dublin and its surroundings by John Rocque*. Introduction by John Andrews to this reprint of the maps. Lympne Castle, Kent: Harry Margary.

Andrews, J.H. (1983a) The oldest map of Dublin, *Proceedings of the Royal Irish Academy*, 83C, pp 205–37.

Andrews, J.H. (1983b) Thomas Aiskew Larcom 1801–1879, *Geographers: Bibliographical Studies*, 7, pp 71–4.

Andrews, J.H. (1985) *Plantation acres – an historical study of the Irish land surveyor and his maps*. Belfast: Ulster Historical Foundation.

Andrews, J.H. (1989) *John Taylor's map of the environs of Dublin*. Booklet to accompany the reprint of the map. Dublin: Phoenix Maps.

See also:

Clark, M. (1983) *The book of maps of the Dublin City Surveyors, 1695–1827*. Dublin: Dublin Corporation, Public Libraries Department.

Ferguson, P. (1998) *The A to Z of Georgian Dublin: John Rocque's maps of the city in 1756 and the county in 1760*. Edited and indexed by Paul Ferguson with an introduction by J.H. Andrews. Lympne Castle, Kent: Harry Margary, in association with Trinity College Library, Dublin.

Kissane, N. (1987) *Historic Dublin maps*. Dublin: National Library of Ireland.

Bibliography

The bibliography that follows does not claim to be comprehensive. Rather it is intended to encourage the reader to explore the development of the city in greater depth. A more comprehensive list of publications on the history of the city of Dublin between 1500 and 1980, published in the period between 1969 and 1993, is that by D. McCabe contained in Nolan, W. and Simms, A. (eds) (1998) *Irish Towns – A Guide to Sources*. Dublin: Geography Publications, pp 227–36. This guide, completed with the assistance of Rionach NíNéill and Yvonne Whelan, also discusses the nature and usefulness of various source materials. A full bibliography on medieval Dublin will appear in 2001 in Clarke, H.B., *Dublin. Part 1, to 1610*, Irish Historic Towns Atlas, 12, edited by A. Simms, H.B. Clarke and R. Gillespie and published in Dublin by the Royal Irish Academy.

The bibliography that follows is arranged by chapter to make it easier to use. This, of necessity, has resulted in some duplication of the entries for key texts. Valuable documents for the history of the city are kept in the City Archive, South William Street, in the National Archives, Bishop Street and the Gilbert Library housed in the Public Library, Pearse Street.

GENERAL TEXTS

Aalen, F.H. and Whelan, K. (eds) (1992) *Dublin city and county from prehistory to present.* Dublin: Geography Publications.

Clarke, D. (1977) *Dublin.* London: Batsford.

Clark, M. (1983) *The book of maps of the Dublin City Surveyors 1695–1827.* Dublin: Dublin Corporation, Public Libraries Department.

Clark, M. and Refaussé, R. (eds) (1993) *Directory of historic Dublin guilds.* Dublin: Dublin Corporation, Public Libraries Department.

Collins, S. (1988) *Dublin: one thousand years.* Dublin: O'Brien Press.

Cosgrove, A. (ed.) (1988) *Dublin through the ages.* Dublin: College Press.

Costello, P. (1989) *Dublin churches.* Dublin: Gill and Macmillan.

de Courcy, J.W. (1996) *The Liffey in Dublin.* Dublin: Gill and Macmillan.

Fitzpatrick, S.A.O. (1907) *Dublin: a historical and topographical account of the city.* London: Methuen.

Gilbert, J.T. (ed.) (1889–1944) *Calendar of ancient records of Dublin in the possession of the municipal corporation.* 19 volumes. Dublin: Dollard.

Gilbert, J.T. (1854–9) *A history of the city of Dublin,* 3 volumes. Dublin: Reprinted by Gill and Macmillan 1978.

Gilligan, H.A. (1988) *A history of the port of Dublin.* Dublin: Gill and Macmillan.

Harris, W. (1766) *History and antiquities of the city of Dublin.* Dublin. Reprinted by Davidson Books, Ballynahinch (1994).

Harvey, J. (1949) *Dublin: a study in environment.* London: Batsford. Reprinted by S.R. Publishers, London (1972).

Kelly, J. and Keogh, D. (eds) (1999) *A history of the Catholic diocese of Dublin.* Dublin: Four Courts Press.

Kissane, N. (1987) *Historic Dublin maps*. Dublin: National Library of Ireland.

Liddy, P. (1998) *Walking Dublin*. London: New Holland.

Liddy, P. (1984) *Dublin today. The city's changing face in text and illustration*. Dublin: Irish Times.

McCullough, N. (1989) *Dublin; an urban history*. Dublin: Anne Street Press.

MacLaren, A. (1993) *Dublin: the shaping of a capital*. London: Belhaven Press.

MacLoughlin, A. (1979) *Guide to historic Dublin*. Dublin: Gill and Macmillan.

O'Donnell, E.E. (1987) *The annals of Dublin, Fair City*. Dublin: Wolfhound Press.

O'Dwyer, F. (1981) *Lost Dublin*. Dublin: Gill and Macmillan.

Somerville-Large, P. (1979) *Dublin*. London: Hamish Hamilton. Revised edition 1996.

Somerville-Large, P. (1988) *Dublin. The first thousand years*. Belfast: Appletree.

Sweeney, C. (1991) *The rivers of Dublin*. Dublin: Dublin Corporation.

Wright, G.N. (1821) *An historical guide to ancient and modern Dublin*, London. Reprinted by
Irish Academic Press (1980).

Wyse Jackson, P. (1993) *The building stones of Dublin*. Dublin: Town House.

ORIGINS AND EARLY GROWTH (PAGES 15–65)

The most important printed collection of sources translated from Latin into English on the early history of Dublin is volume 1 of Gilbert, J.T. (1889–1944) *Calendar of ancient records of Dublin, in the possession of the municipal corporation of that city*, 19 volumes, published by Dollard, Dublin. Also valuable are the edited records of the major monastic institutions in medieval Dublin, Holy Trinity (Christ Church), St Thomas, St John the Baptist and Mary's Abbey. The full references to these can be found below under McNeill (1950), Gilbert (1889), Brooks (1936) and Gilbert (1884–86).

The archaeological evidence comes to us from different sites. It was a unique experience for those who were fortunate enough to have visited one of the places excavated by the National Museum in Dublin, at High Street, Winetavern Street or Fishamble Street. There, three metres under the present street level, archaeologists had exposed the wooden foundations of houses, which were built most likely by Irish craftsmen under the direction of Viking traders approximately a thousand years ago. The publications of the excavation reports permit the study of this material. The excavations at Fishamble Street are published as a detailed series of which Wallace's (1992) two volumes on Viking houses in Dublin are the most important ones for our study of the layout of medieval Dublin. More recently, rescue excavations promoted by Dublin Corporation and Temple Bar Properties have contributed to our knowledge of medieval Dublin. The reports of these excavations can be found below under the editors' names, Gowen and Scally (1995), Walsh (1997), and Simpson (1994; 1999; 2000). Duffy's (2000) volume on rescue excavations in medieval Dublin provides easy access to the archaeological material.

Evidence for the composition of the river bed of the Liffey, sand and gravel over bedrock, comes from bore-hole records compiled by the Geological Survey of Ireland. Finally, early maps are a most important source for the study of the early growth-stages of the city.

Specific References

Andrews, J.H. (1977) *Two maps of eighteenth-century Dublin and its surroundings by John Rocque*.
Introduction by John Andrews to this reprint of the maps. Lympne Castle, Kent: Harry
Margary.

Andrews, J.H. (1983) The oldest map of Dublin, *Proceedings of the Royal Irish Academy*, 83C,
pp 205–37.

Bardon, J. and Conlin, S. (1984) *One thousand years of Wood Quay*. Dublin.

Berry, H.F. (1890–1) The water supply of ancient Dublin, *Journal of the Royal Society of Antiquaries of Ireland*, 21, pp 557–73.

Berry, H.F. (ed.) (1912–13) Minute book of the corporation of Dublin, known as the 'Friday Book', 1567–1611, *Proceedings of the Royal Irish Academy*, 30C, pp 477–514.

Bradley, J. (ed.) (1984) *Viking Dublin exposed: the Wood Quay saga*. Dublin: O'Brien Press.

Bradley, J. (1992) The topographical development of Scandinavian Dublin. *In*: Aalen, F.H.A. and Whelan, K. (eds) *Dublin city and county: from prehistory to present*. Dublin: Geography Publications, pp 43–56.

Bradshaw, B. (1974) *The dissolution of religious orders in Ireland under Henry VIII*. Cambridge: Cambridge University Press.

Brooks, E. St. J. (ed.) (1936) *Register of the hospital of St John the Baptist without the New Gate, Dublin*. Dublin: Stationery Office.

Burke, N. (1972) An early modern suburb. The estate of Francis Aungier, earl of Longford, *Irish Geography*, 6(4), pp 365–85.

Burke, N. (1974) Dublin's north-eastern city wall: early reclamation and development at the Poddle-Liffey confluence, *Proceedings of the Royal Irish Academy*, 74C, pp 113–32; reprinted in Clarke, H.B. (ed.) (1990a) *Medieval Dublin : The making of a metropolis*. Dublin: Irish Academic Press, pp 142–61.

Clark, M. (1983) *The book of maps of the Dublin City surveyors 1695–1827*. Dublin: Dublin Corporation, Public Libraries Department.

Clarke, H.B. (1977) The topographical development of early medieval Dublin, *Journal of the Royal Society of Antiquaries of Ireland*, 107, pp 29–51; reprinted in Clarke, H.B. (ed.) (1990a) *Medieval Dublin: the making of a metropolis*. Dublin: Irish Academic Press, pp 52–69.

Clarke, H.B. (1978) *Dublin c.840–c.1540: the medieval town in the modern city* (map with commentary), Dublin.

Clarke, H.B. and Simms, A. (1984) Early Dublin, 790–1170, and Medieval Dublin 1170–1542. *In*: Moody, T.W., Martin, F.X. and Byrne, F.J. (eds) *A New History of Ireland*. Volume 9. Oxford: Clarendon Press, pp 36–7; pp 104–6.

Clarke, H.B. (1988) Gaelic, Viking and Hiberno-Norse Dublin. *In:* Cosgrove, A. (ed.) *Dublin through the ages*. Dublin: College Press, pp 5–24.

Clarke, H.B. (ed.) (1990a) *Medieval Dublin: the making of a metropolis*. Dublin: Irish Academic Press.

Clarke, H.B. (ed.) (1990b) *Medieval Dublin: the living city*. Dublin: Irish Academic Press.

Clarke, H.B. (1993) The 1192 charter of liberties and the beginnings of Dublin's municipal life, *Dublin Historical Record*, 46, pp 5–14.

Clarke, H.B. (1985) The mapping of medieval Dublin. *In:* Clarke, H.B. and Simms, A. (eds) *The comparative history and urban origins in non-Roman Europe*. British Archaeological Reports, International Series, 255, vol. 2 pp 617–46.

Clarke, H.B. (1996) Proto-towns and towns in Ireland and Britain in the ninth and tenth centuries. *In:* Clarke, H.B., Ní Mhaonaigh, M. and Ó Floinn, R. (eds) *Ireland and Scandinavia in the early Viking age*. Dublin: Four Courts Press, pp 331–80.

Clarke, H.B. (1998) *Urbs et suburbium*: beyond the walls of medieval Dublin. *In:* Manning, C. (ed.) *Dublin and beyond the Pale. Studies in honour of Patrick Healy*. Bray, pp 45–58.

Clarke, H.B. (1999) Conversion, church and cathedral: the diocese of Dublin to 1152. *In:* Kelly, J. and Keogh, D. (eds) *History of the Catholic diocese of Dublin*. Dublin: Four Courts Press, pp 19–50.

Connolly, P. and Martin, G. (1992) (eds) *The Dublin guild merchant roll, c.1190–1265*. Dublin: Dublin Corporation.

Coughlan, T. (2000) The Anglo-Norman houses of Dublin: evidence from Back Lane. *In:* Duffy, S. (ed.) *Medieval Dublin I*. Dublin: Four Courts Press, pp 203–34.

Cotter, C. (1989) Bridge Street Lower, *Excavations*, 30.

Corry, G. (1970) The Dublin bar – the obstacle to the improvement of the port of Dublin, *Dublin Historical Record*, 23, pp 137–52.

Curtis, E. (1942) Norse Dublin, *Dublin Historical Record*, 4, pp 96–108. Reprinted in Clarke, H.B. (ed.) (1990b) *Medieval Dublin: the living city*. Dublin: Irish Academic Press, pp 110–27.

Davis, V. (1987) Relations between the abbey of St Thomas the Martyr and the municipality of Dublin 1176–1527, *Dublin Historical Record*, 40 (2), pp 57–64.

de Courcy, J.W. (1996) *The Liffey in Dublin. Proceedings of the Friends of Medieval Dublin Symposium 2000*. Dublin: Gill and Macmillian.

de Courcy, J.W. (2000) Bluffs, bays and pools in the medieval Liffey at Dublin, *Irish Geography*, 33(2), pp 117–133.

Doherty, C. (1980) Exchange and trade in early medieval Ireland, *Journal of the Royal Society of Antiquaries of Ireland*, 110, pp 67–89.

Doherty, C. (1998) The Vikings in Ireland; a review. *In:* Clarke, H.B., Ní Mhaonaigh, M. and Ó Floinn, R. (eds) *Ireland and Scandinavia in the early Viking age*. Dublin: Four Courts Press, pp 288–330.

Dolley, R.H.M. (1966) *The Hiberno-Norse coins in the British Museum*. London.

Duddy, C. (1990) The role of St Thomas' abbey in the development of the extra-mural settlement of medieval Dublin, 1177–1272. Unpublished MA thesis. Dublin: Department of Geography, University College Dublin.

Duffy, S. (1992) Irishmen and Islesmen in the kingdoms of Dublin and Man, 1051–1171, *Eriu*, 43, pp 93–133.

Duffy, S. (ed.) (2000) *Medieval Dublin I. Proceedings of the Friends of Medieval Dublin Symposium 2000*, Dublin: Four Courts Press.

Edwards, R.W.D. (1939) The beginnings of municipal government in Dublin, *Dublin Historical Record*, 1, pp 2–10.

Elliott, A.L. (1990) The abbey of St Thomas the Martyr, near Dublin. *In:* Clarke, H.B. (ed.) (1990b) *Medieval Dublin: the living city*. Dublin: Irish Academic Press, pp 62–76.

Ferguson, P. (1998) *The A to Z of Georgian Dublin: John Rocque's maps of the city in 1756 and the county in 1760*. Edited and indexed by Paul Ferguson with an introduction by J.H. Andrews. Lympne Castle, Kent: Harry Margary, in association with Trinity College Library, Dublin.

Geraghty, S. (1996) Viking Dublin: botanical evidence from Fishamble Street. *Medieval Dublin Excavations Series C*, 2. Dublin.

Gilbert, J.T. (ed.) (1870) *Historic and municipal documents of Ireland AD 1172–1320 from the Archives of the City of Dublin*. London: HMSO.

Gilbert, J.T. (ed.) (1884–1886) *Chartularies of St Mary's abbey, Dublin and annals of Ireland, 1162–1370*. 2 volumes. London: HMSO.

Gilbert, J.T. (ed.) (1889) *Register of the abbey of St Thomas*. London: HMSO.

Gilbert, J.T. (ed.) (1897) 'Crede Mihi': The most ancient register book of the archbishops of Dublin before the Reformation. Dublin: Dollard.

Gillespie, R. (ed.) (1997) *The Chapter account book of Christ Church Dublin, 1574–1634*. Dublin: Four Courts Press.

Gillespie, R. (2000) The coming of reform, 1500–58. *In:* Milne, K. (ed.) *Christ Church Cathedral – a history*. Dublin: Four Courts Press, pp 151–73.

Gillespie, R. (2000) The shaping of reform, 1558–1625. *In:* Milne, K. (ed.) *Christ Church cathedral – a history*. Dublin: Four Courts Press, pp 174–94.

Gillespie, R. (2000) The crisis of reform, 1625–60. *In:* Milne, K. (ed.) *Christ Church cathedral – a history*. Dublin: Four Courts Press, pp 195–217.

Gowen, M. (1989) Christchurch Place, Dublin. *Excavations*, 32.

Gowen, M. and Scally, G. (1995) *A summary report on excavations at Exchange Street, Upper Parliament Street, Dublin*. Temple Bar Archaeological Report 4. Dublin: Temple Bar Properties.

Gwynn, A. (1949) The origins of St Mary's abbey, Dublin, *Journal of the Royal Society of Antiquaries*, 79, pp 110–25.

Gwynn, A. and Hadcock, R.N. (1970) *Medieval religious houses in Ireland*. London: Longman.

Haliday, G. (1882) *The Scandinavian kingdom of Dublin*. Dublin: Alex Thom. Reprinted by Irish University Press (Shannon) (1969).

Halpin, A. (2000) *The port of medieval Dublin. Archaeological excavations at the Civic Offices, Winetavern Street, 1993*. Dublin: Four Courts Press.

Harris, W. (1766) *History and antiquities of the city of Dublin*. Dublin. Reprinted by Davidson Books, Ballynahinch, Co. Down (1994).

Healy, P. (1973) The town walls of Dublin. *In:* Gillespie, E. (ed.) *The Liberties of Dublin*. Dublin, pp 16–23. Reprinted with additions in Clarke, H.B. (1990a) *Medieval Dublin: the making of a metropolis*. Dublin: Irish Academic Press, pp 183–92.

Heffernan, T.F. (1988) *Wood Quay: the clash over Dublin's Viking past*. Austin: University of Texas Press.

Hennessy, M. (1988) The priory and hospital of NewGate: the evolution and decline of a medieval monastic estate. *In:* Smyth, W.J. and Whelan K. (eds) *Common ground: essays on the historical geography of Ireland*. Cork: Cork University Press, pp 41–54.

Holm, P. (1986) The slave trade of Dublin, ninth to twelfth centuries, *Peritia*, 5, pp 317–45.

Kelly, J. and Keogh, D. (eds) (1999) *A history of the Catholic Church in the diocese of Dublin*. Dublin: Four Courts Press.

Kinsella, St. (2000) From Hiberno-Norse to Anglo-Norman, c.1030–1300. *In:* Milne, K. (ed.) *Christ Church cathedral – a history*. Dublin: Four Courts Press, pp 25–52.

Lamplugh, G.W., Kilroe, J.R., McHenry, A., Seymour, H.J. and Wright, W.B. (1903) *The geology of the country around Dublin*. Memoirs of the Geological Survey of Ireland. Explanation of sheet 112. Dublin: GSI, pp 1–97.

Lennon, C. (1981) *Richard Stanihurst the Dubliner, 1547–1618*. Irish Academic Press, Dublin.

Lennon, C. (1983) Civic life and religion in early-seventeenth-century Dublin, *Archivium Hibernicum*, 38, pp 14–25.

Lennon, C. (1988a) The beauty and eye of Ireland: the sixteenth century. *In:* Cosgrove, A. (ed.) *Dublin through the ages*. Dublin: College Press, pp 46–62.

Lennon, C. (1988b) The great explosion in Dublin, 1597, *Dublin Historical Record*, 42, pp 7–20.

Lennon, C. (1989) *The lords of Dublin in the age of reformation*. Dublin: Irish Academic Press.

Lucas, A.T. (1966) Irish-Norse relations: time for a reappraisal, *Journal of the Cork Historical Society*, 71, pp 62–75.

Lydon, J. (ed.) (1982) A fifteenth-century building account from Dublin, *Irish Economic and Social History*, 9, pp 73–5.

Lydon, J. (1988) The medieval city. *In:* Cosgrove, A. (ed.) *Dublin through the ages*. Dublin: College Press, pp 25–45.

Lynch, A. and Manning, C. (1986) Dublin Castle. *Excavations*, 25.

MacCurtain, M. (1972) *Tudor and Stuart Ireland*. The Gill History of Ireland, volume 7. Dublin: Gill and Macmillan.

Maguire, J. (1974) Seventeenth-century plans of Dublin Castle, *Journal of the Royal Society of Antiquaries of Ireland*, 104, pp 5–14.

Manning, C. (ed.) (1998) *Dublin and beyond the Pale – studies in honour of Patrick Healy.* Dublin: Bray.

Maxwell, C. (ed.) (1923) *Irish history from contemporary sources, 1509–1610.* London: Allen and Unwin.

McCabe, A.M. and Hoare, P.G. (1978) The Late Quaternary history of east central Ireland, *Geological Magazine*, 115, pp 397–413.

McCready, C.T. (1892) *Dublin street names dated and explained.* Reprinted by Carraig Books, Blackrock (1987).

McNeill, C. (1921) New Gate, Dublin. *Journal of the Royal Society of Antiquaries of Ireland*, 51, pp 152–65.

McNeill, C. (1925) Hospital of St John without the New Gate, Dublin. *In:* Clarke, H.B. (ed.) (1990b) *Medieval Dublin: the living city.* Dublin: Irish Academic Press, pp 77–82.

McNeill, C. (ed.) (1950) *Calendar of Archbishop Alen's Register c.1172–1534.* Dublin: Royal Society of Antiquaries of Ireland.

Miller, L. and Power, E. (1979) *Holinshed's Irish chronicle.* Dublin: Dolmen Press.

Milne, K. (ed.) (2000) *Christ Church cathedral – a history.* Dublin: Four Courts Press.

Mills, J. (ed.) (1891) *The account roll of the priory of the Holy Trinity, Dublin, 1337–1346.* Dublin: Royal Society of Antiquaries of Ireland. Reprinted by Four Courts Press (1996).

Mitchell, G.F. (1987) *Archaeology and environment in early Dublin.* Medieval Dublin Excavations 1962–81, series C. 1. Dublin.

Moryson, F. (1735) *The history of Ireland, from 1599 to 1603, with a ... description of Ireland.* Dublin.

Murray, H. (1981) Houses and other structures from the Dublin excavations, 1962–1976: a summary. *In:* Bekker-Nielsen, H. et al. (eds) *Proceedings of the Eighth Viking Congress.* Odense, pp 57–68.

Murray, H. (1983) Viking and early medieval buildings in Dublin. *British Archaeological Reports. British Series*, 119. Oxford.

Ní Néill, R. (1995) Conflict and change in the townscape of the Dublin city quays, with a comparative perspective of the Parisian quays. Unpublished PhD thesis. Dublin: Department of Geography, University College Dublin.

O'Brien, E. (1998) The location and context of Viking burials at Kilmainham and Islandbridge. *In:* Clarke, H.B., Ní Mhaonaigh, M. and Ó Floinn, R. (eds) *Ireland and Scandinavia in the early Viking age.* Dublin: Four Courts Press, pp 203–35.

O'Carroll (1981) The municipal government of Dublin, 1558–1603, *Retrospect*, New Series, 1, pp 7–12.

Ó Conbhuí, C. (1961–4) The lands of St Mary's Abbey, Dublin, at the dissolution of the abbey, *Repertorium Novum*, 3 (1).

Ó Floinn, R. (1998) The archaeology of the early Viking age in Ireland. *In:* Clarke, H.B., Ní Mhaonaigh, M. and Ó Floinn, R. (eds) *Ireland and Scandinavia in the early Viking Age.* Dublin: Four Courts Press, pp 131–65.

Ó Ríordáin, B. (1971) Excavations at High Street and Winetavern Street, Dublin, *Medieval Archaeology*, 15, pp 73–85.

Ó Ríordáin, B. (1976) The High Street excavations. *In:* Almqvist, B. and Greene, D. (eds) *Proceedings of the Seventh Viking Congress.* Dublin, pp 29–37; reprinted in Clarke, H.B. (ed.) (1990a) *Medieval Dublin: the making of a metropolis.* Dublin: Irish Academic Press, pp 165–72.

Prunty, J. (1995) Residential urban renewal schemes, Dublin 1986–1994, *Irish Geography*, 28(2), pp 131–49.

Rae, E.C. (1979) The medieval fabric of the cathedral church of St Patrick in Dublin, *Journal of the Royal Society of Antiquaries of Ireland*, 109, pp 29–73.

Refaussé, R. and Lennon, C. (eds) (1998) *The registers of Christ Church cathedral, Dublin*. Dublin: Four Courts Press.

Ronan, M.V. (1925) Religious customs of Dublin medieval guilds, *Irish Ecclesiastical Record*, Fifth series, 26, pp 225–47, pp 364–85.

Semple, G. (1776) *A treatise on building in water*. Dublin.

Simms, A. (1979) Medieval Dublin: a topographical analysis, *Irish Geography*, 12, pp 25–41.

Simms, A. (1980) Medieval Dublin in a European context: from proto-town to chartered town. *In:* Clarke, H.B. (ed.) *Medieval Dublin: the making of a metropolis*. Dublin: Irish Adademic Press, pp 37–51.

Simms, A. (1994) The Vikings in Ireland: the urban contribution with particular reference to Dublin. *In:* Nilsson, L. and Lilja, S. (eds) *The emergence of towns, archaeology and early urbanisation in non-Roman, north-west Europe*. Stockholm: Stockholm University, pp 50–78.

Simpson, L. (1994) *Excavations at Isolde's Tower*. Temple Bar Archaeological Report, 1. Dublin: Temple Bar Properties.

Simpson, L. (1995) *Excavations at Essex Street West, Dublin*. Temple Bar Archaeological Report, 2. Dublin: Temple Bar Properties.

Simpson, L. (1999) *Director's findings. Temple Bar West*. Temple Bar Archaeological Report, 5. Dublin: Temple Bar Properties.

Simpson, L. (2000) Forty years a-digging: a preliminary synthesis of archaeological investigations in medieval Dublin. *In:* Duffy, S. (ed.) *Medieval Dublin I*. Dublin: Four Courts Press, pp 11–68.

Stone, N. (1990) *The Russian chronicles*. London: Century.

Stalley, R. (2000) The reconstruction of the medieval cathedral. *In:* Milne, K. (ed.) *Christ Church cathedral – a history*. Dublin: Four Courts Press, pp 53–74.

Stalley, R. (2000) The architecture of the cathedral and priory buildings, 1250–1530. *In:* Milne, K. (ed.) *Christ Church cathedral – a history*. Dublin: Four Courts Press, pp 95–128.

Stalley, R. (2000) The 1562 collapse of the nave and its aftermath. *In:* Milne, K. (ed.) *Christ Church cathedral – a history*. Dublin: Four Courts Press, pp 218–36.

Turner, J.S. (1950) The carboniferous limestone in Co. Dublin, south of the river Liffey, *Scientific Proceedings of the Royal Dublin Society*, 25, pp 169–91.

Wallace, P.F. (1981) Dublin's waterfront at Wood Quay, 900–1317. *In:* Milne, G. and Hobley, B. (eds) *Waterfront archaeology in Britain and Northern Europe*. London, pp 109–18.

Wallace, P.F. (1985) The archaeology of Viking Dublin. *In:* Clarke, H.B. and Simms, A. (eds) The comparative history of urban origins in non-Roman Europe. *British Archaeological Reports*, International Series, 255. Oxford, pp 103–45.

Wallace, P.F. (1985) The archaeology of Anglo-Norman Dublin. *In:* Clarke, H.B. and Simms, A. (eds) The comparative history of urban origins in non-Roman Europe. *British Archaeological Reports*, International Series, 255. Oxford, pp 379–410.

Wallace, P.F. (1987) *The layout of later Viking-age Dublin: indication of its regulation and problems of continuity*. Proceedings of the Tenth Viking Congress. Oslo, pp 271–85.

Wallace, P.F. (1990) The origins of Dublin. *In:* Clarke, H.B. (ed.) *Medieval Dublin: the making of a metropolis*. Dublin: Irish Academic Press, pp 70–97.

Wallace, P.F. (1992a) The Viking-age buildings of Dublin. *Medieval Dublin Excavations 1962–81*, Series A(1). Dublin: Royal Irish Academy.

Wallace, P.F. (1992b) The archaeological identity of the Hiberno-Norse town, *Journal of the Royal Society of Antiquaries of Ireland*, 122, pp 35–66.

Walsh, C. (1997) *Archaeological excavations at Patrick, Nicholas and Winetavern streets*. Dingle: Brandon Press.

Walsh, P. (1977) *Dublin c.840 to c.1540: the years of medieval growth*. Map. Dublin: Ordnance Survey.

Watt, J.A. (1986) Dublin in the thirteenth century: the making of a colonial capital city. *In:* Coss, P.R. and Lloyd, S.D. (eds) *Thirteenth-century England*. Proceedings of the Newcastle upon Tyne Conference, 1985. London: Boydell Press, pp 150–7.

Yarraton, A. (1674) Report and map on Liffey estuary 1674. Reprinted in Gilbert, J.T. (1895) *Calendar of ancient records of Dublin.*, volume 5. Dublin: Dollard, plate 1 and pp 573–6.

White, N.B. (1943) *Extents of Irish monastic possessions, 1540–1*, Dublin: Stationery Office.

Wood, H. (ed.) (1933) *James Perrot. The chronicle of Ireland, 1584–1608*. Dublin: Irish Manuscripts Commission.

DESIGNING THE CAPITAL CITY – DUBLIN c.1660–1810 AND LIVING IN THE CAPITAL CITY DUBLIN IN THE EIGHTEENTH CENTURY (PAGES 66–158)

Much reference is made in the text to Gilbert, J.T. (1889–1944) *Calendar of ancient records of Dublin, in the possession of the municipal corporation of that city*, 19 volumes. The reader should also visit the Civic Museum in South William Street, Dublin, which houses the City Archive and is a wonderful resource for anyone interested in the development of the city. This archive houses the Minutes of the Wide Streets Commission (1758–1802) and many of its maps and elevations. The Registry of Deeds, Henrietta Street, Dublin, holds the *Books of Transcripts* referred to in the discussion of the Gardiner estate as well as the *City of Dublin Index* books. The National Archives of Ireland, Bishop Street, Dublin, hold important documentary material on eighteenth-century Dublin, for example wills such as that of the Right Hon. Luke Gardiner Esq. 1755 and pre-Ordnance Survey maps such as those from the Pembroke Estate collection. Eighteenth-century letterbooks, leases and maps of the Fitzwilliam estate survived in the collection of the Pembroke Estate Office in Dublin. In the late 1980s this collection was removed to England but has since been returned. In contrast to the Fitzwilliam estate, the Gardiner estate was broken up by sale in the Encumbered Estates Court in 1846. As a result the Gardiner papers were not kept together as a collection. Readers will also find it useful to refer the directories and almanacks published during this period. The *Treble Almanack* developed as a compendium of the *Gentleman and Citizen's Almanack* (1729), the *Dublin Directory* (1752) and the *English Registry* and provided information on communications, lists of Dublin merchants and traders and, from the 1780s, a street map of the city. Dublin Corporation Public Libraries has recently published (2000) *A Directory of Dublin for the year 1738* which has been compiled from a number of contemporary sources.

Specific References

Anderson, M.S. (1987) *Europe in the eighteenth century 1713–1783*. 3rd edition. London: Longman.

Andrews, J.H. (1977) *Two maps of eighteenth-century Dublin and its surroundings by John Rocque*. Introduction by John Andrews to this reprint of the maps. Lympne Castle, Kent: Harry Margary.

Anon. (1732) *Description of the city of Dublin, 1732. By a citizen of London*. Reprinted in Gilbert, J.T. (1903) *Calendar of ancient records of Dublin*. Volume 10, appendix 7.

Ashe, F.A. (1941) Mountjoy Square, *Dublin Historical Record*, 3, pp 98–115.

Bardon, C. and Bardon, J. (1988) *If ever you go to Dublin town. A historic guide to the city's street names*. Belfast: Blackstaff.

Barker, J. (1762) *A plan of Merrion Square, with the intended new streets*. Pembroke Estate Office.

Brooking, C. (1728) *A map of the city and suburbs of Dublin*. Reprinted in Craig, M. (1983) *Charles Brooking, the city of Dublin 1728*. Dublin: Irish Architectural Archive.

Burke, N. (1972a) An early modern suburb. The estate of Francis Aungier, earl of Longford, *Irish Geography*, 6(4), pp 365–85.

Burke, N. (1972b) Dublin 1600–1800: a study in urban morphogenesis. Unpublished PhD thesis. Dublin: University of Dublin, Trinity College.

Burke, N. (1974) Dublin's north-eastern city wall: early reclamation and development at the Poddle–Liffey confluence, *Proceedings of the Royal Irish Academy*, 74C, pp 113–32.

Burton Conyngham (1810) *Catalogue of an extensive and valuable collection of books* (Burton Conyngham). Dublin: Trinity College Libraries, Early Printed Books Section.

Bush, J. (1769) *Hibernia curiosa*. Dublin.

Butlin, R.A. (1965) The population of Dublin in the late-seventeenth century, *Irish Geography*, 5(2), pp 57–66.

Butel, P. and Cullen, L.M. (1986) *Cities and merchants. French and Irish perspectives on urban development 1500–1900*. Dublin: Trinity College Dublin.

Caldicott, C.E.J., Gough, H. and Pittion, J.P. (eds) (1987) *The Huguenots and Ireland*. Dublin: Glendale Press.

Caldwell (1809) *Catalogue of books, being the library of the late Andrew Caldwell, Esq*. Dublin: Trinity College Libraries, Early Printed Books Section.

Campbell, C. (1715–71) *Vitruvius Britannicus, or The British architect*. London.

Campbell, Revd T. (1777) *A philosophical survey of the south of Ireland*. London.

Casey, C. (1988) Architectural books in eighteenth-century Ireland, *Eighteenth-Century Ireland*, 3, pp 105–13.

Clark, M. (1986) Dublin Surveyors and their maps, *Dublin Historical Record*, 39, 4, pp 140–8.

Clark, M. (1988) Catalogue of Wide Streets Commission architectural drawings. Unpublished catalogue. Dublin: Dublin Corporation Archives.

Cole, R. (1974) Private libraries in eighteenth-century Ireland, *Library Quarterly*, 44(3), pp 231–47.

Cole, H. (1984) Handel in Dublin, *Irish Arts Review*, 1 (2), pp 28–30.

Colley, M. (1991) A list of architects, builders, measurers and engineers extracted from Wilson's Dublin directories, 1760–1837, *Bulletin of the Irish Georgian Society*, 34, pp 3–68.

Craig, M. (1952) *Dublin 1660–1860*. London: Cresset Press. Reprinted many times, references in the text are to the 1969 edition.

Cromwell, T. (1820) *Excursions through Ireland*. London.

Cullen, L.M. (1986) The Dublin merchant community. *In*: Butel, P. and Cullen, L.M. (eds) *Cities and merchants – French and Irish perspectives on urban development 1500–1900*. Dublin: Trinity College Dublin, pp 195–210.

Cullen, L.M. (1992) The growth of Dublin, 1600–1900: character and heritage. *In*: Aalen, F.H.A. and Whelan, K. (eds) *Dublin city and county from prehistory to present*. Dublin: Geography Publications, pp 252–77.

Curran, C.P. (1967) *Dublin's decorative plasterwork of the seventeenth and eighteenth centuries*. London: Alec Tiranti.

Daly, M.E. (1984) *Dublin, the deposed capital – a social and economic history 1850–1900*. Cork: Cork University Press.

de Gomme, B. (1673) *The city and suburbs of Dublin*. National Maritime Museum, Greenwich, England. Reprinted in Gilbert (1854).

Dickson, D. (1987) *The gorgeous mask: Dublin 1700–1850*. Dublin: Trinity History Workshop.

Dickson, D. (1988) Capital and country: 1600–1800. *In:* Cosgrove, A. (ed.) *Dublin through the ages*. Dublin: College Press, pp 63–76.

Dickson, D. (1989) The demographic implications of Dublin's growth, 1650–1850. *In:* Lawton, R. and Lee, R. (eds) *Urban population development in western Europe from the late-eighteenth to the early-twentieth century*. Liverpool: Liverpool University Press, pp 178–89.

Diderot, D. and d'Alembert, J.L. (eds) (1762) *Recueil de planches, sur les sciences, les arts liberaux, et les arts méchaniques, avec leur explication*. Volume 22 of the *Encylopédie*. Paris. Reprinted in 1967 in Stuttgart-Bad Cannstatt.

Fagan, P. (1986) *The second city: portrait of Dublin 1700–1760*. Dublin: Branar.

Fagan, P. (1991) The population of Dublin in the eighteenth century with particular reference to the proportions of Protestants and Catholics, *Eighteenth Century Ireland*, 6, pp 121–58.

Ferrar, J. (1796) *A view of ancient and modern Dublin*. Dublin.

Fraser, A.M. (1964) Messrs Gardiner and Hill – Bankers, *Dublin Historical Record*, 19 (4), pp 127–33.

Frazer, M. (1985) Public building and colonial policy in Dublin 1750–1800, *Architectural History*, 28.

Georgian Society (1909–1913) *Records of eighteenth-century domestic architecture and decoration in Dublin*. Dublin: Irish Georgian Society. Reprinted in 1969 by Irish University Press.

Gilbert, J.T. (1889–1944) *Calendar of ancient records of Dublin, in the possession of the municipal corporation of that city*. Dublin: Dollard.

Gilbert, J.T. (1854–9) *A history of the city of Dublin*. Dublin: McGlashin and Gill. Reprinted by Irish University Press (1992).

Girouard, M. (1985) *Cities and people. A social and architectural history*. New Haven: Yale University Press.

Guinness, D. (1979) *Georgian Dublin*. London: Batsford.

Hall, T. (1997) *Planning Europe's capital cities. Aspects of nineteenth-century urban development*. London: E and FN Spon.

Harris, W. (1766) *History and antiquities of the city of Dublin*. London. Reprinted by Davidson Books, Ballynahinch, Co. Down (1994).

Hochberg, L. and Genovese, E. (eds) (1988) *Geographic perspectives in history*. Oxford: Blackwell.

Jefferys, N. (1810) *An Englishman's descriptive account of Dublin*. London.

Kostof, S. (1991) *The city shaped – urban patterns and meanings through history*. London: Thames and Hudson.

La Tocnaye, le Chevalier de (1796–7) *A Frenchman's walk through Ireland 1796–7*. Reprinted and translated by J. Stevenson (1917). London.

La Touche, J.J. Digges (ed.) (1893) *Registers of the French conformed churches of St Patrick and St Mary, Dublin*. The publications of the Huguenot Society of London 7. Dublin: Thom.

Lewis, R. (1787) *The Dublin guide*. Dublin.

Lewis, S. (1837) *Topographical dictionary of Ireland*. London. Reprinted by Kennikat Press, New York and London (1970).

Loeber, R. (1978) An unpublished view of Dublin in 1698 by Francis Place, *Bulletin of Irish Georgian Society*, 21(1), pp 7–15.

Loeber, R. (1980) The rebuilding of Dublin Castle: thirty critical years, 1661–90, *Studies*, 69, 273, pp 45–69.

Loeber, R. and Stouthamer-Loeber, M. (eds) (1994) An unknown account of Georgian architecture and the arts in Dublin and its vicinity in 1797. Manuscript.

Malton, J. (1792–9) *A picturesque and descriptive view of the city of Dublin*. Dublin. Reprinted in 1981 by Dolmen Press as *James Malton's Dublin views in colour*.

Maxwell, C. (1938) *Dublin under the Georges*. London: Harrap.

McCready, C.T. (1892) *Dublin street names dated and explained*. Reprinted by Carraig Books, Blackrock (1987).

McCullough, N. (1989) *Dublin. An urban history* Dublin: Anne Street Press.

McCullough, N. (1991) *A vision of the city. Dublin and the Wide Streets Commissioners*. Dublin: Dublin Corporation.

McGregor, J.J. (1821) *New picture of Dublin*. Dublin.

McParland, E. (1969) Francis Johnston, architect 1760–1829, *Bulletin of the Irish Georgian Society*, 12(2), pp 124ff.

McParland, E. (1972) The Wide Streets Commissioners: their importance for Dublin architecture in the late-eighteenth – early-nineteenth century, *Bulletin of the Irish Georgian Society*, 15 (1), pp 1–32.

McParland, E. (1985) *James Gandon. Vitruvius Hibernicus*. Studies in architecture 24. London: Zwemmer.

McParland, E. (1986) Strategy in the planning of Dublin 1750–1800. *In:* Butel, P. and Cullen L.M. (eds) *Cities and merchants: French and Irish perspectives on urban development, 1500–1900*. Dublin: Trinity College Dublin, pp 97–108.

McParland, E. (1991) *The Custom House, Dublin*. Dublin: Office of Public Works.

Milne, K. (2000) Restoration and reorganisation 1660–1830. *In:* Milne, K. (ed.) *Christ Church cathedral – a history*. Dublin: Four Courts Press, pp 255–97.

Mumford, L. (1961) *The city in history*. New York: Harcourt, Brace and World. Numerous reprints. References are to the 1966 edition.

Murphy, S. (1984) The Corporation of Dublin, 1660–1760, *Dublin Historical Record*, 38 (1), pp 22–35.

Murnane, B. (1988) The recreation of the urban historical landscape: Mountjoy Ward Dublin *c.*1901. *In:* Smyth, W.J. and Whelan, K. (eds) *Common Ground – essays on the historical geography of Ireland*. Cork: Cork University Press, pp 189–207.

Murray, F. (1985) Public building and colonial policy in Dublin, 1760–1800, *Architectural History*, 28, pp 102–23.

National Council for Educational Awards (1991) *Gardiner's Dublin: a history and topography of Mountjoy Square and its environs*. Dublin: NCEA.

Neve, R. (1703) *The city and countrey purchaser, and builder's dictionary, or the compleat builder's guide, with aphorisms, or necessary rules in building, as to situation, contrivance, compactness, uniformity, conveniency, firmness and form, etc.* London.

O'Kelly, F. (1974) John Rocque on Dublin and Dubliners 1756, *Irish Historical Record*, 27(4), pp 146–7.

Palladio, A. (1736) *Palladio's architecture … containing 226 folio copperplates … revised and redelinieted* by E. Hopkins.

Phillips, T. (1685) *Map of Dublin*. Reprinted in Gilbert (1895), volume 5, Plate II.

Pool, R. and Cash, J. (1780) *Views of the most remarkable public buildings, monuments and other edifices in the city of Dublin*. Dublin. Reprinted by Irish University Press (1969).

Prunty, J.L. (1992) The geography of poverty Dublin 1850–1900; the social mission of the church, with particular reference to Margaret Aylward and co-workers. Unpublished PhD thesis. Dublin: Department of Geography, University College Dublin.

Putland (1847) *Bibliotheca Putlandiana … collection … formed from 1749 to about 1816 …* , Dublin: Charles Sharpe, National Library of Ireland.

Simms, J.G. (1965) Dublin in 1685, *Irish Historical Studies*, 14, pp 212–26.

Shaw, H. (1850) *New city pictorial directory 1850 to which is added a retrospective review of the past year.* Dublin: Henry Shaw. Reprinted in 1988 by Friar's Bush Press, Belfast.

Sheridan, E. (1993) Dublin and Berlin – a comparative geography of two eighteenth-century European capitals. Unpublished PhD thesis. Dublin: Department of Geography, University College Dublin.

Summerson, Sir J. (1945) *Georgian London.* London: Batsford.

Trench, C.E.F. (1985) William Burton Conyngham 1733–1796, *Journal of the Royal Society of Antiquaries of Ireland*, 115, pp 40–63.

Turpin, J. (1987) Continental influence in eighteenth-century Ireland, *Irish Arts Review*, 4 (4), pp 50–7.

Twiss, R. (1776) *A tour in Ireland in 1775.* London.

Walsh, E. (1987) Sackville Mall: the first one hundred years. *In:* Dickson, D. (ed.) *The gorgeous mask: Dublin 1700–1850.* Dublin: Trinity History Workshop, pp 30–50.

Walsh, J.E. (1847) *Ireland sixty years ago.* Dublin. Reprinted as *Rakes and ruffians – the underworld of Georgian Dublin*, Four Courts Press (1979).

Warburton, J., Whitelaw, Revd J. and Walsh, Revd R. (1818) *History of the city of Dublin.* London.

Webb, J.J. (1929) *The guilds of Dublin.* London: Benn. Reprinted by Kennikat Press, London (1970).

Whitelaw, Revd J. (1805) *An essay on the population of Dublin, being the result of an actual survey taken in 1798 with great care and precision, to which is added the general return of the district committee in 1804, with a comparative statement of the two surveys, also several observations on the present state of the poorer parts of the city of Dublin, 1805.* Dublin. Reprinted as *Slum conditions in London and Dublin* (1974). Farnborough, Hants: Gregg International.

Wilson, W. (1786) *The post-chaise companion or traveller's directory through Ireland.* Dublin.

Wright, G.N. (1821) *An historical guide to ancient and modern Dublin*, London. Reprinted by Irish Academic Press (1980).

IMPROVING THE URBAN ENVIRONMENT AND PUBLIC HEALTH AND HOUSING IN
NINETEENTH-CENTURY DUBLIN (PAGES 166–220)

Early (pre-1850s) reports on the sanitary state of the city were produced by a number of individuals and private institutions such as the Cork Street Fever Hospital and are available in the National Library of Ireland pamphlet and report collection. There are two housing inquiries that are relevant to the discussion in this chapter. The first report was published in 1885 and the second in 1914. These are referenced in the text as Housing Inquiry (1885) and Housing Inquiry (1914) respectively.

1885   *Third report of her majesty's commissioners for Inquiring into the housing of the working classes – Ireland.* British Parliamentary Papers c.4547 with Minutes of Evidence etc, c.4547–I. These were reprinted in 1970 by Irish University Press in a volume that also contains the reports of the inquiries for England, Scotland and Wales. The full reference of this volume is – British Parliamentary Papers, *Urban Areas – Housing.* Volume 3, Session 1884–85. Dublin: Irish University Press.

1914   *Report of the departmental committee to inquire into the housing conditions of the working class in Dublin.* British Parliamentary Papers c.7273.

The reports of the Public Health Committee of Dublin Corporation appear in two forms. A reference to *RPDCD* is to *Reports and Printed Documents of the Corporation of Dublin*, a compendium of the various reports produced by the Corporation in a given year. However, the *Report upon the state of Public Health*, referred to in the text as *Report on Public Health*, was also produced annually as a separate volume which included the annual report on the analysis of food, drugs and water. These can most easily be consulted in the City Archive. The Griffith Valuation (1854) is more properly referred to as the *General Valuation of Rateable Property in Ireland*. For the city of Dublin, a separate volume was published for each of the wards of the city. Details of the assigned valuation are provided for each property within the ward.

The journal of the Statistical and Social Inquiry Society of Ireland, formerly the Dublin Statistical Society, is also a very useful source on the housing question in Dublin during the late-nineteenth and early-twentieth centuries. See also the references to the final two chapters.

Specific References

Aalen, F.H.A. (1985) The working class housing movement in Dublin 1850–1920. *In:* Bannon, M.J. (ed.) *The emergence of Irish planning 1880–1920.* Dublin: Turoe Press, pp 101–60.

Aalen, F.H.A. (1987) Public housing in Ireland, 1880–1921, *Planning Perspectives*, 2, pp 175–93.

Aalen, F.H.A. (1989) Lord Meath, city improvement and social imperialism, *Planning Perspectives*, 4, pp 127–52.

Aalen, F.H.A. (1990) *The Iveagh Trust: the first hundred years.* Dublin: Iveagh Trust.

Burke, H. (1987) *The people and the Poor Law in nineteenth-century Ireland.* Littlehampton, West Sussex: Women's Education Bureau.

Cameron, C.A. (1914) *Municipal public health administration in Dublin.* Dublin: Hodges Figgis.

Clear, C. and Johnston, M. (1993) *Growing up poor: the homeless young in nineteenth-century Ireland, Dublin childhoods.* Galway.

Cork Street Report (1802) *Observation of the circumstances which tend to generate and propagate contagion in the Liberties on the south side of the City of Dublin and the means of removing them.* Dublin: Trustees of the House of Recovery or Fever Hospital in Cork Street.

Corrigan, F. (1976) Dublin workhouses during the great famine, *Dublin Historical Record*, 20, pp 59–65.

Coyne, J. Stirling and Bartlett, W.H. (1847) *The scenery and antiquities of Ireland.* London: Virtue.

Cowan, P.C. (1918) *Report on Dublin housing.* Dublin: Cahill.

Crossman, V. (1994) *Local government in nineteenth-century Ireland.* Belfast: Institute of Irish Studies, Queen's University Belfast.

Cullen, M. (1990) Bread winners and providers: women in the household economy of labouring families 1835–6. *In:* Luddy, M. and Murphy, C. (eds) *Women surviving: studies in Irish women's history in the nineteenth and twentieth centuries.* Dublin: Poolbeg, pp 85–116.

Daly, M.E. (1984) *Dublin, the deposed capital: a social and economic history 1850–1900.* Cork: Cork University Press.

Daly, M. (1985) Housing conditions and the genesis of housing reform in Dublin 1880–1920. *In:* Bannon, M.J. (ed.) *The emergence of Irish planning 1880–1920.* Dublin: Turoe Press pp 77–130.

Daly, M. (1986) Dublin in the nineteenth century. *In:* Butel, P. and Cullen, L.M. (eds) *Cities and merchants: French and Irish perspectives on urban development, 1500–1900.* Dublin: Trinity College Dublin, pp 53–66.

Daly, M. (1988) A tale of two cities: 1860–1920. *In:* Cosgrove, A. (ed.) *Dublin through the ages.* Dublin: College Press, pp 113–32.

D'Arcy, F. (1988) An age of distress and reform: 1800 to 1860. *In:* Cosgrove, A. (ed.) *Dublin through the ages*. Dublin: College Press, pp 93–112.

Eason, C. (1899) The tenement houses of Dublin: their condition and regulation, *Journal of the Statistical and Social Inquiry Society of Ireland*, 10 (79), pp 383ff.

Falkiner, F.R. (1881) Report on the homes of the poor, *Journal of the Statistical and Social Inquiry Society of Ireland*, 8 (59), 261–70.

Gamble, J. (1826) *Sketches of history, politics and manners in Dublin and the north of Ireland in 1810*. London.

Gilbert, J.T. (1889–1944) *Calendar of ancient records of Dublin, in the possession of the municipal corporation of that city*. Dublin: Dollard.

Harty, S. (1884) Some considerations on the working of the Artizans' and Labourers' Dwellings Act as illustrated in the case of the Coombe area, Dublin, *Journal of the Statistical and Social Inquiry Society of Ireland*, 8 (62).

Hearn, M. (1989) Life for domestic servants in Dublin, 1880–1920. *In:* Luddy, M. and Murphy, C. (eds) *Women surviving: studies in Irish women's history in the nineteenth and twentieth centuries*. Dublin: Poolbeg, pp 148–79.

Hooper, G. and Litvack, L. (2000) *Ireland in the nineteenth century – regional identity*. Dublin: Four Courts Press.

House of Industry (1818) *Observation on the House of Industry, Dublin and on the plans of the Association for Suppressing Mendicity in that city*. Dublin.

Jordan, T. (1857) The present state of the dwellings of the poor, chiefly in Dublin, *Journal of the Dublin Statistical Society*, 2(8), pp 12–19.

Kearns, K.C. (1991) *Dublin street life and lore*. Dublin: Glendale.

Kearns, K.C. (1994) *Dublin tenement life – an oral history*. Dublin: Gill and Macmillan.

Kearns, K.C. (1996) *Dublin pub life and lore*. Dublin: Gill and Macmillan.

Kennedy, T. (ed.) (1980) *Victorian Dublin*. Dublin: Albertine Kennedy Publishing.

Lennon, C. (1983) Civic life and religion in early eighteenth-century Dublin, *Archivium Hibernicum*, 38, pp 14–25.

Lindsay, D. (1990) *Dublin's oldest charity: the Sick and Indigent Roomkeepers' Society*. Dublin: Anniversary Press.

Maltby, A. and Maltby, J. (1979) *Ireland in the nineteenth century: A breviate of official publications*. Guides to Official Publications 4. Oxford: Pergamon Press.

Martin, J.H. (1988) The social geography of mid-nineteenth-century Dublin city. *In:* Smyth, W.J. and Whelan, K. (eds) *Common ground: essays on the historical geography of Ireland*. Cork: Cork University Press, pp 173–88.

McCullough, N. (1989) *Dublin: an urban history*. Dublin: Anne Street Press.

Mendicity Report (1819) *Report of the Association for the Suppression of Mendicity in Dublin for the year 1818*. Dublin.

McLoughlin, D. (1990) Workhouses and Irish female paupers, 1840–70. *In:* Luddy, M. and Murphy, C. (eds) *Women surviving: studies in Irish women's history in the nineteenth and twentieth centuries*. Dublin: Poolbeg, pp 117–47.

Mosher, A.E. and Holdsworth, D.W. (1992) The meaning of alley housing in industrial towns: examples from late-nineteenth-century and early-twentieth-century Pennsylvania, *Journal of Historical Geography*, 18 (2), pp 174–89.

Murnane, B. (1988) The recreation of the urban historical landscape: Mountjoy Ward Dublin c.1901. *In:* Smyth, W.J. and Whelan, K. (eds) *Common ground: essays on the historical geography of Ireland*. Cork: Cork University Press, pp 189–207.

Murray, T.A. (1801) *Remarks on the situation of the poor in the metropolis as contributing to the progress of contagious diseases with a plan for the institution of houses of recovery for persons infected by fever, prepared by the desire, and at the expence of the society for bettering the condition of the poor.* Dublin.

Neville, P. (1884) Report of Parke Neville, City Engineer for the years 1882 and 1883, *RPDCD*, 2, pp 108ff.

Norwood, J. (1873) On the working of the sanitary laws in Dublin, with suggestions for their amendment, *Journal of the Statistical and Social Inquiry Society of Ireland*, 6 (43), pp 230–42.

Prunty, J. (1992) The geography of poverty Dublin 1850–1900; the social mission of the church, with particular reference to Margaret Aylward and co-workers. Unpublished PhD thesis. Dublin: Department of Geography, University College Dublin.

Prunty, J. (1998) *Dublin slums 1800–1925, a study in urban geography.* Dublin: Irish Academic Press.

Raymond, R.J. (1986) Dublin: the great famine 1845–60, *Dublin Historical Record*, 33 (3), pp 98–105.

Stedman Jones, G. (1971, 1984) *Outcast London, a study in the relationship between classes in Victorian society.* Oxford: Clarendon Press.

Trustees of the House of Recovery or Fever Hospital in Cork-Street (1802) *Observations on the circumstances which tend to generate and propagate contagion in the Liberties on the south side of the City of Dublin and on the means of removing them.* Dublin.

White, F. (1833) *Report and observation on the state of the poor of Dublin.* Dublin.

Whitelaw, Revd J. (1805) *An essay on the population of Dublin, being the result of an actual survey taken in 1798 with great care and precision, to which is added the general return of the district committee in 1804, with a comparative statement of the two surveys, also several observations on the present state of the poorer parts of the city of Dublin, 1805.* Dublin. Reprinted as *Slum conditions in London and Dublin* (1974). Farnborough, Hants: Gregg International.

Willis, T. (1845) *Facts connected with the social and sanitary condition of the working classes in the city of Dublin.* Dublin.

DUBLIN AT THE TURN OF THE CENTURY (PAGES 221–81)

As for previous chapters, an important source of information is the City Archive, especially the published reports. The following are useful for the insights they give into supplying water to the city.

1868 *Reports of the Vartry water.* Charles A. Cameron, City Analyst, Dublin, 1868 (City Archive).

1869 *Report on the general state of public works in the City of Dublin.* Parke Neville, City Engineer.

1875 *A description of the Dublin Corporation waterworks.* Parke Neville, City Engineer.

1877 *Report of the City Engineer on relative advantages of Vartry and Canal water for supply of the Township (Rathmines).* Corporation Reports, No. 48.

1880 *Report of the City Engineer re Rathmines and Rathgar Waterworks Bill 1880.* Dublin Corporation Reports 1880, No. 122.

There are many guides to Dublin that were produced during the nineteenth century. Some were the recollections of travellers and might be part of a larger peregrination. These were sometimes on a grand scale such as that produced by Mr and Mrs Sydney Hall in the 1840s. Others were guides specifically designed for visitors to Dublin and very similar to a present-day tourist guide. These offer immense detail on the changing landscape of the city but unfortunately being ephemeral by nature can be difficult to obtain. Therefore reference is made below to only those used in the text or to those that are relatively easily obtained. The *Dublin Penny Journal*, published for a short time in the 1830s, is also a fascinating source.

Specific References

Aalen, F.H.A. (1990) *The Iveagh Trust – the first hundred years 1890–1990*. Dublin: Iveagh Trust.

Alabaster, E. (1905) *New Dublin*. Dublin.

Abercrombie, P., Kelly, S. and Kelly, A. (1922) *Dublin of the future – the new town plan*. Dublin: Civics Institute of Ireland and Liverpool University Press.

Anon. (1917) *Dublin – Explorations and reflections by an Englishman*. Dublin: Maunsell.

Aspinall, P.J. (1978) *Building applications and the building industry in nineteenth-century towns: the scope for statistical analysis*. Research Memo 68, Centre for Urban and Regional Studies, University of Birmingham.

Bannon, M.J. (1978) The making of Irish geography, III: Patrick Geddes and the emergence of modern town planning in Ireland, *Irish Geography*, 11, pp 141–8.

Bannon, M.J. (ed.) (1985) *The emergence of Irish planning 1880–1920*. Dublin: Turoe Press.

Bannon, M.J. (ed.) (1989) *Planning – the Irish experience 1920–1988*. Dublin: Wolfhound Press.

Bannon, M. (1988) The capital and the new state. *In*: Cosgrove, A. (ed.) *Dublin through the ages*. Dublin: College Press, pp 133–50.

Behan, B. (1978) *Brendan Behan – the complete plays*. London: Methuen.

Behan, D. (1965) *My Brother Brendan*. London: Leslie Frewin.

Black's Guide Books (1908) *Black's guide to Dublin*. London: Adam and Charles Black.

Boundary Commission (1885) *Report of the Royal Commission to inquire into the boundaries and municipal areas of certain cities and towns in Ireland*. Dublin: Alex Thom.

Colivet, M.P. (1943) *Report of inquiry into the housing of the working classes of the city of Dublin, 1939–43*. Dublin: Stationery Office.

Cannadine, D. (1977) Victorian cities: How different?, *Social History*, 2, pp 457–82.

CDVEC (1993) *The old township of Pembroke 1863–1930*. Dublin: City of Dublin Vocational Education Committee.

Cosgrave, E. and Strangways, M. (1907) *Visitor's guide to Dublin and neighbourhood giving a complete dictionary of Dublin*. Dublin: Sealy, Bryers and Walker.

Cosgrave, E. (1909) *North Dublin: city and environs*. Dublin: Catholic Truth Society.

Daly, M. (1984) *Dublin, the deposed capital: a social and economic history 1850–1900*. Cork: Cork University Press.

Daly, M. (1985) Housing conditions and the genesis of housing reform in Dublin 1880–1920. *In*: Bannon, M.J. (ed.) *The emergence of Irish planning 1880–1920*. Dublin: Turoe Press, pp 77–130.

Daly, M. (1988) A tale of two cities: 1860–1920. *In*: Cosgrove, A. (ed.) *Dublin through the ages*. Dublin: College Press, pp 113–32.

D'Alton, J. (1888) *History of the county of Dublin*. Dublin: Hodges and Smith.

D'Arcy, F. (1988) An age of distress and reform: 1800 to 1860. *In*: Cosgrove, A. (ed.) *Dublin through the ages*. Dublin, College Press, pp 93–112.

de Courcy, J.W. (1996) *The Liffey in Dublin*. Dublin: Gill and Macmillan.

Donnelly, N. (1909–1920) Short history of Dublin parishes. 17 parts, 4 volumes. Dublin: Catholic Truth Society.

[Dublin] (1835) *The new picture of Dublin or Stranger's guide to the Irish metropolis*. Dublin: Curry.

[Dublin Charities] (1902) Dublin charities. Dublin: Association of Charities.

Fayle, H. and Newham, A.T. (1963) *The Dublin and Blessington tramway*. Locomotion Papers No. 20. Surrey: Oakwood Press.

Fitzpatrick, S.A.O. (1907) *Dublin – a historical and topographical account of the city*. London: Methuen.

Gilligan, H.A. (1988) *A history of the port of Dublin*. Dublin: Gill and Macmillan.

Girouard, M. (1985) *Cities and people*. New Haven and London: Yale University Press.

Hall, Mr and Mrs S.C. (1841–3) *Ireland – its scenery and character*. London: How and Parsons. Numerous later editions and reprints.

Hely (1917) *An illustrated record of the Sinn Fein rebellion in Dublin 1916*. Dublin: Hely.

Hearn, M. (1990) Life for domestic servants in Dublin, 1880–1920. *In*: Luddy, M. and Murphy, C. (eds) *Women surviving: studies in Irish women's history in the nineteenth and twentieth centuries*. Dublin: Poolbeg, pp 148–79.

Horner, A. (1985) The Dublin region 1880–1982: an overview of its development and planning. *In*: Bannon, M.J. (ed.) *The emergence of Irish planning*. Dublin: Turoe Press, pp 21–76.

Horner, A. (1990) Changes in population and in the extent of the built-up area in the Dublin city-region 1936–1988, *Irish Geography*, 23 (1), pp 50–5.

Hoyt, H. (1939) *The structure and growth of residential neighborhoods in American cities*. Washington: Federal Housing Administration.

Johnston, L. (1989) *Dublin: then and now*. Dublin, Gill and Macmillan.

Jordan, D.P. (1995) *Transforming Paris – the life and labors of Baron Haussmann*. New York: Free Press.

Joyce, P.W. and Sullivan, A.M. (1905) *Atlas and cyclopedia of Ireland*. New York: Murphy and McCarthy.

Kearns, K.C. (1994) *Dublin tenement Life – an oral history*. Dublin: Gill and Macmillan.

Kelly, D. (1995) *Four roads to Dublin – the history of Ranelagh, Rathmines and Leeson Street*. Dublin: O'Brien Press.

Kellett, J.R. (1969) *The impact of railways on Victorian cities*. London: Routledge and Kegan Paul.

MacAlister, A. and McNab, W. (1878) *Guide to the county of Dublin*. Produced for the British Association. Dublin: Hodges, Foster, Figgis.

McCullough, N. (1989) *Dublin – an urban history*. Dublin: Anne Street Press.

McManus, R. (1999) The building parson – the role of Reverend David Hall in the solution of Ireland's early-twentieth-century housing problems, *Irish Geography*, 32(2), pp 87–98.

NCEA (1991) *Gardiner's Dublin. A history and topography of Mountjoy Square and environs*. Dublin: National Council for Educational Awards.

Neville, P. (1874) *On the water supply of the city of Dublin*. Paper No. 1308. Dublin: Institution of Civil Engineers.

O'Brien, J.V. (1982) *Dear dirty Dublin – a city in distress, 1899–1916*. Berkeley: University of California Press.

O'Donnell, E.E. (1993) *Father Browne's Dublin photographs, 1925–1950*. Dublin: Wolfhound Press.

O'Dwyer, F. (1981) *Lost Dublin*. Dublin: Gill and Macmillan.

Ó Fearghail, C. (1992) The evolution of Catholic parishes in Dublin city from the sixteenth to the nineteenth centuries. *In*: Aalen, F.H.A. and Whelan, K. (eds) *Dublin city and county: from prehistory to present*. Dublin: Geography Publications, pp 229–50.

Ó Grada, C. (1982) The rocky road to Dublin, *Studia Hibernica*, 22/33, p. 134 ff.

Osborough, W.N. (1996) *Law and the emergence of modern Dublin*. Dublin: Irish Academic Press.

Pearson, P. (1999) *Between the mountains and the sea – Dun Laoghaire-Rathdown County.* Dublin: O'Brien Press.

Pearson, P. (2000) *The heart of Dublin.* Dublin: O'Brien Press.

Peter, A. (1907) *Sketches of old Dublin.* London: Sealy, Bryers and Walker.

Prunty, J. (1995) From city slums to city sprawl: Dublin in the nineteenth and twentieth centuries. *In*: Clarke, H.B. (ed.) *Irish cities.* Thomas Davis Lecture Series. Cork: Mercier Press, pp 109–22.

Prunty, J. (1998) *Dublin slums 1800–1925. A study in urban geography.* Dublin: Irish Academic Press.

Savage, J. (1878) *Picturesque Ireland.* New York: Thomas Kelly.

Somerville-Large, P. (1979) *Dublin.* London: Hamish Hamilton.

Starratt, R. (1849) *The stranger's guide through Dublin.* Dublin: Browne and Nolan.

Shepperd, W.E. (1974) *The Dublin and South Eastern Railway.* Newtown Abbot: David and Charles.

Wakeman, P. (1890) *Illustrated guide to Ireland for tourists.*

Ward Lock (1918) *Guide to Dublin, Kingstown, Bray.* London: Ward Lock. Numerous editions of this guide were produced during the twentieth century.

Wilson, W. (1989) *The City Beautiful movement.* Maryland: Johns Hopkins Press.

Wright, G.N. (1821) *Ancient and modern Dublin.* London. Many reprints available.

Wright, G.N. (1829) *Ireland illustrated.* London: Fisher and Son. Reprinted by Boethius, Kilkenny (1989).

Whitelaw, Revd J. (1805) *An essay on the population of Dublin, being the result of an actual survey taken in 1798 with great care and precision, to which is added the general return of the district committee in 1804, with a comparative statement of the two surveys, also several observations on the present state of the poorer parts of the city of Dublin, 1805. Dublin.* Reprinted as *Slum conditions in London and Dublin* (1974). Farnborough, Hants: Gregg International.

THE HEART OF THE CITY: COMMERCIAL DUBLIN, *c.*1890–1915
(PAGES 282–340)

Land use patterns in the city are constantly changing. At a broad scale, the pace of change is reasonably sedate – a retail area does not decline overnight. At the level of individual units, however, the pace of change can be quite rapid as buildings change hands and change uses. Keeping pace with this level of detail and recording it is a daunting task and the best that can be hoped-for is to have a snap-shot at regular time intervals. One of the most valuable sources of this information is *Thom's Official Directory* produced annually since the middle of the nineteenth century. The directory for 1911 proclaims that it is the 'sixty-eighth Annual Publication'. It was produced by Alexander Thom and Co. in Middle Abbey Street and is a compilation of a variety of directories containing, *inter alia*, British, foreign and colonial directories, the parliamentary and ecclesiastical directories as well as statistics of Great Britain and Ireland. However of greatest interest to the student of the city are the county and borough directory and the post office Dublin city and county directory.

The post office directory gives a street-by-street breakdown of the land use of the city. The name of the person(s) occupying each building is given as well as the nature of any commercial activity. The information is given for all floors in the building though the various floors above the ground floor are not usually differentiated. The directory is not without its limitations. The coverage is imperfect and an annual updating cannot be guaranteed. It would therefore not be wise to use the directory for precise attribution or dating but it is perfectly adequate when what is being sought is a general impression or overview. As with all directories, it is best used in conjunction with other sources and when the detail it offers make its shortcomings acceptable.

The directories of trades and professions should also be mentioned, in which the location of various commercial activities is listed under a quite detailed classification. For example, the 1911 directory tells us that Henry Smith manufactures billiard balls at 155 Capel Street, the only such manufacturer in the city. This listing provides a useful cross-check for the street listings though it is not without its own shortcomings. The first is that the classification system is not explained so it is not possible to determine with accuracy what criteria were used to place an entry under one heading rather than another. The second is that there is no way in which the scale of operations can be gauged from the list. Thus, Arnotts of Henry Street are described as drapers but they are on a much grander scale to Miss Mary Hand of 60 Camden Street. From a geographical point of view, Thom's directory has a major drawback. It gives no topographical information. No street layout and, more importantly, no plot layout is provided and the user can only imagine the streetscape.

Thom's directory is only one a number of guides and directories produced at this time but it is undoubtedly the most comprehensive. Others include the *Family Physician and Dublin Directory*, published by the pharmaceutical company of William Hayes of Grafton Street and the *Almanac for Ireland* produced by Eason's. The reader is directed to an extensive review of newspapers, directories and gazetteers as data sources in Horner, A. (1998) *Irish towns – a guide to sources*. Dublin: Geography Publications, pp 147–62.

The absence of spatial data is remedied to a degree by the Fire Insurance maps which yield a lot more information on the fabric of the town in the early-twentieth-century. In Britain during the late-nineteenth-century, the need for insurance companies offering fire insurance to know about the physical characteristics of the buildings they were covering and their geographical location led to the development of Fire Insurance Plans. From 1885 on one company, Charles E. Goad, dominated the production of these plans within Britain and Ireland (Rowley, 1984). The plans show, by using colour and symbols, a great deal of information on the streetscape of the city. The size and location of individual buildings is noted. The broad land use, the number of storeys and the nature of the roof are among the other items of information noted on the plan. There is great detail provided on the nature of windows, location of hydrants, skylights, hoists and lifts. It is possible to identify individual buildings by their street number and in conjunction with the street directory build a picture of the streetscape for a given time period. An initial atlas was issued for each town, concentrating on the commercial centre of the city and this was updated at regular intervals. However it is this updating which has caused the plans to be very rare. The Goad company had a policy of only leasing the maps to insurance companies. The atlases were returned to the companies when updates were available; this happened on a regular basis. Minor changes were noted by means of paper overlays which were pasted onto the original plans. Major revisions resulted in new sheets being issued. Therefore the insurance company had only a current atlas at any one time; there were no archival copies. This was useful for the insurance company but not for the researcher. It is relatively rare to find older sheets that have not been updated with the earlier information obliterated. Fortunately some original sets still exist. The Goad company itself has an archive and the British Library has a major holding.

The reader is also directed to the series of short parish histories produced by Bishop Donnelly for the Catholic Truth Society in the early years of the century. Another fascinating, but relatively unused, source is picture postcards. By the end of the nineteenth century there were many companies producing views of the city and not just of the main streets and major monuments. These are excellent in revealing the landscape of the city and the character of its streets. Many of the illustrations in this chapter are from contemporary postcards or from adverstising material. While they belong to the period under discussion, it was not felt necessary to attempt to determine the precise date of each.

Specific References

Aalen, F.H.A. (1985) The working class housing movement in Dublin 1860–1920. *In*: Bannon, M.J. *The emergence of Irish planning 1880–1920.* Dublin: Turoe Press, pp 131–88.

Abercrombie, P., Kelly, S. and Kelly, A. (1922) *Dublin of the future: the new town plan.* Dublin: Civics Institute of Ireland and Liverpool University Press.

Alter, P. (1974) Symbols of Irish nationalism, *Studia Hibernica*, pp 14–123.

Bannon, M. (1988) The capital of the new state. *In*: Cosgrove, A. (ed.) *Dublin through the ages*, Dublin: College Press, pp 133–50.

Barnard, A. (1887) *Whisky distilleries of the United Kingdom.* London: E. Norton Harper.

Bolger, W. and Share, B. (1976) *And Nelson on his pillar, 1808–1966: a retrospective record.* Dublin: Nonpareil.

Butler, R.M. (1916) The reconstruction of O'Connell Street, *Studies*, 5, pp 570–6.

Carter, H. (1995) *The study of urban geography.* 4th edition. London: Arnold.

Christopher, A.J. (1997) The second city of the Empire: colonial Dublin, 1911, *Journal of Historical Geography*, 23 (2), pp 151–63.

Civics Institute of Ireland (1925) *The Dublin civic survey.* Liverpool: Liverpool University Press.

Curriculum Development Unit (1978) *Divided city: portrait of Dublin, 1913.* Dublin: TCD.

Daly, M. (1984) *Dublin, the deposed capital: a social and economic history 1850–1900.* Cork: Cork University Press.

Dublin Chamber of Commerce (1917) *Year book – with which is incorporated Kingstown.* London: Bemrose and Sons.

Dublin Corporation (1913) *Dublin – Ireland's capital – Dublin Corporation guide.* Dublin: Crossley.

Farmer, T. (1995) *Ordinary lives.* Dublin: A&A Farmer.

Gorham, M. (1972) *Dublin from old photographs.* London: Batsford.

Hill, J. (1998) *Irish public sculpture – a history.* Dublin: Four Courts Press.

Harrison, W. (1890) *Memorable Dublin houses – a handy guide.* Dublin: Leckie and Co.

Horner, A. (1985) The Dublin region, 1880–1928: an overview of its development and planning. *In*: Bannon, M.J. (ed.) *The emergence of Irish planning, 1880–1920*, pp 21–76.

Hotelling, H. (1929) Stability in competition, *Economic Geography*, 39, 41–57.

Kearns, K.C. (1983) *Georgian Dublin: Ireland's imperilled architectural heritage.* Newton Abbot: David and Charles.

Kennedy, T. (ed.) (1980) *Victorian Dublin.* Dublin: Albertine Kennedy Publishing.

Killen, J.E. (1992) Transport in Dublin: past, present and future. *In*: Aalen, F.H.A. and Whelan, K. (eds) *Dublin city and county: from prehistory to present.* Dublin: Geography Publications, pp 305–25.

McDermott, M. (1988) *Dublin's architectural development 1800–1925.* Dublin: Tulcamac.

MacLaren, A. (1996) Office development in Dublin and tax incentive areas, *Irish Geography*, 29 (1), 49–54.

Murphy, F.J. (1979) Dublin trams 1872–1959, *Dublin Historical Record*, 33, pp 2–9.

O'Brien, J.V. (1982) *Dear dirty Dublin: a city in distress, 1899–1916.* Berkeley: California University Press.

O'Broin, S. (1980) *The book of Finglas.* Dublin: Kincora Press.

O'Connor, C. and O'Regan, J. (eds) (1987) *Public works. The architecture of the Office of Public Works 1831–1987.* Dublin: Architectural Association of Ireland.

O'Riain, M. (1998) Nelson's Pillar: a controversy that ran and ran, *History Ireland,* 6 (4), pp 21–5.

Osborough, W.N. (1996) *Law and the emergence of modern Dublin.* Dublin: Irish Academic Press.

Plunkett, J. (1969) *Strumpet city.* London: Hutchinson.

Rothery, S. (1991) *Ireland and the new architecture, 1900–1940.* Dublin: Lilliput Press.

Rowley, G. (1984) An introduction to British fire insurance plans, *Map Collector,* 29, pp 14–19.

Royal Commission (1880) *Report of the royal commission appointed to inquire into the sewerage and drainage of the city of Dublin,* (cd. 2605). London.

Savage, J. (ed.) (1884) *Picturesque Ireland. A literary and artistic delineation of its scenery, antiquities, buildings, abbeys etc.* New York: Thomas Kelly.

Scott, W.A. (1916) Reconstruction of O'Connell Street Dublin: a note, *Studies,* 5, p. 165.

Shaffrey, M. (1988) Sackville Street/O'Connell Street, *Irish Arts Review,* pp 144–56.

Shaw, H. (1850) *New city pictorial directory 1850 to which is added a retrospective review of the past year.* Dublin: Henry Shaw. Reprinted by Friar's Bush Press, Belfast (1988).

Stratten and Stratten (1892) *Dublin, Cork and south of Ireland: A literary, commercial and social review.* London: Stratten and Stratten.

Townsend, B. (1997) *The lost distilleries of Ireland.* UK: Neil Wilson Publishing.

Vaughan, W.E. (ed.) (1996) *Ireland under the Union. II, 1870–1921.* A New History of Ireland, volume 6. Oxford: Clarendon Press.

Whelan, Y. (1999) Dublin: The symbolic geography of a capital city in transition, 1900–1966, with a comparative perspective on Helsinki. Unpublished PhD thesis. Dublin: Department of Geography, University College Dublin.

Wren, J. (1988) *The villages of Dublin.* Dublin: Tomar Publishing Enterprises.

Illustrations

Contributors

JOSEPH BRADY, Department of Geography, University College Dublin

JACINTA PRUNTY, Department of Modern History, National University of Ireland, Maynooth

EDEL SHERIDAN, Historisches Seminar, Universität Hannover

ANNGRET SIMMS, Department of Geography, University College Dublin

Index

Numbers in italics refer to illustrations

Clarence Hotel, 57
Clarke, Howard, 19, 28, 29, 31, 46–7, 48, 50–1
Clery and Co., 288, 292, 333, 335, *336*
Clondalkin, 303
Clonliffe Road, 272, 275
Clonskeagh, 246, 250
Clontarf, 163, 250, 272:
    Township, 262, 276–8
Clontarf Island, 22
clothes shopping, 288–92
clothing industry, 312–13
Clyde Road, 267
coaches, 76–7
Coates, William, 88
Coghlan's drapery, 324
coinage, 37–38
Colby, Colonel Thomas, 344
Coldwell and Co., 316
Coles Alley, 180
Cole's Lane, 183
College Green, 65, 120, *137*, 236, 317, 318, 321–2, 328:
    business centre, 282, 283, 285
    development, 127;
    fair green, 51–2;
    hackney stands, 76;
    social class, 145;
    18th century, 110–112;
    trams, 246
College Street, 332
Colles, Mr, 123
Collins, Greenville, 342
Collins Barracks, 63
Colvill, William, 115
commercial life, 282–340:
    clustering, 283–85;
    local retailing, 301–3;
    retailing, 287–96;
    services, 296–301
Commercial Union Insurance Company, 285
Commissioners for Paving, Cleansing and Lighting, 161
Commissioners of Public Works, 192, 194, 201–2
Common Council, 74, 162–3
Commons Street, 256

commuting, 222
Connell, Daniel, 215
Conyngham, William Burton, 114–15
Cook Street, 38, 46, 50, 57, 61, 80, 178
Cooley, Thomas, 124
Coombe, the, 52, 174, 211, 303:
    housing scheme, 195–200, 203–5, 217;
    public transport, 247;
    tenements, 176, 180, 194
Coombe stream, 21, 27
Corey Lane, 274
Cork, 114, 192, 226
Cork Hill, 34, 36, 135
Cork Street, 308
Cork Street Fever Hospital, 168, 196:
    report, 1802, 172, 173, 175–6
Cornmarket, 38, 48
Corporation Market, 293
Corrigan, Alderman, 164
Cosby, Francis, 60
cottages, 189–90
county borough, 55
court, 65
Courtenay Cottages, 185
Cowper Garden Building Estate, 269
Cowper Road, 269
crafts, 37, 50, 138, 150, *153*:
    medieval, 54
Craig Gardner, 299
Cramer, Wood and Co., 328–9
Crampton, Sir Philip, 235
Crampton Buildings, 207
Crokers' Street, 54
Cromwell, Oliver, 67
Cromwell, T., 127
Cross Act, 1875, 192, 195
Crozier, Councillor, 164
Crumlin, 247
Cumberland Street South, 182
Curry, William, 344
Cusack, Sir Thomas, 62
Custom House, 1707, 68, 80, 112
Custom House, medieval, 57
Custom House (Gandon), 21, 57, 70, 115, 116, 127, 133, 222, 237, 253, 260:
    built, 134–5;
    Loop Line, 245;
    social class, 148